Face and Enactment of Identities in the L2 Classroom

NEW PERSPECTIVES ON LANGUAGE AND EDUCATION

***Series Editor*:** Professor Viv Edwards, *University of Reading, Reading, Great Britain*

Two decades of research and development in language and literacy education have yielded a broad, multidisciplinary focus. Yet education systems face constant economic and technological change, with attendant issues of identity and power, community and culture. This series will feature critical and interpretive, disciplinary and multidisciplinary perspectives on teaching and learning, language and literacy in new times.

Full details of all the books in this series and of all our other publications can be found on http://www.multilingual-matters.com, or by writing to Multilingual Matters, St Nicholas House, 31–34 High Street, Bristol BS1 2AW, UK.

NEW PERSPECTIVES ON LANGUAGE AND EDUCATION: 46

Face and Enactment of Identities in the L2 Classroom

Joshua Alexander Kidd

MULTILINGUAL MATTERS
Bristol • Buffalo • Toronto

Library of Congress Cataloging in Publication Data
Names: Kidd, Joshua Alexander, author.
Title: Face and Enactment of Identities in the L2 Classroom/Joshua Alexander Kidd.
Description: Bristol; Buffalo: Multilingual Matters, [2016] |
Series: New Perspectives on Language and Education: 46 | Includes bibliographical references and index.
Identifiers: LCCN 2015036330| ISBN 9781783094998 (hbk : alk. paper) | ISBN 9781783095001 (ebook)
Subjects: LCSH: Identity (Psychology)—Japan. | Second language acquisition—Japan. | Politeness (Linguistics)—Japan. | Language and culture—Japan. | Language and education—Japan. | Classroom management. | Japan—Languages.
Classification: LCC P57.J3 K533 2016 | DDC 428.0071/052—dc23 LC record available at http://lccn.loc.gov/2015036330

British Library Cataloguing in Publication Data
A catalogue entry for this book is available from the British Library.

ISBN-13: 978-1-78309-499-8 (hbk)

Multilingual Matters
UK: St Nicholas House, 31–34 High Street, Bristol BS1 2AW, UK.
USA: UTP, 2250 Military Road, Tonawanda, NY 14150, USA.
Canada: UTP, 5201 Dufferin Street, North York, Ontario M3H 5T8, Canada.

Website: www.multilingual-matters.com
Twitter: Multi_Ling_Mat
Facebook: https://www.facebook.com/multilingualmatters
Blog: www.channelviewpublications.wordpress.com

The policy of Multilingual Matters/Channel View Publications is to use papers that are natural, renewable and recyclable products, made from wood grown in sustainable forests. In the manufacturing process of our books, and to further support our policy, preference is given to printers that have FSC and PEFC Chain of Custody certification. The FSC and/or PEFC logos will appear on those books where full certification has been granted to the printer concerned.

Typeset by Techset Composition India(P) Ltd, Bangalore and Chennai, India.
Printed and bound in Great Britain by the CPI Books Group Ltd.

Contents

Part 2: Overview of Research Methodology

Part 3: Student Insights into Classroom Interaction

Part 4: Reflection and Modification: Teacher Professional Development Model

Acronyms and Abbreviations

ALT	Assistant Language Teacher
B&L	Brown and Levinson
DA	Discourse Analysis
EFL	English as a Foreign Language
ELT	English Language Teaching
ESL	English as a Second Language
FTA	Face-Threatening Acts
ICC	Intercultural Communicative Competence
IRET	Institute for Research in English Teaching
JET	Japan Exchange and Teaching Programme
L1	First language
L2	Second language
MEXT	Japanese Ministry of Education, Culture, Sports, Science and Technology
MP	Model Person
NS	Native Speaker
NNS	Non Native Speaker
S	Student
SAMI	Self-Aspect Model of Identity
SLA	Second Language Acquisition
SR	Stimulated Recall
STEP	Society for Testing English Proficiency
TEFL	Teaching English as a Foreign Language
TESL	Teaching English as a Second Language
TESOL	Teaching English to Speakers of Other Languages
T	Teacher
T/B	Textbook
W/B	Workbook

Acknowledgements

I would like to acknowledge a truly remarkable man – the late Professor Christopher Candlin. I had the privilege of being guided by Professor Candlin throughout the duration of my PhD at Macquarie University, research which has provided the foundations upon which this book has been constructed. Professor Candlin had an extraordinary ability to make the confusing comprehensible through interweaving his vast knowledge of linguistic theory, classroom practice and an endless supply of pertinent and mesmerising anecdotes. A man of passion and boundless energy, he encouraged the pursuit of knowledge and the identification of meaningful ways in which this knowledge could best be employed to serve others. His deep love for his wife Dr Sally Candlin, affection for his children and grandchildren, respect for his colleagues and aspirations for his students characterised the way in which he conducted himself. His uncompromising work ethic and impact within the field of Applied Linguistics will remain a source of inspiration. Professor Candlin had a strong wish for me to publish this study in order to reach a wider audience. I am delighted to have the opportunity to honour his memory by making a contribution, albeit small, to the field he so loved. This dream would not have come to fruition if not for the editorial team at Multilingual Matters whose guidance and counsel have enabled me to reshape the original manuscript. I have been very fortunate to have worked with such a capable and meticulous team.

I am indebted to the teachers and students who participated in the research outlined in this book for their candid feedback and willingness to share personal reflections – never an easy task. As a teacher and researcher, I have found the students insights into classroom interaction enlightening, and at times confronting. They provide a potent reminder that we teachers, irrespective of experience and qualifications, have an ongoing duty to improve our craft through experimentation and evaluation. I would like to extend my deep gratitude to Dr Takashi Suzuki, Ms Megumi Bailey and

Mr Jay Gregory for their generosity with their time and expertise. I am especially grateful for their comprehensive attention to classroom data files, thought-provoking suggestions and the discussions we have shared. I also owe a considerable debt to Dr Jill Murray whose guidance has been critical at all the right times, and Dr Rosalind Kidd for her thorough proof-reading of earlier editions of this manuscript.

This book is the product of discussions I have shared with many stimulating colleagues and students over the past 20 years. I am grateful for their knowledge, experience and observations, all of which continue to challenge me to examine my views and question my assumptions. I particularly wish to thank Mr Hiroshi Komoriya whose extensive knowledge of traditional and contemporary Japanese educational practices I have been fortunate to discuss at length over many an insightful exchange. In addition, I would like to acknowledge my parents, Daryl and Helen, whose decision to always take the road less travelled instilled in me from a young age the conviction that life is an adventure or nothing. My father has been a shrewd proof-reader of several drafts of this book and has contributed invaluable feedback which has helped keep me on track, and enabled me to fashion it into a more coherent and readable form. While the contributions of all of these colleagues and friends have been crucial in producing this book, the opinions expressed and any faults are mine alone.

Above all, this book would not have been possible without the support of my wife Miho, and my daughters, Iysa and Sarika, to whom this book is dedicated with love. With resilience and understanding, for years they have put up with me examining data, scrutinising publications and tapping away at my keyboard. From day one, Miho's sustained support and her creative flair shaped what could have been an isolating endeavour into a family undertaking. Through Miho's vision and ingenuity, an undersized closet space was skilfully transformed to embrace a role far removed from that which it had initially signed on for. Clothes were relocated and the contents of unopened moving boxes once again given their freedom as the tiny space miraculously morphed to accommodate our family of four and much loved dogs, Booma and Pappy. A dynamic space where we could be together, share news, support and encourage each other. As I typed, Sarika would memorise scripts, play the guitar, sing and somehow manage to rehearse dance routines. Iysa would immerse herself in homework, devise running programmes and posit technical questions which soon eroded her misplaced belief that her father is capable of anything. Miho would make seemingly unresolvable obstacles fade away through compassion, humour and love. While bringing balance to our lives Miho would also keep abreast of her own demanding work schedule and troubleshoot my frequent computer problems. I was blessed to have my family by my side to share in every step of this journey. Three determined and inspiring women to remind me that we all need to make time to sing, to dance, to ask the tough questions and to laugh. Days I will forever treasure.

Preface

Factors of face and identity influence the complex and dynamic ways in which individuals present themselves verbally, and non-verbally, during communicative exchanges. While face research has addressed issues such as the degree to which face is individual or relational, public or private, and situation-specific or context-independent, there has been a lack of attention to the central issue of its relationship to identity (Spencer-Oatey, 2007: 639). The study discussed in this book explores the construction of student identities as revealed through the pragmatics of face in the context of second language (L2) classroom interaction between Japanese students and their non-Japanese English teacher. In exploring such classroom interaction and its implications for identity construction, we draw extensively on the voices of students during retrospective interviews following English learning activities with a native speaker teacher.

Classroom recordings, together with retrospective interviews, reveal specific points during learning activities when the students' and their teacher's interpretations of classroom communication deviate from communicative intentions. Candid student feedback allows access to pervasive patterns of language use, attitudes and behaviour from which an understanding of Japanese students' perceptions of issues of face as impinging on their construct of identity begins to materialise. Analysis of the data, structured around four recurring themes, explores issues of cross-cultural pragmatic divergence from the perspective of the students in relation to; (a) spontaneous peer collaboration, (b) characteristics of Japanese identities, (c) use of the L1 (Japanese), and (d) recourse to, and the maintenance of, silence. Such analysis of the classroom interaction and student reflection draws on the multi-dimensional construct of face duality proposed by Brown and Levinson ([1978]1987) combined with theories of politeness and face proposed in Japanese scholarship. Specifically, we draw on Hill *et al.*'s (1986) examination of volition and discernment, Haugh's (2005) theory of place in relation to

Japanese society, Ide's (1989) theory of *wakimae* (discernment) politeness and Matsumoto's (1988) theory of interdependence.

This research study is a potent reminder that what students and teachers may consider as standard and conventionally acceptable language use and behaviour within the classroom context can differ dramatically according to social, cultural and individual frames of reference. Student insights illustrate how, within the classroom context, even an experienced and well-intentioned language teacher's verbal and non-verbal interaction with students may, albeit unintentionally, block or interfere with students' management of face and enactment of identities. Pedagogically, data sources underscore the pressing need to actively build teachers' and students' mutual capacity to recognise and subsequently negotiate pragmatic meaning beyond the literal interpretation of what is said. In pursuit of such inquiry, results of the analyses are directed at the construction of an innovative teacher professional development programme which provides teachers with the tools to reflect on and, where desired, modify existing pedagogic practices.

As a teacher, my primary motive for writing this book was to try and understand what younger students are thinking and feeling when engaged in second language learning activities, and how these activities potentially influence their management of face and the identities they forge. The reader is advised to bear in mind that this book is not intended to be read from end-to-end. On the contrary, I would encourage you to select content relevant to your specific areas of interest and to move back and forth between the chapters as desired. The early chapters explore the field of pragmatics, the constructs of face and identity, and outline the research methodology. For the reader chiefly interested in the examination of classroom data, I would suggest proceeding directly to Part 3, which focuses on the four key themes cited above. These themes, while interwoven, are structured to stand alone and consequently do not need to be read consecutively. It is my hope that the participants insights presented within the following chapters contribute to our understanding of the students' perspective, raise pragmatic awareness and offer a model for teacher professional development.

Research Origins

When I arrived in Japan some 20 plus years ago, I was warmly met at a bustling local station and guided through a fascinating web-like configuration of narrow streets to my new abode; a run-down apartment with an abundance of traditional Japanese charm. The *genkan* entrance area led directly to a modest kitchenette occupied almost in entirety by an oversized *toyu* kerosene heater topped with a *yakan* tea kettle. Behind *fusuma* sliding partitions was a musty *tatami* room with a *futon* placed in the *oshiire* closet space. *Shoji* window screens decorated with a hodgepodge of flower patches artistically concealing puncture holes afforded privacy from the adjacent apartment located but an arm's length away. My employer, an individual of few words, briefly dropped by to hand me the key to a rusted bicycle, my teaching schedule and an employment contract. On leaving, as if by afterthought, an intimidating stack of linguistic theory publications was placed on the *getabako* shoe chest and I was advised to read them over the weekend. I was later to discover that this constituted the entire teacher training programme referred to during the interview process.

I had arrived in Japan brimming with enthusiasm yet distinctly underprepared for the journey that lay ahead. Prior to my departure from Australia, I had been caught-up in a whirlwind of preparation and did not stop to consider that I had, in effect, zero knowledge of Japan, the Japanese people or the Japanese language. At the time these had not presented as concerns. Once capable of navigating my new surroundings and accustomed to operating household appliances such as the *ofuro* bathtub and *gasukonro* gas stove, I shifted my focus to my work – teaching. First and foremost, I sensed that I was failing to engage my students in activities or to encourage interaction in the ways in which I expected to. My desire to shape a dynamic, vibrant and vocal classroom environment was markedly different from the reality I faced. I did the talking while the students listened. There was clearly a gap between what I expected of my students and what they expected of me as their teacher. Attempting to transform the classroom dynamic,

I systematically supplemented course materials with activities such as role-play and information gap tasks designed to foster contextualised communicative exchanges. Despite additions and modifications, I struggled to inspire the level of student involvement I expected or believed necessary to promote second language acquisition (SLA).

Conceding that my limitations in the Japanese language needed to be addressed, I used all available means to search for a Japanese family receptive to accommodating a young Aussie boarder. This was to be far from simple. After a long and fruitless search, a friend, Megumi, offered to intervene and somehow managed to convince her visibly reluctant *obasan* (aunt) and *ojisan* (uncle) that I would not take up too much room or interfere with their lives. Over time, owing to the graciousness and tolerance of my adopted family, the Shimodas, I gradually became more competent using Japanese while gaining first-hand experience of the social dimensions of family, social and professional life. Nonetheless, this knowledge did not have a perceptible impact on my success within the classroom. It became apparent that the difficulties I experienced in communicating my intentions and encouraging student participation were not purely of a linguistic nature. This forced me to address how my teaching practices were, or more accurately were not, meeting the needs of my students. While there were clear disparities in expectations, it was far from evident what these specific points of disparity were, and if or how these points could be pedagogically addressed through adopting, modifying or discontinuing specific teaching practices.

In the light of the foregoing, the following book examines Japanese students of English as they manage face and align with identities through drawing on the field of pragmatics and the analysis of classroom discourse. In the tradition of qualitative research, it is acknowledged that while the following interpretation of classroom discourse is built on the accumulated work of those experts cited throughout the book, it does not claim to be the only possible explanation. As Gee (1999: 113) notes, 'All analyses are open to further discussion and dispute, and their status can go up or down with time as work goes on in the field'. The following study assumes a positive trajectory in the sense that it aims to directly contribute to classroom practices, and thereby serve as a contributing piece to the larger puzzle that is language teaching and learning.

Part 1

Setting the Scene: Exploring the Theoretical Landscape and Context

1 The Research

Overview

Communicative success is not guaranteed by a student's ability to memorise and employ the structural features of a target language. Teaching the grammar, vocabulary and syntax of a language does not prepare the L2 learner for real-world interaction which requires the ability to engage differing interlocutors in diverse and dynamic situations to achieve specific objectives. From the earliest stages of language learning programmes, students, irrespective of age and proficiency level, require pedagogically appropriate and concrete opportunities to compare and contrast pragmatic features of language through attention to cultural, social and individual factors that shape the way language is used and interpreted. It is here that the classroom provides a unique context from which to explore the linguistic systems of the target language and the mother tongue in order to build cultural tolerance through raising awareness of factors that influence language use and behaviour. Awareness raising activities are followed by student-centred interactive opportunities in which authentic language samples stimulate interpretation and production activities designed to rehearse linguistic forms and contextualised pragmatic meaning.

The responsibility falls on the teacher to incorporate pedagogical strategies that are culturally and linguistically responsive in order to enhance student efficacy, motivation and achievement. For pragmatic instruction to be effective, it is critical that pragmatics forms a part of the language teacher's content and pedagogical knowledge. As a first step, in order to recognise, embrace and value cultural diversity, we teachers are faced with the challenge of actively questioning the pedagogies and practices we employ within the L2 classroom, and the impact these potentially have on our students. It is equally important to develop awareness of our students and the sociocultural beliefs, traditions, customs and values associated with their linguistic practices and behaviour, observed in the target language and mother tongue. It is here that identity, as revealed through the construct of face, and face, as revealed through identity (dis)alignment, are examined through attention to the students' subjective interpretation of their own language use and behaviour at specific moments during English activities.

Synopsis

> *The person who learns a language without learning*
> *a culture risks becoming a fluent fool.*
> (Bennett *et al.*, 2003: 237)

Face and identity influence the complex and dynamic ways in which individuals present themselves both verbally and non-verbally during interaction. Language and issues of identity are closely bound together, as too are language and the management and negotiation of face. Nevertheless, there has been surprisingly little attention within the research community to how the constructs of identity and face are interrelated and impact on the student within the language classroom. These two formidable conceptual areas present an opportunity to explore the communicative negotiation of face within the broader framework of identity. Or, simply speaking, theories of identity may enrich our understanding of face and potentially aid the analysis of face by adding layers of description that have traditionally been overlooked (see Spencer-Oatey, 2007; Joseph, 2013). While face research has addressed issues such as the degree to which face is individual or relational, public or private and situation-specific or context-independent, Spencer-Oatey (2007: 639) points out a lack of attention to the one fundamental point underpinning the debate, namely the issue of identity.

The research described in this book explores student identities as revealed through the pragmatics of face as observed during L2 classroom interaction between Japanese students and a native-speaker (NS) teacher. The study is directed at an examination of classroom discourse as interpreted through the voices of the typically neglected perspectives of younger students during retrospective interviews following English language learning activities. Classroom recordings, student retrospective interviews and teacher interviews reveal specific moments during learning activities when the Japanese students' and their non-Japanese English teacher's interpretations of classroom communication deviate from the speaker's communicative intentions. These points of disparity expose ways in which the meanings attributed to language use by both students and teacher are influenced by socio-cultural and individual affiliations. What emerges from this analysis of retrospective data and classroom excerpts is the complexity of separating identity and face in interactions where language and identity constitute part of the subject matter.

Student interpretations of classroom interaction offers compelling evidence that the Japanese students felt threatened by specific verbal and non-verbal features of the L2 classroom that the teacher assumed to be standard practice. This was particularly evident when language use or behaviour viewed by the students as being standard was not recognised, or rejected by the teacher as violating unstated classroom protocol. Candid student insights captured through retrospective interviews highlight that, while language was employed by both students and teacher so as to confront issues of face and to enable them to enact specific identities, meanings attributed to such language were rooted in socio-cultural and individual affiliations of both students and teachers and were not always mutually recognised. Student reflections provide access to pervasive patterns of language use, attitudes, and behaviour from which a picture of the Japanese students' face, as a construct of identity, begins to materialise. Data analysis, organised around four recurring themes, explores cross-cultural pragmatic divergence from the perspective of the students in relation to; (a) spontaneous peer collaboration, (b) characteristics of Japanese identities, (c) use of the L1 (Japanese), and (d) recourse to, and the maintenance of, silence. It is necessary to bear in mind that the themes are interwoven and consequently there is a degree of overlap which aptly reflects the interconnectedness of the constructs of face and identity.

The recurring themes reveal identities that the students actively seek to align with, resist or reject within the language classroom. In the analysis of classroom interaction and student reflections on this interaction, the discussion draws on a critical account of the multi-dimensional construct of face duality as proposed by Brown and Levinson ([1978]1987) (hereafter referred to as B&L) in conjunction with theories of politeness and face proposed by Japanese scholarship. Specifically, the discussion draws on those theories of Japanese politeness as outlined in Hill *et al.*'s (1986) examination of volition and discernment, Haugh's (2005) theory of place in relation to Japanese society, consisting of the dual concepts of the place one belongs (inclusion) and the place one stands (distinction), Ide's (1989) theory of *wakimae* (discernment) politeness and Matsumoto's (1988) theory of interdependence. The position here being that the involvedness of face necessitates comprehensive attention to universalities and socio-cultural specific notions in order to meaningfully contextualise Japanese students' interactive management of face and alignment with identities.

Importantly, the analysis of data sources demonstrates that, within the classroom context, even an experienced and well-intentioned teacher's verbal and non-verbal interaction strategies can inadvertently interfere with or block students' management of face and the enactment of identities. The point being that this accidental teacher obstruction radically influences learning outcomes through shaping student attitudes towards not only the teacher, but also the L2 and assumptions regarding the L2 community. In addressing issues of socio-cultural variance in the negotiation of face and alignment with identities, this book illustrates the importance for language teachers to recognise how misconceptions associated with preconceived cultural stereotypes may result in unintended instances of divergence in speaker communicative intentions and associated meanings as interpreted by the receiver. In this way, the data advocates systematic attention to pragmatics in L2 classrooms as imperative to building and assessing intercultural communicative competence (ICC) (see Byram *et al.*, 2002; Scarino, 2009). ICC is aptly described by Byram *et al.* as the 'ability to ensure a shared understanding by people of different social identities, and [the] ability to interact with people as complex human beings with multiple identities and their own individuality' (2000: 10). The move towards intercultural language teaching in second and foreign language education reflects growing awareness of the need to pedagogically address the interwovenness of language and culture within our increasingly multicultural world. This orientation values the fact that two or more linguistic and cultural systems are at play simultaneously in the learning of additional languages. Accordingly, students engage in a complex process of forging and performing new identities as they adjust to what at times they identify as being the unfamiliar demands of the L2 learning environment (see García, 2009; Ortega, 2013, 2014).

Given that people from different cultural, social and linguistic backgrounds communicate on a daily basis, it is critical to acknowledge that potential variance in the production and interpretation of language within the language classroom can give rise to misunderstandings. For the language teacher, attention to pragmatic forms reinforces the proposition that instruction supporting the acquisition of the lexico-grammar of a language alone does not prepare the student to engage in, or interpret the use and meanings of pragmatic features of the target language (see Archer *et al.*, 2012; Ishihara & Cohen, 2010; LoCastro, 2012; Ross & Kasper, 2013). Furthermore, language education plays a key role in encouraging tolerance and understanding between people from different cultural backgrounds through promoting awareness, interest, respect and tolerance. Pedagogically, data sources affirm that such information has value for teacher professional development and underscores the importance of building teachers' and students' mutual capacity to recognise and subsequently negotiate meaning beyond the literal interpretation of what is said. In cross-cultural classroom contexts, such capacity building requires teacher and student awareness of how pragmatics is intertwined with socio-cultural beliefs, values and contextual information associated with linguistic practices and behaviour.

Research findings are discussed by means of the examination of interaction patterns and behaviours employed by the Japanese students and their non-Japanese teacher. It is through the students' personal reflections on these processes that we seek to develop a particular and perhaps fresh perspective into our actions as teachers, and how students may be interpreting such actions. In pursuit of such inquiry, this book aims to shed light on the students' views of classroom interaction and to outline a teacher professional development model designed to encourage and build awareness of culturally sensitive classroom teaching strategies that acknowledge and offer a means of responding to pragmatic divergence.

Structure of Book

Part 1 of this book contains four chapters (Chapters 1 through 4) which address the research origins, English education in Japan, the field of pragmatics and the focal constructs of face and identity. Chapter 1 provides a discussion of the central research aims. The broader context is described in Chapter 2, which begins with an overview of the history of Japanese contact with the English language, followed by a description of the Japan Exchange and Teaching Programme (JET). The chapter concludes with an overview of the concept of culture and the relationship between language and culture. Chapter 3 overviews the field of pragmatics and sets the scene from which a review of cross-cultural pragmatics is offered. This is followed by a discussion of pragmatic failure and issues regarding resistance to pragmatic forms. We conclude with a look at the role of pragmatic competence within intercultural communicative competence followed by a discussion of pragmatics within the language classroom. Chapter 4 outlines the theoretical basis of the research by means of a critical examination of the key concepts of politeness, face and identity. First, an overview of the central construct of face is given through attention to Goffman's (1955) theory of social interaction and B&L's ([1978]1987) theory, often referred to as the 'face-saving theory' of linguistic politeness. This is followed by a review of literature both for and against B&L's notion of face and universal politeness, and the ground in-between which focuses on Japanese scholarship. The chapter concludes with an overview of identity and discussion of the interrelationship between identity and face.

Part 2 of the book (Chapter 5) outlines the research methodology, reviews the methods and approaches applied and details the theoretical framework guiding data analysis. The chapter begins with an overview of the research methodology, the research context and participants. This is followed by a description of the principal phases in data collection; (1) trajectory of access, (2) video recordings, (3) semi-structured interviews, and (4) stimulated recall sessions. This is followed by an overview of the dissemination of findings and a description of translating and transcribing conventions. Finally, the chapter outlines the theoretical framework employed in the analysis of the primary data sources.

Part 3 consists of five chapters (Chapters 6 through 11), which address the research results through a discussion of key themes revealed through the data sources. Chapter 6 begins with an overview of the findings and outlines the four central themes which guide the discussion of results; (a) spontaneous peer collaboration, (b) characteristics of Japanese identities, (c) use of the L1 (Japanese), and (d) recourse to, and the maintenance of ,silence. Each of the ensuing chapters (Chapters 7 through 10) is dedicated to the exploration of these themes through classroom excerpts discussed with direct reference to the student retrospective comments and teacher interview data.

Chapter 7 examines student peer support strategies as viewed through spontaneous collaborative exchanges. The chapter begins by defining collaboration and follows with an analysis of student collaboration from the perspective of the teacher, as revealed through interview comments and classroom intervention strategies. Classroom data and student reflections reveal three objectives of collaboration which are discussed in turn; (a) to compare and confirm lesson content, (b) to solicit answers, and (c) to avoid error. We conclude with an overview of the pedagogical implications of cross-cultural disparity in classroom collaborative strategies.

In Chapter 8, teacher/student discord associated with the students identifying with what they view as being their Japanese identities is examined through attention to the data sources and framed with reference to the themes of *kokusaika* (internationalisation), ethnocentricity and *nihonjinron* theories of the uniqueness of Japanese culture. Japanese identities and *nihonjinron* are examined in relation to three themes; (a) student resistance to peer correction, (b) teacher correction strategies, and (c) positive feedback following error correction. We conclude with an overview of the implications of Japanese identities in relation to classroom activities.

Chapter 9 addresses diverging student/teacher interpretations regarding the use of the L1, Japanese, within the L2 classroom. The chapter begins with an outline of the teacher's views and practices when employing Japanese during English activities, followed by an examination of code-switching. Analysis of student attitudes concerning teacher L1 use focuses on three key themes; (a) L1 and the assumption of comprehension difficulties, (b) L1 illocutionary force, and (c) erroneous and/or ambiguous use of Japanese.

The chapter discusses the students' attitude to the teacher's regulating of L1 use and concludes with a summary of the pedagogical implications.

In Chapter 10, we examine the students' non-verbal interactive strategies associated with silence during communication. The chapter begins with an overview of silence in communication and the interactive applications within the Japanese classroom. Following a description of the teacher's interpretation of classroom silence, we analyse silence from the students' perspectives through attention to four key themes; (a) fear of failure, (b) L2 limitations, (c) *aizuchi* (backchannels), and (d) processing time. To conclude, the chapter considers the pedagogical implications of classroom silence.

Part 4 of the book overviews the critical relationship linking structural and pragmatic linguistic knowledge in relation to the primary themes examined. The chapter outlines a teacher professional development model designed around the five phases of: Awareness, Knowledge, Critique, Action and Evaluation followed by a sample professional development seminar focusing on Japanese *aizuchi* (backchannels). We conclude with a discussion of culturally responsive teaching in relation to socio-cultural diversity and student individuality.

Research Aims

The research presented in this book began as a relatively straightforward project to examine and evaluate Japanese students' management of face and identities during classroom communication with a non-Japanese teacher. While bearing in mind that every classroom has its own unique ensemble of students with their individual backgrounds, personalities and objectives, it is equally important to remember that these students share assumptions as to what is expected of them within the classroom, and moreover, what they expect of their teachers. The underlying premise here is that during the course of social interaction, interlocutors engage in a negotiation of face relationships and employ strategies to manage face and align with, resist or reject identities. These strategies, verbal and non-verbal, are conditioned by socio-cultural norms of a particular society and informed by the individual's judgment. Given that in most communicative situations speakers mean more than they say in a strictly semantic sense, this investigation sought to identify the communicative intent and meaning assigned to verbal and non-verbal language observed during L2 classroom interaction. Students' personal reflections on their participation during English activities (*eigo katsudo*) provided the framework from which we examined diverse ways in which pragmatic differences in discourse strategies and behaviour are managed through face. In this way, based on the position that face is deeply personal and cannot be assigned or assumed without first-hand participant feedback, the students' subjective interpretations of their own language discourse and behaviour guided the collection and analysis of data.

The public nature of face, as observed during the Japanese students' discursive negotiation and renegotiation of face, serves as the window through which discursive orientations and behaviour are examined from the students' perspective. Through observing how the students claim face, the research study explores a number of identities important to the students, and the process by which they are constructed and enacted during interactional exchanges. The identities salient in a particular exchange are contextually specified and negotiated by the participants involved in that exchange. A central question in the following examination is: what kind of data is needed for research into face and identity? To elaborate, how do we build an adequate and accurate picture of face when it is linked to not only social and cultural contexts, but also shaped by personal agency which impacts the ways in which language is employed and interpreted? This issue is raised in Spencer-Oatey's (2007) theories of identity and the analysis of face, which ask:

> If face is something that people claim for themselves, and if face-threat or face enhancement occurs when there is a mismatch between as attribute claimed (or denied, in the case of negatively evaluated traits) and an attribute perceived as being ascribed by others, then to what extent is discourse data sufficient for research purposes? To what extent is it necessary to obtain people's evaluative reactions? (Spencer-Oatey, 2007: 653–654)

In reference to retrospective feedback of such evaluative reactions, Spencer-Oatey argues that post-event data provides a practical tool for gaining valuable insights as they 'help identify people's face sensitivities and evaluative reactions, and they can provide insights into the cognitive underpinnings of their reactions' (2007: 654). The difficulties facing L2 students as they negotiate identities are raised by Haugh (2007: 658) who observes that the 'discursive dispute between the interconnected layers that constitute identities in the interactional achievement of "(im)politeness" and "face" in communication are the cause of at least some of the dilemmas facing second language learners'. Within the context of the following study, the Japanese students' negotiation of face and alignment with identities is examined through the analysis of L2 classroom discourse and by means of drawing on the students' reflections on this discourse as revealed during retrospective interview sessions.

In light of the above considerations, a qualitative research framework is employed to identify and analyse patterns of language use and behaviour evidenced in recurring themes with attention to social, historical and cultural factors which potentially influence the communicative practices students' engage in to manage face as they construct and enact identities (see Davis, 1995; Erickson, 1986; Lazaraton, 2003). In order to address the notions of face and identity, we employ three primary data sets; (a) interactional data from L2 learning activities involving young Japanese students of English, (b) the narratives from Japanese students collected through retrospective interviews, and (c) semi-structured interviews conducted with the English teacher. In pursuit of understanding classroom interaction as intended and interpreted by the students, we present naturally occurring classroom excerpts examined in conjunction with retrospective feedback provided by the students. Analytic themes drawn from linguistic and applied linguistic research (see Roberts & Sarangi, 2005) link student feedback to focal themes which illustrate how the Japanese students manage face and align with, resist or reject identities.

In the evaluation of the classroom excerpts and student reflections on such excerpts, the analysis explores the multi-dimensional construct of face as proposed by B&L in conjunction with theories of politeness and face proposed by Japanese scholarship. We argue that B&L's model, built around the constructs of positive and negative face, remains a progressive conceptual and analytic tool when used in combination with culturally appropriate descriptions of, in this case, Japanese culture, society and language. The work of Japanese scholarship discussed in the following literature review provides a platform from which to analyse cultural pragmatics in relation to insights gained from the students' reflections. Specifically, the field of pragmatics provides insight into how differing teacher and student assumptions and expectations regarding classroom standards and roles can impose identities and unintentionally interfere with the management and negotiation of face. The themes and associated language practices observed during L2 activities are viewed as socially and culturally informed by the situational context and cultural practices associated with the contexts in which they occur. As face threats represent the primary categories explored, the excerpts discussed reside at the negative pole; however, this is somewhat to be expected given that awareness of face is more likely to emerge in situations when the student feels under threat. In other words, when the interactive management of face proceeds smoothly and without problems, it is likely that the students will not register the need to respond defensively. This examination acknowledges that while there are specific patterns of behaviour and language uses that emerge during the examination, all students exhibit unique interpretations of classroom discourse, which underscore the diversity of students beyond cultural generalisations.

Student views, as revealed through retrospective interview sessions, uncover recurring gaps between the students' communicative intentions and the meaning assigned to language use and behaviour by the language teacher. Similarly, the teacher's interview comments draw attention to recurring gaps between the teacher's communicative intentions and the meaning assigned to his language use and behaviour by the students. Focusing on these gaps, we explore contradictions between communicative intentions as expressed through language use and behaviour and the interpretation as conceived by the interlocutor. The students' personal reflections on their interactions generate insight into a number of identities important to the students, and perhaps a fresh perspective into how the L2 classroom is viewed from the students' perspective. Drawing on the results of this research study, we develop a professional development programme for English language teachers. We argue that heightened awareness, followed by knowledge building activities and critique, can provide a basis from which teachers can be encouraged to adopt, modify, or where deemed appropriate, discontinue specific teaching practices in order to better meet students' needs.

2 English Education in Japan

Tracing English in Japan

The first recorded contact between Japan and the English language was in 1600 when Englishman William Adams was swept ashore on the southern island of Kyushu (Ike, 1995). Adams, known in Japanese as *Miura Anjin* (the pilot of Miura) built Japan's first Western-style ships while cementing his role as an influential advisor to Tokugawa Ieyasu, the founder of the Tokugawa Feudal Government, which saw him play a decisive role in the establishment of trading factories (Hughes, 1999). Following the death of Tokugawa Ieyasu in 1616, a change in foreign policy saw the trading offices suspended, which prompted the English to leave Japan (Reesor, 2002). Distrustful of foreigners and the spread of European imperialism, from 1638, Japan adopted an isolationist policy which saw contact with foreigners limited to Dejima Island off Nagasaki (Hagerman, 2009). It was not until the arrival of the American mission to Japan under the charge of Commodore Matthew Perry in 1853 that Japan was again proclaimed open for trade and isolationist policy ended. With the end of the isolation period *'sakoku'*, English language education was initiated in 1854 following the signing of the Kanagawa Treaty (Hosoki, 2011). A change in the linguistic landscape of Japan followed, which saw Japanese scholars move from the study of Dutch to the study of English and the cultures and social practices of the west (McKenzie, 2010: 7).

The study of English and interest in western cultures was further fuelled by the ensuing Meiji period of modernisation (1868 to 1912) during which western ideas, culture and goods were welcomed. In 1871, English was adopted as an integral part of the national language curriculum and universities initiated an entrance exam system designed to test English grammar and translation skills. This reflected an emerging need for expertise in translating English technical documents, viewed as being essential to Japan's progress (Koike & Tanaka, 1995). The rising status of English was evidenced in

Arinori Mori's 1872 proposal that the Japanese language be abolished and replaced with English as the official language of Japan for reasons of international trade.

> The spoken language of Japan being inadequate to the growing necessities of the people of the Empire, and too poor to be made, by a phonetic alphabet, sufficiently useful as a written language, the idea prevails among us that, if we would keep pace with the age, we must adopt a copious and expanding European language. The necessity for this arises mainly out of the fact that Japan is a commercial nation; and also that, if we do not adopt a language like that of English, which is quite predominant in Asia, as well as elsewhere in the commercial world, the progress of Japanese civilization is evidently impossible. Indeed a new language is demanded by the whole Empire. (Mori, cited in Tukahara, 2002: 8)

In addition to the perception that the Japanese language was of limited value internationally, Mori's proposal was motivated by the conviction that spoken Japanese was of lower status than European languages, the writing system of *kanji, hiragana* and *katakana* was too complex, and that written Japanese was essentially a vestige of Chinese cultural imperialism (Hagerman, 2009). Mori's proposal was rejected with the period that followed during the 1880s, characterised by a backlash against Japan's interest in English and the West (Ike, 1995; Koike & Tanaka, 1995). Anti-Western and anti-English sentiment continued into the 20th century, with calls to alter the status of English from compulsory to elective (Ike, 1995).

It was against this backdrop that in 1921, a lecturer from the University of London, Harold E. Palmer, was invited by the Ministry of Education to Japan as a linguistic adviser, tasked with identifying ways to improve English teaching (see Imura, 1997; Smith & Imura, 2002). In 1923, Palmer established the Institute for Research in English Teaching (IRET) in Tokyo and became the first director. The IRET functioned as a 'semi-official organization, with premises in the Department of Education but with its own independent board of advisers, bulletin and publishing outlets' (Smith & Imura, 2004: 32). In 1925, the IRET conference for English Language Teaching proposed four recommendations for reform suggesting; (a) smaller class sizes, (b) greater freedom for teachers textbook selection, (c) better in-service teacher education and, (d) effective participation of NS teachers. In addition, the IRET recommended that the university entrance examinations be reformed to emphasise 'plain English (as opposed to over-literary words and expressions) and for oral/aural testing to be introduced in counterweight to translation tasks' (Smith & Imura, 2004: 32). The Ministry of Education failed to follow up on Palmer's recommendations as the political climate during the late 1920s and 1930s shifted and anti-English sentiment grew, fuelled by factors such as reaction to the new United States immigration laws which prohibited Japanese immigration (Imura, 2003).

The Japanese military took control of the government in 1932, and in the lead-up to Japan's involvement in World War II, nationalism dominated, with English maligned as the enemy's language (Imura, 2003). Calls for the abolition of English language education led the Ministry of Education to reduce the time allocated to the study of English for boys, and terminate English education for girls (Koika & Tanaka, 1995: 17). Subsequently, Palmer returned to the United Kingdom in 1936, as did a large number of foreign scholars employed at Japanese universities who were dismissed subsequent to the Pacific War in 1941 (Imura, 2003). During the United States occupation (1945 to 52), there was a shift in social attitudes away from extreme nationalism, coupled by a resurgence of interest in the learning of English. Japan's new constitution came into effect in May 1947 and marked the introduction of a new educational structure based on the American system: six years at primary school followed by three years at junior high school. This compulsory nine years of education was to be followed by three non-compulsory years at senior high school, and either two or four years at college or university (Hosoki, 2011). Education reform saw English language teaching reinstated as a compulsory subject in secondary schools. In addition, reforms initiated by the United States recommended that traditional Japanese teaching methods, which emphasised memorisation, be replaced by practices designed to foster independent thinking, the development of personality and democratic citizenship (Shimahara, 1979: 64).

In addition to school-based learning, the end of World War II saw a surge in English learning driven by the fact that 'Japanese administrators and civilians now needed to acquire a practical command of English in order to communicate with US occupation forces' (Butler, 2007a: 131). As the Japanese economy grew, Japanese business leaders called for an improvement in the level of practical English in the Japanese workforce in order to facilitate graduates' ability to conduct international business. Events such as the 1964 Tokyo Olympics, together with the large number of Japanese travelling abroad, motivated interest in learning English and attention to exploring new approaches to teaching (Imura, 2003). In 1963, the Society for Testing English Proficiency (STEP) introduced the first nationwide English examination to test practical English proficiency of the four language skills - reading, writing, speaking and listening. The modern age of English language learning in Japan has been closely associated with *koku-saika* (internationalisation) which 'affirms the urgent need for Japan to emerge from cultural isolation and assimilate a set of Western values' (McConnell, 1996: 447). The Japanese Ministry of Education, Culture, Sports, Science and Technology (hereafter referred to as MEXT) promotes English language policy through stressing the role of English in stimulating economic development, maintaining pace with globalisation and enhancing individual opportunities.

> Globalization advances at a rapid pace in politics, economics, and other fields, and we live in the age of increasing borderless flow of things, people and money. Nowadays, command of English is required in many fields, in contrast to the past when it was only needed in large companies and some industries; it is also pointed out that the level of English-language skills has a great impact on one's future including employment and career advancement. (MEXT, 2011: 2)

In recent years, recognition of the need to keep pace with a rapidly changing world is reflected in MEXT policy, such as the focus on the English curriculum at the elementary school level. In March 2006, the Central Council for Education, an advisory council for MEXT, proposed the inclusion of English for fifth and sixth grade students at all Japanese public elementary schools (Butler, 2004, 2007a). These guidelines for elementary schools became effective in 2011 with compulsory 'foreign language activities' scheduled for a total of 35 lessons per year. This equates to approximately one 45 minute period per week, taught primarily by the Japanese homeroom teachers who are, on occasion, aided by Assistant Language Teachers (ALTs). While dispute pertaining to the role of English at the elementary school level has generated heated debate, reflected in positions ranging from strong support to outright rejection (Ohtani, 2010), MEXT continues to struggle with the development and implementation of an effective English curriculum. In recent years, the tragic 2011 *Higashi Nihon Daishinsai* 'Great East Japan Earthquake', resulting tsunami and partial meltdowns at the Fukushima Daiichi Nuclear Power Plant complex have been cited by MEXT as evidence of the need for the accurate and timely dissemination of information in English.

> After the Great East Japan Earthquake, Japan received much support from abroad, and every Japanese felt connected with the world as a member of the global community; at the same time, we rediscovered the

need for dissemination of information overseas and the importance of the English language as a tool to achieve this goal. (MEXT, 2011: 2)

In regard to English and the private sector, private language schools fall into two major groups: *juku* (cram schools) and *eikaiwa* English conversation schools (McKenzie, 2010: 13). *Juku*, typically attended by junior high school and high school students in the evenings and on weekends, are usually staffed by Japanese teachers with a curriculum structured to prepare students for the notoriously competitive *juken* entrance examinations in key subject areas (Neustupny & Tanaka, 2004: 14). By contrast, *eikaiwa* are by and large staffed by NSs of English, and attended by an extensive range of students with equally diverse learning objectives. For students, the principal motivation for attending *eikaiwa* is often associated with the desire to engage in speaking and listening activities with NSs of English. While younger students are generally enrolled by parents, others regard *eikaiwa* lessons as a recreational activity, and some require English proficiency for professional purposes such as work placements outside of Japan. Kobayashi (2000: 24) makes the point that a key reason for attending *eikaiwa* is the assumption that English equates to *kokusaika* and therefore you 'need to study English to become internationalized'. While Japan's integration of English has been characterised by extremes, the political and economic advantages of English continue to shape public sentiment, private sector commitment and government language policy.

Debate as to the role of English draws attention to ideological tensions in Japan's language policies (both foreign language and Japanese language) which Gottlieb (1994) describes as having always 'been driven by imperatives ranging from modernization to imperialism to democratization to conservationism' (1994: 1195). Reesor (2002) argues that the desire to both acquire and share knowledge through English is weighed against concern that English education will equate to an unwanted and fundamentally corrupting foreign influence. Pro-English versus anti-English attitudes, framed as a rivalry between a Japanese identity and a global identity, are cited by Kobayashi (2011) as having 'contributed not only to the increasing call for English education and multiculturalism but also to a unified identity as we-Japanese' (2011: 1). The point is that pressure to develop a global identity through increased English proficiency has, ironically, evoked a resurgence of nationalism and attention to defending Japanese identity. The current official English agenda highlights the underlying political, social and economic concerns facing Japan as the government and private sector endeavour to prepare Japanese youth for a globalised world in which effective communication is seen as being fundamental to Japans economic future.

JET Programme

The Japan Exchange and Teaching Programme (JET) was established in 1987 by local authorities in cooperation with governmental ministries and the council of local authorities for international relations (Ohtani, 2010). With the focus on promotion of *kokusaika* (internationalisation) through fostering understanding between Japanese students and non-Japanese recruits, participants are typically recruited from foreign universities and contracted for a one year period with the option to extend for up to three years. While those recruited have the opportunity to serve in local government offices, the vast majority are dispatched to elementary, junior high and/or senior high schools where they serve as ALTs assigned to support English education and promote international exchange at the local level.

> The purpose of this programme is to enhance mutual understanding between our country and other countries, and to contribute to the promotion of internationalization in our country through promoting international exchange as well as strengthening foreign language education in our country. (MEXT, 2003: note 5)

Despite the fact that ALTs are valued as integral to MEXT's education policy and are seen as playing a pivotal role in introducing foreign cultures and English language instruction to classrooms (Fujita-Round & Maher, 2008), detractors have raised valid questions regarding the qualifications of ALTs and queried the minimal training provided while employed within Japanese schools (Ohtani, 2010). In addition, Japanese teachers working with ALTs have raised concerns as to the competence and commitment of ALTs given that they are not required to have tertiary backgrounds in education, lack teaching experience and are unaware of Japanese school management systems and daily student routines (Kushima & Nishihori, 2006).

While the JET Programme demonstrates Japan's commitment to improving English language education, success in terms of raising student English proficiency has been far from convincing. Researchers have reasoned that JET is a political rather than an educational initiative (Rivers, 2011a), and that success, if judged by the large number of participating teachers, effectively masks questionable effectiveness in advancing English competency (Butler, 2007b; McConnell, 2000; Okuno, 2007). Challenging MEXT claims that the JET Programme is intended to promote international exchange and language education, Rivers (2011a: 378) argues that it is essentially a product of political and economic factors implemented to improve the Japan – United States economic imbalance of the 1980s. Rivers maintains that the JET

Programme was viewed as 'an ideal humanistic solution focusing on grass-roots internationalization between the two countries' with Japan able to demonstrate to the world that its people were not economic predators, and the United States benefiting from the opportunity to maintain and advance 'native-English linguistic and cultural norms with a non-native context' (Rivers, 2011a: 378).

An often heard criticism of the JET Programme over the years has been the policy of hiring young, inexperienced participants without teacher training based on the assumption that a NS of English will inherently be capable of teaching English and influencing positive learning outcomes (Butler, 2007b; Okuno, 2007). In regard to the eligibility criteria for participants, JET stipulates that candidates have only a bachelor's degree in any field, and as Ohtani (2010: 39) notes, do not require a degree in education or in English. Given that teaching qualifications are optional, the majority of ALTs lack educational experience or content knowledge and find little support in a system that provides limited professional training opportunities once a recruit is allocated a teaching position (Kushima & Nishihori, 2006). Stressing ALT training deficiencies, Ohtani (2010) notes that there is no systematic training provided and that ALT preparation consists of a single post-arrival orientation, one mid-year training seminar and one conference for returning JET teachers. Moreover, it is at the mid-year training, after ALT teachers have been dispatched to schools, that lesson-related training is provided.

Beyond systemic problems in recruitment and training, Kobayashi (2011) cites the JET Programme as consolidating cultural boundaries through emphasising 'ideal whiteness' and placing native teachers 'with no background knowledge of Japanese culture or language' in the school classroom. Challenging the notion that the 'native speaker' is the ideal language teacher, Butler (2007b) maintains that it is far from clear what constitutes a 'native speaker' and that there is no pedagogical evidence to validate the notion that NSs are superior language teachers. Underscoring this lack of pedagogical evidence, Astor (2000) argues that differences among native and non-native language teachers exist not in their nativeness, but in their knowledge of pedagogy, methodology and psycho-/applied linguistics. In short, if lines of demarcation are to be drawn then the focus should be on issues relevant to the practice of teaching as opposed to the flawed notion of nativeness.

Examining the assumption that the NS provides a model of correctness, Pavlenko and Blackledge (2004: 15) write that 'speakers of official languages or standard varieties may be regarded as having greater moral and intellectual worth than speakers of unofficial languages or non-standard varieties'. The clear irony being that the NNS, far from being inadequate, demonstrates capabilities in two or more languages in addition to experience and knowledge gained through exposure to socio-cultural factors associated with the languages and process of acquisition. Kobayashi (2011) argues that the maximum three year JET contract essentially guarantees an uninterrupted supply of 'ideal whiteness' and the likelihood that cultural disparities will remain a focal point of the relationship students build with their non-Japanese teachers (Kobayashi, 2011: 9). Commenting on the standing afforded the NS within Japan, Rivers (2011a) argues that 'native-English speaker models have traditionally been held aloft as prestigious targets for non-native English speakers to aspire to and replicate', creating 'a division between the elite (the native speakers), and the non-elite (the non-native speakers)' (Rivers, 2011a: 378).

Kachru's (1982, 1985) model of the worldwide spread of English describes three concentric circles: the Inner Circle, the Outer Circle and the Expanding Circle. These circles represent 'the type of spread, the patterns of acquisition and the functional domains in which English is used across cultures and languages' (Kachru, 1985: 12). The Inner Circle English, said to be 'norm providing', is dominated by the mother-tongue varieties of English. The Outer Circle English, considered 'norm-developing', consists of non-native settings where English is one of two or more official languages and used in a variety of functions. Most of the countries included in the Outer Circle are former colonies of the United Kingdom or the United States. The Expanding Circle refers to countries where English does not assume a historical or governmental role, but is taught as a foreign language for international communication and is regarded as 'norm dependent'. In Kachru's model, Japan lies in the 'Expanding Circle' meaning that English exists as an international language, is a 'performance variety', and is 'norm dependent'. The implication is that it gets its model from metropolitan varieties of English used in 'Inner Circle' countries.

Kachru's concentric circles bring to light the existence of 'multilinguistic identities, multiplicity of norms, both endocentric and exocentric, and distinct socio-linguistic histories' (Kachru, 1996: 135). The model illustrates that the spread of English has given rise to the diversification with English users from the Outer and Expanding Circles increasing. For example, Morrow (2004) makes the point that there are more English speakers in India than in Australia and New Zealand combined. Moreover, Morrow notes a growing number of English users are bilinguals or multilinguals, while the spread of English has seen the emergence of new varieties of English each reflecting the cultural conditions of the place or places where it is employed (Morrow, 2004: 84). Importantly, research on World Englishes illustrates that English is employed in non-native contexts, and as Morrow concludes, 'has shown

that non-Inner Circle varieties are functionally adequate and valid as varieties of English' (Morrow, 2004: 86). English varieties used in Outer and
Expanding Circle countries are not invalidated by variance from Inner Circle
notions of normalcy, rather, it should be assumed that socio-cultural factors
will shape English grammatically, lexically and pragmatically. McKay (2002:
127) observes that changes in English are to be expected as a result of its
international role and 'those changes that do not impede intelligibility should
be recognized as one of the natural consequences of the use of English as an
international language' while Nihalani (2010) makes the critical point that
'new-English speakers are not just passively absorbing the language, they are
shaping it' (2010: 25).

With recruits from 42 countries for the 2014 to 2015 year, JET has been
widening parameters to include Outer Circle countries, however, overall
recruitment numbers illustrate a preference towards Inner Circle speech for
notions of correctness. Japanese students are primarily exposed to white
middle-class North American or British varieties of English and culture
(Kubota, 2002; Matsuda, 2002, 2003) which Matsuda (2002) views as a
potentially impeding comprehension of unfamiliar English varieties encountered in real-world situations. Moreover, Japanese researchers hypothesise
that awareness of, and exposure to, English varieties encourages students to
accept their own English accent and other non-native English varieties
(Matsuda, 2002, 2003; Morrow, 2004). Stressing that globalisation will
increase opportunities for students to use English with NNS and NS of
English, Butler (2007a) emphasises the importance for the Japanese to 'be
familiar with varieties of English and to develop sufficient skills to communicate with speakers of EIL (English as an international language)' (2007a:
144). To this end, it is hoped that NNS teachers may serve as role models for
English learning and raise awareness of international communication (Butler,
2007a). Even so, Rivers (2011a: 378) argues that the native-English speaker is
still very much the 'preferred linguistic other', an argument that in the case
of Japan, can be supported by the pervasiveness of white, young, attractive
faces plastered on English advertising mediums, and further supported by a
glance into any of the numerous *eikaiwa* language schools, or browse through
teaching employment opportunities.

Understanding Culture

The term culture is often characterised by a lack of clarity illustrated in
the diverse and complex array of definitions presented in literature. This
sense of prevailing ambiguity is borne out in the words of Scollon and Scollon

(2001: 128) who reason that 'the word culture brings up more problems than it solves'. Rendering culture a 'vacuous notion', Watts (2003: 101) notes that within politeness literature, the classifications of culture range across national groupings, languages, gender, social classes, subcultures and so on. While potentially divisive, the multiplicity observed in contemporary literature is testament to the fact that culture is recognised as being of critical importance to the process of language teaching and learning. Moreover, difficulty in reaching agreement regarding a working definition underscores that culture, constantly constructed and reconstructed through human interaction and communication, is not a static entity, but rather dynamic and multidimensional.

Earlier models have tended to consider culture through the examination of surface level features or what Hinkel (2001) refers to as that part of culture that is 'visible' and easily discussed. Hinkel argues that this can include the folklore, literature, arts, architecture, styles of dress, cuisine, customs, festivals, traditions and the history of a particular 'people'. This 'visible' framework is evident in the tendency to equate cultures with nations and overlooks 'invisible' aspects of culture Hinkel describes as including socio-cultural norms, worldviews, beliefs, assumptions and value systems. These 'invisible' aspects of culture are considerably more difficult to access given that people may not even be aware they exist. Weaver (1986) depicts the layers of culture through the image of an iceberg in which only a small visible portion sits above the waterline while the greater area rests unseen below the surface. The position here being that those areas above water constitute external elements of culture which are linked with objective knowledge and include behaviour and some beliefs. Internal elements, depicted below the waterline are linked with subjective knowledge such as beliefs, values and thought patterns. Weaver's model posits that external culture is explicitly learned and easily changed, whereas internal culture is implicitly acquired and difficult to modify.

Contesting the correlation between cultures and nations, Ros i Solé (2003: 143) speculates that 'the fallacy of identifying cultures with nations should be demolished' given the failure to account for perpetually shifting global and cultural diversity and the flawed implication that there is an accepted set of quantifiable cultural norms that are able to define the people of a nation. Reasoning that correlations are misleading and discriminatory, Park (2005) speculates that the term culture is employed as a euphemism for 'race' and 'ethnicity' and expresses deficit in the sense that 'different from' equates to 'less than'. Park hypothesises that through using the white mainstream as a point of comparison, there is an assumption 'that culture is that which differentiates minorities, immigrants and refugees from the rest of society' and that the preservation of stereotypes is made possible by culture as a category defined by essential, fixable traits (2005: 19). Promoting a position that moves beyond nations, Ros i Solé (2003) outlines a set of cross-national influences that shape an individual's culture including communities of work, social groups, ethnic origins and gender, while Diaz-Rico and Weed (2006) stress that culture is not static or solitary, but rather evolving and influenced by human agency over time and space.

> The explicit and implicit patterns for living, the dynamic system of commonly agreed upon symbols and meanings, knowledge, belief, art, morals, law, customs, behaviors, traditions, and/or habits that are shared and make up the total way of life of a people, as negotiated by individuals in the process of constructing a personal identity. (Diaz-Rico & Weed, 2006: 232–233)

The role of human agency and the inevitably of variation is addressed by Streeck (2002) and Spencer-Oatey (2008) who underscore that culture, while shared by a group of people, is not predetermined. Given that culture is dynamic, variable and influenced by human agency it follows that membership within a cultural group does not prevent differences between members from contributing to deviation in judgment.

> The old model of patchwork of cultures and cultural identities, which is to a large extent a product of late-19th century anthropology and its context, colonialism, has now begun to recede, giving way to a mode of thinking about culture and social life that, in the first place, regards cultural difference as a product of human agency, not as a part of a seemingly natural order of things, and is utterly aware of the contested and shifting nature of cultural identity and cultural borders. (Streeck, 2002: 301–302)

> Culture is a fuzzy set of basic assumptions and values, orientations to life, beliefs, policies, procedures and behavioural conventions that are shared by a group of people, and that influence (but do not determine) each member's behaviour and his/her interpretations of the 'meaning' of other people's behaviour. (Spencer-Oatey, 2008: 3)

The bond between culture and language has generated intense interest within the linguistics research community fuelled by wide-spread consensus that 'culture is no longer an invisible or incidental presence in language learning but instead is ... a strand with equal status to that of language'

(Newton *et al.*, 2010: 1). Teachers have a responsibility to pedagogically address issues of culture and language within the classroom given that communicative practices are shaped and transmitted by culture, just as language functions as a tool by which culture is communicated (see Atkinson, 2002; Byram, 2012; Kramsch, 1993, 2003, 2004, 2009; Liddicoat, 2004a, 2009). This is succinctly summarised by Mitchell and Myles (2004: 235) who observe that 'language and culture are not separate, but are acquired together, with each providing support for the development of the other'. The evolving dynamic, personal and interconnected connection between language and culture is well captured by Liddicoat as follows:

> Every message a human being communicates through language is communicated in a cultural context. Cultures shape the ways language is structured and the ways in which language is used. A language learner who has learnt only the grammar and vocabulary of a language is, therefore, not well equipped to communicate in that language. (Liddicoat, 2004b: 17)

In defining culture in reference to the following examination, our position draws on Streeck's (2002) and Spencer-Oatey's (2008) views which embrace both collective elements and factors of human agency as informing culture. This position is captured in Christensen's (1992) definition which understands culture as formed in a historical context, and Streeck's position which argues the need to move beyond culture as a static notion. In short, culture describes an ongoing process of learned and shared human patterns of behaviours and interactions acquired through socialisation. Like all social units, the classroom has its own unique and developing culture observable in collaboration between the students, the processes of teacher/student interaction, specific classroom activities, materials and so forth. These shared characteristics are termed 'commonalities' by Christensen (1992), who explains culture as consisting of 'commonalities around which people have developed values, norms, family values, social roles, and behaviours, in response to the historical, political, economic, and social realities they face' (1992: 86). It is these shared patterns of explicit and implicit commonalities which provide insights into not only how the students express themselves, but also how they interpret the teacher's language use and behaviour. The point that people within a culture tend to interpret meaning in similar ways is expressed in Lederach's (1995) definition that 'Culture is the shared knowledge and schemes created by a set of people for perceiving, interpreting, expressing, and responding to the social realities around them' (1995: 9). These shared reactions provide insight into potential areas of pragmatic failure which unintentionally bring about an assumption of meaning that does not correspond with the speaker's intent.

In relation to culture and its associated generalisations, a further point of caution is the tendency in research to reference politeness orientations and face within 'western' culture or societies. As Watts (2003) points out, it is all too easy to talk about 'western societies' without acknowledging that there are of course differences in politeness between the United States and Western Europe (2003: 83) and indeed within both political entities. For example, McKay (2002) cautions that contrasting western and eastern assumptions of cultures of learning 'can perpetuate differences, promote the concept of otherness, and lead to simple dichotomies and stereotyping' (2002: 121). Accordingly, for the following examination, the objective is not to define culture in terms of nation, but rather to explore the teacher and students' shared patterns of language use and behaviour in relation to a series of L2 learning activities. Understanding the influence of culture is deemed important in that insight into the students' interpretation of classroom interaction can be enhanced through an understanding of the knowledge and schematic framework that they bring to the classroom. As Scollon and Scollon (2001) point out, 'cultures do not talk to each other; individuals do' (2001: 138). With this in mind, we maintain that culture alone does not define students or account for all classroom behaviour as individuals bring their own unique perspective to the classroom. At the same time, within the culture of the classroom there are shared patterns in how the students behave, express themselves, interact, and interpret language and behaviour. These discernible patterns of behaviour among the students are examined with attention to the students' views of their own classroom participation, and an analysis of the underlying assumptions which inform these behaviours.

3   Pragmatics

What is Pragmatics?

The term pragmatics, originally coined by Charles Morris in 1938, was identified as the branch of semiotics that studies the relation of signs to interpreters, in contrast with semantics, which examines the relation of signs to the specific objects to which they refer (Levinson, 1983: 1). Introduced into linguistics in the 1980s through Leech's *Principles of Pragmatics* (1983) and Levinson's *Pragmatics* (1983), the field of pragmatics has attracted growing attention over the past three decades as interest in the social aspects of language move beyond literal interpretations of linguistic forms to the manner in which the meanings of such forms are interpreted by interlocutors in context. Evolution in the field of pragmatics has been motivated by what Archer *et al.* (2012) describe as 'the realization that we need a broad theory of human communication going beyond what is treated in semantics, which can explain how human beings use language to express what they mean on different levels' (2012: 4). The field of pragmatics, referred to by Archer *et al.* as 'a full-blown theory of communication and language use' (2012: xxiii), goes beyond the literal interpretation of language to explore the ways in which the use of language and context affect meaning. In short, pragmatics is concerned with linguistic and non-linguistic signals framed with attention to the specific socio-cultural features of the context and its participants. Accordingly, at base pragmatics embraces the view that communication represents an inherently complex process in which the speaker/writer will not always communicate directly what he means, correspondingly, the manner in which listener/readers interpret meaning will not always coincide with the intended communicative objective of the speaker(s).

With regard to second/foreign-language teaching and learning, the mainstream relevance afforded pragmatics can be observed in the array of publications available, the diverse range of research areas and the expanding role of pragmatics within teacher education. Notwithstanding this exposure and engagement, Archer *et al.* (2012: 3) note the diversity of possible definitions and a persisting lack of clear boundaries regarding 'how pragmatics should be delimited from semantics and grammar, the scope of the discipline of linguistic pragmatics and terminology we need to describe pragmatic phenomena'. Indeed, the field of pragmatics, referred to by Bar-Hillel (1971) at that time as the 'wastebasket' of linguistics (1971: 405), extends over such a range of phenomena that it has become notoriously difficult to answer the question 'What is pragmatics?' Despite varying views on how pragmatics could best be characterised and indeed in some circumstances quantified, there exists nevertheless a shared focus within all approaches to pragmatics on discovering; (a) the communicative intentions of the speaker and/or writer, (b) the meanings assigned by the listener and/or reader, and (c) the situational variables which impact on the use and interpretation of language forms during communication. As a consequence, the process of interpreting pragmatic meaning depends on the accretion of a wide range of language data; the examination of the verbal and non-verbal cues employed by interlocutors to jointly construct meaning through the 'interweaving of linguistic analysis, local contextual information, and socio-linguistic dimensions such as socio-cultural and historical information' (LoCastro, 2012: xi). It is these inferences drawn from language in use, both linguistic and non-linguistic, that provide essential information as to how such forms and behaviours are intended to be interpreted, or might be, within the given context. In this way, essential to pragmatics is the recognition that there may be gaps between the literal and denotative meaning of an utterance and the connotative meanings of any message being conveyed. A simple example being that if a father were to remark to his son, 'It's a relief when you get your homework done' is he; (a) praising the boy for completing his homework, (b) reminding the boy that he should be doing his homework, or (c) admonishing the boy for neglecting his homework?

Individuals from different cultures, societies and speech communities interact in accordance with beliefs, values and behavioural conventions that may not always be obvious to the listener or even apparent to the speaker. The pragmatic rules for language use, as Bardovi-Harlig and Mahan-Taylor (2003) point out, 'are often subconscious, and even NS (native speakers) are often unaware of pragmatic rules until they are broken (and feelings are hurt, offense is taken, or sometimes things just seem a bit odd)' (2003: 1–2).

> In different societies and different communities, people speak differently; these differences in ways of speaking are profound and systematic, they reflect different cultural values, or at least different hierarchies of values;

different ways of speaking, different communicative styles, can be explained and made sense of in terms of independently established different cultural values and cultural priorities. (Wierzbicka, 1991: 69)

While pragmatic norms influence the communicative strategies by which one elects to express himself and the meaning assigned to language, a shared native language, culture and social influences do not automatically equate to the consistent application or interpretation of pragmatic conventions which do not constitute a singular set of rules. For example, Schneider and Barron (2008) note that potential impact of variation both across and within socio-cultural groups such as regional, socio-economic, ethnic, gender and age-related. Variation in language is addressed by Ishihara and Cohen (2010) who observe that pragmatic norms denote 'a range of tendencies or conventions for pragmatic language use that are not absolute or fixed but are typical or generally preferred in the L2 community' (2010: 13). While core speech acts may follow in regular and predictable patterns for members of a given community, the researchers highlight that the challenge lies in 'knowing whether they are applied in the given language context, and if so, determining when, how, and why' (2010: 10). To illustrate diversity in the use of language, albeit in a limited way, one can look at the use of language in conducting speech acts such as thanking and refusing as negotiated in Japanese and English. As Bouchard (2011) notes, the Japanese receiver of a gift will typically register gratitude through responding 'sorry' (*sumimasen*) whereas non-Japanese are likely to regard expressions such as 'Thank you' or 'Oh, you shouldn't have' as pragmatically appropriate (2011: 82). Bouchard theorises that 'in Japanese, "Thank you" as an expression of gratitude does not always sound sincere enough' (2011: 82). Shedding light on this gap in pragmatic expectations, Kondo (2008) points out that the Japanese expression *sumimasen* is multi-functional and used for both apologising and thanking, yet tends to be translated in English as 'I'm sorry'. Consequently, while a non-Japanese speaker may assume that it is an inappropriate expression of thanks, the Japanese speaker tends to view the communicative expression of thanks as requiring one to simultaneously convey indebtedness as well as thanks (Ide, 1998; Kumatoridani, 1999). Consequently, for the receiver of a gift, *sumimasen* serves as an appropriate expression of gratitude while at the same time registering indebtedness for the generosity and potential inconvenience that has resulted from the purchase.

The capacity to effectively make use of the pragmatic features of a language refers to one's ability 'to go beyond the literal meaning of what is said or written, in order to interpret the intended meanings, assumptions, purposes or goals, and the kinds of actions that are being performed' (Ishihara

& Cohen, 2010: 5). Moreover, the facility to effectively comprehend and produce a communicative act requires knowledge of factors such as social distance, social status and cultural knowledge among participants. Barron (2003) describes competence in one's ability to use pragmatic features of language as 'knowledge of the linguistic resources available in a given language for realising particular illocutions, knowledge of the sequential aspects of speech acts and finally, knowledge of the appropriate contextual use of the particular languages' linguistic resources' (2003: 10). Taking these factors into account, pragmatics examines the varying ways in which interlocutors express and assign meanings to wordings and behaviours in order to effectively communicate while making choices regarding appropriateness, word choice, structures, suitability within the specific context and the anticipated impact of their verbal and non-verbal actions on the listener. In this respect, a primary challenge for researchers of pragmatics is to ascertain the principles and systems that motivate the speaker or writer when producing an utterance, and the listener or reader when interpreting the given message.

Pragmatic Failure

The term pragmatic failure denotes a wide range of communicative dysfunctions and misunderstandings explained by Riley (2006) as resulting from 'an interactant's applying inappropriate social rules or knowledge to the production and interpretation of discourse and related communicative behaviours' (2006: 313). In short, individuals may express themselves and interpret meaning according to socio-culturally informed patterns of language use that are not readily identifiable without an insider's perspective. Described by Thomas (1983) as 'the inability to understand "what is meant by what is said"', cross-cultural pragmatic failure is explained by Thomas as a mismatch of schema and interpretive frame in which interactants from different cultural backgrounds misunderstand or miscommunicate intended meanings (1983: 91). Simply put, during communication the speaker produces language and the listener assigns meaning in accordance with his own socially and culturally informed worldview. Pragmatic failure affects language production and interpretation in the sense that interlocutors are bound by their own socio-cultural norms and will typically use these as the basis from which to evaluate each other.

Thomas (1983), based on Leech's (1983) distinction between socio-pragmatics and pragma-linguistics, discusses two kinds of pragmatic failure: socio-pragmatic failure and pragma-linguistic failure. Pragma-linguistic failure occurs when the illocutionary force of the utterance is different from the force assigned to it by the NSs of the target language, or when speech act strategies are inappropriately transferred from the L1 to L2. On the other hand, socio-pragmatic failure deals with the social conditions placed on language in use and occurs when the speaker fails to perform the required speech act in the right context and in using the appropriate language forms. For this reason, socio-pragmatic failure stems from different intercultural perceptions of what constitutes appropriate linguistic behaviour and as a consequence, engages one's beliefs and value system. This engagement refers to implicit social meanings and deals with mismatches in social aspects of language use such as the miscalculation of size of imposition, cost/benefit, social distance, and relative power, which may be caused by cross-cultural differences in understanding certain social values. Thomas (1983) makes clear that while pragma-linguistic failure is basically a linguistic problem caused by differences in the linguistic encoding of pragmatic force, socio-pragmatic failure stems from cross-culturally different perceptions of what constitutes appropriate linguistic behaviour.

The distinctions between pragma-linguistic and socio-pragmatic failure are useful, however the borderline is often blurred in the sense that both are fundamentally concerned with perceptions of socio-cultural norms. To illustrate, in Japanese when handing a gift to a business associate, a Japanese speaker may say: *'kore wa tsumaranai mono desu ga yoroshikattara douzo'* which can be translated literally as 'This is trifling thing. If you don't mind please accept it'. The speaker intentionally understates the value and appeal of the gift however, it is understood by the recipient that this is not a reflection of the true value of the gift. On the contrary, gifts are often given to those of higher status or someone who is regarded as having the power to positively benefit the gift giver. Consequently, as a display of respect, the gift has in all likelihood been carefully selected as the value is determined in proportion to the debt incurred and importance of the relationship. If a Japanese speaker were to directly translate this phrase into English when presenting a gift to English speaking associates it is not clear whether this would represent pragma-linguistic or socio-pragmatic failure. As the act of giving gifts as an indication of the value placed on a relationship is closely associated with rank, role and power within Japanese culture, it is of questionable merit to specify an equivalent socio-cultural context or pragmatically appropriate English speech act as expressions such as 'This is just a little something for you' fail to capture the communicative intent. Given that pragma linguistic failure represents a problem with the linguistic encoding of pragmatic meaning or force, an important source of this type of error is pragma linguistic transfer which occurs when L1 speech act strategies are inappropriately transferred from to L2. On the other hand, a distinctive feature of socio-pragmatics is the interdependent relation between linguistic forms and socio-cultural contexts (Harlow, 1990). It is the knowledge of how to vary the language output in speech acts according to different situations and/or social considerations which is why Thomas (1983) sites socio-pragmatic failure as being more difficult to correct than pragma linguistic failure.

The implications of pragmatic failure are considerable given that pragmatic errors are not usually marked as clearly as grammatical errors. In other words, while a grammatical error when refusing an invitation may disclose difficulties a non-native speaking interlocutor may be experiencing in interpreting the invitation or formulating a response, deviation from L1 pragmatic forms tend to go unnoticed. For this reason, an individual may not recognise or respond to the pragmatic deviation and instead, evaluate the refusal based on what he views as L1 standards. As LoCastro (2012) notes, 'Grammatical errors made by a non-native English speaker may be forgiven, a mistake attributed to low proficiency in the target language. However, speakers are less willing to explain away pragmatic failures' (2012: 85). The stakes become higher when the pragmatic infringement directly threatens the interlocutor or in some way contradicts standards associated with the specific interactional context.

Resistance to a Native Speaker Model

Student resistance to socio-pragmatic norms and their pragma linguistic manifestations can generate insight into underlying ideologies, cultural values, social practices and assumptions that inform the individual's worldview regarding the native language and the target language. Language students bring to the classroom a diverse and unique set of socio-cultural backgrounds, experiences and beliefs which inform their expectations regarding the L2, the classroom, and the roles they associate with both the teacher and the student. This worldview, even within a homogenous group, will manifest itself through varying expectations and learning styles. In addition, we can add to this mix the teacher whose background, experiences, beliefs, and professional knowledge will influence the learning environment (see Borg, 2006, 2013; Ishihara, 2010; Shulman & Shulman, 2004 for discussion of teacher education and beliefs.). Ishihara and Tarone (2009) note that within most classrooms in which pragmatic features of the target language are taught it is the 'native-speaker model' or 'native norms' which students are expected to emulate. This theme is taken up by McKay (2002) who reasons that the primary objective of the student is to effectively communicate their ideas and culture in the L2, and consequently, may not aspire to align with the NS model. Challenging the assumption that a NS model of language use is the accepted objective for the student, Haugh (2007) reasons that L2 users may be receptive to some pragmatic features of the target language while resisting others particularly when 'underlying values formed through first language experiences are perceived to be inconsistent with values underlying language use in the second language' (2007: 658). This position is reflected in the work of Dewaele (2008) which observes that the L2 user may not elect to perform 'appropriately' even if aware of appropriateness associated with a new language or culture. Amongst other alternatives, options the student has include the avoidance of interactions that may lead to inappropriate behaviours or accommodation to the L1 norm to achieve a desired outcome.

Divergence from or alignment with the pragmatic norms of a speech community is not a definitive choice given that students may at times 'model themselves after native speakers or follow culturally acceptable norms in the community' while at other times elect to 'intentionally behave rather uniquely in order to preserve their subjectivity' (Ishihara & Tarone, 2009: 301). In this way, whether intentional or unintentional, students constantly evaluate pragmatic choices in line with their own worldview and their own subjective position. Students may demonstrate affective resistance toward the use of certain NS norms and to maintain identity, may deliberately engage pragmatic features of the L1 even when known to be inappropriate (Al-Issa, 2003; Ishihara & Tarone, 2009; Siegal, 1996). Speaking to this issue, Ishihara and Tarone (2009) found L2 Japanese speakers' unwilling to embrace specific pragmatic norms that they felt challenged their values. For example, one participant elected to use *keigo* (Japanese honorifics) when interacting with a younger employee even though aware that this conflicted with Japanese pragmatic forms as this was consistent with his views of human equality. Similarly, LoCastro (1998) offers a personal examination of her own Japanese acquisition which discusses pragmatic development and the distinctly hierarchical ways in which factors such as age, status and gender differences are linguistically marked. LoCastro examines her resistance to and lack of motivation in acquiring pragmatic norms associated with *keigo* which she describes as conflicting with her ideological position formed by more egalitarian, less-gendered societal structures. Illustrating that Japanese students share these feeling, LoCastro's (2001) examination of the relationship between Japanese EFL learners attitudes to self-identity and receptiveness to the accommodation of L2 pragmatic norms found that students expressed a desire to build an L2 identity compatible with their Japanese identities. The students articulated positive orientations towards achieving English proficiency in order to increase academic and future possibilities, yet also noted that a reluctance to abandon their identities as Japanese which influenced and constrained attitudes to NS pragmatic forms. Of note in these cases is that acquisition and application of pragmatic forms was associated with an attempt to construct an L2 identity that was consistent with the learners self-identity and world view.

A final and essential point concerns the idealised and misleading view of a NS model of pragmatic competence as somehow guaranteeing the language student communicative precision. Specifically, the NS model begs the question whether the NS is in fact always an effective communicator. Speaking to this concern over 20 years ago, Coupland *et al.* (1991: 3) state that 'language use and communication are (...) pervasively and even intrinsically flawed, partial, and problematic'. In many ways this underscores the obvious point that the NS is not always the model communicator in every situation. There are of course NSs who struggle to effectively communicate and conversely, NNSs who excel at communicating even when faced with limited L2 proficiency. Accordingly, idealising a NS model as the target for language students promotes expectations and assumes standards that may not only be inconsistent with student goals, but also create a false sense of universal standards of pragmatic forms that students should aspire to. The deeply flawed NS model tasks the teacher with accepting the validity of the language student as an acceptable and capable communicator.

Intercultural Communicative Competence

The term communicative competence, defined in different ways by different scholars, is built on the premise that understanding a language requires more than the ability to assemble and use lexical items according to grammatical rules. To become a competent L2 user, one needs to be able to produce language which is both structurally accurate and appropriate to the context in which it is being used. The concept of communicative competence was initially introduced by Hymes (1966) in reaction to Chomsky's (1965) notion of linguistic competence and its perceived inadequacies in its failure to account for contextual appropriateness. Stressing the role of context, Saville-Troike (1996: 362) explains communicative competence as 'what a speaker needs to know to communicate appropriately within a particular speech community'. While definitions vary, there is agreement that students cannot master a target language without adequate knowledge of the culture related to that language (see Bachman, 1990; Canale & Swain, 1980, 1981; Celce-Murcia *et al.*, 1995; Saville-Troike, 1996). Bachman's (1990) model identifies communicative competence as consisting of language competence, strategic competence, and psychological mechanisms. Based on this model, language competence comprises both organisational competence and pragmatic competence, which is further explained as encompassing illocutionary and socio-linguistic competence. Pragmatic competence is characterised by Bachman as 'the relationships between utterances and the acts of functions that speakers (or writers) intend to perform through these utterances, which can be called the illocutionary force of utterances, and the characteristics of the context of language use that determine the appropriateness of utterances' (1990: 89–90). Importantly, Bachman's model regards pragmatic competence as interacting with 'organizational competence' to enhance communicative competence.

In recent years, there has been a shift as the concept of communicative competence has been transformed into the concept of intercultural communicative competence (ICC). Intercultural dimensions draw attention to the fact that humans are complex, dynamic and diverse and consequently, effective interaction requires learners to be attentive to their own identities and those of their interlocutors. As Byram *et al.* (2002: 7) emphasise, 'It is the hope that language learners who thus become "intercultural speakers" will be successful not only in communicating information but also in developing a human relationship with people of other languages and cultures'. Scarino (2009) explains intercultural language learning as being primarily about the way in which 'language and culture come into play in creating and exchanging meaning' (2009: 69). For this reason intercultural language learning focuses on the development of students' ability 'to recognise and integrate into their communication an understanding of themselves as already situated in their own language(s) and culture(s)' and when communicating, 'to recognise that others also approach communication from the background of their own experiences within their own language(s) and culture(s)' (Scarino, 2009: 69). Additionally, Scarino highlights that intercultural language learning recognises that individuals 'interpret communication and relationships through the frame of reference of their cumulative experience within their own language and culture' and this cumulative experience is 'constantly reconsidered and re-articulated, and re-shapes the frame of reference that people draw upon in creating and interpreting meaning' (2009: 69). The shift towards ICC reflects a holistic approach to communicative competence stimulated by recognition that language and culture are profoundly interconnected and students' require intercultural skills for effective cross-cultural communication. Accordingly, ICC stresses the mediation between different cultures, namely, the ability to look at oneself from an 'external' perspective, analyse and adapt one's own behaviours, values and beliefs (Byram & Zarate, 1997).

Within the ICC framework, building knowledge of both the native and target language cultures and culturally-shaped identities is viewed as critical given that during intercultural communication, interlocutors with potentially diverse sets of values and world views interact by means of considerably different linguistic codes (Beneke, 2000). Awareness of one's own cultural dimensions, often not apparent at a conscious level, enhances mediation of interaction as interlocutors can interpret cultural contexts and interact within them. Accordingly, ICC is linked not only to one's sensitivity to features of the target language culture, but also represents the ability to recognise the culture, behaviours, values and beliefs that one brings to any interaction. Liddicoat *et al.* (2003) describe intercultural language learning as follows:

> Intercultural language learning involves the fusing of language, culture and learning into a single educative approach. It begins with the idea that language, culture and learning are fundamentally interrelated and places this interrelationship at the centre of the learning process. (...) Intercultural language learning involves developing with learners an understanding of their own language(s) and culture(s) in relation to an additional language and culture. It is a dialogue that allows for reaching a common ground for negotiation to take place, and where variable points of view are recognised, mediated and accepted. (Liddicoat *et al.*, 2003: 43)

Byram *et al.* (2002: 10) stress that 'The acquisition of intercultural competence is never complete and perfect, but *to be a successful intercultural speaker and mediator does not require complete and perfect competence*'. Consequently, the learner is not expected to assimilate to L2 cultural norms as it is the development of an intermediate position which is central to mediating between cultural frameworks. Learners follow the norms of an 'intercultural speaker' that require them to acquire the 'competences which enable them to mediate/interpret the values, beliefs and behaviours (the "cultures") of themselves and of others and to "stand on the bridge" or indeed "be the bridge" between people of different languages and cultures' (Byram, 2006: 12). In short, students learn to recognise the culturally-shaped worldviews that form their personal identities and to engage with their own and others' languages and cultures in order to move between these worlds. Not only does intercultural teaching involve developing the students' critical cultural awareness, but also focuses on teaching the skills and attitudes needed to understand and effectively interact with people from different cultures. Liddicoat (2002, 2005) outlines a pathway for acquiring intercultural competence as a model of student's internal processes of noticings, reflections and language production (see Figure 1).

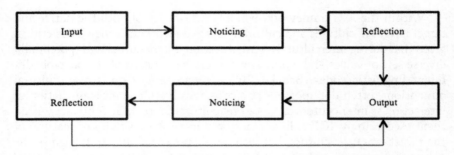

Figure 1 A pathway for developing intercultural competence (Liddicoat, 2002: 11)

The student begins with knowledge of the practices of their own first culture and gradually acquires an approximated system of practices through exposure to new input. This involves awareness-raising opportunities to reflect on one's own culture, experimentation with the new culture, and deciding how to respond to cultural variance. Crozet (2007) maintains that this requires 'the turning inward of cultural information through self-reflection leading to an enhanced understanding of the role of culture/language in the construct of worldviews (one's own and others) and allowing for conscious positioning of self when confronting difference (...)' (2007: 5). Students infer, compare, interpret, discuss and negotiate meaning through a process referred to as the finding of a 'third place' (Kramsch, 1993). This 'third place' is described by Kramsch (1993: 236) as 'the interstices between cultures that the learner grew up with and the new cultures he or she is being introduced to'. The third place is where learners synthesise elements of different cultures and establish their own understanding of the cultural differences between those cultures. Learners are encouraged to understand their own identities in relation to others and to recognise that identities change and develop as a result of exposure to new cultures. The intercultural speaker is charged with building a new place for himself based on an understanding of, and respect for cultural diversity. The last section of the pathway involves intercultural negotiation in action captured as a cyclical process. In this way, developing ICC is viewed as a cyclical process of acquiring and acting with intercultural understanding.

Teaching Pragmatics

Research from as early as the 1980s demonstrated that language students who achieved a high level of structural proficiency in a target language did not necessarily attain equal proficiency in pragmatic aptitude (Schmidt, 1983; Swain, 1985; Thomas, 1983). Illustrating this critical gap, Cohen (2008: 226) observes that 'many advanced language learners are able to utilise complex linguistic systems, but are unable to express and interpret meaning in order to perform language functions (e.g. apologies, requests) appropriately'. Among other things, students have been found to exhibit considerable differences from NSs in the execution and comprehension of speech acts, and in the management of conversation through reactive tokens such as back channels, silences and short responses (see Archer *et al.*, 2012; Ishihara & Cohen, 2010; Kasper & Rose, 1999). Given that learners often struggle to acquire L2 pragmatic competence on their own, it is vital that attention to pragmatics within the classroom be pedagogically addressed from the earliest stages, and at every stage, of learning. The importance of methodically integrating pragmatics into language learning is succinctly expressed by Childs as follows:

> Pragmatics is not an optional add-on. It is a necessary facet of language and of language learning. This is because the whole point is no longer grammatical form but communication of meaning and that is based on situations. The emphasis is on appropriate patterns, whether they are grammatical or not. (Childs, 2005: 23)

The teaching of pragmatics is a complex undertaking given that the use of language, both the target language and native language, is intricately connected with socio-cultural and individual affiliations, values, social factors, interlocutors, and other variables that are not always evident. As early as 1983, Thomas outlined the teachers' responsibility as being to 'equip the student to express her/himself in exactly the way s/he chooses to do so – rudely, tactfully, or in an elaborately polite manner' (1983: 96). In such, awareness of the target language pragmatic devices and practices is necessary for students to develop the capacity to make informed linguistic choices. Through appropriate contextualised use of language the student can communicatively preserve identities and manage face by means of extending greater control over language selections. Moreover, this knowledge allows the speaker to predict how interactive choices are potentially being interpreted by interlocutors.

Recognising that pragmatic forms are not always shared by NSs, welcomed by the language student or incorporated in language curriculum, the teacher is tasked with determining what role pragmatics instruction should play within the classroom. Ishihara and Tarone (2009) make the distinction between receptive and productive pragmatic competence, that is, even if students choose not to produce native-like language and behave in a native-like manner, it is critical to learn to recognise and understand intentions, nuances, politeness and rudeness in others' linguistic production. This issue has been addressed by Bardovi-Harlig and Mahan-Taylor's (2003: 38) who argue that 'The goal of instruction in pragmatics is not to insist on conformity to a particular target-language norm, but rather to help learners become familiar with the range of pragmatic devices and practices in the target language'. This position finds support in Rose and Kasper (2001) who caution that 'Teaching target norms, which learners are then forced to use, does not seem to be an appropriate way to teach pragmatics, as learners' pragmatic choices are connected with their cultural identities' (2001: 153). The problem is intensified if the student is forced or expected to comply with unfamiliar communicative practices and not presented explicit detail outlining how and why NSs conventionally use the target language as they do.

As attention to the need for pragmatics instruction within the language classroom intensifies, there has been an increase in pedagogical suggestions outlining techniques and activities to develop pragmatic awareness specifically through noticing, understanding and producing pragmatic forms (see Archer *et al.*, 2012; Bardovi-Harlig & Mahan-Taylor, 2003; Ishihara & Cohen, 2010; Martínez-Flor & Usó-Juan, 2006). To raise pragmatic awareness, Bardovi-Harlig and Mahan-Taylor (2003) promote moving away from a teacher centred classroom and creating options for practicing L2 pragmatic abilities through student-centred interaction. The focus on empowering the language learner is expressed in Kondo's (2008: 153) view that students need to be given 'the opportunity in the classroom to reflect on their own linguistic choices, compare those choices with pragmatic features of the target language and then to try out the various other options available to them'. Among other matters, Kasper (1997) notes that student-centred activities extend students' speaking time, provide opportunities to practice conversational management, perform communicative acts and interact with peers.

In terms of pedagogical steps, Kasper (1997) stresses that the acquisition of pragmatic knowledge requires pertinent and recognisable input in addition to opportunities to develop a 'high level of processing control in order to access relevant knowledge quickly and effectively in different communicative contexts' (1997: 148). The two primary types of activities frequently cited in research are awareness-raising activities and activities that focus on communicative practice. Kondo (2008) mentions awareness-raising activities as a means by which to sensitise students to cultural differences and variables involved in language use. Awareness-raising activities are followed by interactive opportunities and hands on student-centred interaction designed to rehearse linguistic forms and contextualised pragmatic meaning.

To achieve this, Kasper (1997) advocates the inclusion of activities such as role-play, simulation and drama to engage students in different social roles and speech events. The intention is for the student to rehearse linguistic forms and contextualised pragmatic meaning through activities that simulate real-world interactive situations.

4 Face/Identity and Politeness Theory

Overview

Linguistic politeness, viewed as a key focus of the field of pragmatics, attends to 'meaning in interaction' (Thomas, 1995: 23) and the possible ways in which information can be communicated in order to protect the participants and the appropriateness of the context. Chapter 4 outlines the theoretical basis for the study by means of a critical examination of the key fields of politeness, face and identity. First, an overview of the central construct of face is developed through attention to Goffman's (1955) theory of social interaction and B&L's ([1978]1987) influential politeness theory. The chapter continues with a review of literature both for and against B&L's notion of face and theory of universal politeness with a concentration on Japanese scholarship and in the context of the Japanese language. The chapter concludes with a discussion of identity which branches into an examination of the interrelationship between identity and face.

Goffman on Face and Facework

The concept of face, widely understood in the fields of sociology and linguistics as 'the negotiated public image, mutually granted each other by participants in a communicative event' (Scollon & Scollon, 1995: 35) is derived from the basic assumption that as social beings we are united by an intrinsic concern for how we are perceived by others (Haugh & Hinze, 2003). Located in the flow of daily communication, face denotes the public self-image human beings wish to maintain and as such can be drawn upon to explicate an extensive range of phenomena including those emotional and social aspects that 'a person expects others to recognise and acknowledge' (LoCastro,

2003: 110). During interaction, the collaborative practice of attending to mutual face claims is viewed as a dynamic process by which one petitions an interlocutor in order to develop and/or maintain those positive aspects of face that the individual values, in accordance with cultural, social and individual notions of appropriateness. In addition to these private face claims, one's linguistic motivations are seen as being guided by an awareness of the need to engage in the reciprocal process of attending to an addressee's face claims. In order to understand this two-fold negotiation of both petitioning and granting face and how it relates to contemporary theories of linguistic politeness, it is necessary to begin with American sociologist Erving Goffman's concept of face.

Through the 1950s and 1960s, Goffman developed a theory of social interaction which maintained that people process certain variables when deciding the form of their speech. Goffman (1955) referred to these variables as matters concerning face and hypothesised that during the process of interaction individuals consciously or sub-consciously structure their verbal and non-verbal behaviour through accounting for these variables. These variables include aspects such as one's relationship to the interlocutor, the situation in which the exchange takes place, and the nature of what it is we wish to communicate.

> Face is an image of self-delineated in terms of approved social attributes – albeit an image that others may share, as when a person makes a good showing for his profession or religion by making a good showing for himself. (Goffman, 1967: 5)

Goffman's examination of face-to-face interaction presents a framework for the interpretation of social exchanges based on the notion that the construct of face can potentially explain how people elect to present themselves in social situations. The actions taken by an individual in order to make whatever he is doing consistent with face are referred to as facework (1967: 12). Bargiela–Chiappini's (2003) re-examination of Goffman's (1955) original conceptualization of face notes that, 'For Goffman, "facework" has to do with self-presentation in social encounters, and although individual psychology matters, it is the interactional order that is the focus of Goffman's study' (2003: 1463). In this sense, facework represents the speaker's endeavours to interact in a positive manner when publicly presenting himself and responding to an interlocutor's face claims in order to maintain what he identifies as social appropriateness. According to Goffman's publication 'On face-work' (1955; republished 1967):

> In any society, whenever the physical possibility of spoken interaction arises, it seems that a system of practices, conventions, and procedural

rules comes into play which functions as a means of guiding and organiz-
ing the flow of messages. An understanding will prevail as to when and
where it will be permissible to initiate talk, among whom, and by means
of what topics of conversation. (Goffman, 1955: 33–34)

The 'understanding' that Goffman (1955) speaks of assumes that interlocutors will recognise a system of practices, conventions and procedural
rules that will enable the speaker to project positive value, support the interlocutor's face and work to preserve the equilibrium of the encounter. Goffman
defines face as 'the positive social value a person effectively claims for himself by the line others assume he has taken during a particular contact' (1955:
213). The line taken refers to 'a pattern of verbal and nonverbal acts by which
he expresses his view of the situation and through this his evaluation of the
participants, especially himself' (Goffman, 1967: 5). When a line and image
are in agreement, the speaker is regarded as maintaining face, however if
there is discontinuity between the desired line and image then this is
described as being 'in the wrong face' (Goffman, 1955: 339). Watts (2003)
characterises Goffman's concept of face as 'the conceptualization each of us
makes of our "self" through the construals of others in social interaction and
particularly in verbal interaction, i.e. through talk' (2003: 124). In other
words, the line an individual takes in social encounters is formulated according to how he wishes to be recognised and valued, how he views the interlocutor and how he perceives the situation.

According to Goffman's (1967) theory of face, social encounters are
enacted in such a way that mutual face claims are maintained through self-
respect and considerateness. Watts (2003) makes the point that Goffman's
face is not regarded as a permanent aspect of our construction of the self, but
rather is impacted by the flow of events that transpire during interaction. To
highlight this shifting status, Watts defines face as a 'socially attributed
aspect of self that is temporarily on loan for the duration of the interaction
in accordance with the line or lines that the individual has adopted' (2003:
125). In this sense, an individual who is granted face during interaction may
subsequently find that a line he employs results in face being withdrawn.
Throughout the process of interaction, the individual not only seeks to claim
face but also responds to the face claims of an interlocutor. Goffman maintains that these 'actions' may be conscious or unconscious, and often become
habitual. In this way an individual, through verbal and non-verbal strategies
employed to enact face, may elect to uphold, enhance or potentially challenge another person's face. The link between the maintenance of one's face
and preservation of the specific social situation is explained in Manning's
(1992) account of Goffman's work in which he comments that 'there is a

general conspiracy to save face so that social situations can also be saved' (1992: 38). The implication being here that facework not only defines the individual, but serves to regulate conduct according to the specific situation. Consequently, the strategies engaged during interaction and the ways in which one chooses to conduct himself in public are profoundly influenced by one's interpretation of social appropriateness and the social image he desires to construct, preserve and build on.

Brown and Levinson on Face and Politeness

In 1978, building on Goffman's definition of face, B&L identified what they termed 'a most remarkable phenomenon' claiming that there exists 'extraordinary parallelism in the linguistic minutiae of the utterances with which persons choose to express themselves in quite unrelated languages and cultures' (1987: 55). On this premise, B&L outline an all-embracing model of face and politeness that reasons motivation behind politeness and linguistic devices are remarkably similar across languages and cultures. Essentially, B&L's theory is built on the assertion that every speech act, referring to the function or the action performed by a particular utterance, carries with it a potential threat to the speaker/writer and the listener/reader. This paradigm, the first to incorporate the notion of face as fundamental in politeness systems, proposes that there is a broad set of polite linguistic conventions for mitigating the force of speech acts and these linguistic mechanisms serve the same interactional and social purpose across languages. This theory, often referred to as the 'face-saving theory' of linguistic politeness, brings together three key concepts:

- Goffman's (1967) notion of face as 'the public self-image that every member wants to claim for himself' (1967: 61).
- The view of communication as a rational activity.
- Grice's (1967, published in 1975) Cooperative Principle and associated maxims of conversation which assumes that communication is a cooperative effort in which interlocutors will recognise and contribute appropriately to a common purpose or purposes (1975: 45).

At the heart of 'face saving theory' is the notion of face defined as 'something that is emotionally invested, and that can be lost, maintained, or enhanced, and must be constantly attended to in interaction' (1975: 61). In a significant departure from Goffman's (1967) theory of face and facework, however, B&L (1987: 61) delineate face as consisting of two related sets of human wants: positive face, the want to be approved of by others, and negative face, the want to be unimpeded by others. They are defined as follows:

(a) *negative face*: the basic claim to territories, personal preserves, rights to no distraction – i.e. to freedom of action and freedom from imposition.
(b) *positive face*: the positive consistent self-image or 'personality' (crucially including the desire that this self-image be appreciated and approved of) claimed by interactants.

This dual concept of face assumes that during interaction an individual will seek positive recognition as a contributing member of the social world, while at the same time strive to preserve his independence. Face is viewed as being constantly at risk given that any kind of linguistic action which has a relational dimension is seen as positing a threat to either the speaker or the hearer via what are called face-threatening acts (FTAs), regarded as pivotal to politeness theory. FTAs are characterised according to two parameters:

• Which type of face is being threatened (positive or negative face)?
• Whose face is being threatened (speaker or addressee)?

Acts characterised as threatening the negative face of either speaker or hearer are those which do not account for the desire for freedom of action. Damage to the addressee's negative face include acts that pressure the hearer to perform, or not perform, a certain act (e.g. orders, requests, threats), acts that express the speaker's attitude towards the addressee (e.g. expressions of admiration, hatred) or acts that may result in the addressee incurring debt (e.g. promises). Those acts that threaten the positive face of either speaker or hearer are acts which do not account for the interlocutor's feelings or wants. Threats to the hearer's positive face include those acts in which the speaker expresses a negative assessment of the hearer (e.g. insults, contradictions or complaints) or indifference to the hearer's positive face such as disregard for their values or well-being. Acts that threaten the speaker's positive face might include apologies, acceptance of a compliment, self-humiliation, confessions or emotion leakages such as uncontrollable tears. For example, an apology or an admission of personal fault by the speaker may damage his positive face.

B&L (1987) propose that during face threatening moments a Model Person (MP), 'a willful speaker of a natural language' who possesses both rationality and face, will generally employ linguistic strategies to mitigate the conflict (1987: 58). It is assumed that all individuals are realisations of the MP and therefore when a speaker decides to commit an act that potentially causes the speaker or hearer to lose face, he will use an appropriate politeness strategy in order to minimise the risk. The researchers outline various politeness strategies for negotiating FTAs based on the assumption 'that the mutual knowledge of members' public self-image or face, and the social necessity to orient oneself to it in interaction, are universal' (1987: 62). The theory states that the speaker will evaluate the weightiness of a FTA (x) based on the social distance between the (S) speaker and the hearer (H), the power the hearer has over the speaker, and the ranking of the imposition:

$$W (x) = D (S, H) + P (H, S) + R (x)$$

(B&L, 1987: 76)

In the above, W(x) refers to the weightiness of the FTA, D (S, H) the social distance that exists between S and H, P (H, S) the power that H has over S and R(x) the extent to which the FTA is regarded an imposition within the culture in which S and H are situated. The speaker's assessment of whether and how to employ a FTA requires balancing the need for maximum efficiency with the desire to preserve the hearer's face or speaker's face. In cases in which the latter is more highly prioritised, the speaker will seek to minimise the threat to face generated by the FTA through choosing from a number of strategies of varying risk. At the heart of linguistic politeness lies the speaker's desire to mitigate face threats in order to:

- Protect one's public self-image.
- Protect the public self-image of the addressee.
- Preserve socio-cultural norms appropriate to the situation.

As communication is a dynamic, two-way process of mutual interdependence, it is assumed that it is in the best interest of interlocutors to protect each other's face by softening or avoiding the impact of FTAs. Accordingly, as recognition of face wants and needs is key to linguistic politeness, it is presumed that interlocutors will instinctively adjust their language based on what they believe to be shared face values. B&L (1987) outline five politeness strategies available to the speaker when linguistically communicating face-threatening information which are hierarchically arranged according to the degree to which they threaten the hearer's face (see Figure 2). The theory being that by virtue of 'payoffs' or 'advantages', 'any rational agent will tend to choose the same genus of strategy under the same conditions' (1987: 71). The higher number of the strategy, as seen in the diagram, corresponds to the increasing weightiness of the FTA. It is assumed that the speaker will select from

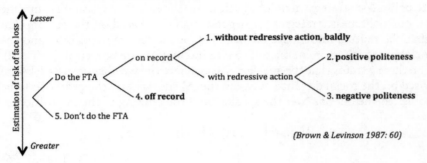

Figure 2 B&L's politeness strategies

strategies with a higher degree of politeness in order to reduce the potential threat to face and that MPs will not select a strategy less risky than required.

In situations when the FTA is regarded as highly threatening, the speaker has the option not to do the FTA (strategy 5). At the other end of the spectrum, if a speech act is regarded as having minimal weightiness it can be executed baldly, on record, with no redressive action (strategy 1). In this case the speaker produces the FTA without attempt to minimise the threat to the addressee's face and therefore follows Grice's (1975) Maxims in order to achieve maximum efficiency; Quality (be non-spurious), Quantity (be informative but don't say more than is required), Relation (be relevant), and Manner (be perspicuous) (Grice, 1975). With the exception of avoidance (strategy 5), the chart makes a distinction between doing a FTA on record (strategies 1, 2 and 3) and doing it off record (strategy 4). If a speaker goes 'on record' then there is 'one unambiguously attributable intention with which witnesses would concur' while if the speaker elects to go 'off-record' then there is 'more than one unambiguously attributable intention so that the actor cannot be held to have committed himself to one particular intent' (1975: 69). For example, if a student requires teacher assistance and inquires, 'Can you help me with this?' he would be on record, however if he were to state, 'I've been thinking about this problem all night' he would be going off record as a direct request for assistance has not been submitted.

As the model indicates, the two key strategies by which politeness can be expressed are positive and negative politeness (strategies 2 and 3). Positive politeness, referred to by Scollon and Scollon (1983, 1995) as 'solidarity politeness' aims at supporting or enhancing the addressee's positive face through emphasising the common ground interlocutors share. Positive politeness is orientated towards the positive face that the addressee claims and consequently the speaker demonstrates that he values the listener and wishes to affirm his positive self-image. In contrast, negative politeness strategies, defined by Scollon as 'deference politeness strategies', are orientated towards addressing the listener's desire to maintain claims of territory and self-determination (B&L, 1987: 70). Scollon and Scollon (1983) point out that 'In any particular case, of course, because of individual differences, differences in the imposition being advanced, or differences in the context, any strategy might be used by a speaker' (1983: 169). Accordingly, the types of politeness strategies that are to be expected in each system are regarded as being predictions, which will or will not be confirmed during conversational exchanges. Importantly, B&L's (1987) theory assumes that negative politeness is the universally preferred approach to facework: 'It is safer to assume that H (hearer) prefers his peace and self-determination more than he prefers your expressions of regard, unless you are certain to the contrary' (1987: 74). The focus is therefore on recognising and upholding the addressee's freedom of action through avoiding imposition or softening the encroachment on the addressee. In other words, positive politeness contributes to the creation of a polite conversational style: to stress in-group knowledge, shared attitudes and values, and appreciation of addressee; and features of negative politeness contribute to the aim of distancing and non-imposing that defines negative politeness (Coates, 1993: 94).

Challenging Brown and Levinson

B&L's ([1978]1987) linguistic politeness theory, based on the premise that face is a basic and universal underlying concept of politeness which transcends cultures and languages, has received both support and criticism from the research community. Challenging claims of universality, critics have questioned the validity of face as a construct for explicating politeness across cultural contexts given that the model is expanded through data from three entirely unrelated languages: Tamil (a South Indian, aboriginal language unrelated to the Indo-European languages of North India), Tzeltal (spoken by Mayan Indians), and English within the United States and England. In particular, B&L's paradigm has been broadly disputed from both a theoretical and empirical standpoint by researchers working with languages other than English, who among other things, accuse the framework of expressing a culturally biased interpretation of politeness that oversimplifies linguistic strategies and neglects factors such as the presence of audience, social status and hierarchical influence.

Reasoning that a universal politeness theory cannot adequately account for the diversity of languages as observed in varying socio-cultural contexts, Nwoye's (1992) examination of interactional norms in African Igbo society outlines a distinction between individual and group face. Arguing that group face conforms to culturally expected norms institutionalised and sanctioned by society, Nwoye's conceptualisation of face prioritises concern for the collective image of the group over the individual self-image, with the group defined as 'any social unit larger than the individual' (1992: 315). The researcher found that within Igbo society, few matters were regarded 'as strictly personal, and therefore, there is a high degree of what in Western societies would be regarded as meddlesomeness or not minding one's business' (1992: 327). Nwoye's analysis of requests, offers, thanks and criticisms found that they are rarely considered impositions, leading the researcher to theorise that while face is associated both with self and the group, it is attention to the group which is ranked higher.

Chinese face, frequently conceptualised through the dual concepts of *mianzi* (or '*mien-tzu*') and *lian* (or '*lien*'), is characterised as embracing the placement of individuals in social hierarchies rather than the accommodation of individual wants or desires (Gu, 1990; Hu, 1944; Mao, 1994). In an early study of the Chinese concept of face conducted through the examination of set phrases, Hu (1944) asserts that *mianzi* refers to prestige or reputation achieved by means of personal effort which is dependent on the external environment, while *lian* constitutes the respect assigned by one's social group on the basis of confidence in one's moral character and is 'both a social sanction for enforcing moral standards and an internalized sanction' (1944: 45). Mao (1994) outlines two fundamental discrepancies between Chinese face and B&L's concept as being the conceptualisation of face as a public 'self-image' as opposed to a 'communal' construct, and the constituents of face, namely negative and positive face. By way of explanation, Mao posits that Chinese *mianzi* is interconnected with the Confucian principle of subordinating the individual to the group and consequently, the desire to seek acknowledgment does not equate to the desire to be free of imposition, but rather 'foregrounds one's dependence on society's recognition of one's social standing and of one's "reputable" existence' (1994: 460). Mao maintains that 'the social and moral connotations evidenced in *mianzi* and *lian* lie well beyond the semantic boundary marked by negative and positive face' (1994: 483) raising concerns as to the extent to which Chinese discursive practices can be accounted for by B&L's paradigm.

Félix-Brasdefer's (2006) investigation of the linguistic strategies employed by Mexican Spanish-speakers found that the notion of negative face 'does not seem to operate in Mexican society because Mexicans do not emphasise the protection of their freedom of action, but rather stress their need to be included in the group and conform with the expected cultural norms of a community that recognises social distance, social power, and closeness in given interactional contexts' (2006: 2180). The examination of the linguistic strategies employed in refusal interactions found that politeness is accomplished largely by means of formulaic/semi-formulaic expressions that utilise ritualised linguistic forms to convey *respeto*, and linguistic forms that weaken the illocutionary force of a refusal. The researcher argues that the negotiation of face and selection of linguistic strategies is accomplished by means of indirect attempts at (re)negotiating a successful resolution politely according to a shared sense of *respeto* based on knowledge of social power and social distance. In contrast with B&L's theory, direct refusal is not interpreted as being impolite and consequently does not impose on the interlocutor's negative face. On the contrary, direct refusals were often accompanied by in-group identity markers, diminutives, and given names between equal-status friends which were interpreted as expressing closeness or affiliation (2006: 2179). Moreover, Placencia's (1996) examination of telephone conversations shows that deference, achieved through strategic lexical choices, is a key value in an Ecuadorian concept of face. Placencia notes that this is not due to the desire to protect one's individuality or territory, but rather to 'conform to the social norms of the group ... and dictate respect to the elderly and parents' (1996: 21).

Bargiela-Chiappini (2003: 1461) observes that criticism has been directed at B&L's conceptualisation of negative and positive politeness as mutually exclusive and the implication that negative politeness is approach based, while positive politeness is avoidance-based. In addition, Spencer-Oatey (2007: 639) identifies opposition to related issues such as the extent to which face is an individual or relational phenomenon, whether it is a public or private phenomenon, and whether it is a situation-specific or context-independent phenomenon. Three recurring criticisms levelled at the model are the prominence given to FTAs, the implementation of a MP, and accusations of Western prejudice relating to the individual. In reference to FTAs, Archer et al. (2012) explain that resistance challenges the fact that the politeness model is centred on FTAs and how to manage them. Secondly, the adoption of an MP is criticised as equating to 'decontextualised pragmatics' as it 'uses rational, goal-oriented means to calculate the politeness strategies required in a given interaction'. Finally, criticism of Western bias contends that B&L's understanding of politeness contradicts collectivist communities orientation to the group and overlooks significant differences when assuming that 'interlocutors share the same "wants", regardless of their cultural heritage' (2012: 87).

The issue of 'Western bias' and the application of face to politeness theory have dominated and polarised the debate (Haugh & Bargiela-Chiappini, 2010: 2073) with Leech (2005) going so far as to argue that 'focus on the individual, however appropriate to the West, is quite inappropriate to the group orientation of Eastern cultures' (2005: 2). As the breadth of investigation into face continues to embrace non-Western cultures and languages other than English, these questions and others pertaining to claims of universality are increasingly being examined with an emphasis on elucidating specific cultural and linguistic orientations as opposed to conforming to a definitive standard. It is this attention to cultural diversity which brings into focus concerns with B&L's formulaic variables of social distance (D), power (P) and imposition when calculating and determining politeness strategies:

> Being defined as static entities that determine polite meanings, these variables represent a narrow approach to social realities, an approach that neglects the dynamic aspects of social language use – aspects that may have no systemic status in the traditional view, but should be at the very heart of a modern one. (Werkhofer, 1992: 176)

Criticism highlights the question that, by quantifying linguistic politeness through variables presented as an uncontextualised formula, how can we accurately address the depth and nature of real-world language use as observed in dynamic and fluid situations? Moreover, how does a formulaic rendering of politeness based on a MP account for the linguistic choices made by real people interacting with different interlocutors, in different situations and communicating in a range of languages? In short, the model has been challenged with regard to its ability to respond to the diversity associated with the linguistic, cultural and social backgrounds and contexts that people bring to any real-world communicative exchange. On these grounds, opponents of universal politeness have rightly exhorted a position that argues that politeness principles need to be re-examined in line with cultural considerations. Intense criticism has generated divisiveness within the research community leading MacMartin *et al.* (2001) to advocate 'moving away from the use of face concepts in actual doing analysis, at least for the time being' (2001: 223). Similarly, Watts (2003) points out that B&L's theory is not a model of politeness but is essentially oriented to face management, and therefore ushers in a call for separating the notion of face from politeness. While acknowledging the prominence of face in politeness research, Haugh and Bargiela-Chiappini (2010) observe that the conflation of politeness with face and culture-specific elements of face remains problematic and suggest theorising face on its own terms (2010: 2073). The point being that as controversy is principally associated with the application of face to B&L's politeness theory, a separation of face from politeness may herald a broader theory of face which better accommodates culture-specific constituents of face.

Universal Politeness Theory: Japanese Scholarship Opposition

The notion that positive and negative face represent universal human wants, and in particular B&L's focus on autonomy and negative politeness, have been intensely contested by Asian scholars. The primary argument being that western attention to individualism fails to accurately account for the value assigned to group belonging and status within Asian society.

> Contrary to the original Asian construal of face, then, the scientific term found in the socio-pragmatics literature is characterized by an emphasis on Other's face (with the concomitant notion of non-imposition), an emphasis on the individual rather than the group, and an emphasis on saving face and the possibility of threatening face. Since these features are inherited from Western folk terms, it should not come as a surprise that this scientific term seems ill-fitted to serve the demands of a universalizing principle. (Terkourafi, 2007: 321)

Matsumoto (1988) and Ide (1989) contest B&L's politeness theory on the grounds that within Japanese culture the group is observed as being of higher importance than the individual. Hence, the desire to belong, relative social status and situational appropriateness are valued over preservation of one's individual territory or negative face. As Matsumoto (1988) puts it, 'A Japanese generally must understand where s/he stands in relation to other members of the group or society, and must acknowledge his/her dependence on the others' (1988: 405). Matsumoto rationalises her position as follows:

> What is of paramount concern to a Japanese is not his/her own territory, but the position in relation to others in the group and his/her acceptance of others. Loss of face is associated with the perception by others that one has not comprehended and acknowledged the structure and hierarchy of the group. (Matsumoto, 1988: 405)

The desire to acknowledge and maintain the relative position of others, not the content of what is being communicated, is seen as dictating the appropriateness of Japanese linguistic forms. To illustrate the researchers submit that Japanese honorifics, the use of which B&L's model classifies as a negative politeness strategy ('Give deference'), occur routinely in non-FTA utterances. Citing honorifics, formulaic expressions, and verbs of giving and receiving, Matsumoto (1988) posits that as Japanese people identify themselves as being part of social networks, the notion of personal autonomy 'cannot be considered as basic to human relations in Japanese culture and society' (1988: 405). In contrast, universal politeness theory focuses on redressing the potential threat to the interlocutor's face that arises from specific conversational moves.

> The use of different speech levels in Japanese is not a matter of showing concern for the addressee's desire to be free from imposition, nor does it involve showing approval for their want. Instead, it is often a matter of acknowledging the addressee's place relative to oneself. (Haugh, 2005: 44)

Matsumoto (1988) and Ide (1989) maintain that Japanese face and politeness strategies can be understood through consideration of culturally sensitive factors as revealed through cultural and social interdependence and discernment or conformity to socially prescribed conventions. Pizziconi (2003) characterises this position as 'one that stresses the role of appropriateness over individual motivations as the prevalent regulating criterion in the speaker's manipulation of the utterance' (2003: 1472) or as Matsumoto (1988) puts it, 'the Japanese politeness system places a higher value on recognition of the interpersonal relation than on mitigating impositions on freedom of action' (1988: 421). Matsumoto asserts that 'preservation of face in Japanese culture is intimately bound up with showing recognition of one's relative position in the communicative context and with the maintenance of the social ranking order' (1988: 415). The choice of stylistic level and address forms are associated with socio-cultural conventions derived from a group-centred hierarchy-based ethos with 'relation-acknowledging devices' such as formulaic expressions, honorifics and verb forms employed by the speaker to indicate differing social status of the interlocutors as opposed to offering redress for FTAs. By way of explanation, Matsumoto argues that 'one's commitment to the social structure and to the other members of a group is so strong that one's actions become meaningful and comprehended only in relation to others' (1988: 408).

The formalised system of marking the relative status of the speaker, addressee, referent and bystanders is examined by Brown (2007) who explains that Japanese verb forms not only have plain (e.g. *da*) and polite (e.g. *desu, masu*) forms, but also have humble, neutral or honorific forms, while 'certain nouns can be prefixed with "o-" or "go-" in order to honor the addressee or referent' (2007: 37). Matsumoto (1988) explains that even plain or neutral forms 'carry specific social and interactional information and can be used only in certain situations' (1988: 418). Illuminating this position, Matsumoto (1989) stresses that as speech level markers are obligatory, 'a Japanese speaker cannot avoid conveying the setting and the relationship among the addressee, the third person(s) or objects(s) in the utterance, and him/herself' (1989: 208). Consequently, even in non-threatening situations, the speaker is obliged by linguistic structures to indicate his social standing in relation to the addressee. This position is reflected in the findings of Hill *et al.* (1986) which argue that 'specific linguistic forms, at a conventional level of politeness' in Japanese are determined after 'the factors of addressee status and general situation relative to speaker's own' (1986: 362). On this basis, Matsumoto deduces that 'a theory of politeness must account for the use by Japanese speakers of honorifics in the absence of FTA's, or must count all utterances as intrinsically face-threatening' (1989: 217).

Underlying Matsumoto's (1988) claim that B&L's face is incongruous with Japanese politeness is her argument that the expression *doozo yoroshiku onegaishimasu* (lit. I ask you to please treat me well/take care of me), while polite in situations where the interactants are meeting for the first time, can also constitute an imposition upon the addressee's freedom of action (1988: 409). Akin to the English expression 'Nice to meet you', this common expression articulates the desire that the relationship be positive. It is cited as illustrating the complexity of Japanese politeness as the person with whom the speaker desires the addressee to benefit from a good relationship may be a third party such as *shujin o doozo yoroshiku onegaishimasu* (lit. I ask you to please treat/take care of my husband well) (1988: 409–410). Matsumoto reasons that as *yoroshiku onegaishimasu* serves as a direct request it represents an imposition on freedom, yet at the same time, is considered polite given that it acknowledges the higher status and deference as the addressee has the power to perform the action requested. Noting that these expressions could be interpreted as positive politeness strategies as they enhance the addressee's face, Matsumoto maintains that this is not the case as 'it is not done straight-forwardly', and there is no 'manifestation of intimacy' (1988: 410). Matsumoto reasons that within Japanese society recognition of interdependence is encouraged and that 'it is an honor to be asked to take care of someone in that it indicates that one is regarded as holding a higher position in the society' (1988: 410). In short, the speaker humbles himself to the addressee by placing himself in a subordinate position and acknowledging the need for support.

Matsumoto (1988) explains that contrasting speech levels in Japanese are commonly used to articulate equivalent content with different interlocutors in order to mark relative social status as, 'Acknowledgment and maintenance of the relative position of others, rather than of an individual's proper territory, governs all social interaction' (1988: 405). The researcher cites Japanese verb-form selection as dependent on 'the social and psychological attitude of the speaker towards the particular referents expressed by the subject and object of the verb' (1988: 416). By way of example, frequently applied forms of the expression 'Today is Saturday' are offered to illustrate how identical propositional content is structured according to the social context. While the expression could be used between any interactants in English, in Japanese the speaker is obliged to select from polite and honorific forms.

(1)   *Kyoo wa doyoobi da*
    (a)   Today TOPIC Saturday (COPULA-PLAIN)
    (b)   (Today is Saturday)
(2)   *Kyoo wa doyoobi desu*
    (a)   Today TOPIC Saturday (COPULA – POLITE)
    (b)   (Today is Saturday)
(3)   *Kyoo wa doyoobi degozai masu*
    (a)   Today TOPIC Saturday (COPULA – SUPER POLITE)

(Matsumoto, 1988: 415)

Matsumoto submits that the expression cannot be socio-pragmatically or grammatically neutral as the copula's allomorph is varied according to social order and stratification imbedded in the obligatory honorific markers, *da, desu, degozaimasu*. The argument being that sentence (1) is not appropriate when used with an interlocutor of a higher status, while sentence (2) is appropriate because the deferential copula *desu* is used in its copula and therefore conveys attention to the listener's relative social position to the speaker. In addition, sentence (3) would only be used on formal occasions between adults as the copula verb *degozaimasu* ('super' deferential) indicates a high level of politeness and formality although the statement itself does not directly impinge on the addressee. Importantly, as the example does not carry a FTA, Matsumoto maintains that the use of honorifics reflects the status difference of the interlocutors rather than serve the listener's negative face wants (1988: 414). Matsumoto surmises that 'there is no socially unmarked form' and that 'in any utterance in Japanese, one is forced to make morphological or lexical choices that depend on the interpersonal relationship between the conversational participants' (1988: 418).

Proposing an alternative framework to universal politeness, Hill *et al.* (1986) advance a theory based on the notions of *wakimae* (discernment) and volition with politeness defined as one of the constraints on human interaction, whose purpose is to consider others' feelings, establish levels of mutual comfort and promote rapport. Based on this definition, a system for polite use of a particular language will exhibit two major aspects: the necessity for speaker discernment and the opportunity for speaker volition. While the researchers observe that no single English word can satisfactorily translate *wakimae*, the term discernment is employed to describe the sense of strict adherence to expected norms and 'almost automatic observation of socially-agreed-upon rules' applicable to verbal and non-verbal behaviour (1986: 348). Ide (1989) explains *wakimae* as a set of socially expected norms 'appropriate behavior people have to observe in order to be considered polite in the society they live' (1989: 299). As a counterpart to *wakimae*, Hill *et al.* use the term volition, defined as an aspect of politeness that 'allows the speaker a considerably more active choice, according to the speaker's intention, from a relatively wider range of possibilities' (1989: 348). In this sense, volition refers to the creative use of communicative strategies to achieve politeness as realised through verbal strategies. In short, the intention of volition politeness is to save face, while *wakimae* guides the selection of appropriate linguistic forms based on social convention. Drawing on the concepts of *wakimae* and volition, the researchers assessed how much speech is obligatory (discernment) and how much variation or volition is allowed in a given culture and specific situation.

Examining requests made in Japanese and American English, Hill *et al.* (1986) administered a three-part questionnaire to measure; (a) the degree of politeness of expressions, (b) the distance participants perceived between themselves and different addressees, and (c) which request forms they would use towards these addressees. Findings indicated that there were similarities between the politeness strategies employed by the participants, such as neither group using expressions regarded as being the most uninhibited with addressees considered as requiring the most care. At the same time, in regard to the expressions required for each addressee, the findings reported that the agreement on proper forms for each addressee was high among Japanese participants while low amongst the American participants. In particular, when addressees were characterised by 'occupation/status, relative age, degree of acquaintance with the speaker and particular situation, Japanese speakers showed very high agreement on the appropriate form(s) for making certain requests while American participants demonstrated a wider spread between person/situation and suitable form(s) for making requests' (1986: 361). The conclusion being that while discernment and volition are evident in politeness strategy selection in both socio-linguistic systems, the weight assigned differs in that for Japanese students, discernment was prioritised over volition, while American participants considered volition to be the primary consideration and discernment secondary.

Ide (1989) and Ide and Yoshida (1999) have challenged universal politeness theory as not being applicable to honorific languages and reason that within Japanese society *wakimae* (discernment) is of greater importance than volition politeness directed towards the preservation and maintenance of face. In particular, Ide (1989) criticises B&L's view of politeness as a strategic means by which to minimise the impact of a FTA, while failing to recognise socio-pragmatically obligatory communicative strategies in Japanese. For Ide, volition-based politeness serves to save face, in accordance with B&L, however discernment-based politeness represents a grammatical requirement, constituting a socio-pragmatic concordance system. Consequently, Ide maintains that the purpose of Japanese honorifics is not exclusively to save face for the reason that honorifics are obligatory even when there is no FTA. In Ide's words:

> For the speaker of an honorific language, linguistic politeness is above all a matter of showing discernment in choosing specific forms, while for the speaker of a non-honorific language, it is mainly a matter of the volitional use of verbal strategies to maintain the faces of the participants ... However, the two aspects are integral to the universals of linguistic politeness, working potentially in almost all languages. (Ide, 1989: 245)

In support of this position, Ide *et al.* (1992) examined notions of politeness by having approximately 200 Japanese and 200 American subjects associate ten adjectives with the most appropriate scene from 14 interactional situations. Results indicated that the American subjects tended to connect polite with friendly, whereas the Japanese subjects judged *teineina* 'polite' and *shitashigena* 'friendly' as being distinct. The conclusion being that in American culture, volition guides politeness, whereas the Japanese politeness is guided by *wakimae* (discernment). Ide's position assumes that the Japanese speaker will select linguistic forms consistent with social convention rather than seek to uphold face needs. For this reason, *wakimae* involves language use consistent with common schemes of socio-culturally informed perceptions realised through appropriate linguistic forms and the modes of speaking according to contextual factors. The speaker is orientated to roles and situations based on 'the choice of linguistic form or expression in which the distinction between the ranks or the roles of the speaker, the referent and the addressee are systematically encoded' (1992: 230). Ide maintains that honorifics are not a negative politeness strategy and cautions against confusing linguistic forms and verbal strategies. Based on this distinction, linguistic forms are viewed as socio-pragmatically obligatory and employed irrespective of whether the referent is or is not present:

(1) Sensee-wa   kore-o   yon-da.
    Professor-TOP   this- ACC   read-PAST
    'The professor read this'.

(2) Sensee-wa   kore-o   oyomi-ni-nat-ta.
    Professor-TOP   this- ACC   REF.HONO-read-PAST
    'The professor read this'.

(Ide, 1989: 227)

According to Ide's discernment model, only sentence (2) is appropriate within Japanese society as the speaker is obligated to use honorific forms when one refers to a person of higher status, in this case the professor. The speaker is compelled to choose between honorific and non-honorific forms based on the premise that the 'use of an honorific verb form is the socio-pragmatic equivalent of grammatical concord, and it is determined by social rules' (1989: 227). Ide cites a second reason to separate linguistic forms and verbal strategy as being that 'strategies are oriented only to the hearer, whereas linguistic forms are used not only for the hearer, but also for the referent and the speaker' (1989: 229). While volition characterises the strategically-motivated practice of politeness, Ide maintains that the above example illustrates *wakimae* (discernment) in which an obligatory polite form is required 'independent of the speaker's rational intention' (1989: 242). Consequently, while volition-based politeness serves to save face, discernment-based politeness is a socio-pragmatic requirement. On this basis, Ide argues that B&L's theory fails to explain Japanese politeness in which language choices are governed firstly by *wakimae* (discernment). Support for the notion of discernment is offered by Hasegawa (2012), who emphasises that the Japanese speaker does not have total freedom of linguistic choices as 'failure to observe the social norm of polite language (*tameguchi*) is frequently ridiculed and penalized' (1989: 245).

Criticism of B&L's politeness model challenges whether imposition can be interpreted as carrying a fixed value across cultures, and therein questions the significance of negative politeness. The implication here being that the notion of threat to face is based on the disputed tenet that negative face is inherently valued more highly than positive face. The influence of social expectations on interaction is addressed within Nakane's (2006) research into intercultural communication between Japanese university students and their Australian lecturers. Nakane found that Japanese students regarded the hierarchical structure delineating teacher and student roles as a primary motivation when interacting within the classroom environment. These perceptions regarding hierarchy and linguistic behaviour practices were not altered by the cross-cultural context of the investigation. In other words, students adopted the same classroom behaviour they recognised as appropriate within a Japanese education setting when interacting with Australian lecturers in an Australian setting.

Challenging universal politeness, Matsumoto (1988) poses that 'a modification in the requirement that the constituents of face be universal' (1988: 425) could generate enhanced agreement between theory and practice and recommends a 'general notion of "face"' with the inclusion of 'a certain spectrum of styles that can be chosen, according to the culture and the situation, to affect face preserving ends' (1988: 424). Matsumoto's attention to disparities between an Eastern group-orientation and a Western individual-orientation of politeness may to some extent disguise the fact that B&L (1987) acknowledge that cultures may differ in the degree to which negative and positive face wants are valued. Nevertheless, there remains intense interest in whether universal politeness theory, and in particular that relating to negative face, is relevant, particularly when it appears that the dimensions proposed by B&L may not account for the use of different speech levels in Japanese in the absence of threat to the addressee's face.

Universal Politeness Theory: Japanese Scholarship Support

Descriptions of Japanese politeness offered by Matsumoto (1988) and Ide (1989) have been critically labelled as polarising by Pizziconi (2003) for the reason that they advocate a position which characterises 'some languages as conforming to individualist behaviour' and others as attending to 'fixed social norms' (2003: 1471). Indeed Matsumoto's (1988) contention that negative face is 'alien' to Japanese culture (1988: 405) and that B&L's politeness theory is incompatible with Japanese linguistic orientations insofar as self-image is based on group rather than individual alignment, appears to validate Pizziconi's criticism. In any case, universal politeness theory has not been categorically rejected by Japanese scholarship (see Fukada & Asato, 2004; Fukushima; 2000; Haugh, 2005; Ishiyama, 2009; Pizziconi, 2003; Takano, 2005). Moreover, studies examining conversational data have demonstrated that negative politeness strategies and place affirming discernment are not exclusive to Japanese polite speech (Cook, 2011; Geyer, 2008; Okamoto, 1998).

For the most part, challenges to Matsumoto and Ide's positions have not disputed what Brown (2007) characterises as Japanese's 'much richer and more formalised system than English of marking the relative social status of the speaker, addressee, referent and bystanders' (2007: 37). Rather, the point of contention relates to whether Japanese honorifics are in fact inconsistent with B&L's model of face and politeness. Fukushima (2000) reasons that Matsumoto and Ide have not invalidated B&L's theory by showing that some choices of politeness forms are obligatory in specific situations as their data amounts to 'simply discuss[ing] some socio-linguistic characteristics of the Japanese language, which are not significant pragmatically' (2000: 61). Comparing requests and responses to requests in British English and Japanese, Fukushima argues that 'the variables determining politeness strategies proposed by Brown and Levinson are valid', and consequently the 'framework is still valid for cross-cultural comparison' (2000: 19).

Pizziconi (2003) proposes that while Japanese scholarship has claimed that interactional markers operate independently of the imposition to the addressee's action, 'Politeness (as "appropriateness") is better observed, even in Japanese, in the polite stances constituted by strategic use of polite devices rather than in unmediated polite meanings conveyed by the plethora of dedicated honorific' (2003: 1471). Pizziconi maintains that as opposed to demonstrating that identity markers are not a negative politeness strategy, Matsumoto (1988) has merely managed to illustrate that identity-marking devices make the interlocutors' roles more explicit. Similarly, Fukada and Asato (2004: 1992) contend that identity-marking devices are indeed consistent with the preservation of face and accordingly 'there is no need to set up a separate kind of politeness, such as discernment'. In the researchers' words:

> We suspect that both Ide and Matsumoto were misled by the superficial correspondences between linguistic forms and social rules. The rigid Japanese social rules require precise control on polite language use, depending on a person's social status, occupation, familiarity, sex, formality of the situation, etc. The well-developed system of Japanese honorifics enables the Japanese to express subtle differences in the degree of deference, making it appear that these social rules dictate the use of honorifics. (Fukada & Asato, 2004: 1996)

In what amounts to a distinctly different interpretation, Fukada and Asato (2004) expound the following arguments which lend support to B&L's politeness theory.

(1)   Failure to employ correct honorific usage in Japanese has much to do with face-preservation for if the speaker neglects to employ honorifics when expected, this may sound presumptuous and rude, in turn generating a threat to both the speaker's and the addressee's face (2004: 1997).

(2)   Even when a person is in a position customarily deserving of obligatory honorifics, an honorific form 'sounds bizarre' when addressing dishonourable acts. To illustrate, a series of examples are presented in which 'dishonourable acts' are framed through levels of honorifics typically assigned to social superiors (2004: 1998):

> Senseega   dookyuusei   o   koroshi-ta
> teacher NOM classmate ACC kill-PAST
> 'My teacher killed my classmate'.

> ¿Senseega dookyuusei   o   o-koroshi-ninat-ta
>   Kill-HONO-PAST

> Senseega   dookyuusei   o   gookanshi-ta
> teacher NOM classmate ACC rape-PAST
> 'My teacher raped my classmate'.

> ¿Senseega   dookyuusei   o   gookannasat-ta
>   rape-HONO-PAST

> Sensee   ga   ginkoogootoo o hatarai-ta
> teacher NOM bank robbery ACC commit-PAST
> 'My teacher committed a bank robbery'.

> ¿Sensee   ga   ginkoogootoo o o-hataraki-ninat-ta
>   commit-HONO-PAST

(3)   Honorifics are employed by social superiors when interacting with subordinates in both non-formal and formal situations when the rank of imposition is sufficiently high to trigger the usage. Alternatively, the formality of a situation creates a temporary distance between the interlocutors which triggers the use of honorifics by the superior. By way of example, the researchers present an exchange in which a lecturer requests the assistance of a student intern in grading work through employing the underlined honorific *yoroshiku onegai shimasu.*

Jaa, isogasete   sumimasen kedo   yoroshiku onegai shimasu.
Well, having you hurry I am sorry, but please beg - POLITE
'Well, I'm sorry to rush you, but thank you very much for
taking care of this'.

(Fukada & Asato, 2004: 1998)

(4)   B&L's formula provides an explanation of a particular social perception in Japan, i.e. that it is a good quality for young people and women not to speak too much in front of their seniors and superiors. Fukada and Asato argue that contrary to Japanese social standards, 'Ide's rule incorrectly predicts that a junior employee can speak as much as seniors and superiors in a meeting as long as he uses honorific forms' (2004: 2000). However, if interpreted according to B&L's 'Don't do the FTA' (fifth strategy), the high values associated with power and distance variables elevate the total FTA regardless of whether an act is intrinsically face-threatening or not. As such, anything said can be counted as a FTA and consequently the FTA is avoided.

While friction concerning universal politeness theory may be declining, arguments presented by Japanese scholarship both for and against face and politeness theory indicate that the face framework, in conjunction with culturally specific dimensions, has a valuable role to play in analysing interaction. The challenge is to establish a middle-ground position in order to account for features of Japanese culture, society and language, while also facilitating meaningful comparisons across cultures.

The Ground In-Between

B&L's ([1978]1987) theory that positive and negative face represent universal human attributes is described by O'Driscoll (1996) as being 'just too valuable to be jettisoned' on the basis of 'false assumptions about what it entails' (1996: 4). In line with this position, researchers have attempted to account for culture-specific values and in so doing, assert that the dual notion of face remains relevant and can be successfully adapted to account for cultural variance (see Fukushima, 2000; Haugh, 2005; Mao, 1994; Spencer-Oatey, 2000, 2005, 2007, 2008). Bringing together common underlying principles associated with the notion of face, a number of alternative frameworks look to explicate diversity observed within languages and cultures while avoiding the tendency to rely on cross-cultural generalisations. For example, drawing from

Matsumoto's (1988) claims and B&L's theory, Mao (1994) proposes that there are two views of face in any given society:

> An underlying direction of face that emulates, though never completely attaining, one of two interactional ideals that may be salient in a given speech community: the ideal social identity, or the ideal individual autonomy. The specific content of face in a given speech community is determined by one of these two interactional ideals sanctioned by members of the community. (Mao, 1994: 472)

This view of face is built on the premise that understanding cross-cultural politeness requires an understanding of these individual and social manifestations of face, and recognition that one may be more prevalent in accordance with socio-cultural expectations. Rapport Management theory as developed by Spencer-Oatey (2000, 2008) proposes a move away from a singular view of communication in terms of positive or negative politeness in acknowledging the complexity of communication as a dynamic phenomenon with a multiplicity of factors influencing communication. Spencer-Oatey's model conceives of communication as aimed at transmitting information and establishing, maintaining or modifying social relationships. The researcher maintains that interaction, governed by socio-pragmatic interactional principles that social groups internalise and tacitly take for granted, is influenced by a rich combination of both social and contextual factors that need to be taken into consideration when defining the rules of the appropriate use of the language. Outlining a broader framework than B&L's politeness theory, Rapport Management looks to explain how language is used to promote, maintain or threaten harmonious social relations. In Spencer-Oatey's model, rapport refers to 'people's subjective perceptions of (dis)harmony, smoothness-turbulence and warmth-antagonism in interpersonal relations' while rapport management describes 'the ways in which this (dis)harmony is (mis)managed' (Spencer-Oatey & Franklin, 2009: 102). Importantly, Spencer-Oatey's Rapport Management theory presents a social component in that it distinguishes between face needs which refer to a person's personal or social value, and sociality rights which refer to a person's personal or social entitlements.

With the term 'rapport' replacing politeness, Spencer Oatey (2008) argues that the motivation for politeness is not only the desire to maintain face, but also the desire to maintain sociality rights defined as 'fundamental personal/social *entitlements* that individuals effectively claim for themselves in their interactions with others' (2008: 14). Spencer-Oatey proposes a three-dimensional model of rapport management: (i) the management of face,

(ii) the management of sociality rights and obligations and (iii) the management of interactional goals (Spencer-Oatey, 2008: 14). The concept of face is explained as 'people's sense of worth, dignity and identity, and is associated with issues such as respect, honour, status, reputation and competence' (2008: 14). The relation between face and a person's self-identity is viewed in three respects: self as an individual (individual identity), self as a group member (collective identity) and self in relationship with others (relational identity). Within the management of face we have quality face, concerned with personal qualities and self-esteem, and identity face, concerned with values effective in social or group roles. The management of sociality rights, on the other hand, involves the management of social expectancies. Sociality rights are social or personal expectancies or entitlements that individuals claim for themselves, some of which are constantly negotiated, while others are culturally or situationally determined beforehand. Within the management of sociality rights we have equity rights and association rights. Equity rights refer to our right to receive personal consideration and be treated fairly, while association rights account for our entitlement to association or dissociation with others such as the degree of closeness-distance in relations. The third component determining the rapport of interaction is the interactional goal of the conversations which may be transactional and/or relational. Interactional goals may damage social interaction if they come into conflict, and if they do not, their management may result in rapport maintenance or rapport-enhancement. Rapport can be threatened by face-threatening behaviour, rights threatening/obligation-omission behaviour and goal-threatening behaviour (Spencer-Oatey, 2008: 17). Spencer-Oatey (2005) explains the management of rapport as 'not only behavior that enhances or maintains smooth relations, but any kind of behavior that has an impact on rapport, whether positive, negative, or neutral' (2005: 96) and outlines four key rapport orientations as being to; (a) enhance, (b) maintain, (c) neglect and (d) challenge (2008: 32). Importantly, cultural differences in language use can influence an individual's assessment of rapport management outcomes and orientations can change during the course of an interaction during which an individual will determine, consciously or unconsciously, whether their rapport has been enhanced, maintained or damaged (Spencer-Oatey, 2005: 96).

Haugh (2005) marks out a middle ground position arguing that positive and negative face may be valuable in explicating politeness in English, yet 'not sufficiently broad in nature to effectively account for politeness phenomena in Japanese' (2005: 42). Haugh proposes that in order to circumvent theoretical shortcomings and supplement B&L's paradigm, the concept of 'place' may serve to explicate Japanese politeness. Haugh's model of Japanese face and politeness orientations hypothesises that 'politeness in Japanese arises primarily from acknowledging the place of others, or compensating for impositions on that place, rather than trying to compensate for possible impositions on the individual autonomy of others' (2005: 45). In other words, the speech levels in Japanese focus on recognising the addressee's place in relation to the speaker as opposed to attending to the imposition or acknowledgement of the individual's wants. Emphasising the role of place in Japanese politeness, it has been argued that Japanese speakers, when using *keigo* (honorific system) determine the appropriate level of speech based on whether the addressee is a member of the in-group *uchi* (inside), or the out-group *soto* (outside) (see Bachnik, 1994; Harada, 1976; Ikuta, 1983; Niyekawa, 1991; Wetzel, 1994). The concept of *uchi* and *soto* is described by Bachnik (1994) as 'a major organizational focus for Japanese self, social life, and language' and consequently, 'the organization of both self and society can be viewed as situating meaning, through the indexing of inside and outside orientations' (1994: 3). Bachnik explicates that while *uchi* represents 'we, us, our group, me, my, I', *soto* tends to be more 'abstract, objective, and unanchored' (1994: 28). Intimacy is linguistically manifested by the use of plain forms in conversation, while the use of honorifics can be seen as a means of maintaining or acknowledging distance. Plain forms, when used by a superior, can potentially be seen as evoking a sense of camaraderie, while if used by an inferior, represent a departure from the rules of acceptable social conduct. According to Niyekawa (1991), hierarchy is invoked if the interlocutor is determined to be *uchi* (inside) while non-polite or minimal polite language is reciprocally engaged in the case that the interlocutor is considered *soto* (outside). Lebra (1976) explains that the intimacy and distance associated with the *uchi* 'in-group' and *soto* 'out-group' requires consideration of the given situation as demarcations are not determined by social structure, rather influenced by constantly varying situations (1976: 112).

Haugh (2005) proposes that place, consisting of the dual concepts of the place one belongs (inclusion) and the place one stands (distinction), is a culturally specific manifestation that underlies Japanese politeness orientations. Inclusion is depicted as being a part of something else such as a particular set or group, while distinction is defined as being different or distinguishable from others (2005: 47). This model of inclusion comprises groups fashioned both socially and psychologically; social groups depict the family structure and metaphorical extensions such as the workplace or class, while psychological groups are derived from an affinity-linking individuals such as friends (2005: 49). In contrast, distinction involves one's public persona or social standing and is based on the individual's role (*ichi, yakuwari*), rank or status (*mibun, chi'i*) and circumstances (*jookyoo*) (2005: 54). Roles are subdivided to include institutional positions and non-institutional positions. Institutional positions are characterised as 'those that are given to people with recognition from others that this position/role has been bestowed upon this person' and tend to have well defined boundaries such as an individual's occupation. Non-institutional positions are described as being context sensitive and less well-defined such as roles arising from social connections (2005: 54). The framework argues that in non-institutional positions the situation defines the individual's position and consequently there is greater variation in roles. Identifying and preserving position in relation to others is rooted in one's social standing in accordance with the social and cultural value attached to the specific place.

Pizziconi (2003) makes the point that, 'The need for an unbiased terminology for cross-cultural comparison is more urgent than ever, and the task of creating one as problematic as ever. Terms like "deference", "tact", "superior", even "politeness" itself, clearly carry multiple connotations in different cultures' (2003: 1502). While management of face is intimately linked to verbal and non-verbal communication strategies, it is far from clear whether all people intrinsically share and attach the same priority to negative and positive face. It is here that we turn to the notion of identity which promises to present a broader approach to understanding the fractal complexity and diversity of face and language.

What is Identity?

Over the past two decades, growing interest in understanding the relationship between identity and language learning has been reflected in the wealth of publications within the field of applied linguistics. Joseph (2013: 36) describes identity as being related to who individuals are in relation to 'the groups to which they belong, including nationality, ethnicity, religion, gender, generation, sexual orientation, social class and an unlimited number of other possibilities'. Identity research in language education has tackled diverse issues including identity and ideology, identity and race, identity and gender, identity in writing, language student identity and teacher professional identity. This expanding scope of research has been fuelled by awareness that issues of identity and language are closely bound together. In short, identity research has demonstrated that as we move towards a view of language as being more than a fixed linguistic system of grammar, vocabulary and syntax, there is the need for greater recognition of contemporary notions of self and identity in order to better understand how students, as complex social participants, interact with and acquire a target language (see Block, 2003, 2007; Joseph, 2004; Kanno, 2003; Kanno & Norton, 2003; Kinginger,

2013; Kramsch, 2009; Kubota & Lin, 2009; Lee, 2008; Miller & Kubota, 2013; Norton, 1997, 2000, 2006; Norton & Toohey, 2002; Pavlenko, 2003). Importantly, identities are not bestowed upon an individual but are 'forged – created, transmitted, reproduced, performed – textually and semiotically' through signs (Joseph, 2013). Joseph emphasises that language is the ultimate semiotic system and that 'every identity ideally wants a language of its own' (2013: 41). This relationship between language learning and identity is framed by Norton and Toohey (2002) as follows:

> Language learning engages the identities of students because language itself is not only a linguistic system of signs and symbols; it is also a complex social practice in which the value and meaning ascribed to an utterance are determined in part by the value and meaning ascribed to the person who speaks. Likewise, how a language learner interprets or constructs a written text requires an ongoing negotiation among historical understandings, contemporary realities, and future desires. (Norton & Toohey, 2002: 115)

Antrim (2007) explains that language, as a channel for self-identification, is a significant part of who we are and who we identify with culturally, ethnically and socially. For this reason, Antrim proposes that identities can be public, private, perceived and projected and 'while language is only one means of constructing these identities, it provides a foundation for those identities' (2007: 2). As a result, L2 competence cannot be viewed in isolation from social practices both within and beyond the classroom context. In essence, identity is connected to one's sense of self which is 'lived, negotiated, on-going, changing constantly across time and space, social, multiple, it is also a learning process with its pasts and future incorporating the present' (Wenger, 1998: 163). Identity explores the complex, dynamic and potentially contradictory ways in which a person views himself and others, explained by Jenkins (2004: 5) as 'our understanding of who we are and of who other people are, and, reciprocally, other people's understanding of themselves and of others (which includes us)'. Mendoza-Denton (2002: 475) describes identity as 'the active negotiation of an individual's relationship with larger social constructs, in so far as this negotiation is signalled through language and other semiotic means'. The researcher points out that identity 'is neither attribute nor possession, but an individual and collective-level process of semiosis' (Mendoza-Denton, 2002: 475). In short, identity does not represent a state of being automatically acquired at birth, ascribed by others or assigned within a classroom, but rather evolving, multifaceted and negotiated. Hall (1990) refers to a process of 'becoming' and proposes that identity should be thought of as a 'production which is never complete, always in process and always constituted within, not outside, representation' (1990: 222). While the individual maintains a degree of control when constructing identities this is not merely a process of aligning to desired identities. The multiple identities one occupies are not always freely chosen given that they are influenced by culture, society and the social groups with parameters necessitating ongoing renegotiation in order to assimilate new experiences.

The complex nature of identity is illustrated in Simon's (2004) Self-Aspect Model of Identity (SAMI) which offers an integrated approach to identity in proposing that a person's self-concept comprises beliefs about his own attributes or self-characteristics. SAMI considers two levels of identity; namely 'collective identity' which arises where self-interpretation focuses upon a socially shared self-aspect and 'individual identity', which is the consequence of self-interpretation based upon a complex configuration of self-aspects. The number of attributes or self-characteristics attached to the individuals can be extensive as these constitute the basic units of identity. Explaining the multiplicity of identities, Ushioda (2011) describes identities as being 'socially forged and negotiated through our relations and interactions with other people' (2011: 202) while Norton and Toohey (2011) view identities as personally valued constructs which focus on how the individual relates to the social world and how one interprets his possibilities for the future. Impacted by social constructs, these facets of identities are forged to shape the way in which the individual understands his relationship to the world and possibilities for the future. The context-dependent nature of identities as constructed during interaction is captured by Zimmerman's (1998: 91) three types of identity: discourse identity, situated identity and transportable identity.

(1) Discourse identity – This refers to the identities an individual adopts within the immediate interaction which are 'integral to the moment-by-moment organization of the interaction' (1998: 90). Discourse identity relates to the sequential development of the talk as interlocutors engage (i.e. speaker, listener, questioner, challenger).

(2) Situated identity – This refers to the alignment of roles with reference to the social situation the participants are in and their contribution in 'engaging in activities and respecting agendas that display an orientation to, and an alignment of, particular identity sets' (1998: 90). For example, within the context of the classroom, the teacher and students will behave according to rank and roles viewed by the participants as being socio-culturally consistent with the classroom environment.

(3) Transportable identity – This refers to identities transported across a variety of interactions and are 'usually visible, that is, assignable or claimable on the basis of physical or culturally based insignia which furnish the intersubjective basis for categorization' (1998: 91).

These levels of description underscore that identity is constructed across time and space as an individual conducts social negotiations based on his perceptions of self and his relationship to the changing contexts. Identity, associated with self-identification, is defined by Antrim (2007: 1) as 'our behavior, values and self-concepts. This is reflected in the language we use, our word choices in identifying ourselves as well as in the words we choose not to use'. As language is a key form of self-representation associated with how we identify ourselves culturally, ethnically and socially (Day, 2002; Morita, 2004; Norton, 2000, 2006, 2010, 2013; Pavlenko & Norton, 2007), it follows that the learning of 'other' or 'additional' languages may challenge the student to expand personal, social and cultural identities in order to accept or potentially reject the new language and all that it symbolises. Through exploring the relationship between the individual and the social world, identity research conceptualises an integrative approach to understanding the complex interaction of the language student in relation to learning processes and the socio-cultural learning context. The importance of recognising students' identities is emphasised by Norton (2000) who argues that '... it is only by acknowledging the complexity of identity that we can gain greater insight into the myriad challenges and possibilities of language learning and language teaching in the new millennium' (2000: 154).

Insight into the negotiation of identities and its deep connection with language learning is offered in Norton Peirce's (1993) qualitative study of five immigrant women in Canada. In diaries, the women recorded daily interactions in English with bosses, co-workers and landlords and frequently found themselves silenced due to their marginal positions as immigrants and language learners. Reflecting on the participants' experience, in 1995 Norton Peirce introduced the term investment, hypothesising that the women invested in English as linguistic capital. Norton Peirce's definition of the construct of investment, inspired by the work of Bourdieu (1977, 1984, 1991), 'signals the socially and historically constructed relationship of learners to the target language, and their often ambivalent desire to learn and practice' (1991: 5). Norton (2010: 3) proposes that learners invest in the target language with the knowledge that they will acquire a wider range of symbolic and material resources, which will in turn increase the value of their cultural capital and social power. The line of reason here being that as the value of the learners' cultural capital increases, their 'sense of themselves, their identities and their opportunities for the future are reevaluated' (2010: 3). Acquisition of the target language is viewed by the learner as positively impacting on his life such as through generating access to educational or employment opportunities. Speaking to future possibilities, Kanno and Norton (2003) refer to imagined communities as 'groups of people, not immediately tangible and accessible, with whom we connect through the power of the imagination' (2003: 241). This sense of imagined communities extends across time and space and speaks to the connections and a sense of community one imagines sharing with others at a future time (Pavlenko & Norton, 2007). Norton (2010) writes, 'Thus in imagining themselves bonded with their fellow human beings across space and time, learners can feel a sense of community with people they have not yet met, including future relationships that exist only in a learner's imagination' (2010: 3). For this reason, multiple identities continually react to changing structural conditions and socio-cultural contexts in order to transform the learner's relationship with interlocutors and potentially claim alternative identities.

> Our language choices reflect not only how we view ourselves, but how we are viewed by society. An individual's identity is reflected in various language constructed identities: ethnicity, gender, and cross-cultural/counter cultural. In turn these identities are projected by society on the individual/ethnic group by the language choices society makes in describing and addressing these individuals. (Antrim, 2007: 2)

In the following analysis, the terms identity and identities refer to the Japanese students' evolving awareness of their roles and relationships within social and cultural forms of practices, values, and beliefs. Consequently, the individual may at times have the freedom to align with particular positions yet at other points be expected to align with socially determined restrictions placed on their choices. These identities, viewed as dynamic, hybrid and fluid, are forged by social, cultural, and individual interpretations of how the individual wishes to align or disalign himself in the present and with an eye to the future.

Interrelationship Between Identity and Face

Face and identity influence the complex and dynamic ways in which individuals present themselves verbally and non-verbally during interaction. It is recognised that language and issues of identity are closely bound together, as too are language and the management and negotiation of face.

Nevertheless, somewhat surprisingly, researchers have shown little interest in how the constructs of identity and face are interrelated and impact on the student both within and outside of the language classroom (Joseph, 2013; Spencer-Oatey, 2007). These two formidable conceptual areas, namely identity and face, present an opportunity to explore the communicative negotiation of face within the broader framework of identity. Or, simply speaking, theories of identity may enrich the understanding of face and aid the analysis of face by adding layers of description that have been overlooked. While face research has addressed issues such as the degree to which face is individual or relational, public or private and situation-specific or context-independent, Spencer-Oatey (2007: 639) points out a lack of attention to the one fundamental point underpinning the debate, namely the issue of identity.

With these issues in mind, Spencer-Oatey (2007) proposes a new approach to analysing and conceptualising face through attention to insights gained from identity theories. Spencer-Oatey (2007) promotes the inclusion of the multiple perspectives offered for 'a richer and more comprehensive understanding of face and the frameworks needed for analyzing it' (2007: 639). By way of explanation, Spencer-Oatey notes that while face literature routinely makes reference to identity there has been little attention to the interrelationship of these two concepts. The researcher points out that as opposed to exploring associations, face and identity research have tended to assume a parallel trajectory with points of intersection a rarity. The assumption that conceptualisations of face and identity are intrinsically contradictory has created a situation in which a number of key questions have failed to generate interest within the research community:

> To what extent are identity and face similar or different?
> How may theories of identity inform our understanding of face?
> How may they (theories of identity) aid our analyses of face?'
>
> (Spencer-Oatey, 2007: 639–640)

Concurring that there is a tendency within literature to stress the perceived distinctions rather than explore the interrelationship between face and identity, Haugh and Bargiela-Chiappini (2010) note a recent shift towards conceptualising face in the context of identity which, in their view, begs the question whether 'research on face can be (or need be) distinguished in any meaningful way from broader work on identity' (2010: 2073). The distinction between face and identity, as outlined by Haugh and

Bargiela-Chiappini, rests primarily on the argument that face represents an individual's claims as to who he is within an interaction, while identity is a more enduring concept that encompasses how an individual sees himself and identifies himself. In this way, conceptualisations typically paint a picture of identity as attending to the whole person whereas face is seen as related to those aspects one elects to publicly reveal. Questioning this distinction Haugh and Bargiela-Chiappini state:

> The problem facing this distinction is that, on the one hand, identity has increasingly been conceptualised as rooted in interaction and thus less enduring than previously thought, while, on the other hand, according to emic or folk conceptualisations, face is often seen as enduring across interactions unless otherwise challenged. (Haugh & Bargiela-Chiappini, 2010: 2073)

In short, face is conceptualised as being stable unless challenged, while identity is continually negotiated in line with the specific context in which the interactions takes place. Arguing that identity and face have much in common, Joseph (2013: 35) points out that 'each is an imagining of the self, or of another, within a public sphere involving multiple actors'. Nevertheless, Joseph submits that as identity and face have entered into language and discourse research from different directions, researchers have tended to frame them so that they appear to be 'no more than tangentially related to one another' (2013: 35). To illustrate, Joseph argues that in research there has been a fundamental, and in the researcher's view, dubious, distinction drawn between how face and identity relate to time with face viewed as being 'punctual' while identity is seen as a 'durative' phenomenon (2013: 36). Challenging this distinction, Joseph emphasises that an individual's face should not be considered inconsistent or facework as not enduring. Similarly, Joseph notes that identity is generally conceived as being the property of a person, even when an individual's awareness of his identity 'may lie below the surface until a particular contact creates a tension that brings it to the fore' (2013: 36). The researcher's point being that face and identity are far more complex, variable and dynamic than outlined in traditional definitions.

Spencer-Oatey (2007) notes that face and identity are socio-cognitively similar in that they both have to do with one's self-image, yet points out that face is distinct from identity in that the attributes it is associated with are sensitive to the claimant (2007: 644). For this reason, the construct of face deals specifically with those aspects of identity that the student elects to claim in accordance with the desired public-self-image.

(…) face is only associated with attributes that are affectively sensitive to the claimant. It is associated with positively evaluated attributes that the claimant wants others to acknowledge (explicitly or implicitly), and with negatively evaluated attributes that the claimant wants others NOT to ascribe to him/her. (Spencer-Oatey, 2007: 644)

It is perhaps inevitable that the demarcation of face and identity has given rise to disagreements regarding the depth to which and areas in which these two notions differ. Two key areas of division that differentiate face and identity are; (a) the role of the interlocutor, and (b) the focus on positive claims. In essence, when claiming face an individual petitions for desired face, however, claims are reliant on the evaluation of the interlocutor who may elect to corroborate or challenge the desired public front claimed. In short, both negative and positive face claims are dependent on the appraisal of the interlocutor and cannot be claimed without joint construction. On the other hand, identity speaks directly to the individual's perceptions of self, and while invariably influenced by the interlocutor and restrained by social constructs, does not require ratification. This distinction is highlighted by Arundale (2006) who characterises face as a dyadic phenomenon while identity is referred to as an individual phenomenon. The second point of divergence pertains to face as concerned with positive claims and avoidance of negatively evaluated attributes that the individual does not wish to have ascribed. As a public self-image, face is associated with positive claims in accordance with how the individual desires to be valued by interlocutors within specific situations. Identity however, is much broader in scope in that it is orientated towards the individual's perceptions of self and therefore may be characterised as negative, positive or neutral. This distinction is noted by Spencer-Oatey (2007) who argues:

Face is not associated with negative attributes, except in so far as we claim NOT to possess them. In this respect, there is a clear distinction between face and identity. A person's identity attributes include negatively and neutrally evaluated characteristics, as well as positive ones, whilst the attributes associated with face are only positive ones. (Spencer-Oatey, 2007: 643)

Nevertheless, Spencer-Oatey emphasises that there will be differences in how individuals evaluate a given attribute impacting face claims. For example, a Japanese child who has acquired English competence abroad may elect to hide these skills at school in Japan so as to avoid losing face among peers by appearing too accomplished or out of the ordinary. However, the same student, if participating in an English proficiency interview may make face claims based on his English competence. Spencer-Oatey refers to affective sensitivity to illustrate that self-presentation operates in foreground and background modes. When self-perceived identity equals other-perceived identity, face perception is viewed as running in a background mode (Schlenker & Pontari, 2000) or passing unnoticed, however becoming salient when the two perceptions are in conflict. Accordingly, claims of face happen only when self-perceived identity is not in harmony with other-perceived identity, either in a positive way or in a negative way. This is summed up by Spencer-Oatey (2007: 644) who writes 'When everything is going smoothly, we may barely be aware of our face sensitivities (they are operating in the background mode), yet as soon as people appraise our face claims in an unexpected way (either positively or negatively) our attention is captured because we are affectively sensitive to those evaluations'. Accordingly, face differs from self-perceived identity, as face can never be claimed unilaterally, and must include the consideration of other's perception of self-attributes, which is essentially other-perceived identity. Identity, on the other hand, is individual and can be claimed without regard to the other's perspective.

While this distinction is clear, if face and identity are socio-cognitively interpreted they are similar to the extent that they both have to do with one's self-image and accordingly, different factors that constitute a person's identity may also influence his/her face. The key point here being that identity and face can potentially offer valuable insights into the individual's interpretation of self through highlighting different levels of self-perception. This is demonstrated in Spencer-Oatey's (2007) approach to face-analysis, which seeks to describe how the face-gain/loss occurs from the perspective of the interactant(s) involved in ongoing interaction. What causes the loss or gain of face; in other words, to find the specific face-sensitive attribute(s) and to determine what face means or represents for the interactant(s) involved in a particular situation. Spencer-Oatey argues that as face entails claims on the evaluations of others, it follows that it should be evaluated as an interactional phenomenon unfolding in real-time interaction. The focus on real-time interaction illustrates that claims to face, and an anticipation of an interlocutors face claims, can vary dynamically during an exchange. Individual, relational and collective factors need to be considered when examining the underpinnings of face for as Spencer-Oatey cautions, 'analysing face only in interaction is comparable to studying just one side of a coin.' The researcher goes on to stress that 'face, like identity, is both social (interactional) and cognitive in nature' (2007: 648). The researcher's point being that 'there are cognitive underpinnings that influence (but do not determine) how face unfolds in interaction, and that considering these will inform and enrich an interactional analysis' (2007: 648). For this reason it is argued that the construct of face, examined alongside theories of identity, potentially provides a broader and richer platform from which to approach varying levels of explanation of how face unfolds during the dynamic process of interaction.

This line of reasoning is useful for face research given that in order to examine face it is critical to first determine how a face phenomenon occurs; and then determine the underpinnings related to the occurrence. It follows that as the face attributes an individual claims are in essence those that he regards as being of importance to this public self-image, they can provide insights into the identity he wishes to construct or maintain. Face, as the positively evaluated attributes one wants others to acknowledge, and the negatively evaluated attributes that one may not wish ascribed, entails claims on the evaluations of others. Accordingly, face is evaluated as an inter-actional phenomenon unfolding in real-time interaction, and face claims, jointly constructed during interaction, are examined with attention to identity claims and (dis)alignment.

Part 2

Overview of Research Methodology

5 Methodology and Data Collection

Overview

The following chapter describes the process of data collection, presents the rationale behind methodological decisions, and discusses the analytical framework underpinning the analysis of language use as revealed in the management of face and (dis)alignment with identities. I take a two-fold approach and examine students' interpretations of classroom events while at the same time analysing discourse in order to explore both lexico-grammatical features and characteristics of actions in the social context in concert. This chapter begins with an overview of the research methodology followed by a description of the phases involved in the process of data collection and the piloting process of the research instruments. This includes a presentation of the types of data collected, namely transcriptions of classroom interactions (English/Japanese), results of stimulated recall interviews (Japanese), and transcriptions of semi-structured interviews (English).

Research Methodology

Given that cultural, social and linguistic diversity are fundamental to communicative practices, the subsequent analysis employs a composite model combining theories of politeness and face within the qualitative framework. The research methodology is based on the view that face, as a culturally influenced construct with a diverse range of conceptualisations across cultures and between individuals, is basic to all human beings. Face, as observed during the Japanese students' discursive negotiation and renegotiation of face while participating in L2 English activities, serves as a window through which discursive orientations and behaviour may be examined from the students' perspective. Identity, as a multi-faceted and dynamic concept-of-self, generates insight into face within the context of the classroom, and does so from multiple perspectives. The interconnections between face and identity shed light on the Japanese students' verbal and non-verbal discursive strategies while insights from theories of identity provide multiple perspectives from which the phenomenon of face can be studied. The participating students, and indeed all students, are not mere observers of social norms, but, rather, active agents constructing their own social worlds. The classroom is an evolving network in which discursive and non-discursive tools are employed by the teacher and students in real time to achieve specific goals. Mediated action, as the focus of analysis, holds that the utterance is but one example of a mediated action, and that all other actions, whether it be opening a book or pointing at a board, are just as much mediated actions that constitute parts of interaction (see Scollon, 2001). Informed by the students' evaluative judgments of both verbal and non-verbal communicative strategies, the examination draws attention to interpretations of not only classroom roles, but also variation in classroom practices as viewed by the teacher and students and how these perceptions influenced interaction as students manage face and align with identities.

Through combining the recording and transcribing of naturally occurring interactions with techniques of observation and interviewing, we observe what the students were thinking through focusing on the students' interpretations of their classroom performance and how language both shapes and is shaped by the classroom socio-cultural context. The study maintains that within the classroom there are inevitably moments during which the communicative competence of the participants will be challenged. Critical moments constitute moments within the processes and practices of the classroom during which the participants (teacher and/or students) identify and orient to the occurrence of contradictions arising among conflicting orders of discourse (Candlin, 1987). During critical moments the participants' actions, beliefs and competencies may be challenged and subjective realities questioned (Candlin & Lucas, 1986). As the direction of communication may deviate from what participants regard as being situationally appropriate, the communicative skills of interlocutors are challenged in order to avoid or resolve potential misunderstandings. In short, the interactions that occur may develop in unanticipated ways, and therefore may require the teacher and/or students to employ differing communicative strategies to clarify or explain. The students' interactional management of critical moments through verbal and non-verbal communicative strategies shed light on the individual personalities and ideologies in a manner which at times requires them to reveal cultural, social and individual positionings through the communicative strategies they employ.

Recognising the construction of identities as a reflection of the students' socio-cultural knowledge, beliefs and values, the analysis explores how language is both used during L2 learning activities, and how language is transformed by these activities. Data analysis is inductive with key patterns and themes emerging from primary data sources examined with attention to the participants' experiences within the research site. Discourse analysis (DA) provides a broad platform from which to delve beneath the structural features of the language employed by the students in order to gain insight into socio-psychological characteristics and features of communication through concentrating on the meaning of language in interaction and 'language in situational and cultural context[s]' (Trappes-Lomax, 2004: 134). Discourses, defined by Merry (1990) as 'aspects of culture, interconnected vocabularies and systems of meaning located in a social world', are not isolated, but rather constitute 'part of a shared cultural world'. While interlocutors are confined by the socio-cultural structure of discourses, Merry emphasises that there is room for creativeness as 'actors define and frame their problems within one or another discourse' (1990: 110).

DA is employed 'to show how micro-level social actions realise and give local form to macro-level social structures' and thereby constitutes 'a way of linking up the analysis of local characteristics of communication to the analysis of broader social characteristics' (Jaworski & Coupland, 1999: 12–13). This dynamic interplay between discourse in structuring areas of knowledge, and the social and institutional practices which are associated with them, is explained by Candlin (1997) as follows:

'Discourse' ... refers to language in use, as a process which is socially situated. However ... we may go on to discuss the constructive and dynamic role of either spoken or written discourse in structuring areas of knowledge and the social and institutional practices which are associated with them. In this sense, discourse is a means of talking and writing about and acting upon worlds, a means which both constructs and is constructed by a set of social practices within these worlds, and in so doing both reproduces and constructs afresh particular social-discursive practices, constrained or encouraged by more macro movements in the overarching social formation. (Candlin, 1997: ix)

Discourse analysis is explained by Sarangi and Candlin (2003: 117) as engaged with bringing three distinct methodological perspectives together; in particular 'the requirement to describe discourse phenomena, the need to incorporate participants' interpretations and perspectives on such phenomena, and to locate such descriptions and such interpretations within a particular institutional order seen historically and social structurally.' Importantly, Sarangi and Candlin (2003: 116) stress that DA 'is not reducible to analysis of language: it systematically examines non-verbal, extra-linguistic behaviour in the ethnographic tradition'. Consequently, discourse is viewed as embedded within specific socio-cultural contexts and impacted by any number of factors salient to the context. Gee (1999) refers to this as being 'situated' or in other words, grounded in the specific contexts and practices of use associated with socio-cultural groups (1999: 54). It is the interpretation of the context and related factors such as relationships and roles that help the analyst build meaning and thereby more deeply understand the communicative intent behind discourse as intended by the speaker or writer, and as understood by the listener or reader (see Gee & Handford, 2011; Jones, 2012).

A qualitative interpretive methodology structured around fieldwork, feedback and analysis, draws on a broad range of data collected through classroom recordings and retrospective interviews in order to provide a contextually rich account of the classroom under investigation and the participants language use and behaviour (Davis, 1995; Erickson, 1986; Lincoln & Guba, 1985, 2000; Richards, 2003). Thick description (Geertz, 1973) or a descriptive-explanatory-interpretive account of the students' interaction with the teacher and each other is adopted through incorporating both an emic perspective, that is the culturally specific framework used by the Japanese students for interpreting and assigning meaning to their experiences, and an etic perspective, based on a framework which explores concepts and categories relevant to the Japanese students through the academic frameworks, concepts and categories of face and identities (Watson-Gegeo, 1988). Thick description is accomplished through a holistic approach (Lutz, 1981), that is, the verbal and non-verbal behaviours are investigated in the context in which the students and teacher produce them, and interpreted and explained in terms of their relationship to the entire system of which they are a part. At the heart of qualitative research lies the contextualised elucidation and exposition of the meanings of actions from the participants' perspective which Creswell (1998) succinctly explains as follows:

> Qualitative research is an inquiry process of understanding based on distinct methodological traditions of inquiry that explore a social or human problem. The researcher builds a complex, holistic picture, analyzes words, reports detailed views of informants and conducts the study in a natural setting. (Creswell, 1998: 15)

A frequent criticism of qualitative inquiry is that as data is interpreted in an explicitly subjective manner there will inevitably be concerns with reliability and validity (Stake, 1995). This criticism assumes that the procedures for validating qualitative research claims are inferior to standardised quantitative research paradigms which, among other things, are better able to monitor variables and less affected by the researchers agenda. Claims of inconsistency and bias frequently overlook that the contemporary qualitative research paradigm typically employs multiple research methods and references diverse data sources. Moreover, it is accepted practice to validate research data collection, analysis and interpretations through engaging the expertise of more than one researcher. Within the qualitative paradigm, triangulation of data sources, investigators and methods is periodically conducted through attention to validity checks which afford analytical mechanisms to promote impartiality and receptiveness to diverse interpretations of the data. Among other things, Richards (2003: 287) advocates the methodical comparison of codings with other codings and classifications, seeking out new relationships, and active attention to negative evidence which can be assessed for relevance to interpretations.

The research methodology can be collapsed into the following five broad phases:

(1) Access – to identify a suitable English conversation school in order to conduct a pilot study, preliminary observations and the central study.
(2) Video recordings – to conduct classroom recordings of naturally occurring classroom-based interaction.
(3) Teacher interviews – to conduct a sequence of semi-structured interviews and administer a questionnaire on teaching beliefs, attitudes and practices.
(4) Stimulated recall – to conduct retrospective interviews with participants using video recorded classroom interaction.
(5) Dissemination of findings – to develop a professional development teaching programme based on the research findings.

Research Site and Participants

Research was carried out at a private language school situated approximately 100 km north of Tokyo in Utsunomiya, the capital city of Tochigi Prefecture (see Ohzeki et al., 2012 for a history of Tochigi Prefecture). Utsunomiya, a medium sized city with an estimated population around 520,000, is surrounded by the scenic mountain ranges of Nikko and Nasu in the northwest and the Kanto Plain in the southeast. With stretches of flat arable land scarce in mountainous Japan, the Kanto Plain serves as a central rice and vegetable producing area. Prior to World War II, the primary crops grown in Tochigi Prefecture were rice, wheat, hemp, 'kanpyo' (dried gourd shavings) and tobacco. A shift away from agriculture towards the creation of an industrial prefecture followed the end of World War II when Prime Minister Ikeda Hayato (1899–1965) established an 'Income Doubling Plan' (Ohzeki et al., 2012: 227). Newly conceived factory zones enticed large corporations to relocate resulting in what is now recognised as the largest inland industrial zone in Japan. Today, Utsunomiya is home to a large number of multinational corporations including Canon, Japan Tobacco, Sony and Honda Design Center. Rural areas juxtaposed with cutting edge industrial zones give Utsunomiya the distinctive feel of a rural city with a modern and progressive outlook.

The study observed two classes of 15 Japanese school students aged from 10 to 12 attending a beginner English conversation programme with one-hour lessons scheduled twice weekly. The teacher instructing the class, Mr Wheaton, is a 35-year-old native-English-speaking male who has taught English in Japan for twelve years. In addition to instructing children, Mr Wheaton conducts training courses for Japanese teachers of English designed to enhance teaching skills primarily through the use of music, flash cards and picture books. Providing insight into his view of teaching Japanese children Mr Wheaton commented that 'Japanese kids are much harder to teach than adults because they don't have the basic English skills or desire to learn. Often they don't see the need'. Reflecting on his work training teachers in Japan, Mr Wheaton remarked 'Experience is everything (...) You get a sense for what works and what doesn't in the classroom. When I train teachers I rely a lot on my experience as a teacher and the things that I know work'.

Phase 1: Trajectory of access

A pilot study was conducted involving self-selecting Japanese students and NS English teachers who were not participants in the main study. Systematic piloting at all stages of development generated insight into how the instruments worked and whether they performed the purposes for which they were designed therein increasing reliability, validity and practicability (Cohen et al., 2000: 260). The analysis of pilot study results led to modifications to SR protocol, time allocation, revision of technical considerations and the rewording of interview items. In addition, the pilot revealed points of SR ambiguity, clarity concerns in instructions, and several omissions that were duly addressed (see Dörnyei & Skehan, 2003).

Following the pilot study, a period of preliminary observation was undertaken during which research objectives were discussed with the teacher, technical requirements trialled and rapport with the students established. Semi-participant observation; that is when the researcher engages only partially in activities in the community observed, provided both time and space to experiment with recording equipment, and crucially, to dissociate myself from the role of 'teacher'. This was critical given that I was to administer SR sessions intended to elicit language beliefs and ideologies from the students. Moreover, these observations allowed time to foster a trusting and collaborative relationship with the teacher which proved constructive to the quality and candid nature of interview dialogue. During this access phase, use of video-cameras was explained to the students and recording equipment positioned to nurture familiarization. Located on either side of the classroom in order to reduce potential distraction and to capture a wide angle-shot of the classroom and the students, camera and audio recording devices allowed for the recording of both dyadic talk and multi-partied talk which was crucial as recall sessions required the use of tangible, high quality visual and audio prompts (see Gass & Mackey, 2000; Mackey & Gass, 2005).

Phase 2: Video recordings

Video recordings of classroom interaction provide a powerful means by which to observe and understand classroom language and behaviour by capturing students and teacher, in real situations, doing real things (see Derry et al., 2010; DuFon, 2002; Jacobs et al., 1999). A primary advantage of video recorded data is that it can be readily replayed, reviewed and reinterpreted (DuFon, 2002) and allows for control of observer fatigue or drift (unintentionally going off on a tangent). Moreover, visual contextual information aids the negotiation of ambiguity in verbal messages by reducing the potential number of accurate interpretations (Iino, 1999) while enabling the researcher to contemplate and deliberate prior to drawing conclusions (DuFon, 2002).

While the intention of video recording is to maximise the richness of data, there are potential limitations associated with issues such as camera intrusiveness (Derry et al., 2010). The chief concern being that people may change their behaviour when aware they are being videotaped which can influence the behaviour of interest. Commonly referred to as participant reactivity or reflexivity to awareness of being observed, Labov (1972) notes that, 'the aim of linguistic research in the community must be to find out how people talk when they are not being systematically observed; yet we can only obtain these data by systematic observation' (1972: 209). A further criticism of videotaped data is that it captures only what is observable, and therefore does not provide insight into the thoughts and feelings of those being recorded (Derry *et al.*, 2010). As this information cannot be seen or heard on recordings, visual data needs to be triangulated with other data sources such as researcher's field notes and/or interviews with participants. The use of retrospective interviews to inspire students to recall and describe their thoughts, feelings and reactions at different points in time during a given event is a valuable means of generating triangulation (see Clarke, 2001; DuFon, 2002).

Despite drawbacks, the recording of English activities is an opportunity to examine the real-life dynamics of classroom interaction without the potentially more distracting presence of the researcher (DuFon, 2002). The inclusion of a technical familiarisation period aided in creating a level of participant acceptance, and attention to placing equipment on the recording function prior to the commencement of classes further reduced intrusiveness. Video recordings enabled the identification of who was speaking, gestures, facial expressions and other visual interactional cues relevant to the negotiation of meaning (see Derry *et al.*, 2010). In addition, recordings generated contextual and non-verbal information regarding the type of activity speakers were engaged in and non-verbal features of exchanges such as silence, gestures and *aizuchi* (backchannels). Accordingly, the video recordings engaged in the analysis of classroom discourse and SR sessions yielded rich insights into factors that influenced the participants' language use and behaviour.

Phase 3: Teacher interviews

The teacher took part in a sequence of one-on-one semi-structured interviews and completed a questionnaire designed to gain insight into his use of Japanese during English activities. By the notion of 'semi-structured', the interviews were conducted in a way that is, as Kvale (2007) puts it, 'neither an open everyday conversation nor a closed questionnaire' (2007: 11). The teacher was given opportunities to articulate his thoughts on a set of questions tapping into his beliefs about language teaching and learning, as well as his thoughts regarding the previous class. The semi-structured format allowed flexibility to follow up on ideas which the teacher raised during the interviews in addition to the planned questions to been covered. The questionnaire, drawn from previous field work, examined the teacher's views regarding the use of the L1 (Japanese) during learning activities (Auerbach, 1993; Cook, 2001; Levine, 2003; Nation, 2003; von Dietze *et al.*, 2009; von Dietze *et al.*, 2010). Interview data, supported by observations of classroom interaction together with questionnaire data, were used to gain contextualised insight into the teacher's classroom teaching practices and beliefs.

The objective here being to tap into the rationale behind the teacher's language and behaviour in order to build a multidimensional description of his performance within the classroom.

Phase 4: Stimulated recall

Stimulated recall procedure, a retrospective technique based on retrieval cues, was employed in order to gain insight into the students' thoughts (see Gass & Mackey, 2000; Mackey & Gass, 2005). Viewed as a subset of introspective research methods, SR uses audio and/or visual stimulus to assist the student to recall and report on thoughts and motivations entertained during specific activities or tasks. The line of reasoning being that tangible stimulus will help 'stimulate recall of the mental processes in operation during the event itself' and thereby 'access to memory structures is enhanced' (Gass & Mackey, 2000: 17). Video recorded data was used to play back classroom interaction to the students so as to assist them to 'recall and describe their thoughts, feelings and reactions at different points in time' during the English activities and therein providing insight in 'the unobservable' (DuFon, 2002: 44). In this way, the use of multimedia sources such as video in recall sessions has the advantage of replaying and reintroducing cues that were present at the time of the task (Sime, 2006; Stough, 2001).

Focusing on the recollection of retrievable information as opposed to rationalisation, the SR methodology is a popular tool in educational research for exploring the connection between discourse and cognition within the classroom practice and interaction (Clarke, 2001; Keyes, 2000; Morris & Tarone, 2003; Plaut, 2006; Sime, 2006; Yoshida, 2008). For example, Morris and Tarone (2003) employed SR to shed light on contextual factors and human relationships and how they impact on classroom language learning while Yoshida (2008) examined Japanese language learners' perceptions of peer corrective feedback in pair work situations. Plaut (2006) utilised SR to investigate students' and teachers' constructs of 'confusion' in their study of transferring teacher expertise to student teachers. Similarly, Sime (2006) explored the perceived functions that teachers' gestures perform in the EFL classroom when viewed from the point of view of students through SR. Mackey et al. (2000) utilised SR in order to examine how students perceive feedback and its target, that is, what feedback is being provided for, and whether their perceptions affect their noticing. A key advantage of conducting video-stimulated interviews is that video records provide 'a specific and immediate stimulus that optimises the conditions for effective recall of associated feelings and thoughts' and the verbal reports obtained with the assistance from such a stimuli, can offer 'useful insights into those individuals' learning behaviour' (Clarke, 2001: 16). Moreover, as verbal reporting is based on the use of a tangible prompt, SR does not place the same demands on memory retrieval as *post hoc* interviews, and is less demanding than think-aloud protocols which require extensive participant training (Gass & Mackey, 2000: 18). Reduced demands on the student enhances researcher access to 'what the respondents actually perceived about each situation (e.g. what they perceived about the relative role status of the interlocutors) and how their perceptions influenced their responses' (Cohen, 2004: 321).

Despite its popularity, SR methodology has generated a number of concerns in regard to issues such as falsifiability, replicability, reliability and validity given that it is far from conclusive whether it is indeed possible to observe internal processes in the same way as external events. The point being that if it is assumed cognitive processing is unconscious, then cognitive processes are inaccessible or potentially vulnerable to inaccurate reporting (Dörnyei, 2007). Moreover, while recall revelations are directly reported on by students, this does not guarantee that they accurately reflect the individuals thought processes (Plaut, 2006; Sime, 2006). For example, during the process of viewing the recording of a lesson, students may pick up new or additional information which they did not attend to during the class and consequently accounts might be vulnerable to problems of unintentional misrepresentation (Clarke, 2001). Consequently, students may establish new connections with material which unintentionally inform their reflections and undermine data reliability. Furthermore, it is conceivable that students may censor or distort their thoughts and ideas in order to present themselves more favourably (Sime, 2006). A further concern is that once information is established in the long-term memory it may no longer be a direct report of the experience and what the person was thinking, but rather a reflection or a combination of experience and other related memories (Plaut, 2006; Sime, 2006). Given that SR can only access information the participant is conscious of, we can assume that pre-existing strategic moves that are routinized may not be detected during recall as the procedural knowledge governing such strategy-use enters long-term memory and is not available for verbal reporting (Ericsson & Simon, 1993).

While surface behaviours may not always reflect underlying strategic processing, SR can assist the researcher to identify students' strategic thoughts and to obtain constructive, though of course not perfect, insight into what they were. Nevertheless, the aforementioned limitations highlight the need to complement SR methodology with observational methods so as to obtain a fuller understanding of what constitutes management of face and enactment of identities. Within the current study, recordings of classroom interaction between students and their teacher provide information concerning actual verbal and non-verbal behaviours to complement reflective reports of such behaviours. In this way, when combined with other data sources, SR serves as a window into an individual's thoughts and feelings and can identify subjects that are of interest and importance to the students (Pomerantz, 2005). This position is underscored in Theobald's (2008: 14) examination of recall with children which surmises that the 'examination of the video-stimulated accounts brings us closer to the children's standpoint' and uncovers matters that are important to children, but which may be disregarded by adults. Triangulating SR data with observational data builds in layers of description and therein increases validity as it is possible to provide thicker description and question the degree to which the reported thought processes were taking place during the event rather than being constructed after the event.

Stimulated recall methodology is particularly appropriate in investigating the negotiation of face not least because students' face is essentially a matter of subjective perception and consequently should not be evaluated as being true or false (Spencer-Oatey, 2007). In other words, while face and identity are informed by socio-cultural factors that provide a useful perspective on the interpretive and comparative analysis of language and behaviour, it is important to bear in mind that personal agency affects the way language is used and interpreted. SR offers a method of obtaining information directly from the students which is then examined with close reference to classroom interaction. To facilitate reporting, SR interviews were carried out in the learners L1 and within 24 hours in order to minimise the impact of time lapse on students' ability to accurately reflect on discourse and behaviour motivations.

Priority was placed on establishing a simple, informal and comfortable approach to retrospection that did not place excessive demands on the students. An inviting student friendly environment was created through measures such as limiting technical demands, the use of unobtrusive recording devices and a choice of seating including beanbags, chairs and cushions. The use of the video recordings in the interviews changed the social structure of the interview, which rather than being depicted as researcher-instigated discourse (Wood & Kroger, 2000), could frequently be described as student instigated. At times the interviewer initiated conversation using the interview protocol while at other points students volunteered their reasoning or provided accounts of the action. Every time when the video was stopped and the student reported constituted an episode. An episode comprises the video playback of a related clip, the prompt (if any) by the researcher and the prompted or unprompted reporting of a student. The analysis of classroom discourse was cross-referenced to retrospective verbal reports on the students participation through a back and forth analysis. Classroom excerpts were examined with attention to how language was used and for what purposes, and further discussed in reference to SR data which provided insight into the students' interpretations of these exchanges.

Phase 5: Dissemination

The final stage of the methodology consisted of designing a professional development programme by which the research findings could be communicated to teachers and employed to improve teacher professional judgment and classroom performance. The approach to dissemination was to focus on a pedagogic and exploratory cycle of teaching and learning through attention to the five phases of: Awareness, Knowledge Building, Critique, Action and Evaluation (see Candlin *et al.*, 1995; Candlin, 1997; O'Grady, 2011). The model composition holds that the informed and self-aware teacher has the capacity to discern if, when and how to adopt, modify or discontinue teaching practices in order to effectively meet students' needs.

Translating/Transcribing Conventions

Stimulated recall, and corresponding moments during learning activities which triggered feedback, were transcribed in Japanese and then translated into English using a colour coding system. Recorded feedback was logged on a coding sheet in which the left column provided a detailed description of the segment of classroom discourse that triggered the recall; the second recorded the recall prompt if employed; the third a transcription of Japanese retrospective feedback; and the fourth an English translation. An extensive inventory of retrospective interviews was created through multiple viewings.

In transcribing and translating recall sessions, I was conscious that both talk and transcription are social acts and the transcriber brings his own perspectives and language ideology to transcribing discussion (Roberts, 1997). In order to maintain objectivity in translations, particular attention was paid to preserving and recording the mood and content through multiple viewings. Colloquial and word-by-word translations are employed to communicate the meanings and structures recorded in line with the context and participants communicative intentions. In cases where differences in the grammatical structure between English and Japanese colloquial translations interfered with the accuracy of translations, word-by-word translations are provided. Classroom and retrospective data is transcribed using transcription symbols adapted from the system developed by Jefferson (Wood & Kroger, 2000: 193) with descriptions of non-verbal action included in the transcripts.

The presentation of classroom exchanges is structured with Japanese presented in italics and English in standard font (non-italicised). As can be expected within a language classroom, often participants shifted between languages. Following the original participant comment is a translation of the Japanese in single quotation marks. In keeping with Jefferson's conventions all non-verbal activity is enclosed in a double bracket. Classroom excerpts are numbered and a brief outline of the classroom exchange provided to contextualise the scene. The presentation of retrospective feedback is structured with the original Japanese text recorded in *italics* and the English translation directly following in single brackets. In classroom excerpts Japanese speech is recorded in *italics* with the corresponding English translations identified in single quotation marks. Pseudonyms have been employed to afford anonymity to the participants.

Data Analysis

Triangulation through the use of multiple sources of data was employed as a means of crosschecking the validity of the findings and establishing a naturalistic description of the students' language use and behaviour. The analysis benefited markedly from the detailed and candid insights provided by the students' retrospective feedback, teacher interview data and classroom recordings which generated three different points of entry to the examination of classroom interaction. Two issues that needed to be addressed concerned the selection and balance of data to be analysed, and the way in which to integrate the multiple types of data collected. The importance of identifying suitable discourse for analysis is noted by Wood and Kroger (2000: 88) who maintain that 'the identification of segments should be comprehensive in order to include all possible instances (because their relevance may not be apparent until analysis is done and because it is often the marginal cases that are most important)'. The following section outlines the six stages of description, analysis and interpretation by which the corpus of data were managed. Data analysis was carried out in tandem with the data collection to the extent that retrospective and classroom data was being transcribed and translated from the first week of observation. Accordingly, this was a gradually evolving process in which the dataset, coded categories and research objectives, were continually re-evaluated and reformulated.

STEP 1. Video recordings were systematically organised using a comprehensive labelling system. Repeated viewings of data were employed to classify and log for identification information including the time,

instructional focus of the lesson, specific learning activities and student configurations.

STEP 2. SR data was transcribed and translated through a back and
forth process so as to develop a comprehensive verbatim of transcripts.
Classroom excerpts that triggered student retrospective feedback were
re-examined, transcribed and presented in textual format for comprehensive analysis.

STEP 3. SR data was segmented and coded with *Nvivo* codes in order to
reveal subtle connections within the data. Emerging patterns were
examined, interpreted and advanced through the analysis of classroom
discourse and data acquired from teacher interviews.

STEP 4. SR data was coded thematically and redundancy among codes
reduced while overlapping codes were clustered together. Themes identified were predominantly 'folk categories' in that they focused directly
on the students' thoughts and feelings in relation to classroom participation (Delamont, 1992: 150). Codes were collapsed into four broad
themes, namely; (a) peer collaboration, (b) Japanese identities, (c) use
of the mother tongue, and (d) interactive silence.

STEP 5. Teacher interviews and transcribed questionnaire feedback
were examined with attention to internal connections within the
data. Data was coded and examined in conjunction with classroom
interaction and retrospective data framed within the four primary
themes in a back and forth process. Correlations were coded.

STEP 6. Retrospective feedback was triangulated with teacher interviews, questionnaire data and examined alongside transcribed points
from learning activities. Through a cyclical process analysis moves
between the data sources in order to explore recurring patterns of student attitudes, behaviour and shared language that shed light on identity construction, identity enactment and the management of face
within the L2 classroom.

Theoretical Framework and Data Analysis

Discourse analysis is employed in order to probe classroom interaction,
interviews and retrospective data in relation to the primary themes and to
explore 'patterns and links within and across utterances in order to form
hypotheses about how meaning is being constructed and organised' (Gee,
1999: 118). Utterances are analysed for their force as social acts during
the negotiation of face and enactment of identities with attention to what
is said, the audience addressed, the responses from interlocutors, voice

intonation, gestures and facial expressions. In order to incorporate students' interpretations of their own discourse their voices, that being the range of observable student language use in the classroom and during interviews, are examined to construct an account of how the students both use and interpret verbal and non-verbal communication during English activities (see Bakhtin, 1981, 1986). Through the interpretation of classroom interaction and the meanings students bring to them we link up the analysis of the associations between local patterns/functions of the students' verbal and non-verbal communication strategies within the classroom to wider socio-cultural patterns of language use and behaviour.

The Japanese students' identity alignment, as revealed through facework, is examined in relation to 'acts of identity' (LePage & Tabouret-Keller, 1985) based on the position that these are more than attempts to align with specific identities as they involve rejection, resistance and modification of imposed identities (Ellwood, 2008). Consequently, the analysis explores ways in which language is both intentionally and unintentionally employed by students to protect the speaker's public self-image, protect or challenge the public self-image of the addressee, and preserve socio-cultural norms deemed appropriate within the Japanese L2 classroom context. Ellwood (2008) argues that the language classroom, as a forum for identity construction where the individual may be forced to assume specific identities, imposes restrictions on the student given that, 'society makes available identity categories with which individuals, in a drive to "be", seek to align or disalign' (2008: 539). From such a position we discern that teacher/student assumptions as to classroom roles and rank, influenced by social, cultural and individual interpretations of appropriate language use and behaviour, at times give rise to identities that are derived from unfamiliar or even contested positioning.

With regard to Japanese students' core expectations as to teaching and learning, Rohlen and LeTendre (1996) have put together an enlightening volume which presents a diverse assortment of ethnographic and experimental studies from varying Japanese social contexts. The wide-ranging contributions draw attention to common themes associated with Japanese theories of teaching and learning through the analyses of observations from formal school based education and non-school based research sites. These research sites include the Rinzai Zen monastery, Kumon schools, training in the art of Noh theatre and the Suzuki method of music instruction. Based on first-hand researcher observations, these diverse contexts generate insight into socio-culturally informed Japanese teaching and learning philosophies which the editors link to larger patterns of practice. It is these underlying patterns which suggest unifying themes reflected in shared expectations with regard to the processes and practices of teaching and learning.

Examining school based pedagogical models of learning Rohlen and LeTendre (1996: 6) posit that the educational process within Japanese elementary schools is oriented primarily toward socialisation to group procedures associated with central values and norms. Contrary to the assumption that this equates to the restriction of individuality, the researchers argue that this process is rooted in a fundamental belief that 'children up to the age of 10 develop best when allowed to follow their own inclinations'. The organisation and management of the classroom is seen as fostering collective identity through encouraging the individual to function productively within group contexts; a skill viewed as imperative to both success as a student and in later adult life. This period of socialisation provides the foundations from which students draw on when faced with the increased demands and discipline associated with the transition to junior and later senior high school where the focus rapidly shifts to club activities, academic achievement and demanding entrance examinations. Rohlen and LeTendre (1996) reason that through both school and non-school based learning, Japanese students acquire shared expectations of appropriate behaviours and a strong sense of collective identity which influences the way in which they perceive the classroom and conduct themselves.

The classroom, as Ellwood (2008) states, 'provides a highly differentiated context with its own specific constellation of rules and roles and where the expected performances of participants are interlinked in relatively codified ways' (2008: 539). It is these constellations which Ellwood cites as manifesting aspects of both cultural differences and cultural alignment. Specifically, Ellwood notes the positioning of the students in relation to the teacher and the 'cluster of identities around the role category "student"' (2008: 539). Positioning theory is described by Linehan and McCarthy (2000: 441) as 'an analytic tool that can be used flexibly to describe the shifting multiple relations in a community of practice'. In this way, positioning theory describes the way in which individuals metaphorically locate themselves within discursive action in everyday conversations. Barnes (2004) explains that 'How people are positioned in any situation depends both on the context and community values and on the personal characteristics of all the individuals concerned, their personal history, their preferences and their capabilities' (2004: 3). For this reason, positioning theory holds that during interaction each person positions himself while simultaneously positioning the other person based on assumptions regarding rights and duties. Accordingly, the examination of positionings requires attention to what interlocutors say and do during interaction with consideration of these presumed rights and duties.

Position is flexible and dynamic, and accordingly, positions can be assumed, abandoned or maintained in relation to the context. When interacting within the classroom environment the teacher and students have obligations and roles to perform. While they have a degree of agency in determining their positioning during interaction, 'this agency is inter-laced with the expectations and history of the community, the sense of "oughtness"' (Linehan & McCarthy, 2000: 442). The asymmetrical nature of power relations that exist between teacher and students, coupled with classroom conventions and boundaries, raise questions as to the extent to which the student is free to harness a range of pragmatic and socio-linguistic abilities. In other words, there are assumptions of appropriateness regard-ing rights and duties one assigns to oneself and interlocutor however within the classroom environment observed within the study, the balance of power clearly lies with the teacher. As positionings are associated with socially and culturally constructed relations, within the language class-room the teacher and students may position themselves and each other in distinctly different ways. In order to maintain relative position the stu-dents and teacher behave in accordance with socio-cultural patterns, which reveal expectations in-group, and individual subjectivity that may go unnoticed.

A final and important point is that the study aligns with Spencer-Oatey's (2007: 648) view that 'face, like identity, is both social (interactional) and cognitive in nature' with the cognitive underpinnings associated with values and sociality rights or obligations which affect face claims and face sensitivi-ties. For this reason, the effective management of face entails an understand-ing of why certain occurrences are regarded by interlocutors as threatening. The examination embraces Spencer-Oatey's argument that theories of iden-tity can offer a richer and more comprehensive understanding of face than has been achieved thus far. Accordingly, attention to identities alongside the examination of face is embraced in order to establish a framework for the analysis of face and provide a broader perspective for conceptualisation and analysis of student interaction. This constitutes an important theoretical basis for the ensuing back and forth analysis of the Japanese students' inter-action during English activities. These conceptualisations, alongside the notion of face, constitute the fundamental structure of the theoretical frame-work. Leech (2005) makes the point that:

There is little doubt that the Eastern group-orientation and the Western individual-orientation are felt to be strong influences on polite behav-iour. But do the East and the West need a different theory of politeness? I would argue that they don't, because the scales of politeness can be used to express such differences in values, both qualitative and quantita-tive. (Leech, 2005: 27)

Aligning with the view that scales of politeness can provide insight into both similarities and differences within and across cultures, the following analysis of student talk is carried out through a composite theoretical framework which draws on a critical account of both B&L's concept of face duality and notions of social and cultural interdependency, discernment and place as advocated by Japanese scholarship (see Matsumoto, 1988, 2003; Hill *et al.*, 1986; Ide, 1989; Haugh, 2005). A primary reason for adopting a composite theory lies in the fact that an increasing body of empirical research examining a diverse range of languages and cultures has demonstrated that a single notion of face cannot adequately account for linguistic politeness across cultures, societies and languages. All the same, the following analysis maintains that the concept of positive and negative face as proposed by B&L remains a dynamic conceptual and analytic tool particularly when used in combination with culturally appropriate descriptions of Japanese culture, society and language. In short, in addition to B&L's model of politeness in which the notion of 'self' is independent and highly individualistic, we maintain that the examination of Japanese students classroom interaction requires language to be appropriately framed in order to display appropriate attitudes consistent to the cultural and social context.

The ensuing examination draws on Hill *et al.*'s (1986) examination of volition and discernment, Haugh's (2005) theory of place inclusion and distinction in relation to Japanese society, Ide's (1989) theory of *wakimae* (discernment) politeness, and Matsumoto's (1988) theory of interdependence. Supported by a growing number of empirical studies targeting languages other than English, varying cultural parameters illustrate the need for a modified approach to face in order to construct culturally inclusive frameworks. The ground in-between, as proposed in Haugh's 2005 notion of place, offers valuable insights into the management and negotiation of face and as such, provides a balance between an opposed rhetoric associated with collective and individual theories of face and communication strategies. Allowing for differing perspectives facilitates cultural comparison and the acknowledgement of specific cultural features, while importantly avoiding the assumption that intercultural communication is inherently a collision of cultures. For this reason, while comparisons and contrasts between the Japanese students and their non-Japanese teacher shape the ensuing discussion of interaction within the classroom, it is critical to recognise that each of the participants is influenced by factors unique to his own background.

Part 3

Student Insights into Classroom Interaction

6   Results

Overview of Findings

> (…) however open towards, curious about and tolerant of other people's beliefs, values and behaviours learners are, their own beliefs, values and behaviours are deeply embedded and can create reaction and rejection. Because of this unavoidable response, intercultural speakers/mediators need to become aware of their own values and how these influence their views of other people's values. Intercultural speakers/mediators need a critical awareness of themselves and their values, as well as those of other people. (Byram *et al.*, 2002: 13)

Students come to the language classroom with individual and varied histories and experiences that mediate their understandings of the environment and provide them with tools to negotiate such understandings within it. In order to examine the construct of identity as revealed through the pragmatics of face, cross-cultural communication within the L2 English classroom is examined from the perspective of the participants and as articulated in the participants' own words. Student face, as the public way in which students engage and petition interlocutors when claiming recognition, sheds light on discursive practices, attitudes and behaviour important to how students perceive themselves in the present and regard possibilities for the future. Data sources closely integrated with relevant literature are explored in a back and forth analysis targeting how students construct, negotiate and at times oppose identities when interactively managing face. Identity, as an ongoing negotiation between individuals, cultural and social contexts, is framed with attention to the lived histories students bring to the classroom activities as they negotiate and co-construct their views of themselves and the world.

Socio-cultural factors influence pragmatic and interactional norms, and the ways in which politeness and appropriateness are realised through communication strategies. At the same time, the following analysis aligns with the position (Tobin, 1999) that excessive preoccupation with cultural differences may lead to over-simplification of cross-cultural interaction and thereby work to legitimise an oppositional paradigm that is counterproductive to understanding students as complex individuals. Scollon and Scollon (1995) posit that in order to avoid oversimplification and stereotyping 'comparisons between groups, one should always consider both likenesses and differences, that is, they should be based upon more than a single dimension of contrast, and it must be remembered that no individual member of a group embodies all of his or her group's characteristics' (1995: 157). The cultural comparisons introduced through a selection of emerging, multi-layered and often overlapping themes do not in any way imply that interpretations of face for Japanese and non-Japanese occupy opposite ends of a spectrum. This is not to say that I have avoided comparative discussion. On the contrary, comparative analysis is a key feature of the pragmatics literature and emerges as a priority for the students in their attempts to negotiate face and align with identities. As Valdes (1986) points out, not only are similarities and contrasts in the native and target languages useful teaching tools, but when applied to teaching practices they can become an advantageous learning tool.

Given that empirical research examining face as claimed by young students represents an area largely uncharted, the investigation focuses on discussing classroom interaction as framed through students' views as revealed through retrospective interviews and recordings of classroom interactions. To recap, the analyses examines ways in which the participants employ verbal and non-verbal communication strategies in order to; (a) claim and maintain face, (b) avoid face threat, (c) attend to the addressee's face needs and wants, and (d) preserve socio-cultural norms viewed as being appropriate within the context. In short, it is through these communication strategies that the participants seek to express and preserve the speaker-addressee relationship in accordance with cultural, social and individual interpretations of appropriateness. In order to attend to conventions governing interaction within the classroom, the students encode language based on perceptions of the nature of the relationship shared with peers and the teacher, and on perceptions regarding how the addressee views the relationship in accordance with the context. These activities and contexts are instilled with, and represent specific cultural values and ideologies (which privilege certain practices over others), and these shape the dynamics of the interactions.

Data reveals that the participants aligned with various identities that shed light on their interpretation of the classroom context and their roles within the classroom. At the same time, student comments highlight that within the teacher/student hierarchy of the classroom identities are not always freely chosen by students as they may be assigned by the teacher. Dynamic nominalism (Hacking, 1986) referred to in SLA as identity categorisation (Pennycook, 2001) argues that people come to fit categories themselves, as a form of social construction, and these come to define positions or subjectivities available to people. According to Hacking, 'If new modes of description come into being, new possibilities for action come into being in consequence' (2001: 231). Within the context of the current study, the language school in which the research takes place has its own institutionally and culturally defined categories which are ranked according to values, beliefs and practices. Moreover, these categories are inscribed in the teacher's cultural models of schooling and transmitted through his interactions with students. The teacher and school have the power to impose identity categories, and there exists potential tensions between agency and imposition of these identity categories when viewed from the students' perspective. Discourses are seen as having the power to impose however individuals can accept or reject the imposition and at the same time contribute to shaping the discourses.

The identities assigned by the teacher were not always consistent with how students aligned themselves or claimed face as competent members within the classroom. Conflicting interpretations of what constitutes appropriate classroom rank, role and associated behaviour gave rise to a number of competing identities. While the similarities and differences discussed should not be taken to be representative of Japanese and non-Japanese students in general (the samples are too small in number and limited in scope to permit that), the results underscore that social and cultural factors influence the negotiation of face and identity (dis)alignment. In other words, while there may be similarities across cultures in the face that people claim, there may also be variation at a more detailed level such as the overall importance and weight that people attach to face wants and needs.

The presentation of results here is organised around four areas of investigation which provide the framework from which I discuss the students' negotiation of face and expression of identities. These themes, each of which is discussed in an independent chapter, are not organised in order of importance as each raises essential questions and highlights potential problems that can result from a lack of awareness of cross-cultural variation between the Japanese students and their non-Japanese teacher's assumptions regarding face and identities. Student feedback underscores that the classroom, as a dynamic context in which students seek to construct identities through identifying roles and expectations, maintains appropriate behaviours and a regulatory frame of responsibility. These expectations are informed by cultural values and social practices which govern both behaviours in public and within the culture of the school. In this sense, the classroom is a decidedly independent setting which embraces detailed systems regarding behaviour and interaction. It follows that students are expected to uphold these roles in order to preserve the classroom environment. It also follows that within the cross-cultural context, these expectations are not always going to be equally apparent to interlocutors who will not always share cultural and social frames of reference. Identified through the examination of student retrospective feedback, the four following themes emerged as being intimately associated with the students' alignment to identities and negotiation of face.

- Peer collaboration – spontaneous collaboration between students during learning activities.
- Japanese identities – students' resistance to L2 classroom practices deemed to be inconsistent with what they held to be standard Japanese classroom behaviour and/or language use.
- Teacher use of the L1 (Japanese) – students' interpretations of the teacher's use of Japanese during L2 learning activities.
- Student silence – recourse to, and maintenance of, silence; students' reflections on periods of extended silence and/or the teacher's intervention during these silent periods.

Analysis of these four categories takes into account a number of factors including the students' language proficiency, educational practices and beliefs about teaching and learning. The analysis focuses on the process of identity construction as students endeavour to align to the teacher's expectations while simultaneously upholding Japanese identities and avoiding loss of face. Although discussed here in separate chapters, these key acts of identity, examined through the construct of face, do not occur independently of each other as they are interrelated and often intersect or emerge in parallel. Among other matters, the Japanese students' retrospective feedback generates insights into patterns of cross-cultural variation regarding: (a) interpretations of classroom appropriateness, (b) expectations pertaining to teacher/student role and rank, (c) acceptable discursive practices and behaviour within the L2 classroom.

United by a desire to project a positive image and align with specific identities within the L2 classroom, the students and their teacher employ culturally, socially and individually informed communicative strategies and behaviour in order to demonstrate individual worth and maintain classroom appropriateness. As Tateyama and Kasper (2008) explain, 'In order to be academically successful students have to become competent members of their classroom community, and such membership critically involves class-room specific ways of participation' (2008: 45). It follows that students are influenced by their interpretations of what they assume to be 'good student' behaviours and practices when aligning with identities. The term 'good student', while open to the interpretation, is used in the following analysis to express how the students feel they are expected to participate in classroom activities in order to achieve a positive teacher evaluation. The analysis agrees with Ellwood's (2008) characterisation of a 'good student' as 'one who con-forms not only to notions of capability and, by implication, intelligence, but also to certain culturally influenced attitudes and behaviours' (2008: 544). As Ellwood notes, 'students prefer to be seen as "good" by their teachers and seek to avoid the exclusion and marginalisation that can derive from any kind of negative student identity' (2008: 544). In short, a 'good student' performs in harmony with culturally informed expectations regarding rank, role, expected levels of aptitude and behaviour within the classroom.

The examination of data illustrates that unbeknownst to the teacher, the four themes outlined above were associated with pragmatic miscommunica-tion and resulted in student frustration, resentment and loss of confidence. Moreover, these themes are shown to have interfered with the management of face and identities claimed, in that miscommunication resulting from dif-fering pragmatic expectations within the classroom impacted on the stu-dents' participation and negatively influenced attitudes towards the teacher and, to some extent, the learning of English. Data highlights that the teacher and students maintained significantly different interpretations of what was occurring in the classroom. For example, following English activities, the teacher's impression of two lessons were expressed in positive reflections such as; 'Great class. A lot of happy faces', 'everyone had a really good time', 'the students really like to talk to me' and 'we can joke around and have a lot of fun together'. In contrast, student feedback following the same English activities paints a very different picture as illustrated by the blunt assess-ments *'tada jugyou ga hayaku owatte hoshii'* (I just want the class to finish quickly), *'kono sensei hontou ni kirai'* (I really hate this teacher) and the descrip-tion of the teacher as being *'zenzen yasashikunai'* (not kind at all). Student feedback underscore that unfamiliar expectations impacted on the Japanese students' ability to maintain face and in consequence interfered with their ability to present themselves in the way in which they wanted to be viewed by the teacher. Frequent retrospective feedback characterised by comments such as *'nani itte ii ka wakaranai'* (I didn't know what to say), *'sasaretaku nai'* (I didn't want to be chosen) and *'iya da'* (I don't like [it]) disclose that the students were not sure what to do and felt that a reasonable solution was therefore to avoid participation. In addition, retrospection such as *'itsumo to chigau na to omotta'* (I thought it was different from usual), and *'odoroita sore wa mezurashii'* (I was surprised, that was unusual) underscored a sense of cross-cultural variance which left the students feeling at times surprised, and at other points uncomfortable or defiant.

Throughout the course of the investigation, it is the Japanese students' own assessment of their language use and behaviour that brings to light identity negotiations and the interactional achievement of face within the L2 classroom. Student feedback illustrates that the L2 classroom, as a cultural and social construct, supports behaviours, discursive practices and roles that reflect cultural values and social practices that are not always consistent with Japanese student expectations. When student Akari was expected to adapt to unfamiliar classroom interaction practices and role relationships she revealed experiencing feelings of anxiety and uncertainty: *'sensei no seito e no kitai ga kowaku kanjita'* (I felt scared by the teacher's expectations of students) and *'nani o sureba ii no ka wakaranakute kuyashikatta shi shinpai datta'* (I didn't know what I was meant to do so I was frustrated and worried). Moreover, retrospective feedback such as that offered by student Miu, highlighted that the implications are significant and worthy of close consideration given that she resists participating when uncertain as to teacher expectations: *'sensei wa nani o shiyou to shiteru no ka shiranakatta kara kuyashikatta sukoshi shitara akiramechatta'* (I didn't know what the teacher was trying to do so I was frustrated. After a while I gave-up). The use of the term *'shiranai'* shows that Miu is speaking from an observer perspective and implies a sense of detachment in that she does not care what the teacher is trying to do and consequently resolves to give-up *'akiramechatta'* on trying. Miu's desire for the teacher to *'yasashiku oshiete ageta hou ga ii ka na'* (It would be better to teach in a kinder way) highlighted her sense of vulnerability and illustrated that the threat to her face and her classmates, at times unintentionally alienated or silenced the Japanese students. While the experience and positive intentions of the teacher are not in doubt, the students' reflections on classroom interaction indicate that face, or rather a lack of cross-cultural awareness regarding cultural variance in face wants, influences the complex process of identity construction and enactment. In this sense it is hoped that the students candid feedback is not rejected as being applicable to the less competent teacher in a specific situation, but rather interpreted as a reminder to teachers and teacher educators of the importance of our impact on students and the need to constantly reflect on what we and our students are doing in the classroom and how this is being interpreted.

7 Face and Student Collaboration

Overview: Student Collaboration

In this chapter, we draw on classroom excerpts and participant interpretations of those excerpts in order to explore the management of face and the miscommunication that results as students attempt to uphold what they describe as an appropriate classroom behaviour, namely spontaneous collaboration, while simultaneously attempting to gain teacher recognition as competent and participating members of the class. Collaboration surfaced during retrospective interviews as a recurring cause of cross-cultural classroom friction between the students and the teacher. For example, throughout classes the students were observed directly soliciting and receiving peer assistance, offering assistance, continuing peers' responses and contributing corrections and suggestions. The chapter begins with an overview of student spontaneous collaboration followed by an examination of the teacher's critical interpretation as revealed through interview comments and intervention strategies employed to block collaboration. Collaboration is then examined from the students' perspective through attention to classroom participation illuminated by retrospective feedback which uncovers the motivation behind frequent peer exchanges.

Student reflections outline three primary objectives of collaboration which are discussed in turn; (a) to compare and/or confirm responses to classroom tasks, (b) to solicit answers from peers in order to complete learning exercises, and (c) to compare/solicit/verify responses in order to avoid failure. These themes are examined through attention to the specific ways in which the students' construct, align with and display identities through the negotiation of face in order to uphold cultural, social and individual expectations. The multi-layered nature of identity as revealed through student collaboration underscores that the students routinely construct and enact new selves which are not always in sync with expectations held by the teacher. In this sense, collaboration exposes cross-cultural disparities in the management of face and the impact this has on the students' ability to maintain crucial student alliances.

The teacher's resistance to student initiated collaboration is relevant to student classroom participation given that it effectively silences students and gives rise to a negative student impression of the teacher. Publicly rebuked for accessing the support of peers, the students specifically indicate feeling anxious and tentative as to how they can productively become involved in language activities. Moreover, threatened by the teacher's intervention, the students expressed and demonstrated resistance to further engagement in English activities. Data sources reveal cross-cultural inconsistencies in interpretations of the discursive functions and appropriateness of unplanned L1 collaboration during classroom activities which ultimately interfered with student and teacher ability to understand each other. These conflicting interpretations of collaboration were found to interfere with the interactional management of face and impede progress of learning activities.

The examination of classroom excerpts draws attention to the students' experiences of competing identities, that is, the choices that they potentially face in aligning with identities the teacher values and identities that they value. This is of importance given that while the teacher clearly opposed collaboration, classroom recordings revealed the pervasiveness of spontaneous student collaboration during the performance of a range of activities. By spontaneous collaboration, I refer to situations in which a student actively engaged a peer, typically in the L1, in order to solicit, transmit or corroborate information related to some aspect of the learning task. A distinctive feature of student collaboration was that students initiated exchanges without being directly instructed to by the teacher and seemingly unconcerned if these exchanges were being viewed by the teacher. As the initiators of peer collaboration, the students controlled the timing, content, participants and format of these exchanges.

Recordings demonstrated that as collaboration during activities was typically not sanctioned by the teacher, it tended to draw a negative teacher reaction with offending students abrasively directed to work *'hitori de'* (alone). It was this critical view of collaboration which students' critically challenged during retrospective sessions. Specifically, feedback illustrated resistance to what was felt to be the teacher's implication that collaboration represented a violation of acceptable classroom practices. Students avidly rejected what they interpreted as being the teacher's assumption that collaboration was associated with negative student behaviours and English competency limitations such as; (a) inability to comprehend task requirements, (b) inability to formulate correct responses, and (c) lack of willing student participation in classroom activities. Moreover, the students expressed frustration at the teacher's tendency to intervene or directly admonish those students who collaborated with peers based on these flawed assumptions.

The implication that by collaborating with classmates, one had failed to perform as a 'good student' draws attention to the potential difficulties students encounter when maintaining face and claiming identity within the classroom. What is particularly interesting to note is that collaboration transpired, even at points when students were specifically directed by the teacher to work 'hitori de' (alone) or chastised for collaborating 'hanasanai de' (don't talk). Moreover, while teacher intervention evidently threatened the students' desire to be recognised and valued as competent and conscientious, recordings evidenced that collaboration was almost never concealed from the teacher. On the contrary, collaboration occurred seemingly irrespective of what was taking place during the lesson and was actively employed by students throughout a wide range of learning tasks. Furthermore, peer collaboration repeatedly occurred in one-on-one teacher/student exchanges such as when the teacher directly nominated an individual student to contribute. During these moments, it was common to observe the nominated student overtly turn to consult a classmate or alternatively, being offered assistance by a peer prior to venturing a response. Such collaboration recurrently drew a stern caution from the distinctly unamused teacher.

In the following analysis, we argue that collaboration, as a channel for self-identification, is important to the students as it maintains and develops affective bonds and solidarity between peers. We hold that collaborative practices are consistent with the cultural code of appropriate behaviour students are socialised to from the early stages of schooling within Japan. During student socialisation to the larger group context 'shudan seikatsu' the teacher performs in a facilitative capacity while prioritising student-student interaction (Rohlen & LeTendre, 1996: 7). Additionally, we posit that peer collaboration serves as a crucial communicative tool by which students' resource collective peer knowledge in order to minimise the potential of an incorrect contribution when faced with the threatening situation of preparing to directly interact with the teacher or in front of the whole class. In this way, collaboration represents a means by which students align with what they interpret to be a 'good student' identity through planning responses prior to sharing them on the larger stage. Collaboration was viewed as both acceptable and constructive as illustrated in student Risa's reflections on aiding a classmate, 'jibun ga Yuki-chan no kotaeru tokoro o wakatteru toki wa Yuki-chan ni oshieyou tte (...) dakara kono toki oshieteta' (When I know the answer to the question Yuki is being asked, then I will tell her [...] so, at this time I told her [the answer]). Risa further reflected on collaboration stressing that she viewed it as a natural process to engage in: *'minna de yatteru no ga atarimae'* (It's natural for everyone to help [each other]).

Classroom data illustrates that the students, faced with the decision as to whether to uphold collaborative interactional patterns even when aware of the negative teacher evaluation, expressed a prevailing desire to uphold collaborative exchanges. For this reason, collaboration sheds light on the students' orientation to communicative interdependence as seen through how students situate themselves in relation to the teacher and peers. As Mercer (1992) argues, 'any task or activity does not exist independently of the ways in which participants (experimenters and subjects, teachers and learners) contextualize it' (1992: 33). Along these lines, we maintain that the linguistic and socio-cultural knowledge which inform collaboration have been acquired through observation and participation in specific socio-educational contexts that need to be understood in order to accurately frame such practices. In the following section, we outline the teacher's interpretation of student collaboration as revealed through interview feedback.

Teacher Interpretation of Collaboration

Student collaboration, particularly in cases when initiated by students during tasks that the teacher viewed as being suited to individual participation, gave rise to a negative teacher evaluation of the students involved. Acting on this negative interpretation, the teacher intervened firstly to reprimand 'offending students', and then reasserted that he expected individual participation. Providing insight into his views, the teacher commented that student collaboration outside of predetermined pair or group work tasks was disrespectful and reflected a lack of adequate student motivation or engagement in the activities. In the teacher's own words: 'It's incredibly frustrating when students keep talking to each other. They ask for help. It shows they're not motivated. I expect more. Students should expect more of themselves. You have to get involved and try if you want results'. This critical view was further expressed in the observation: 'If I ask students a question and they have to think about the answer, they look at the person next to them to say "What's the answer?" or "Give me the answer!"' The teacher expressly noted that he did not approve of students 'getting classmates to do the hard work' and qualified this position by stating 'there's never a good reason to look for an easy way out'.

The assumption that collaboration constituted the act of a less motivated or less proficient student soliciting information from a classmate assumed to have higher motivation and to be of higher English proficiency, and that this potentially sabotaged learning, was a recurring theme: 'There's no benefit in relying on the smart students all the time. If you want to improve or you want to learn you have to be prepared to try yourself'. An additional point raised by the teacher was concern that a primary motivation behind student collaboration was an inherent fear of failure: 'Japanese students rely on each other and ask each other for help because they're afraid of messing-up. They want to get it right the first time because they think it's embarrassing to mess-up'. Implying that fear of failure constitutes a Japanese cultural trait which interferes with effective learning the teacher stated, 'From my culture we're encouraged to make mistakes, we're encouraged to try our best, do what we can, make a mistake, learn from it, and move on. Making mistakes is the way we learn'. The teacher went on to express his desire for Japanese students to align with his views of 'making mistakes' and to embrace error as a critical part of the learning process: 'I don't care even if they get the answer wrong. It's a learning process. It holds them back if they're scared to try. I want them to learn that trying to get the answer is more important than actually getting the answer right'. Underscoring the priority he attached to deterring what he deemed as constituting excessive collaboration and the challenge this represents for English teachers based in Japan, the teacher reasoned:

> A challenge for English teachers in Japan is trying to get students to answer on their own without asking someone who knows. It happens all the time. Students believe if you don't know you can just ask someone who does before trying. Students just go ahead and ask someone else for the answers even when the teacher's right there watching.

Student collaboration was a demotivational factor for the teacher who viewed it as counterproductive to L2 learning, interfering with his ability to demonstrate content knowledge and limiting opportunities to display his approachability. In short, the students' reliance on peer collaboration challenged the teacher's face in that it threatened his ability to direct the class and facilitate learning in line with the professional role he desired. In the teacher's own words: 'I want the students to know that I'm approachable. Let's have fun, relax, enjoy, and don't be afraid to make mistakes. Come and talk to me about anything, don't ask a classmate when I'm available'. By soliciting classmate support, the teacher assumes students are ignoring or undervaluing his professional standing as expert and authority figure within the classroom and therein blocking his ability to align with the professional identities he desires. Consequently, his rank and role within the classroom become somewhat ambiguous. Of relevance here is that in order to align with the identities he desires, the teacher is reliant on the students assuming corresponding roles. In other words, in order to be a 'successful teacher' he must have students take on and embrace the behaviours he associates with 'good students'. In the classroom excerpts which follow the teacher seeks to align students with what he views as being a 'good student' identity through encouraging individual participation and actively intervening in order to block and discourage students from collaborating. Throughout English activities, the teacher employed Japanese and English to verbally intervene and reinforce that collaboration was not recognised as permissible classroom behaviour:

- *jibun de* (by yourself);
- *hitori de* (alone);
- *shizuka ni* (be quiet);
- *hanasanai de* (don't talk);
- by yourself;
- listen.

Student feedback indicated that teacher intervention during collaboration reinforced that the teacher had the 'right' to hold the floor and that student talk that was not directly teacher sanctioned violated classroom protocol that was not known to the students. In the following section, the students' reflections on collaboration are discussed with respect to the corresponding classroom excerpts which when viewed together provide insight into the language use and motivations behind collaboration.

Collaboration to Compare/Confirm Responses

The following two classroom excerpts explore points during which students collaborated in order to confirm and compare answers to questions asked by the teacher. Of relevance here is that the students did not construe collaboration as a breach of appropriate classroom behaviour and accordingly, teacher intervention intended to block collaboration was interpreted as a threat to the management of face as it implied students had consciously violated classroom standards. In both excerpts 1 and 2, the students collaborated with peers to check answers while the teacher was moving about the classroom offering his assistance. The first excerpt begins with two students discussing answers to a homework activity from the previous week when the teacher, only metres away, looks directly at the students while vigorously shaking his head. The teacher then holds up his right hand in a chopping position and rapidly moves it from left to right in front of his face. This gesture, commonly employed in Japan to indicate refusal, plainly conveys that he does not approve of, and will not permit, the exchange to continue. When the directive fails to bring an end to the collaboration, the teacher again intervenes by moving directly towards the students. The students respond to the seemingly imminent threat of reproach by promptly breaking-off the exchange and falling silent.

[Classroom excerpt 1: Hikari (H) asks Fuuka (F) about a homework activity and the teacher (T) intervenes.]

1H: *nani o sureba ii ka* (.) *wakannai* ((H points at W/B, turns to F))
'I'm not sure what to do'

2F: ((F points at vocabulary box in H's W/B, twists body toward H, leans closer)) *ee* (1) *kore ja nai⸮* (1) I went to ((inaudible))
'Well, isn't it this⸮ I went to ((inaudible))'

3H: ((T shakes head, moves hand back and forth in front of face. H/F look at T questioningly. T frowns, turns, moves in direction of whiteboard. H/F resume exchange)) *kou iu fuu ni yatta yo* ((H points at W/B, touches F's hand))
'I did it this way'

4F: ((F places finger on W/B, taps specific area)) *nan ka* (1) *kore tte sa* (1) *kou iu fuu ni kakeba ii* (2) in the morning (turns to H, nods)
'Well, this is, you write it like this, in the morning'

5H: ((H erases answer in W/B, picks up pencil, writes)) *kou ka na⸮* (turns to F)
'Like this⸮'

6F: *u::n u::n u::n* ((F nods several times to indicate agreement))
'Yes, yes, yes' (that's right)

7T: ((T paces towards H/F shaking head irritably))

8H/F: ((H/F look at T stunned, whisper together then fall silent))

9T: ((T stops directly in front of H/F, places hands on hips, makes an X shape with forearms. F/H look down at desks in silence)) (4) That's better ((turns, nods, moves towards front of classroom))

Student Hikari begins in turn 1 by indicating that she is not sure how to complete the task and in doing so petitions the student seated next to her for assistance *'nani o sureba ii ka wakannai'* (I'm not sure what to do). Hikari does not appear to regard the admission of difficulty as representing a threat to her face or inappropriate within the classroom context and does so in full view and hearing range of the teacher who is located only metres away.

The use of the non-past-negative form *wakannai*, the contracted form of *wakaranai* (see Sadler, 2010) draws classmate Fuuka closer in that it conveys a sense of immediacy and empathy. Reciprocating this closeness, classmate Fuuka, openly responding to the request for assistance without hesitation (turn 2), twists and leans over towards Hikari offering a suggestion as to how she thinks the activity should be carried out, *'ee kore ja nai?'* (Well, isn't this it?). Fuuka's use of the expression *'ja nai'* serves to mitigate the potential threat to Hikari's face in that it provides interactional space for her to respond. Characterised by Manita and Blagdon (2010) as an expression engaged to 'make assertions more vague', *ja nai* allows the Japanese speaker to express opinions without overt displays of confidence and thereby avoid pushing their positions on others (2010: 428). Hayashi (2010: 2689) explains that *ja nai* consists of the copulative expression *ja*, the contracted form of *de wa*, and the negative morpheme *nai*. The function of *ja nai* is not to enhance the propositional content of the sentence, but rather 'as a sentence extension seeking agreement/confirmation from the addressee.' Translated as a negative question, Fuuka employs *ja nai* to convey rather than impose her confidence in her evaluation, and through rising intonation, invites a subsequent turn from Hikari who can assume that she may indeed understand the material as well as her classmate. Hikari, empowered by her peer's receptiveness and the implication that she too harbours doubts, orients to her turn by revealing her answer in turn 3, *'kou iu fuu ni yatta yo'* (I did it this way).

The construction of Fuuka's response, beginning with *'nan ka'* in turn 4, is a frequently used Japanese expression which functions as a non-confrontational means of evaluating Hikari's views. *Nan ka*, translated by Manita and Blagdon (2010: 428) as, 'I have a vague feeling about this' or 'I don't really understand the reason, but ...' serves to uphold Hikari's face by implying that both students share equal status given their compatible levels of English competence. This approach provides a platform from which Fuuka then launches into a more direct explanation of how she believes the task is to be negotiated, *'nan ka kore tte sa kou iu fuu ni kakeba ii'* (Well, this is, you write it like this ...). Peer collaboration as a means of ascertaining solutions to assessment tasks is consistent with Tang's (1993) examination of spontaneous collaborative learning which found that Chinese tertiary students were able to discover solutions and generate ideas in an environment characterised by mutual respect. Student initiated and structured collaboration was found to enable students to view 'problems from new perspectives, to develop relationships between new and previously learned information, to internalise ideas and criticism and also to enhance perceptions of positive support from the other group members' (1993: 116). Determining that student collaboration generated performance at higher cognitive levels and lead to superior understanding and interest in content, Tang hypothesises that 'the students' thinking is likely to be stimulated to higher cognitive levels when they try to express their own opinions, argue for their points, relate, compare and apply the information' (1993: 127).

Similarly, this open approach to peer collaboration is consistent with Foster and Snyder Ohta's (2005) cognitive and socio-cultural investigation of classroom negotiation, which found that students actively sought peer co-construction and prompting when engaged in classroom tasks. Observing that learners actively assisted each other to conduct tasks through co-construction and prompting, the researchers demonstrate that 'Learners expressed interest and encouragement while seeking and providing assistance and initiating self-repair of their own utterances, all in the absence of communication breakdowns' (2005: 402). Moreover, they note that maintenance of a supportive and friendly discourse was prioritised by students over achieving entirely comprehensible input concluding that learners 'are sharing their meanings while monitoring and modifying their own and each other's utterances, minimizing overt communication breakdowns, and the accompanying frustration' (2005: 425). In the above exchange, the participating students are able to express uncertainty without discomfort or concern that revealing an inability to complete the task will result in loss of face as a competent member of the class. Moreover, the students are willing to seek peer assistance and express self-doubt in the presence of the teacher and other classmates. As noted, the teacher is well within hearing range of the students and due to the relative simplicity of the Japanese and the teacher's level of Japanese proficiency, it can be assumed that the students would have been aware that the content of the exchange, a homework activity, would be evident to the teacher.

The teacher expresses his disapproval of the students' collaboration (turn 3) by way of emphatically shaking his head from side to side then waving his hand in front of his face. The students can be observed briefly looking up at the teacher, however, suggesting their opposition to his demand for individual participation, immediately resume their exchange when the teacher moves off in the direction of the whiteboard. In turn 7, the teacher indicates that his tolerance has come to an end as he marches in the direction of the students' desks while vigorously shaking his head from left to right. In this movement, the teacher unequivocally asserts his opposition to the students' negotiation and this brings an abrupt end to the exchange. The students' silence has implications for the teacher as the threat to his face associated with his sense of powerlessness to have the students work alone can only be restored by such student silence. This is evident in turn 9 when the teacher, in a defensive and agitated manner, places his hands on his hips, then crosses his arms forcefully in an X shape in front of his body. This frequently employed Japanese gesture explicitly expresses that the teacher wants closure. He does not approve of the students' persisting with the exchange after he has indicated his opposition and demands that they discontinue.

Acknowledging the students have ceased talking and this is no less than he expects, the teacher responds 'That's better' (turn 9) before returning to the front of the classroom. Within the small classroom, the intervention poses a direct threat to both the students' negative and positive face as it impedes their freedom of action and the desire to be free from imposition, while also failing to ratify the students' desire to be appreciated and approved of. The teacher's intervention, initiated in view of the entire class, implies that the students' tendency to collaborate is a violation of expectations associated with the context of the classroom. In this way, the teacher is non-verbally placing constraints on student interaction through delineating what he determines to be acceptable classroom verbal interaction between students without allowing for variation. This is relevant to the students for as Walsh (2006) points out, teacher control over activities such as turn taking can lead to control over topics and activities. Predictably, recordings evidenced that the teacher's intervention was not contested by the young students during classroom activities. By contrast, students were both eager and willing to defend themselves during retrospective interviews during which the teacher was not present. A point in case being Hikari's decision to shed light on the content of her above exchange with Fuuka and the effect of the teacher's negative critique:

shukudai toka machigaeta tokoro toka no hanashi o shiteta (...) futsuu ni suru koto da to omou (...) nani mo warui koto shitenai no ni nande sensei ga sonna ni okotta no ka wakannai hazukashikatta (...) kore kara wakaranai koto ga attara dou sureba ii no tte kanji

We talked about things like the homework and places we had made mistakes. I think it's a usual thing to do. We weren't doing anything wrong. I don't know why the teacher got so angry. I felt embarrassed. What should I do if I don't understand something in the future?

Importantly, Hikari's feedback illustrates that she viewed the exchange as two directional and thereby as serving to facilitate both her and Fuuka's understanding of the homework material. Moreover, Hikari notes that she views classroom collaboration in this case as a *'futsuu ni suru koto'* (a usual thing to do) and consequently she finds it difficult to understand precisely why the teacher reacts angrily when *'nani mo warui koto shitenai no ni'* (we weren't doing anything wrong). Hikari explains that the teacher's highly critical intervention in full view of classmates leaves her feeling *'hazuka-shikatta'* (embarrassed) and confused.

Hikari's identity claims illustrate that language learning is a complex social practice as the value and meaning ascribed to an utterance or behaviour, in this situation peer collaboration, may at times be differently determined by the value and meaning ascribed by the teacher and the students. Hikari's interpretation of peer collaboration represents her understanding of the classroom and her role in regard to contemporary realities and future desires. Hikari's classroom behaviour demonstrates the identities she assumes as she seeks to align with her classmate, Fuuka, through working collaboratively in order to understand the homework task. At the same time, Hikari desires to be recognised by the teacher as an engaged and motivated member of the class, as evidenced in turn 8 when she embraces the teachers demand for individual participation by means of terminating her exchange with Fuuka (turn 8). In line with the teacher's expectations, intervention during student initiated collaboration is correctly interpreted by Hikari as an indication that collaboration is not an acceptable strategy for negotiating gaps in comprehension. Not only does this represent a threat to face and a challenge to identity alignment, it may also represent a potential impediment to Hikari's learning as she does not appear to have explicitly been made aware of alternative strategies or acceptable practices for dealing with lesson content she finds challenging or would like to discuss. Hikari's frustration is evident in her concluding remark: *'kore kara wakaranai koto ga attara dou sureba ii no tte kanji?'* (What should I do if I don't understand something in the future?).

In contrast with Hikari's implication that peer collaboration represents a standard practice, the teacher's intervention effectively aligns the students with a negative student identity and implies that failure to work alone reflects calculated noncompliance with what are effectively unstated classroom rules and standards. The implication being here that the collaborative approach represents the avoidance of engagement through sharing the workload in order to make life easier for the less competent, or possibly both students. Hikari's frustration at being positioned as a less capable student is further evident in the following retrospective comment:

> *sensei wa watashi ga wakaranai to omotte ite dakara tomodachi to hanasu to okoru (...) zuru shiteru to omotteru tte wakaru (...) demo sore wa chigau (...) sore ga sugoku hazukashiku kanjiru shi hanasenaku naru (...) nande itsumo doori soudan shinagara yatte wa ikenai no ka ga wakaranai (...) nani ga warui no*

The teacher thought that I didn't understand so he gets angry when I talk with friends. I know he thinks that I'm cheating, but that's wrong. This makes me feel really embarrassed and I (feel like) I can't say anything. I don't get why we aren't allowed to consult like we usually do. What's wrong with it?

Hikari's perceptive feedback intimates that she is cognisant of the identities favoured by the teacher within the classroom and as a result, cannot avoid feeling a sense of pressure to conform to the demands for individual participation. Hikari notes feeling really embarrassed *'sugoku hazukashiku kanjiru'* when the teacher intervenes, and indicates that as a direct consequence she feels unable to say anything *'hanasenaku naru'*. Conscious of the teacher's expectations within the classroom, Hikari and Fuuka register their initial opposition through continuing their collaboration (turns 3 and 4), and again in retrospective feedback. Nevertheless, when the threat to face becomes too great, and it is apparent that the teacher not only has misinterpreted the exchange but will not let it persist, the students conceded and align to the teacher's expectations through falling silent. Recall presents an opportunity for Hikari to defend and explain her views during which she defiantly responds to the teacher's theory as being *'chigau'* (wrong). As Hikari does not view her behaviour as violating normative classroom practices, she reacts to the implication that she should refrain from collaboration as follows: *'nande itsumo doori soudan shinagara yatte wa ikenai no ka ga wakaranai (...) nani ga warui no'* (I don't get why we aren't allowed to consult like we usually do. What's wrong with it?).

Collaboration on certain tasks potentially provides an opportunity for students to benefit from peer experience and knowledge and contributes to willingness and success in negotiating classroom activities. A point in case being De Guerrero and Villamil's (2000) examination of the spoken discourse between Spanish-speaking ESL students during peer editing sessions for a writing class. The researchers found that particular attitudes and behaviour displayed by students such as humour, sensitivity and politeness advanced valuable peer interaction and collaboration. Effective use of discourse strategies such as advising, eliciting and requesting clarification resulted in co-constructed learning which served as valuable scaffolding for students. Similarly, patterns of co-construction and mutual assistance were evident at points during the English activities when the students assisted classmates with activities including textbook based questions, the translation of specific vocabulary, error correction and pronunciation. In particular, classroom recordings demonstrated the frequency with which students collaborated in order to formulate responses to teacher initiated questions even in cases when it was understood that the teacher had directly nominated an individual student to respond. In other words, the teacher would nominate a student by name or gesture to answer a question after which the student would openly turn to a classmate and proceed to discuss the question in Japanese. To illustrate, the following exchange occurs when the students are instructed to take turns working one on one with the teacher on a short conversation drill. The teacher intervenes when the student nominated to participate directly seeks assistance from a classmate.

[Classroom excerpt 2: When Kana (K) solicits assistance from classmate Ami (A) the teacher (T) intervenes.]

1T: ((T clears throat, points at K, nods once)) Let's start (.) I will read the first part ((points at activity)) <u>are you ready</u>¿ (3) ((nods, gestures towards K by raising chin))

2K: ((K turns face, shifts body position to the left to speak with A)) *kore ka na*¿ ((A glances at K, leans closer, looks down at K's T/B)) 'Is it this¿'

3A: ((A points at section in K's T/B)) *kore da to omou* 'I think it's this'

4T: ((T knocks loudly on desk several times with knuckles. K/A look up startled)) Ask me (1) <u>ask me</u> (3) ((grabs his T/B impatiently))

5K: ((K turns toward A, leans closer)) *dou yatte yomu no*¿ 'How do you read this¿'

6T: ((T looks at K, points at and hits his chest)) Ask me (1) <u>what's the problem</u>¿ (2) *wakaru*¿ (1) *WAKARANAI*¿ ((raises shoulders)) 'Do you understand¿ You don't understand¿'

7K: (2) ((K turns, leans toward A) *dou sureba ii*¿ (2) *nani o sureba ii no*¿ 'What should I do¿ What do I need to do¿'

8T: ((T claps suddenly to get K's attention. Ss look up at T startled. T holds up one finger to indicate that K should work/answer alone))

9A: (5) (A leans closer to K, points at T/B)) *kono mama yonda hou ga ii to omou* ((K tilts head to side)) 'I think you should just read it like this'

10K: (2) *ee* (2) ((looks at A)) *dekiru ka wakaranai* 'I don't know if I can do it'

11T: ((T takes several steps directly towards K/A)) (2) *HITORI DE* (2) ((stops in front of K, holds up one finger, shakes finger rapidly. Folds arms, turns, moves to front of classroom)) 'Work alone'

12K/A: ((K/A glance at each other, silently look down at T/Bs))

In turn 1, the teacher clears his throat to gain the students attention, points to indicate that it is Kana's turn to take part in the conversation drill and proceeds to inquire whether she is prepared, 'Are you ready?' Following several seconds of silence, the teacher expressly nods and raises his chin in Kana's direction so as to affirm that he intends to commence the drill. Contrary to the teacher's expectations, Kana does not respond to either the initial verbal request for confirmation or the non-verbally expressed intent to commence. On the contrary, Kana looks away from the waiting teacher and repositions her body on the chair so that she is able to face the student seated next to her. It is here that Kana commences to ask her classmate, Ami, whether she has correctly identified the dialogue she has been asked to read with the teacher, 'kore ka na' (Is it this?) The teacher, assuming that his offer to assist has been overtly rejected by Kana who appears to prefer the assistance of a classmate, reacts indignantly in turn 4 by abruptly rapping his knuckles loudly on his desk in rapid succession. The animated and unexpected reaction visibly startles Kana and Hikari who instantly fall silent and apprehensively look up at the teacher. Having gained Kana's attention, the teacher appears to recognise the students uneasiness and takes a decidedly softer tone as he instructs them to 'Ask me, ask me', as opposed to a classmate, for assistance.

In turn 5 Kana, appearing oblivious or indifferent to the teacher's demand that he be consulted and by implication, the warning that student collaboration will not be tolerated, once again turns to her classmate Ami and asks: 'dou yatte yomu no?' (How do you read this?) In turn 6, reacting without delay to the face threat generated by the student's failure to uphold his request to be directly consulted, the teacher vigorously points at and slaps his chest while reiterating that students are to 'Ask me'. Altering his approach, the teacher then attempts to avert further student interaction through ascertaining specifically what the obstacle to comprehension may be: 'What's the problem?' When Kana is unresponsive, the teacher employs Japanese to unequivocally resolve whether the she has understood what he requires: 'wakaru? wakaranai?' (Do you understand? You don't understand?) Without directly responding to the teacher's offer of assistance or attempt to confirm comprehension, once again Kana directly turns and leans toward Ami (turn 7) and attempts to clarify what is required: 'dou sureba ii? nani o sureba ii no?' (What should I do? What do I need to do?)

The teacher, seemingly unable to encourage the student to raise any need for assistance she may have directly with him, elects to disrupt the students exchange through capturing their immediate attention as he abruptly claps his hands together. When the students promptly look up, the teacher holds their attention by raising one finger in a gesture that signals that with the exception of consulting himself, he expects students to work alone. Seemingly unconcerned as to the teacher's physical proximity and attempts to offer of assistance, Ami directs Kana's attention to a vocabulary box in the textbook which is to be used in the drill. In turn 10 Kana, responding to Ami's assistance, openly indicates that she is uncertain as to whether or not she can answer as required in the task, *'dekiru ka wakaranai'* (I don't know if I can do it), yet does not appear to view teacher assistance as an option in addressing her concerns. Throughout this exchange the students do not attempt to conceal that they are working together. The teacher's physical presence or his attempts to block collaboration in order to provide assistance do not appear to interfere with the students' intent to exchange information. When the students continue to collaborate, the teacher elects to assert his authority (turn 11) by moving directly towards the students and stopping a short distance in front of Kana. He then holds up one finger and shakes it in front of her while directing her in Japanese to work *'hitori de'* (alone). The intervention, delivered in a raised and frustrated tone of voice in the students' mother tongue, has the desired effect when the students terminate their exchange and look down at their textbooks in silence.

The teacher's serious countenance orients to the fact that he seeks to establish that he will not permit the collaborative exchange to continue. His intervention conveys his disapproval of the students in front of the class and in this way threatens the students desire to be recognised as 'good students' while at the same time setting barriers that place limitations on the type of interaction students are permitted to engage in. While the student's communicative intention throughout the exchange was to establish what she was required to do and how it was to be done, this was interpreted by the teachers as being inappropriate classroom behaviour. The point being that it was not so much the content of the exchange, but the fact that the teacher's professional identity was threatened by the student collaboration that led to his uncompromising response. The intervention eventually resulted in the students being silenced (turn 12).

The frequency of student collaboration throughout the recorded classes registers that the students did not view open collaboration as either detracting from their positive face claims as valuable and competent members of the class, or contradicting what they viewed as acceptable classroom practices. On the contrary, it appears that collaboration was an avenue for the students to connect with classmates and to clarify information without feeling intimidated or that they were imposing. This appears to be in keeping with Haugh's (2005) theory of 'place' based on inclusion and distinction which as noted is built on the premise that face in Japanese culture is inherently associated with 'place' in relation to group membership and social connections and role. Haugh (2005) proposes that inclusion is depicted as being a part of something else such as a particular set or group, while distinction is defined as being different or distinguishable from others (2005: 47). Accordingly, the attributes or factors of an individual's group members, in this case students and teacher, contribute to the perceived identities and/or status of the individuals. Within the context of the classroom the student is expected to acknowledge and uphold the rank and status of the teacher as an expert and engage an appropriate level of politeness to make this clear to the teacher and other members of the class. These factors suggest that even simple requests for assistance, such as those expressed by Kana in the above excerpt, represent a potentially face threatening exchange for the student whereas soliciting a classmate provides a means of acquiring the same information without necessarily exposing oneself to the associated risk to face.

Classroom exchanges illustrate that while student collaboration was typically on task, the teacher nevertheless discouraged exchanges and viewed their occurrence as interruptive. Interview feedback highlighted that from the teacher's perspective, there was the added concern that as student collaboration was conducted in the L1, the teacher was at times linguistically excluded from access to the students' inner circle. For example, the teacher was unable to identify the precise nature of comprehension difficulties or gain insights into other issues that may have been impacting on student performance within the classroom. Stating that he was at times linguistically challenged, the teacher remarked 'I don't get it right every time, my Japanese is not perfect. I'm not fluent'. As a result, the teacher's face is at times threatened by limitations in his capacity to perform professional functions such as assessing comprehension, providing remedial instruction and coordinating the class. Reflecting on L1 collaboration between students as observed throughout learning activities, the teacher commented, 'The students have a responsibility too in their participation and attitudes in class'. The implication being here that L1 interaction between students not only was viewed as limiting participation, but also was seen as reflecting what was considered to be a substandard attitude towards L2 learning activities. In this way the teacher's positioning of the students imposed cultural assumptions and values that the teacher associated with a successful student identity. At the same time, retrospective student feedback indicated a gap in perceptions regarding the appropriateness of student collaboration and the specific functions it served. Moreover, it is important to note that the teacher's rejection of student collaboration made it difficult for students to take proactive steps to clarify their own understanding, while also interfering with the students' efforts to align with identities they associated with the classroom environment.

Reflecting on the exchange in excerpt 2, Ami commented, *'nan ka jibun de nani o ieba ii no ka wakannai kara tomodachi ni kiku to omou (...) sore ni tokidoki nani o sureba ii no ka hakkiri setsumei saretenai kara wakannai'* (Well, I think that the reason you ask a friend is because you don't know what you should say [...] and sometimes you don't know what to do because it's not explained clearly). The student's observations reveal that she regards collaboration as being an obvious way of negotiating comprehension difficulties and consequently she can reasonably assume the teacher is aware of and receptive to peer collaboration. In addition, the feedback underscores that in part she believes the need for classmate assistance is a result of the teacher's inability to adequately explain lesson content, *'hakkiri setsumei saretenai'* (It's not explained clearly). The solicitation of peers to compensate for what was felt to be a lack of teacher direction was again noted at a different point during English activities by Ami in the following: *'Ami ga wakaranakatta (...) sore de Kaori-chan to shabettete Kaori-chan ga Iori-chan ni kiite nan ka sou iu no wa sensei kara setsumei o motto shite moraitai na tte'* (Ami [I] didn't understand so I was talking to Kaori, then Kaori asked Iori. Well, like in this case [of having to ask classmates] I would like to receive more instruction from the teacher). From Ami's perspective, the fact that she is admonished by the teacher for seeking classmate assistance in order to compensate for what she regards as an insufficient teacher explanation is unfair and objectionable. Rejecting the implication that she has done anything wrong, Ami indicates that while she was conscious of the negative teacher evaluation, *'sensei wa watashitachi ga issho ni hanashite hoshiku nai tte koto ga wakaru'* (I know the teacher doesn't want us to talk together), she rejects this position and affirms her desire to continue engaging in peer collaboration *'watashitachi ga tetsudaiau no o sensei ga okoru no ga okashii (...) sensei wa sore ga iya demo watashi wa narete iru yarikata de yaritsuzuketai'* (It's strange that the teacher gets angry about us helping each other. Even if he doesn't like it, I just want to keep doing things the way I'm used to). This display of resistance to the teacher's demands through the continuation of peer collaboration, while likely to be critically viewed by the teacher, demonstrates the student's desire to align with what she regards as a familiar classroom identity she associates with her role as an engaged student, while at the same time illustrating her willingness to assume an identity of resistance to achieve this, albeit outside of the classroom where her objections will not go on record.

Resistance to the teacher's implication that student collaboration violated standard classroom practices was also voiced by other students. A case in point being when student Akari, reflecting on an episode when instructed by the teacher to carry out a classroom activity *'jibun de'* (by yourself) later commented: *'sonna ookina koe de hanashite nai shi (…) shitsumon shita dake de yokei na koto dewa nai no ni kyuu ni "shhh" tte iwareta'* (We weren't talking in a loud voice, we were just asking questions, not talking about irrelevant things and then suddenly the teacher told us to be quiet). The student's reflections differentiate collaboration recognised as being on task from collaboration that she characterises as, *'yokei na koto'* (irrelevant/unnecessary). The reference to *'yokei na koto'* displays that Akari recognises the teacher's intervention as based on conjecture that the exchange was not related to lesson content. Moreover, Akari's reference to the low-volume at which the students collaborated affirms that as the exchange does not interfere with other members of the class it was not regarded as being a threat to classroom practices. When viewing a further point of teacher intervention when reacting to a student initiated exchange Akari went on to comment: *'nande sensei ga okoru no (…) watashitachi ga kanningu shiteru to sensei ga omotteru mitai de waruku omowasetai'* (Why does the teacher get angry? It sounds like he thinks we are cheating and wants to make us feel bad). The feedback illustrates not only that the student is aware of the implication that she and her classmates are engaged in cheating, but also believes that the teacher is deliberately setting out to make her feel uncomfortable for reasons that she does not agree with, yet appears powerless to change.

In both excerpts 1 and 2, the students finally responded to the teacher's demands for individual participation by breaking-off communication with classmates. The threat to face resulting from the implication that students had violated classroom practice, namely the requirement for individual participation, surfaced as being a concern for the students during retrospective feedback. While aware of the negative identity alignment, the students' decision to withdraw into silence rather than present identities potentially undesirable to the teacher illustrates that the students' classroom verbal behaviour was in part guided by an awareness of the uneven teacher/student power dynamic. This appeared to impact on the students' decision as to whether to continue taking part in collaborative exchanges with classmates. Students may have felt obliged to comply with the teacher's expectations regarding collaboration in order to manage and possibly work towards restoring lost face. To this end, silence represented a means of minimising the threat to face. While demonstrating a willingness, albeit reluctant, to adopt the teacher's expectations during the learning activities, retrospection highlighted that students resisted positioning where they were aligned with a less capable student identity. While perhaps unable or unwilling to express their views directly when addressing the teacher during English activities, retrospective feedback demonstrated that student collaboration was viewed by the students as a practice that aligned students with a good student identity through serving to maintain both student and teacher face. Essentially, student collaboration provided a readily available means by which students could resource collective peer knowledge and maintain the teacher's position of authority by avoiding imposing on his time. In other words, from the students' perspective it appears that collaboration was viewed as a means by which students demonstrated they were capable of participating and finding solutions, and did not wish to use the teacher's valuable time for comprehension difficulties or questions that may not have been shared by the class. It is the role of collaboration and the view that soliciting answers from peers was a positive practice which maintained rather than challenged face to which we now turn.

Collaboration to Solicit Answers

The following three classroom excerpts (excerpts 3, 4 and 5) demonstrate cases of collaboration observed when students directly solicit answers from classmates with the intention of responding to teacher initiated questions. Of relevance here are the students' insights into their views regarding collaboration and their reaction to the implication that they were failing to uphold classroom practices that the teacher associated with a 'good student' identity. It is also of consequence that the teacher indicates that he feels justified in challenging the students' motivations for collaboration and assigning negative identities. In the three excerpts, the students, nominated by the teacher to respond to specific questions, can be seen shifting their line of gaze away from the teacher in order to consult classmates. The teacher expresses opposition through direct intervention and makes clear his concerns during follow-up interviews when commenting, 'I expect the students to take responsibility for their own work' and 'by asking someone it's clear that they're just taking the easy option'. The management of face, as discussed in the excerpts, reveals the students' dilemma as they try to align with teacher expectations while expressing themselves in line with what they appear to recognise as standard classroom interactional patterns. In the first selection, excerpt 3, a student can be seen assisting her classmate who is unable to answer a question when asked by the teacher.

[Classroom excerpt 3: Sayaka (S) is nominated by the teacher (T) to answer a question and classmate Risa (R) assists her.]

1T: ((T turns to S, clears throat)) Sayaka (1) can you do (2) <u>number</u> SEVEN (.) please ((nods once, holds up open T/B, points at question))

2S: ((S looks down at T/B, looks up at T)) *koreʔ* ((points at T/B, taps page lightly))
'Thisʔ'

3T: ((T hastily moves closer to S's desk, leans forward)) Yep ((nods once, smiles, takes several steps back to centre of classroom))

4S: (2) ((S looks down at T/B)) She is (4) she (3) she is ((looks at R seated to her left, twists toward R, leans over))

5T: ((T takes several hasty steps toward S, points down at T/B, makes circular motion with index finger on T/B around series of illustrations)) LOOK (1) it's ALL here ((takes one step back))

6S: ((S looks down at T/B)) (3) She is (2) ((turns to R)) *nan da kkeʔ*
'What is it againʔ'

7R: ((R looks at T/B, rotates body toward S)) (2) Waking up (S looks at R, nods twice)

8S: ((S looks up at T)) (2) She is (1) waking up ((smiles))

9T: (4) ((T frowns, shakes head back and forth slowly in exaggerated movement, points at S)) Next time (1) ((raised voice) *JIBUN DE YARI NASAI*
'Do it by yourself'

10S/R: ((S/R look at each other, then down at desks))

In turn 2, Sayaka, nominated to answer a question, without delay seeks to confirm that she has understood what she is being asked by enquiring *'koreʔ'* (Thisʔ), while pointing at her textbook and tapping lightly on the precise area. The teacher, appearing to want to proceed with the activity promptly, swiftly moves over to Sayaka's desk and leans forward to confirm that she is indeed referring to the correct point. Satisfied that Sayaka is ready to continue, the teacher responds with a crisp 'Yep' accompanied by an assured nod of the head and a smile. Implying that his job has now been done and he is confident in Sayaka's ability to take control, the teacher physically distances himself as he takes several steps back toward the centre of the classroom (turn 3). In turn 4, taking the reins, S looks down at her textbook, briefly pauses, then begins to haltingly formulate a response 'She is, she, she is'. Appearing uncertain as to how to finish the sentence Sayaka then rotates her body and leans over toward classmate Risa who is seated on her left. Responding without delay to this shift, the teacher hastily moves over to Sayaka's desk and redirects her attention to the question. To further assist her he then, with his finger, circles a series of illustrations on the opposite page which are to be referred to in order to complete the question. Noting that all the required information is available for a successful answer, 'Look, it's all here', the teacher then takes one step back, and therein gives the floor back to

Sayaka (turn 5). After briefly examining her textbook and hesitantly venturing a response 'She is', Sayaka once again appears unsure as to how to respond and elects to turn to classmate Risa in order to solicit assistance *'nan da kkeč'* (What is it again?) Although the teacher is observing the exchange separated by only a single stride, Risa does not appear to hesitate as she confidently turns to Sayaka and provides the answer 'waking up' (turn 7). In turn 8, Sayaka looks up at the teacher who has been monitoring this exchange and responds 'She is waking up'. The teacher registers his frustration in turn 9 by his critical demeanour, communicated through several seconds of deliberate silence, his exaggerated frown and disapproving shaking of his head. His dissatisfaction is confirmed when he rebukes Sayaka in front of her classmates by directly pointing at her while sternly demanding in a raised voice: 'next time jibun de yari nasai!' (Next time do it by yourself!) Japanese is used by the teacher to convey, without the possibility of miscommunication, that Sayaka has failed to provide an individual student contribution as is expected.

On viewing this classroom excerpt during retrospection, Sayaka responded directly to the teacher's implication that she was failing to meet his expectations for individual participation when she stated that: *'imi wakaranai (…) nan ka warui koto shichatta mitai (…) minna yatteru shi futsuu no koto da shi betsu ni himitsu ja nai shi'* (I don't get it, it's like I did something wrong. Everyone does it [collaborates], it's a usual thing, it's not like it's a secret). Sayaka's response presents as a rejection of being positioned as a less capable student through emphasising that collaboration represents what she views as being a typical Japanese classroom practice. In making her case, Sayaka stresses that collaboration is a reciprocal process in which all students are engaged, *'minna yatteru'* (everyone does it) and is not a practice concealed from others *'himitsu ja nai shi'* (It's not a secret). The implication here being that the point of soliciting information from a classmate is not to avoid contributing to activities, but rather is motivated by the desire to participate accurately. As a result, it appears that through assisting one another, classmates are mutually empowered in that they are able to maintain a degree of control over their ability to effectively take part in conversation tasks without having to be dependent on the teacher to bridge potential gaps in understanding task requirements. This link between collaboration as a means of proving a pathway by which students are able to actively seek and establish ways to take part in classroom activities was captured in Sayaka's comment: *'sensei ni kikanai de kurasumeito to hanashiatte kaiketsu dekiru to jishin ga moteru'* (It gives me confidence when I can work out what to do by confirming with my classmates without having to ask the teacher).

Underlying the student's retrospective feedback is a prevailing sense of student interdependence, expressed through collaboration and recognition that peer interaction represents a mutually beneficial practice. As Sayaka did not recognise collaboration as being a breach of standard classroom behaviour, the teacher's penchant to intervene and express disapproval represented a direct threat to the students' face through projecting an interpretation on students that was inconsistent with the face they were claiming. Reflecting on a point during English activities, when she responded to a classmates request for assistance in order to answer a question initiated by the teacher, student Akari commented *'wakatteta kara mochiron Satoko-chan ni oshieta'* (I knew the answer so of course I told Satoko). Akari's willingness to volunteer assistance and the assumption that this is essentially an automatic response given her classmate Satoko appears to be uncertain is a conviction shared by student Marin who commented: *'moshi dareka ga sensei ni kikareteru shitsumon no kotae o watashi ga wakaru nara oshiete ageru (...) dareka ni kikaretara tetsudatte ageru shi minna mo onaji you ni shite kureru'* (Well, if I know the answer to a question someone is being asked by the teacher then I will tell them. If someone asks me I will help them and everyone [classmates] will do the same for me). Marin's interpretation of the exchange illustrates that she regards providing the required answer to a question directed to a classmate as representing an acceptable practice that she willingly engages in. Importantly, Marin notes that it is assumed that sharing information will be reciprocated by classmates when she is the one in need. This is illustrated at another moment during English activities when Marin, uncertain as to how to respond to a question, commented during retrospective feedback: *'hitori de dekinai (...) atama no naka de kangaetemo wakaranakute de "nan da kke" tte omotte minna ni "nan da kke" tte kiite chotto tasuke o motometa'* (I can't do it alone. I searched for the answer in my head and I didn't know, so I was like, 'What is it again?' I asked 'What was it again?' to everyone [classmates] to get some help). While prone to draw a negative teacher appraisal, feedback exhibits that identity as a member of the class as evidenced through the interdependent sharing of information was prioritised over the potential loss of face that may stem from failing to meet the teacher's demands for individual classroom participation.

Assuming that peer collaboration was viewed by the Japanese students as acceptable practice, it comes as no surprise that in retrospective interviews the students articulated a desire to be able to collaborate with peers unimpeded by teacher intervention. Moreover, students' specifically indexed frustration that collaboration attracted a negative teacher evaluation as can be seen in the following two classroom excerpts. Excerpt 4 begins with the teacher moving throughout the classroom checking whether students have completed a homework task.

[Classroom excerpt 4: Risa (R) consults classmates Miu (M) and Ayaka (A) about a homework activity when the teacher (T) intervenes.]

1T: ((T paces around classroom checking W/B homework)) OK (1) <u>who</u> did their <u>homework</u>⸮ (5) ((takes out red pen, begins to tap pen on palm repetitively)) what's the homework⸮ (1) do you <u>remember</u>⸮ ((looks from left to right at Ss several times)) (3) did you do your <u>homework</u>⸮ ((raises eyebrows))

2S: (5) ((Ss glance around at classmates))

3T: ((T turns from left to right, notices two Ss on either side of classroom with bandaged fingers)) Oh ((raises eyebrows)) (1) we've got <u>two broken fingers</u>⸮ (1) it's like the <u>bad finger</u> club (2) ((smiles and laughs)) yeah (1) the BROKEN FINGER GROUP ((laughs and smiles, continues to pace around checking homework))

4R: ((R turns to M on her left)) *ne* (1) *yatta no⸮*
'Hey, did you do it (the homework⸮)'

5M: ((M turns to R)) *umm::* ((tilts head))
'What⸮'

6R: *shukudai atta⸮* ((R opens W/B))
'Did we have homework⸮'

7M: ((R places finger on W/B)) *un* (1) *kore* ((T stops walking, crosses arms, focuses gaze on M/R))
'Yeah, this'

8R: *da yo ne* ((R nods)) (10) ((looks down at W/B)) *a::re::* (.) *chotto matte* (2) ((turns to A on her left, places hand on W/B)) *kore tte sa* (↑) *kore tte shukudai da kke⸮* (tilts head to side)
'That's right. Wait a second, this, was this homework⸮'

9A: ((A points at page in W/B)) *kore da ne⸮*
'It's this, right⸮'

10R: *u::n* (.) *kore da ne* (↑) *nan-ko ka* (↑) *oshiete⸮*
'Yeah (you're right), it's this. Can you tell me how many are there⸮'

11A: (4) ((A points at her W/B, slides W/B across desk to R))

12T: ((T clears throat loudly, shakes head back and forth irritably, raises shoulders with palms faced upward. Crosses arms in front of body, raises one finger to indicate Ss should work alone)) *hitori de yatte* (.) *HANASANAI DE* ((Ss look at each other then down at W/Bs))
'Work alone, don't talk'

As is the case in earlier excerpts, the student exchange initiated by Risa was audible to the teacher indicating that she was not concerned that revealing that she had not finished the task or did not know the answer would reflect negatively on her face as a competent member of the class, nor bring about a negative evaluation of the classmates she sought to engage. Risa solicits peers on either side of her, in full view of the teacher, and checks her work even though the teacher has intervened on a number of earlier occasions and registered his displeasure. During this exchange, Risa consults peers with increasing urgency particularly after the teacher indicates (turn 1) he will be checking homework and starts to move around the classroom. In turn 4, seemingly unconcerned at the risk of attracting teacher or additional peer attention to herself or her classmates, Risa inquires whether the student sitting next to her has done her homework, *'ne yatta no?'* (Hey, did you do it [the homework]?) Risa, after reviewing what she assumes to have been the homework *'da yo ne'* (that's right), finds a problem and turns to another classmate (turn 8) in order to substantiate homework requirements and check her answers, *'chotto matte kore tte sa kore tte shukudai da kke?'* (Wait a second, this, was this homework?) In turn 10, Risa, in clear view and audio range of the teacher who clearly displeased, has by now stopped moving around the classroom in order to observe Risa's movements, requests the answer to the homework task *'oshiete'* (tell me). Appearing to have reached the threshold of his tolerance, the teacher dramatically intervenes in turn 12 when he gains the classes attention by noisily clearing his throat, then proceeds to vigorously shake his head from side to side. With outstretched arms palms faced upward, the teacher looks toward the ceiling as if requesting divine intervention. He then shifts his gaze back to Risa, crosses his arms in front of his body and holds up one finger. In a raised voice the teacher instructs Risa and the students seated on either side of her to *'hitori de yatte'* (work alone) and fortifies this by demanding that the students do not consult or converse with anyone *'hanasanai de'* (don't talk). The teacher's intent to have students comply, explicit and threatening, results in the three students exchanging nervous glances before looking down at their workbooks.

During retrospection, Risa was clearly frustrated as she reflected, *'kocchi mo yappari dou shiyou tte omotte (...) tomodachi ni kiita'* (This point too I also felt like, 'What am I going to do?' I asked a friend). Risa's classroom interaction and feedback illustrates that she views collaboration as a valid means of soliciting information during classroom activities when unable to arrive at an answer herself or provided with a viable alternative course of action. From Risa's perspective, collaboration should not be associated with either a lack of competence or potential loss of face. Revealing that the teacher's decision to intervene was at times interpreted as both atypical and threatening student Akari stated, *'itsumo to chigau na to omotta* (…) *itsumo nara hanashitari shite mo daijoubu dakedo kono sensei wa hanashi o sasete kurenai kara kowai na to omotta'* (I thought it was different from usual. Usually we are allowed to collaborate in class but this teacher wouldn't let us so I felt he was strict/scary). Akari's reference to unfamiliar discursive and behavioural expectations within the L2 classroom draws attention to the teacher's non-Japanese status, and the threat to face that arises from disparities in conceptions of classroom rank and role. Characterised as being *'chigau'* (different) when weighed against familiar *'itsumo'* (always) practices, the feedback implies that cross-cultural discrepancies interfered with the students' ability to interact as the teacher did not accommodate the Japanese students' desire for peer collaboration. Furthermore, Akari stresses that the teacher's unfamiliar expectations resulted in her feeling afraid within the classroom *'kowai na to omotta'* (I felt he was strict/scary).

The students' conviction that collaboration is acceptable, and standard student behaviour, is also supported by student Hikari's reaction to being instructed by the teacher to work alone. In Hikari's own words: *'jibun dewa tomodachi toka no o mite naoshitari shita kedo sore de mata machigattetara dou shiyou tte iu ka nani mo warui koto shitenai no ni'* (Well, I looked at my friends [homework] and I fixed it [my answers] and stuff, but then, well, I felt like, what will I do if I make another mistake. I mean, we weren't even doing anything wrong). Hikari's feedback implies that within the classroom context, the teacher's objection to collaboration and clear preference for individual contributions restricted the Japanese students' ability to interact freely with classmates. Thus the students, isolated from a key resource, namely the student body network, at times felt uncomfortable and unable to interact and perform at the level they would have liked within the classroom.

In the following classroom exchange, students are instructed by the teacher to work alone in order to identify and write the names of a number of countries from a vocabulary box in order to label a map of the world. The excerpt begins when a student, unable to answer, seeks assistance from a classmate sitting next to her. Prior to this exchange, the students have been instructed by the teacher on several occasions to work alone.

[Classroom excerpt 5: Kaori (K) asks classmate Mimi (M) for assistance with a workbook activity when the teacher (T) intervenes.]

1T: ((T looks from side to side, holds right hand up)) I want you to write down your answers <u>here</u> ((holds up W/B, points to world map in W/B))

2K: (5) ((K turns and leans toward M)) *ne* (1) *kore muzukashii* (↑) ((points at W/B map))
          'Hey, this is difficult'

3M: ((M turns toward K)) *u::n::* (nods) (5) *naruhodo ne* (1) ((looks down at W/B)) *kore dekiru kamo*
'Yeah. I see. I think I can do this'

4K: ((K points at blank space on map)) (3) *nani kakeba ii no⸮*
'What should we write⸮'

5T: (2) ((T places hands on hips, looks at K then slowly around classroom from left to right)) <u>Alone</u> ((holds pen at eye level, makes writing motion in the air)) (3) <u>alone</u> (1) LET'S GO ((taps fingers on W/B map))

6K: ((K turns to M, points at blank space on W/B map)) *nani kore⸮*
'What's this⸮'

7M: ((M leans closer to look at K's W/B)) *kore kaite* ((points at answer in W/B vocabulary box))
'Write this'

8K: (2) ((K begins to write, glances up at M)) *kore desho⸮*
'This, right⸮'

9M: *u::n* ((M points out answers from W/B vocabulary box in turn, K fills in map))
'Yeah, (that's right).'

10T: OK ((T holds hand up palm facing away from body in stop gesture)) HEY (1) listen ((shakes head back and forth rapidly)) (1) NO talking (2) work alone ((frowns irritably))

11K/M: ((K/M look up probingly. T shakes head back and forth. K/M look down in silence))

Student Kaori informs classmate Mimi in turn 2 that she regards the map labelling task as being *'muzukashii'* (difficult) and therein non-directly petitions her assistance. Kaori proceeds in turn 4 to specifically outline what she requires help with when she asks Mimi what she should write in order to complete the task, *'nani kakeba ii no⸮'* (What should we write⸮) In turn 5 the teacher responds to the attempt to collaborate by placing his hands on his hips, staring silently in the direction of Kaori, and then shifting his gaze to a deliberate inspection of her classmates. The expectation that students work unaided is confirmed when the teacher twice states that he demands they perform *'alone'*. This is reinforced when the teacher holds up his pen, gestures as if writing, and directs students to resume work, 'Let's go', while tapping his fingers on Kaori's workbook. Appearing oblivious or indifferent to the teacher's demand, in turn 7 Mimi responds to Kaori's request for assistance by directing her attention to the required country name *'kore kaite'* (write this) to which Kaori responds *'kore desho⸮'* (This, right⸮) *Desho*, an auxiliary of conjecture, when spoken with rising intonation functions on a discursive level to seek conformation as to the speaker's conjecture (Hayashi, 2010). Mimi, confirming accuracy with the casual-style positive response *'un'* (Yes/Uh-huh/Yeah), goes on to point out the remaining answers to the activity by referring to the vocabulary box (turn 9). The exchange is open and upfront in the sense that neither student attempts to conceal what they are doing from the teacher or other members of the class. The teacher, within close physical proximity, reacts to Kaori and Mimi's exchange in turn 10 by rebuking the students, 'Hey, listen', while at the same time rapidly shaking his head from side to side to indicate that a collaborative effort will not be permitted. The teacher reaffirms his demands by stating his expectations that there should be 'no talking' and students should 'work alone'. From the Kaori and Mimi's perspective, it appears that the confrontational nature of the teacher's intervention captures them by surprise as they can be observed furtively stealing glances at the teacher as if to confirm whether they are being directly referred to. After inquiringly shifting their line of gaze to the teacher and establishing that they are indeed being reprimanded for not working alone (turn 11) Kaori and Mimi react by promptly terminating their collaboration and looking down at their desks in silence. Following the class, the teacher specifically commented on this and other points of student collaboration stating that, 'the students know what I will and won't accept in class' and 'they (the students) know that I'm not going let them take the easy option'. The teacher's position intimates that the students concur with his view of collaboration and are aware of what this means in terms of communicative practices that are held up as being acceptable within the classroom.

The student's perspective was articulated during retrospection when Kaori stated: *'kono tango atteru tte kakunin shitara atteru tte itte kureta'* (I was checking to see whether the word was correct and [Mimi] said it was right). Explaining the rationale behind her decision to seek peer assistance Kaori states *'wakannai kara kikitai (…) dou suru no toka kikitai'* (I didn't know so I wanted to ask. I wanted to ask 'What do we do?' and other things). The fundamental need for assistance in order to understand lesson content coupled with her desire to actively seek this assistance from a classmate underscores that the teacher's intervention potentially threatens Kaori's ability to engage in classroom activities. For Kaori, being admonished by the teacher for soliciting her classmate for help amounts to an outright denial of the fact that she is on task and actively engaged in carrying out the activity in a way she feels is appropriate. Rejecting this implication that she has performed inappropriately, Kaori asserts that the need for peer support on this, and *'toka'* other things, is the result of a lack of direction offered by the teacher, *'wakaranai kara tatoe o daseba iinda kedo tatoe ga nai kara zenzen wakannai (…) koko no imi ga yoku wakaranakatta'* (It would have been fine if the teacher gave us an example, but there wasn't an example. I had no idea what to do. I didn't really understand what this part meant). Responding to the threat to face, Kaori's proposal that the teacher *'tatoe o daseba ii'* (should give us an example) presents as a criticism of the teacher's professional skills. The use of the Japanese verb + *ba* indicates a conditional 'if', and with the additional *ii* (good) expresses her conviction that a particular course of action would be beneficial. Kaori's choice of expression, typically used for making suggestions and giving advice, implies doubts in the teacher's abilities. As the teacher is not present, Kaori's submission does not directly threaten the teacher's face, however it does serve to intimate a lack of confidence in his ability perhaps as a result of her frustration at his critical intervention within the classroom. Indeed it appears that Kaori is objecting to being tagged with an identity which insinuates that she has failed to uphold norms associated with what the teacher views as constituting 'good student' behaviour particularly when she has been proactively seeking peer assistance in order to take part in English activities and to compensate for what she views as being a lack of sufficient teacher direction.

Collaboration and Error Avoidance

The third theme to emerge from the data sources pertaining to peer collaboration that will be discussed in this section is what can be described as the students' desire to avoid error in order to align with a 'good student' identity. Classroom recordings and student reflections revealed that in order to align with identities they associate with competence, the students assumed that they had to avoid making errors when interacting with the teacher and that collaboration with classmates provided a readily available means of achieving this objective. As distinct from the data excerpts discussed to date, the following interaction traces an interesting practice whereby students engaged in not only joint construction of responses, but also delivered responses to questions together. This practice of tandem responses was observed frequently throughout learning activities. Student retrospective feedback affirmed that jointly proffered responses reduced the perceived threat to face through the sharing of responsibility shouldered by individual students. On the other hand, the teacher's critical intervention during co-construction and delivery represented a failure to acknowledge an important identity issue for the students.

In the following excerpt, the teacher stands at the front of the class from where he indicates that he intends to check the answers to workbook questions with the whole class. When students appear reluctant to voluntarily contribute responses, the teacher takes control of the activity by nominating students in succession. In the following exchange, the designated student can be observed turning to consult a classmate after which the two students proceed to respond to the question in unison.

[Classroom excerpt 6: Satoko (Sa) consults classmate Marin (M) after being directed by the teacher (T) to translate.]

1T: ((T holds up W/B, taps on cover, opens W/B)) SECTION one (.) number one (1) onegai shi::ma::su or (.) *dou::zo* (2) IN ENGLISH¿ ((looks around at Ss, raises shoulders))

2Sa: (5) ((Ss look down at desks in silence, glance at classmates))

3T: ((T looks around at Ss, claps hands together forcefully, Ss look up at T startled)) What's the <u>English</u> word¿ ((looks directly at Sa, points at Sa))

4Sa/M: (3) ((Sa turns to M seated on her right (inaudible))) Please ((Sa/M respond in unison)) (1) <u>please</u>

5T: (3) ((T looks from Sa to M in slow exaggerated left/right movement)) <u>Please</u> (1) ((nods slowly with bemused expression)) <u>now</u> (1) let's try <u>again</u> (2) ALONE ((places hands on hips, points at M))

6Sa/M: ((M turns to Sa and whispers (inaudible)))

7T: ((T gestures to M with chin)) Number 2 is (.) *OO-KII* (2) <u>how</u> do you say that (.) <u>in English</u>¿ (2) ((raises shoulders))

8Sa/M: (4) ((M turns to Sa and whispers (inaudible), Sa/M respond in unison)) <u>Large</u> ((M/Sa look up at T))

9T: ((T frowns, shrugs shoulders with palms faced upwards, turns to look first at Sa, then M)) WHO is answering¿ ((scratches head while raising eyebrows in exaggerated movements)) (1) are you TWINS¿ ((shrugs, looks from Sa to M with confused expression, raises eyebrows while shrugging)) What is this¿ ((crosses arms in front of body, turns body, walks away))

In both turns 4 and 8, while one of the students has been markedly solicited by the teacher to respond, the students proceed to briefly collaborate before responding in unison. Although the answer given by the students is accurate, the response results in a critical teacher reaction (turn 5) exemplified when he looks from Satoko to Marin in an exaggerated and disconcertingly measured left/right movement. Punctuating the move with a slow nod, the teacher adopts a bemused expression as he instructs the students to 'try again' but this time 'alone', after which he looks directly at the students and places his hands resolutely on his hips. The teacher demonstrates that he does in fact intend to have the students 'try again' and proceeds to nominate

Marin to respond to a new question. Once again, (turn 8) the students consult each other before delivering a joint response. On this occasion, the teacher does not even bother to indicate that the response is correct and instead focuses on addressing what he implies is an unacceptable response strategy, namely a collaborative answer. This is evident when in turn 9, the teacher shrugs his shoulders and appears both confused and frustrated as he looks at both of the students in turn while asking 'Who is answering?' The threat to the students face is further intensified when the teacher proceeds to scratch his head while raising his eyebrows in an exaggerated display of confusion while asking 'Are you twins?', and proceeds to look around the classroom petitioning the students to comprehend his dissatisfaction. The teacher's reference to twins as he looks at both students with overstated uncertainty, intimates that the joint response borders on humorous as the students not only lack the ability to work alone, but are essentially indistinguishable from each other. The teacher's irritation is punctuated when he asks 'What is this?' and abruptly terminates the exchange by crossing his arms, turning his back on the students and walking away.

This animated display of exasperation motivated by his view that the students' joint response represented a failure to uphold standard classroom behaviour is revealed as being radically different from student Marin's interpretation. Underscoring her sense of confusion, Marin commented *'ano futago tte dou iu koto?'* (What was that about the twins?) and articulated her view of the collaborative student response as, *'nan ka minna de ieba anmari medatanai shi umm machigatte mo minna ga kaba-a shite kureru kara anshin'* (Well, if we all say it together you don't really stand out and if you make a mistake, everyone can cover for you so it feels safe). Consequently, in the above excerpt, the students' solicit and receive classmate assistance leading to a joint response which shifts the focus away from the individual. This facilitates the maintenance of face as the risk of teacher attention faced by the individual student is substantially reduced. Similarly, commenting on a moment when she collaborates with classmates student Hikari notes: *'jibun de nani o iu ka daitai wakatteru kedo jishin ga nai'* (I kind of knew what to say but I didn't have any confidence) and goes on to explain *'hitori yori wa minna to issho ni itta hou ga jibun teki ni wa yariyasui'* (Rather than by yourself, it's easier for me to respond together [with my classmates]).

These findings are consistent with Japanese students' concern over making mistakes as reported by Nakane (2006) who commented, 'Japanese students perhaps tend to have differing criteria for relevance and correctness of student comments in the classroom, and hence frame classroom participation as a risky act' (2006: 1819). The assumption that an errant response during classroom participation involves a risk of face loss infers that peer collaboration serves as a means of exploring safe and ideally advantageous identities. Moreover, the student's reference to feeling *'anshin'* (safe) and the collective tendency to *'kaba-a shite kureru'* (cover for each other) highlights the emergent nature of identities as the students seek to align to the group and avoid teacher positioning as less competent students. For this reason collaboration between students did not replace classroom contributions, but rather appeared to serve as a first decisive step regarded by students as being acceptable and offering a degree of protection. This observation is supported by Foster and Snyder Ohta (2005), who maintain that 'assistance given and utilized creates a discourse that is a joint performance, something which can be seen as an important precursor of individual production' (2005: 414). Hence, the teacher's automatic rejection of identities associated with acts of student collaboration unintentionally interfered with classroom participation as it resulted in a negative teacher evaluation of students resourcing collaboration, and frequently led to students being forced to avoid a valuable interactive response strategy.

The suggestion that Japanese students may embrace different criteria for relevance and correctness of student comments in the classroom, and the implication that this may influence views of the weight associated with classroom participation, was reflected in views expressed by student Mika who commented *'wakatteta kedo nani mo iitaku nai no wa kotaeru koto ga ookina koto dakara'* (I knew [the answer], but I didn't want to say anything, mostly because it's a big thing to answer). It is revealing to note that even when confident in her ability to correctly respond to a question, Mika still identifies commenting in the classroom as a threat to face for the reason that it is *'ookina koto'* (a big thing). Nakane's (2006) research into intercultural communication between Japanese university students and their Australian lecturers noted that Japanese students regard speaking in front of the class as a potential source of embarrassment and view it as a 'big deal'. This position is echoed in Tani's (2008) large-scale survey of Asian students' in-class participation at the National University of Singapore. The survey explored the links between learning experience and beliefs, motivations and personal characteristics. Among the questions addressed, Tani asked students 'Are you comfortable asking questions in class?' and found that the majority expressed feeling uneasy about in-class participation. The primary reason for unease cited by students was the belief that in-class participation was too risky as students feared making mistakes and 'looking stupid' (2008: 350). Tani, observing that the distributions evidenced in the survey can be applied to the overall population of Asian students in Western higher education institutions, surmises 'that low levels of in-class participation from Asian students are mostly caused by anxiety and fear of making mistakes in public rather than individual characteristics or learning approaches' (2008: 351). Students communicated an intense sense of vulnerability associated with making mistakes and a dominant assumption that classroom participation represented a risky and significant undertaking. Students, conscious that participation contributed to the teacher's overall assessment of performance, indicated a predilection for collaborative responses which communicatively aided in negating threats to face and supported identities associated with competent and engaged classroom performance.

The students' insights into their views regarding collaboration illustrated that joint responses were perceived to be standard classroom practice that aligned the students with peers. Collective responses functioned on a number of levels to support face as they enabled students' to proactively reduce anxiety associated with an individual student response, provided a sense of security in numbers and was a tangible means of negotiating classroom material deemed difficult to comprehend alone. Moreover, retrospective feedback underlined that students prioritised the avoidance of individual errors when responding to teacher-initiated questions. The reason being that while a correct contribution was seen as resulting in a positive teacher appraisal, an incorrect contribution was associated with the loss of face and the possibility of being aligned with an undesirable identity. In the final excerpt in this chapter, student collaboration ensues when the teacher nominates a student to take part in a short substitution activity. After struggling to respond the student seeks assistance from a classmate.

[Classroom excerpt 7: Risa (R) seeks classmate Hikari's (H) assistance when asked by the teacher (T) to take part in a drill.]

1T: ((T moves over to R's desk, stands in front of her, points down at T/B)) What's he doing↗

2R: (2) ((R looks up at T, smiles and tilts head))

3T: (2) What (2) is (2) he (1) doing↗ ((T points at illustration in R's T/B))

4R: (2) He is (4) ((R turns to H on her right)) (5) ((inaudible))

5R/H: (2) ((R/H respond in unison)) Watching T.V.

6T: (2) ((T shakes head, points at R)) Watching T.V. ((holds up index, turns and paces toward whiteboard))

7R: (6) ((R looks over at H, tilts head, raises eyebrows, furrows forehead in comical display. T looks back at R, nods)) (.) He is watching T.V.

After having been asked by the teacher to respond to the prompt 'What's he doing↗' Risa (turn 2) appears uncertain and tilts her head to the side in a gesture typically employed to communicate confusion or uncertainty. Acknowledging this uncertainty, the teacher repeats the question in turn 3 at a markedly slower speed, while pointing down at the textbook in order to direct the student's attention to a series of illustrations which are to serve as visual support. Risa hesitates when attempting to answer the question in turn 4 and following a brief silence, turns to the classmate seated next to her. Here, Risa's collaboration with classmate Hikari gives her the opportunity to co-construct a response after which the students contribute a joint response, 'Watching T.V.'. The teacher responds by shaking his head vigorously from left to right to index his displeasure and pointing toward Risa to indicate that he expects her to answer alone. He then repeats the response 'Watching T.V.' and raises his index finger to underline that he is indeed waiting for her to respond alone. As the teacher turns toward the whiteboard, Risa, unnoticed by the teacher, takes the opportunity to convey to her classmates her confusion by adopting a quizzical expression, tilting her head and furrowing her forehead in a comical display (turn 7). Body language and facial expression combine to align her with her classmates, the in-group, and indicates that she contests the teacher's directive while at the same time she accepts that she has to respond as directed by the teacher. Reflecting on her position, Risa later commented, *'nan ka kuraku naru'* (I kind of felt down) and *'sensei ga itte hoshii koto o iu no wa motto kantan'* (It's easier to say what the teacher wants). These competing identities intimate that Risa felt that she had to construct and enact classroom identities that did not always reflect how she viewed herself or wished to be viewed by her classmates. Irrespective of her personal desires, when the teacher glances back and nods in Risa's direction she accommodates his expectations by hastily responding 'He is watching T.V.' (turn 7). In this way Risa is able to create the appearance of aligning with an identity consistent with the teacher's expectations.

Students' attention to maintaining face through the avoidance of error illustrate that while they are willing to exchange opinions with classmates, there is an extra significance attached to giving opinions to the teacher. In contrast with Western face, Matsumoto (1988) hypothesises that Japanese face is not motivated by self-preservation, but arises from interdependency and a high value placed on the creation of harmonious relationships. Reflecting on the instruction to work alone a student, Iori, comments: *'jibun de tte iwareru to nani o kikeba ii no ka yokei wakaranaku naru'* (When you're told to do it by yourself, it makes it even harder to decide what to ask). The feedback indicates that Iori felt that class activities could potentially be complicated by a lack of access to the established peer network intimating that she may have struggled to adapt to a system in which the basic unit of the classroom was the individual. The perception of a collaborative identity as a means of protecting threat to face is reinforced by additional student feedback which highlighted the sense of empowerment when responding with the support of peers. For example, students Marin and Hikari expressed almost identical positions when stating: *'minna issho ni iu toki wa futsuu ni ieru kedo hitori de iu toki ga kinchou suru'* (I can simply say it when we say it together [as a class], but when I have to say it by myself I get nervous) and *'minna de issei ni iu to ieru kedo hitori de iu no wa sugoku kinchou suru kara'* (I can say it when we say it together [as a class], but when I say it by myself I feel really nervous).

Implications: Cross-Cultural Disparity in Collaboration

In the course of collaborating, the students enacted cultural identities through upholding the legitimacy of peer co-construction as an appropriate classroom linguistic practice. As such, the examination of collaboration as seen from the Japanese students' perspective shines light on the varying teacher/student interpretations of the cultural and situational appropriateness of collaboration during L2 activities. The teacher's preference for individual participation was perceived by Japanese students as threatening, restrictive and inconsistent with what they considered to be standard classroom communication strategies. On the one hand, throughout learning activities, the students were urged to actively engage in speaking activities, while at the same time, there were restrictions placed on how students chose to participate. Students were time and again cautioned for resourcing classmates and explicitly directed to work alone. Within the classroom, given the teacher controlled the balance of power the students were faced with the challenge of negotiating their participation in order to avoid a negative appraisal within limits that were not always evident. While the teacher assumed that the students would acknowledge and accept the legitimacy of the direction to work alone this was not the case. Students expressed feeling a strong sense of vulnerability at what they cited as constituting an unreasonable imposition. In opposition to the teacher's appraisal of collaboration, the Japanese students did not regard the solicitation or sharing of information as breaching classroom protocol and consequently, did not conceal when they were working collaboratively with classmates. From the students' perspective, collaboration was positively viewed as a means by which to negotiate potential challenges associated with L2 activities, maintain group unity and achieve legitimacy through upholding student roles. In this way, collaboration represented an identity associated with student interdependence and often preceded classroom participation.

It is important to note that from the teacher's perspective, the timing or points during lesson activities at which the students elected to seek collaborative support were central to whether collaboration resulted in a negative student appraisal. For example, the teacher decisively blocked collaboration in cases when a student had directly been requested to contribute to an activity. Fundamental to this critical positioning was the supposition that these points of student collaboration exposed an inability to initiate an individual response on the basis that a less competent or unmotivated student was unacceptably avoiding 'hard work' through soliciting a more competent peer. This perceived failure to perform in the way the teacher expected of a competent student was interpreted as a violation of normative classroom 'good student' roles and associated behaviours and therein, presented an open threat to the teacher's authority. Intervention strategies embraced by the teacher clearly stressed that collaboration was at best inappropriate, and at worst, deceitful. The implications for classroom practice merit prudent consideration given that the majority of students indicated that they were indeed alert to the teacher's disapproval and moreover, assumed that all student collaboration between classmates irrespective of the nature of the activity or exchange, was negatively viewed by the teacher. The point being that the students were unable to differentiate between collaborative practices sanctioned by the teacher and those which was viewed as being objectionable. Illustrating this sense of uncertainty, student Iori commented: *'sensei wa watashitachi ga kurasumeito to hanashite hoshiku nai no ga hakkiri wakaru (...) sensei to dake hanashitemo ii rashii'* (It's clear that the teacher doesn't want us to talk to each other. It's like we're only allowed to talk to the teacher). Similarly, student Kaori expressed concern about communicating with peers and noted that even the performance of routine tasks such as borrowing an eraser would be considered objectionable within the classroom: *'sensei wa minna hanasu no ga sugoku kirai mitai de keshigomu o kariru koto sae kikenai kanji ga suru'* (It's like the teacher really hates it when we talk [between classmates]. I feel like I can't even ask to borrow an eraser).

The teacher promoted his view of personal autonomy through making obvious that individual classroom contributions were highly valued and assumed that this would resonate with the students. On the contrary, the students' feedback highlighted that they did not view an independent classroom contribution as being more meaningful than a contribution arrived at through collective efforts. Students employed collaborative interactional practices to draw on peer alliances in order to facilitate comprehension and formulate responses. Collaboration was a means to establish the space required to process input and potentially modify output in a non-threatening and mutually beneficial exchange which functioned to create affective bonds and reinforce solidarity between classmates. For this reason, students indicated that they viewed collaboration as constituting an acceptable strategy for engaging in, and negotiating, classroom tasks as it was a means by which they could confirm assumptions and/or seek assistance before attempting the face threatening leap of venturing a classroom contribution in full view of their peers. Noting that this was perceived as a standard practice, student Akari commented *'gakkou wa betsuni zenzen minna futsuu ni hanashiteru shi'* (At school, it's absolutely normal that everyone talks [with each other]). As a collective effort to share group knowledge, collaboration enabled students to achieve the best possible results in a given task and consequently, was positively interpreted by students as demonstrating active interest in lesson content. While aware that collaboration resulted in a negative appraisal, students did not see it as in any way diminishing the effort invested and stanchly resisted aligning their communicative practices to the teacher's expectations. Moreover, students took exception to teacher intervention which interfered with their capacity to interdependently seek solutions to comprehension difficulties through sourcing assistance from peers.

For the students, seeking peer collaboration was an active process of engagement through which they might make sense of lesson content in a manner over which they could exercise control and was in many cases not an indication of student comprehension difficulties, nor intended to undermine the teacher's authority. Retrospection illustrated that students shared ownership of a classroom contribution arrived at through collaboration rendered it less threatening for to venture a classroom contribution as it minimised the risk to student face associated with errant classroom contributions. Accordingly, the classroom data underscores the need for teachers working with Japanese students to be cautious of negatively interpreting student initiated collaboration as an indicator of student comprehension limitations, the pursuit of an easy option, or a lack of motivation. Through specifically targeted training, teachers can be guided to identify their own views of collaboration as well as those held by their students. Greater teacher awareness can ultimately lead to a situation in which the students inclination to collaborate, rather than viewed as being an obstacle to learning, can be effectively integrated within the classroom to promote learning. Teacher exposure to adequate training and culturally sensitive teaching/learning strategies can promote acknowledgement and acceptance of differing interpretations of collaboration. Besides increasing the amount of time students spend actively engaged in classroom activities, collaboration enables students to avoid the 'anxiety and self-consciousness that prevent some students from speaking up in front of the whole class' and creates as positive learning environment which 'allows the teacher more opportunity for individual instruction' (Foster, 1998: 1).

Through collaboration, students are empowered to manage face and align with identities they associate with membership within the student group and competent student performance. Research has demonstrated advantages of collaborative learning associated with activities such as 'engaging with the task, trying to understand other people's thinking, explaining and justifying one's own thinking, critically monitoring what others are doing, and being supported in carrying out complex tasks' (Barnes, 2004: 14). Consistent with these observations, Foster and Snyder Ohta (2005) citing Long's (1985, 1996) insights into ways in which input is made comprehensible, explain that in negotiations through which interlocutors seek to overcome comprehension difficulties, 'problem utterances are checked, repeated, clarified, or modified in some way (lexically, phonologically, morphosyntactically) so that they are brought within the optimum i + 1 level' (Foster & Snyder Ohta, 2005: 405). The optimum i + 1 level refers to Krashen's (1982, 1985) theory that L2 acquisition is enhanced through exposure to comprehensible input slightly beyond one's current L2 knowledge. Students' negotiation for meaning and other forms of peer assistance and repair are a means by which they seek to comprehend the L2. This is demonstrated in Kobayashi's (2003) qualitative examination which found that through peer collaboration, students at a Canadian university were able to succeed on a task that would have potentially been beyond their capabilities if attempted alone. The positive outcomes associated with collaboration illustrate the need for educators to consider the potential applications of collaborative learning activities within the language classroom.

8 Alignment to Japanese Identities

Overview: Japanese Identities

This chapter examines the students' management of face as explored through alignment with Japanese identities and resistance to, and/or rejection of, classroom practices interpreted as threatening these identities. Retrospective interviews revealed that the students were highly aware of what they felt to be conflict that existed between what they viewed as being Japanese identities and their obligatory alignment with the expectations they associated with the L2 classroom under the instruction of the non-Japanese teacher. Frequent references to perceived differences between Japanese and non-Japanese classroom practices such as the teacher's approach to error correction are of interest as they illustrated overt sensitivities to what students interpreted as fundamental differences threatening their national identity. Specifically, retrospection underscored that when the students believed that they were being negatively evaluated by the teacher or found unfamiliar classroom expectations objectionable, that there was a distinct tendency to explicitly cite incompatibility between non-Japanese and Japanese classroom teachers and teaching practices. In short, students reacted to unfamiliar practices during learning activities by assuming that the teacher, as the bearer of English language and culture, represented a challenge or threat to their national identities and responded by taking a protective stance.

Students' references to cultural incompatibility were employed to draw a rigid boundary between Japanese culture and an abstract notion of 'Other'. This is important for the reason that the students approached aspects of the English classroom and target language carrying assumptions that not only would there be differences, but that these differences would inevitably be threatening and irreconcilable. As opposed to reflecting cultural differences, student assumptions tended to perpetuate stereotypes capitulating in resistance to the L2 classroom and the teacher. Student criticism of the teacher illustrated that rather than upholding the teacher's *'tachiba'* (standing in relation to others) the students were intent on demonstrating that they did not routinely accept his position of authority within the classroom. In this way, the students' line of approach directly brings into focus the teacher's non-Japanese status within the classroom which is juxtaposed to the students' sense of shared Japanese status. Of note here is that student awareness of national identities comes into focus when students feel that aspects of these identities are threatened by routine classroom practices that are not intended or recognised by the teacher to being divisive.

The students' suggestion that Japanese and non-Japanese identities are intrinsically far removed and at times seemingly irreconcilable set the stage for competition between what retrospective feedback identified as being a sense of conflict between Western and Japanese identities. For example, students Miu and Iori commented: *'watashitachi no kimochi o rikai shite kureru no wa nihonjin no sensei dake'* (Only Japanese teachers would understand how we feel) and *'sensei wa nihon no yarikata ga iya mitai'* (It's like the teacher doesn't like the Japanese way of doing things). The students referred to themselves, and by extension all Japanese, as verbally and behaviourally unified. It was this identity of Japaneseness and the feeling that it was at times being denied or outright rejected which was cited when classroom practices conflicted with student expectations or perhaps how they desired the classroom activities to be managed. Students expressed feeling *'kinchou'* (nervous), *'hazukashii'* (embarrassed) and *'iya da'* (I don't like [it]) when reflecting on unfamiliar practices or approaches to instruction which varied from the *'nihon no yarikata'* (Japanese way). In addition, the students' apprehension was indicated in comments such as Marin's feedback *'sensei wa watashi no kimochi o rikai dekinai kara kono jiten dewa kotaetaku nai'* (At this point I didn't want to answer because the teacher couldn't understand how I feel), and Sayaka's comment that *'sensei no yarikata de yaranakya ikenai to omou to ochikonjau (…) nihonjin no sensei ga shidou shite itara kono you na mondai wa nai no ni'* (I feel down when I think I have to do things the teacher's way. If it was a Japanese teacher instructing us there wouldn't be any problems like this). In this way, student attention to an abstract notion of what constitutes the 'Japanese way' served as a means by which students negotiated loss of face through rationalising uncomfortable classroom situations, distancing themselves from the teacher and building solidarity with classmates.

References to cultural incongruity not only highlighted a general assumption among the students that points of miscommunication or discomfort that occurred during lessons were culturally motivated, but also a compelling sense of frustration that they would ultimately have to embrace these practices in order to gain a positive teacher evaluation. In the words of Sayaka, *'gaikoku no yarikata to nihon no yarikata ga aru* (...) *nande gaikoku no yarikata ni awasenakya naranai no٤'* (There's a foreign way of doing things and the Japanese way. Why do we have to fit in with the foreign way٤) Student Hikari not only noted what she felt to be differing teaching/learning practices, but used these differences as a point from which to critically evaluate the teacher while aligning herself with the Japanese student group: *'nihonjin dakara nihonjin no sensei no oshiekata ga suki* (...) *socchi no hou ga wakariyasui'* (I'm Japanese so I like the way Japanese teachers teach us. It's easier to understand). The rejection of what were viewed by students as being non-Japanese classroom practices, and resistance to the expectation that conforming to these practices was the only valid option was highlighted by Iori: *'kowai to omotta* (...) *sensei wa nihon no yarikata ja nakute watashitachi ga sensei ni awasenakucha ikenai* (...) *yaru kedo iya da* (...) *nihonjin no sensei no hou ga zettai ii'* (I felt scared. He doesn't do things in the Japanese way and we have to do it in his way. I do it, but I don't like it. Japanese teachers are definitely much better). Resigned to complying with classroom practices that may not always be agreeable, the sense of powerlessness and vulnerability was expressed by students through reference to feelings of dislike and unwillingness *'iya da'* combined with critical comparisons between the NS teacher and the *'zettai ii'* definitely better approach associated with the *'nihonjin no sensei'* Japanese teacher.

Retrospection sheds light on the students' enactment of Japanese identities through language use and behaviour, and brings to light assumptions regarding their relationship to the international community. The discussion draws on a critical account of the interrelated themes of *kokusaika* (internationalisation), ethnocentricity and *nihonjinron* theories of the uniqueness of Japanese culture. These themes, as revealed through issues of cultural stereotyping, are highly relevant to the experiences of the young students as they grapple with their own cultural identities and how they perceive these to both impact on, and impacted by the acquisition of English. The point being that with the current focus on *kokusaika* and enhancing *kokusai rikai* (international understanding) within Japanese language policy, attention to the classroom implementation of English activities has yet to examine the perspectives of younger Japanese students as they wrestle with competing identities.

Adopting a position that does not see national identities as necessarily threatened, Kubota (1998) argues that modern Japanese education policy as revealed through the discourse of *kokusaika* seeks to welcome Westernisation while simultaneously promoting Japanese nationalistic values through the learning of English. Examining the link between English and *kokusaika*, Kubota states that: 'In this discourse of *kokusaika*, creation of cultural identity and patriotism as resistance to Westernization harmoniously coexists with promotion of learning English and English "logic" that would enable Japanese to become a respected member of the West' (1998: 301). The basic premise being that effective English education policy will enable Japan to attain an active and prominent role within the global community through increased English proficiency.

Nihonjinron, popularised during the 1960s and 1970s during a time of extensive economic growth accompanied by industrialization and Westernisation (Kubota, 1999, 2003), is based on the premise that the Japanese identity is held to be distinct from non-Japanese identity. *Nihonjinron* argues as a central premise that the Japanese are a culturally homogeneous people (*tan'itsu minzoku*) and there exist distinctive characteristics associated with race, language and culture which constitute Japaneseness. Founded on the disputed claim that Japanese society is unique and group orientation is the dominant cultural pattern which shapes behaviour (see Mouer & Sugimoto, 1986, 1995), *nihonjinron* views groupism as moderating diversity and promoting conformity to group goals and homogeneity (Kubota, 1999). Japanese anthropologist Befu (2001) asserts that *nihonjinron* serves as a prescriptive model or ideology that characterises an idealised vision of what Japanese society should be like:

> In short, a claim is made for equivalency and mutual implications among land, people (that is, race), culture, and language, such that those and only those who practice the culture also speak the language and have inherited Japanese 'blood' from their forebears, who have always lived on the Japanese archipelago, and that no other person speaks the language natively and practices the culture. (Befu, 2001: 71)

Claiming that attributes exclusive to the Japanese include 'the Japanese brain, social customs and language' (Liddicoat, 2007: 34) *nihonjinron* promotes a 'Japanese identity [that] is the anti-image of foreignness and, as such, can only be affirmed by formulating the images of the Other, namely the West' (Yoshino, 1992: 11). Highlighting the *nihonjinron* distinction between Japanese and Western ideology, Takayama (2008) explains that Japanese society is depicted as 'group-oriented, harmonious, ethnically homogeneous and reliant on shame', while the West is viewed as being 'individualistic, fond of conflict, ethnically plural and reliant on guilt' (2008: 24–25). The nationalistic self-positioning not only sees Japan and the Japanese as being distinct from outside world, but implies that the world outside Japan is essentially a singular collective group that represents a potential threat to Japanese uniqueness.

Critics have undermined claims of uniqueness proposed by the *nihonjin-ron* genre through systematically demonstrating that the portrayal of Japan as being homogeneous is fundamentally inaccurate. For example, Parmenter (1999) points out not only a failure to account for indigenous minorities such as the Ainu, but also social diversity resulting from immigrant populations, children with one foreign parent and children who have lived abroad (1999: 456). While claims of homogeneity cannot be substantiated, Liddicoat (2007) notes that there remains a focus on Japanese distinctiveness which essentially represents 'an ideologically constructed worldview rather than an accurate reflection of the nature of Japan' (2007: 34). Consequently, as a prescriptive model that characterises an idealised vision of what Japanese society should be like (Befu, 1993, 2001) discourses of *nihonjinron* retain a significant influence in structuring both national identity and social reality as reflected in language policy. Yoshino (2002) goes so far as to argue that cultural nationalism, as instilled in English classrooms, is achieved by the Japanese language and culture being considered in opposition to the language and culture of English speaking countries. The point being that learning English reinforces an ethnocentric agenda which cultivates a sense of fundamental uniqueness (McVeigh, 2004) and supports cultural nationalism associated with the perceived threat of Westernisation. Underscoring the perception that national identity is threatened, Schneer's (2007) examination of internationalism and English textbooks endorsed by MEXT found that the 'images and cultural explanations presented in high school English readers initiate cross-cultural discussions from a position of opposition, which is established to maintain a fixed Japanese cultural identity' (2007: 605). Schneer surmises that this identity is intricately linked with the discourse of patriotism/nationalism arguing that there is a strong motivation at a governmental and corporate level to see that this view is upheld. The juxtaposition of national concerns and the perceived threat is framed by Rivers as follows:

> As a non-colonized country, the Japanese are typically proud and protective of their national language, culture, and perceived ethnic homogeneity. This symbiotic-like relationship is often used to evoke patriotic sentiment and unity among the Japanese people, especially when sensing physical or ideological threat. (Rivers, 2010b: 105)

Assigned symbolic status framed as being in direct conflict with traditional Japanese values, Tsuda (1990) refers to negative attitudes towards the English language as xenophobia caused by 'English allergy' brought on by excessive and/or unsuccessful attempts to acquire English and identify with native English speakers. Opposition to the linguistic influence of English focuses primarily on the perceived cultural, social and linguistic implications associated with the adoption of a non-Japanese world-view. The argument being that as the Japanese language and Japanese identity share an innate bond, so too is the English language bound to English identity. Hence, to acquire English will inevitably result in the acquisition of aspects of the culture and values typically associated with English, or rather Western, culture.

With attention to the interrelated themes of ethnocentricity, *kokusaika*, and *nihonjinron* the following data draws attention to areas of systematic variance in teacher and student attitudes pertaining to specific teaching practices which the students found objectionable and specifically referred to as conflicting with the 'Japanese way'. Three teaching practices identified by students as being incompatible with standard Japanese classroom practices which are explored in the following analysis are; (a) student involvement in the correction of classmates' errors, (b) classroom correction strategies, and (c) positive feedback following error correction. The subsequent classroom excerpts reveal differing teacher and student assumptions regarding roles and practices within the classroom and how they interfered with the students' attempts to claim positive recognition. Among other matters, student feedback illustrated that alignment with and a desire to protect what was felt to be threatened Japanese identity was viewed as being of significance to the students and influenced their management of face. In this way the feedback points to the shifting and conditional nature of identities as students construct and enact new selves which reflect both national and international motivations.

Resistance to Peer Correction

The following three data excerpts illustrate student acts of alignment to a Japanese identity through resistance to the classroom error correction practices employed by the teacher throughout English activities. In particular, the students took exception to the teacher's practice of inviting class members to actively take part in the correction of classmates' incorrect responses. Points at which students were encouraged to contribute corrections typically occurred following an incorrect student contribution after which the teacher would directly solicit corrections from the class with invitations such as: 'Is that OK?', 'What should it be?', 'Does anyone know what the correct answer is?' In these cases the teacher would solicit voluntary responses and/or directly nominate an individual student who was then instructed to correct the mistake while the student responsible for the original error generally watched on in silence. Interview feedback highlighted that the teacher felt that student initiated corrections enhanced student confidence and persuaded those students not directly engaged in the exchange to remain focused: 'It's better when the answers come from students because it shows them that they do know. It keeps the students involved because they might be asked to help out at any time. They have to be prepared to answer'. Reflecting on what he interpreted to be the Japanese students' reluctance to contribute corrections when invited or directly nominated, the teacher referred to what he viewed as being a cultural predisposition to shyness, 'The students are shy when you ask them to correct something. I know they can do it but they're just too shy. It's a cultural thing. You see it a lot with Japanese students'. Providing insight into how he felt this should be addressed within the classroom the teacher noted that this was a tendency that should and ultimately could be overcome: 'I get the students used to correcting each other. It's important that they all get used to thinking about solutions because that's how they learn. Taking on an active role and not just waiting for me to do the correcting'.

Disparities regarding interpretations of classroom correction were revealed in student retrospective feedback, which exposed a strong aversion to directly correcting classmates' errors and the expectation that correction was principally the responsibility of the teacher. Accordingly, the correction of classmates not only clashed with expected classroom norms, but also represented a threat to the face of both the correcting and the corrected students by negatively impacting on the symmetry of the peer bond. In other words, the students' reluctance to participate, even when directly solicited by the teacher, was largely motivated by the desire to maintain mutual face through upholding the equal status of classmates. In order to support face, students expressed solidarity through rejecting the teacher's invitations to offer corrective suggestions on the grounds that to remark on a classmate's contribution was to effectively pass judgment on the classmate in a highly public manner. Among other things, feedback illustrated that this was interpreted as implying that the student commenting possessed superior English proficiency and that this would inevitably lead to a proficiency hierarchy within the classroom that the students were not comfortable with. In the words of student Akari: *'hanasu to minna kinchou suru (...) eigo de hanasu koto wa ranku zuke sareru mitai dakara nani mo iitaku nai'* (We all feel nervous when we speak [in English]. I don't want to say anything because it's like our spoken English is being ranked).

For the students, maintaining bonds associated with acknowledging equal status were more highly prioritised than potentially being aligned with a 'good student' identity by the teacher for contributing a correct response.

Excerpt 8 begins with the teacher asking a student to respond to a question after which he solicits corrective feedback from another member of the class.

[Classroom excerpt 8: Yuki (Y) is unable to answer a question and the teacher (T) instructs student, Risa (R) to correct her response.]

1T: ((T holds up T/B and points to series of illustrations)) Do they exercise↗ (2) ((nods in direction of Y))

2Y: ((Y looks down at T/B)) (3) No (2) they (3) doesn't ((looks up at T, tilts head to side))

3T: NO ((shakes head from left to right several times)) NO ((Y looks down at desk, T points at questions in T/B, looks around at Ss)) (4) everybody ((T paces around classroom looking at Ss)) (6) no they doesn't (2) is that OK↗ ((lifts shoulders, raises eyebrows while looking at Ss))

4Ss: (12) ((Ss remain silent, glance at classmates, and/or look down at desks/pencil cases/T/Bs))

5T: ((T moves to centre of classroom)) No (.) they doesn't (3) ((raises shoulders, animatedly scratches head)) is that OK↗ ((looks from left to right at Ss))

6Y: (3) ((Y glances up at T, picks up pencil case and shows *purikura* stickers to classmate))

7T: ((T slams T/B closed, Ss look up surprised)) (4) YES↗ (1) NO↗ (1) ((purposefully looks from left to right)) (4) is that OK↗ ((raises shoulders))

8S: (5) ((Ss glance at each other uncomfortably, fiddle with pencil cases and handouts, look down at desks))

9T: What should it be↗ ((T points at R))

10R: (2) No (.) they DON'T ((R glances across at Y, then looks down at desk))

11T: Right (3) ((claps)) NO (.) they don't ((nods deliberately at Y, Y looks down at desk, fidgets with pencil case))

In turn 1, the teacher directly nominates Yuki to respond to a question from the textbook as her classmates watch on in silence. Following a short delay, Yuki haltingly responds in turn 2 after which she looks up from her textbook to the teacher and then tilts her head to register uncertainty. Yuki's face is threatened when the teacher, as opposed to acknowledging her hesitation as the appeal for his assistance intended, twice states that the response is in fact incorrect 'No' (turn 3). After indicating that the response is incorrect while animatedly reinforcing this by means of shaking his head from left to right, the teacher then proceeds to move around the classroom while inviting the class to comment on the accuracy of Yuki's response 'Everybody, No, they doesn't. Is that OK?' In view of the fact that the teacher has emphatically stated that the answer is incorrect, the invitation to the class is met with silence given that a response would be essentially to reiterate a foregone conclusion. This is highlighted by student Risa who expresses her confusion as to what the students are required to do during retrospection: *'sensei ni chigau tte iwareta (…) sensei ga nani o itte hoshii no ka shiranai (…) sakki sensei ga kotae o itta kara'* (The teacher said 'No'. I don't know what the teacher wants us to say because he had already answered the question). Risa's use of *shiranai*, the no-past-negative form of the verb *shiru* 'to learn/to know/to find out' (Manita & Blagdon, 2010: 21) is telling in that it implies that she is not interested, and does not regard the teacher's expectations or objectives to be within her territory of information. The nuance being conveyed here is that there is no apparent logic behind the teacher's approach. The teacher's question, 'Is that OK?', not only draws attention to the error, but also implies that Yuki's mistake will be obvious to her classmates who he judges capable of making the required correction. From the teacher's perspective, while restating the error is not intended to illicit a Yes or No response but rather to encourage students to provide a correction, this is clearly lost on the students and a lengthy silence ensues.

In turn 6, after the teacher again asks the students: 'No, they doesn't. Is that OK?', Yuki responds by shifting her attention away from the teacher and begins to talk to the student seated next to her. After initially glancing up at the teacher, Yuki's simple act of classroom resistance can be observed in her decision to ignore the teacher's search for a student correction, and as such may be seen as a visible demonstration that she has lost interest and no longer upholds the teacher's central classroom position. Yuki's resistance to the teacher's unwanted attention is amplified when she proceeds to engage a classmate in conversation as she points at and describes various *purikura* (sticker photographs) attached to her pencil case. The students' conversation, in full view of the teacher and clearly off-topic, illustrates Yuki's desire to protect her face by diverting attention from the impasse while simultaneously serving as a challenge to the approach the teacher has outlined for error correction. In turn 7, the teacher reacts to Yuki's display of indifference and the lack of general student participation by abruptly slamming his textbook closed and in doing so, signals that he will not proceed with the lesson until an acceptable level of student involvement or a correct response is forthcoming.

In turn 8, in what appears to be an effort to avoid eye contact with the teacher, students can be seen stealing glances with each other, looking down at their textbooks, fiddling with pencil cases and shuffling notes. Through their non-participation the students effectively index resistance to the request for contributions and thereby uphold their classmate Yuki's face. Without a correct student response, the assumption that the correct answer should be common knowledge to the students cannot be validated. In this sense, while contributing a response may represent an opportunity for an individual student to align with the teacher's notion of a 'good student' identity, the students nevertheless elect to align themselves with their classmate. This was reflected in student Risa's retrospective comment, *'Yuki mo watashi mo iya na kimochi o suru dake (…) nani mo iitaku nai'* (I didn't want to say anything [because] Yuki was just going to feel bad and so would I). In turn 9, the teacher elects to react to the lack of student response to his requests for participation by gesturing towards an individual student, Risa, and thereby nominating her to respond. Risa, having been directly solicited is compelled to answer and after a short pause responds, 'No, they don't'. The apparent ease with which Risa responds indicates that the question is indeed within her level of English competence. Following her response, Risa does not wait for teacher confirmation of whether the answer is accurate as may be expected, but instead can be seen immediately glancing in the direction of Yuki and then down at her desk. Her behaviour expresses confidence in the accuracy and appropriateness of her answer while also registering concern for her classmate Yuki's feelings. While Risa's did not volunteer to contribute a correction, she nevertheless appears reluctant to refuse the teacher's direct request to participate. During retrospective feedback Risa commented, *'Yuki ga machigaeta ato kurasu zen'in no mae de shitsumon ni kotaetaku nai (…) Yuki ga iya na omoi o suru dake dakara sensei ga watashi ni kiite hoshiku nakatta'* (I didn't want to answer the question in front of the whole class after Yuki has just made a mistake. She would just feel bad so I wish the teacher hadn't asked me). Risa went on to further comment: *'chigau iikata ni shite hoshii (…) nihonjin no sensei wa iwanai shi motto aite no kimochi o kangaeru to omou'* (I wanted him [the teacher] to say it in a different way. Japanese teachers wouldn't say that. I think they consider others' feelings more). Her reaction to the exchange draws attention to what she outlines as being a distinct contrast between Japanese and non-Japanese classroom correction methods and motivations. Specifically, Risa suggests not only that the teacher has not approached error correction in a way that the students find familiar, but that she regards his approach as uncomfortable and something that she would ultimately like him to modify. The position that peer based correction practices are not a standard Japanese classroom procedure is unequivocally noted when she states that *'nihonjin no sensei wa iwanai'* (Japanese teachers wouldn't say that). Offering both an explanation and condemnation of the teacher, Risa goes on to spell out that she thinks this is because Japanese teachers *'motto aite no kimochi o kangaeru'* (consider others' feelings more). Similarly, commenting on a point during English activities when the teacher asked a student to correct a classmate's errant response to a question, student Kaho observed: *'iya datta (...) tte iu ka itsumo sensei ni awasenakucha ikenai (...) chou yada'* (I didn't like it. I mean we always have to do it in the teacher's way. I really don't like this).

A perceptible 'we-they' distinction is manifested in both Risa and Iori's distinction expressing as it does underlying tones of a value judgment associated with superior-inferior rhetoric in which the familiar Japanese approach is viewed as being superior to what the students assume to be a standard non-Japanese approach. Hinenoya and Gatbonton (2000) maintain that it is common for a sense of distinctiveness to be 'associated with attitudes reflecting better-worse, positive-negative, or even superior-inferior comparison with others' (2000: 227). The researchers note that 'The uniqueness or distinctiveness that characterizes Japanese-style ethnocentrism seems to be limited to a feeling that there is something positive about being Japanese or, at the very least, that being Japanese is a focal point from which all things are to be viewed or interpreted' (2000: 227–228). Of interest here is that student Risa directly states that she assumes Japanese inherently *'motto aite no kimochi o kangaeru'* (consider each other's feelings more), and by implication, that non-Japanese are generally unable or unwilling to prioritise the feelings of others. Hence, the teacher's failure to perform in line with or uphold standards the students maintain for Japanese teachers is seen as a mark of his limited and inferior by Japanese standards, capacity to teach. The implication being that while he has failed to execute his role according to Japanese cultural standards that the students associate with the role of the teacher and the context of the classroom, that this is to a certain degree to be expected as he is not Japanese.

Risa's critical appraisal of what she regards as being the teacher's lack of awareness and concern for the students feelings was consistent with comments offered by other students. For example, in aligning with a Japanese identity viewed as being distinct from values held by the teacher, student Marin commented: *'wakaranakute mo nani mo dekinai shi sensei ni otagai naoshiatte tte iwareru no wa kirai (...) machigaeta hito ni sugoku waruku kanjiru kara kotaetaku nai (...) minna ni totte muzukashiku naru'* (You can't do anything because you don't even understand. I don't like it when the teacher asks us to correct each other. You feel really bad for the person who made the mistake and you don't want to answer. It makes it difficult for everyone). In addition, student Iori spoke about what she felt to be a greater sense of mutual concern for classmates held by Japanese students when she commented *'mawari motto kizukatte'* (we consider others (feelings) more) while Kaori noted the importance of the class student body working as a unit: *'nihon de wa seito minna ga chi-mu mitai'* (In Japan the students are all like a team). The students' insights highlight that they have taken the position that the teacher's perceived lack of concern for their feelings is in point of fact indicative of a larger non-Japanese cultural tendency. In the above excerpt the teacher did not appear to regard the solicitation of oral contributions following the student's error as threatening either the face of the incorrect student or an imposition to her peers. Of relevance here is that the teacher's approach to error correction is interpreted and rationalised by the students during retrospective feedback as representing a fundamental difference between Japanese and non-Japanese teaching practices. The students' understanding of the situation being both that Japanese teachers retain greater concern for their feelings, and that Japanese students are in general more unified than they assume non-Japanese students to be. For this reason, taking a position that underscores attention to perceived cultural divisions and a desire to uphold Japanese identities they view as being valuable, the students' focus on interdependence as registered through attention to the unity of the group. The following classroom excerpt provides a further example of a point during English activities when a student was asked by the teacher to correct a classmate.

[Classroom excerpt 9: The teacher (T) nominates Sayaka (Sa) to correct classmates Marin's (M) incorrect answer.]

1T: ((T points at M, nods twice)) It's your turn (2) here we go ((points at M's W/B, nods for M to begin)) (2) what is <u>he doing</u>¿

2M: ((M looks down at W/B, then up at T)) (3) He <u>watch</u> sports

3T: ((T shakes head from left to right)) he (.) <u>watch</u> sports¿ (1) WATCH (2) ((raises eyebrows)) what's wrong with this¿ ((looks around at Ss, points toward Sa))

4Sa: (3) ((Sa whispers with classmate next to her)) *nande watashi na no* ((looks up at T, tilts head to side))
'Why me¿'

5T: (3) ((T nods at Sa, gestures towards Sa by raising chin)) WHAT'S WRONG WITH THIS¿ ((points in M's direction, M looks down))

6Sa: (4) ((Sa looks at T, tilts head to side))

7T: ((T looks directly at Sa, clicks fingers rapidly several times, points at W/B, looks around at Ss)) (5) What's <u>wrong</u> with this¿ (2) ((raises shoulders)) <u>come:: on::</u> ((drums fingers on W/B)) (4)

8Sa: ((Sa looks down at desk, rummages through pencil case, shuffles papers))

9T: (5) WatchES (1) he WATCHES sports ((T looks at M, then Sa)) (2) you know this ((taps W/B, looks at Sa, looks around class))

Following the student's incorrect response (turn 2) the teacher swiftly reacts by vigorously shaking his head from left to right after which he repeats Marin's answer 'he watch sports' (turn 3), stressing the incorrect verb form in order so as to draw the class's attention to the error. The teacher asks 'What's wrong with this?', however as opposed to seeking volunteers (excerpt 8), promptly nominates Sayaka to contribute the desired correction. Sayaka, flaunting 'good student' conventions, unobtrusively registers her apprehension to the student seated next to her when in turn 4 she asks *'nande watashi na no'* (Why me?). After a short pause it appears that Sayaka is not going to respond and the teacher gestures towards her with his chin while radically increasing the volume of his voice to demand 'What's wrong with this?' The teacher then points in the direction of Marin in order to affirm that it is Marin's inaccurate response that Sayaka has been directed to modify. In turn 6, Sayaka reinforces that she is unable or unwilling to revise her classmate's response by looking directly at the teacher and in silence holding his gaze while tilting her head to the side. The teacher appears to be agitated at Sayaka's failure to contribute the necessary correction to what he may assume to be a request within her L2 capacity when in turn 7 he clicks his fingers together in rapid succession. The teacher, attempting to diffuse the threat to his face associated with his powerlessness to stimulate student involvement, alters his approach by methodically scanning the classroom while inviting contributions: 'What's wrong with this?' When the students fail to take the lead and verbally engage, he theatrically raises his shoulders and impatiently interjects 'Come on' which he punctuates by his impatiently drumming his fingers on his workbook. The demand for a response reinforces that the teacher deems Sayaka and her classmates capable of rectifying Marin's response. Their failure to do so is consequently interpreted as a lack of student engagement in the activity which threatens the teacher's face by way of both challenging his authority and impeding the lesson flow. Rejecting the teacher's appeal for participation, in turn 8 Sayaka can be seen looking away from the teacher as she begins to go through the contents of her pencil case and shuffle handouts in a move that expresses that she does not wish to take part in the exchange.

Contrary to the image she projects as being unable to respond to the teacher's question, during retrospection Sayaka indicated that she did in fact know the answer yet objected to being asked *'kotae wa wakatteta kedo kou iu fuu ni kikareru no wa iya da'* (I knew the answer but I don't like to be asked like this). Illuminating her resistance to correcting Marin, Sayaka reasons that the process of error correction is the teacher's responsibility, *'nani mo iitaku nai (...) nihonjin no sensei wa oshiete kureru'* (I didn't want to say anything. Japanese teachers tell us [the answers]). This subtle display of resistance illustrates that Sayaka is prepared to risk a negative teacher appraisal and forego the opportunity to claim face as a competent student in order to uphold what she views as appropriate classroom practices. Moreover, her refusal to respond conveys that she is willing not only to risk face, but also to threaten the teacher's face in order to align with classmates. The teacher, seemingly resolved to the fact that he will not be able to elicit a response from the students elects to bring closure through providing the verb form 'watches, he watches sports' and then admonishing the students by stating 'you know this' (turn 9).

Student dissatisfaction with being invited or directed to participate in peer correction was a view expressed by other students such as Kaori, who on viewing a point during English activities commented, *'sensei ga minna ni kiitara kotaerarenaku naru (...) kotaerarenai wake dewa nai kedo machigaeta hito no kimochi o kangaeru to kotaerarenai'* (If the teacher asks everyone I can't answer. It's not that I'm not able to answer, rather when I think about how the person who made the mistake feels then I can't answer). Kaori elects to conceal her ability to respond as this is superseded by her concern for the feelings of the classmate being corrected. Again, the student makes a point of emphasising that this is not an issue of English proficiency, but one of maintaining classroom standards and student relationships which she priorities more highly than the opportunity of claiming positive face through individual success.

As noted, retrospective interviews imply that the students assumed that the teacher did not share their concern for feelings or an awareness of appropriate Japanese classroom roles regarding student correction. Through framing disparities within the classroom as related to broader issues of perceived cultural disparities between Japanese and non-Japanese attitudes, the students illustrate that they feel threatened by unfamiliar expectations that they view as extending beyond the four walls of the classroom. Murata (2011) argues that Japanese students' *'tanin no me'*, or awareness of how one is perceived by others, is influenced by cultural assumptions and values associated with the desire to maintain public image in accordance with the mother tongue culture. In the above cases (excerpts 8 and 9) the students viewed correcting peers, irrespective of whether capable of doing so, as conflicting with Japanese classroom practices and consequently resisted participation. Drawing on Abe (2002, 2004), Murata (2011) hypothesises that *'seken'*, described as 'the web of human relationships in the local community and the concern of those involved to maintain a positive public image', restrains students behaviour and the desire to avoid being perceived as different or distinct from other students (2011: 14).

The orientation of English language education in Japan is characterised by Liddicoat (2007) as prioritising Japanese nationalistic perspectives rather than developing intercultural perspectives. Liddicoat argues that the Japanese government language policy views the acquisition of English as a tool for internationally articulating Japaneseness as opposed to a means of mediating Japanese perspectives with those of other countries (2007: 41). In other words, English serves not as a tool for developing a deeper understanding of non-Japanese cultures, but rather as a method by which Japanese society can communicate national identity to people who do not speak the Japanese language. The implication being here that English language education within Japan is implemented under a larger context in which the articulation of Japaneseness is prioritised. To some extent this position fails to acknowledge that English language education in Japan is diverse in that students often study at both public and private institutions, with NS teachers and curriculum materials frequently crossing over. In short, student exposure to English is influenced not only by government language policy but also by other key factors, namely that teachers and curriculum which particularly in the private sector, are not always determined or monitored by government policy.

While is not possible to comprehensively evaluate the students' individual worldviews, it is imperative to note that students at times viewed Japanese identities, and in particular their awareness of classmates, as being challenged by expectations associated with L2 error correction practices as implemented by their non-Japanese teacher. To express defiance, students could be observed demonstrating alliance with their peers through the most basic and non-threatening of strategies – non-participation. To recap, for the students, expressing group solidarity and shared social purpose appears to have been more important than identifying with the teacher's version of the 'good student' identity.

Us and Them: Teacher Correction

The following classroom exchanges are excerpts during which the teacher can be seen directly correcting the Japanese students' verbal contributions to speaking activities or homework tasks. During retrospective interviews students specifically noted that the teacher's approach to correction at these points differed from Japanese classroom correction practices as managed by Japanese teachers. Referencing what they viewed as being disparity between the Japanese and non-Japanese ways of teacher correction, student feedback highlighted what they viewed as being incongruity in teacher/student values and classroom practices. For example, the students expressed concern that the teacher was intent on finding error with their work and was deliberately targeting less competent members of the class when asking questions, a practice they cited as being inconsistent with Japanese classroom norms. Citing these unfamiliar classroom practices the students noted feeling threatened and expressed reluctance to take part in L2 activities. In order to deal with this sense of threat, students registered their resistance in ways that were not immediately obvious to the teacher. For example, students appeared distracted, communicated in low voices, and displayed a lack of interest through behaviours such as leisurely looking through their pencil cases or other items in their bags. One result of such actions evidenced was the frequent breakdown of communication and the assumption, held by the teacher, that the lack of student participation was associated with limited English proficiency. In the following classroom exchange, the teacher begins the lesson by moving among the students in order to check if the students have completed the homework task from the previous week.

[Classroom excerpt 10: Teacher (T) checks Iori (I), Hikari (H) and Yuki's (Y) workbooks.]

1T: ((T strolls around classroom checking homework)) Did you do your homework⸮ (2) ((stops in front of I, looks down at W/B))

2I: (3) ((I looks up at T, nods, looks down))

3T: ((T leans over desk, corrects I's homework)) (9) OK (.) it's all very good (2) <u>except</u> for one ((points at question in I's W/B))

4I: ((I looks at T's correction)) (3) *Aaa::: aaa:::*
          'Ah, I see'

5T: ((T mimics I's reaction)) *Aaa:::aaa:::* ((moves on to next student, picks up H's W/B)) (7) ((begins writing in H's W/B))
          'Ah, I see'

6H: (10) ((H looks up at T, then looks around at classmates))

7T: (2) ((T replaces W/B on H's desk)) OK (.) <u>good</u> (3) ((moves to next student)) did <u>you</u> do your <u>homework</u>⸮ ((looks down at Y))

8Y: (5) ((Y hastily writes in W/B, turns W/B to face T))

9T: ((T leans over desk to correct Y's homework)) (7) This <u>should be</u> an I (2) this should be an I ((points at book)) GOOD ((T nods, moves to next student))

In turns 1 and 7 the teacher seeks verbal confirmation from the students that they have completed the homework activity asking the question: 'Did you do your homework⸮' The teacher then either picks up the students workbooks or leans over the desk for a closer examination of the homework. At these points, the students can be observed talking with peers, looking around the classroom, and occasionally glancing up at the teacher. The teacher selects two students' workbooks for closer observation and proceeds to make corrections indicating that in both cases that an error has been made: 'It's all very good except for one' (turn 3) and 'This should be an "I"' (turn 9). In turn 4, the student, Iori, recognises her error and communicates that she has understood what appears to be an oversight, 'Aaa aaa' (Ah, I see). In turn 5, the teacher employs humour by comically mimicking Iori's response and therein restores her face by confirming that he views the error as a minor lapse that does not require a detailed explanation. While the teacher's corrective feedback and verbal mimicking were intended to support Iori's face, retrospective comments offered by the student highlight disparities in teacher/student views of this exchange and what is held to be a resulting negative impact on student face.

On viewing this exchange during retrospection, Iori elected to stop the recording and irately reflect: *'nihonjin no sensei wa machigae o sagasanai kedo kono sensei wa machigae o mitsuketai dake (…) kono mae shukudai o yatte kite ikutsu ka machigae ga atte sensei wa watashi no koto o kurasu minna no mae de baka ni shita'* (Japanese teachers don't look for mistakes but this teacher just wanted to find mistakes […] Last time I did the homework and I made a few mistakes. The teacher made fun of me in front of the whole class). Of note here is that Iori assumes the teacher's approach to correction is motivated in part by a desire to identify student errors. The loss of face is intensified by the assumption that the teacher's mimicking of her response is not intended to minimise the threat to face, but rather to publicly embarrass her in front of her classmates. This is puzzling for her for the reason that from Iori's perspective, she has fulfilled her student obligations by doing the homework task. Whether or not her answers to the task are correct do not appear to be the issue and consequently the teacher's approach to correction is viewed as being both inappropriate and humiliating. Aligning with Japanese identities in order to validate her criticism and the accuracy of her position, Iori states that the public correction practices employed by the teacher are inconsistent with how her Japanese teachers approach students and the process of correction, *'nihonjin no sensei wa machigae o sagasanai'* (Japanese teachers don't look for mistakes). The implication being not only that she favours the approach to instruction she associates with Japanese teaching methods, but that this approach is inherently better as it does not seek to humiliate or threaten students.

Objecting to the correction strategies employed by the teacher as being incompatible with, and by implication inferior to, Japanese correction strategies, student Hikari comments on the teacher's correction of a classmate's work. When the student answers incorrectly, Hikari comments *'sensei wa waza to wakaranai hito o sasu kedo nihonjin no sensei wa wakatteru hito o erabu (…) gaikoku no sensei wa wakaranai hito o mitsukeru mitai na kanji'* (The teacher deliberately points to someone who doesn't understand but Japanese teachers choose someone who understands. It's like foreign teachers find someone who doesn't know). The teacher's selection process is characterised as being a strategy employed deliberately *'waza to'* to identify a student thought to be unable of correctly answering. Framed by the feedback as constituting a fundamental difference between Japanese and non-Japanese teachers, Hikari assumes that the Japanese teacher will seek to identify a capable student *'wakatteru hito'* (someone who understands) while a non-Japanese teacher will deliberately select those who do not understand *'wakaranai hito o sasu'* (points to someone who doesn't understand). Hikari's feedback conveys that she has interpreted the teacher's correction strategies as an indication that Japanese teachers on a whole, place a higher value on avoiding threats to face than do their non-Japanese counterparts. Hikari sheds further light on how she perceives the teacher's role when she goes on to state *'sensei wa minna no no-to o mite wakatteru hito o eranda hou ga ii to omou'* (I think the teacher should look at everyone's notebooks and then choose someone who does know). In other words, Hikari believes that the teacher should identify a student capable of responding correctly and then invite that student to contribute an answer. This position was also expressed in feedback contributed by student Ami when reflecting on a moment when a classmate was unable to answer a question correctly: *'kawaisou tte iu ka wakaranai tte itteru no ni waza to sasu (...) kotae o kaite nai hito ya wakaranai hito ja nakute wakatteru hito o saseba ii no ni'* (I felt sorry for her, I mean she said she didn't understand but he (the teacher) deliberately chose her. Rather than choosing someone who didn't have the answer written or didn't understand it would be better if he chose someone who understood).

Similarly, the assumption that less competent members of the class were being deliberately targeted and embarrassed was implied in retrospective comments made by student Kaori following the nomination of a classmate who was unable to answer a question: *'moshi nihonjin no sensei ga sashita hito ga wakaranakattara sono shitsumon wa tobasu ka tsugi no hito ni mawasu'* (If the person our Japanese teacher chose didn't know (the answer) then the teacher would skip the question or ask the next person). Presumably, in contrast with what she interprets as being the non-Japanese teacher's approach, Kaori maintains that Japanese teachers will nominate a student capable of responding correctly and in doing so, will presumably avoid potential imposition or loss of face to a student who lacks confidence or competence with the material. In the event that a student is unable to answer, Kaori implies that it is standard practice for a Japanese teacher to skip the individual or redirect the question to a different member of the class. In line with Kaori's observations, classroom recordings did in fact demonstrate that the teacher typically responded to student errors not by skipping or redirecting the student, but through techniques such as offering additional instruction or by inviting contributions from other class members. Moreover, the teacher sought confirmation that an understanding of the material had been reached before proceeding with learning activities. The teacher's intentions, while evidently unclear to Kaori, were not to threaten or humiliate the students, but rather to facilitate comprehension as evidenced in the teacher's comment 'If a student doesn't understand I'm going to try different approaches until he gets it. I don't want students leaving the class feeling confused'.

As articulated in the above retrospective feedback, student criticism of classroom practices tended to specifically outline how Japanese teachers conducted classes or interacted with students in order to validate or strengthen arguments. Students' references to an idealised image of the Japanese classroom and the desire for Japanese teaching practices to be upheld intimated that the students at times felt their Japanese identities within the context of the L2 classroom to be under threat. Typically the threat to face associated with unfamiliar teaching practices were expressed by the students through resistance to L2 classroom teaching strategies employed by the teacher during English activities. The following classroom excerpt illustrates a student's resistance to teacher positioning, borne out in part in silence, and more strongly registered in her frustration expressed during the retrospective interview. In the excerpt student Akari is asked to read a series of words she has been able to construct in a word search activity.

[Classroom excerpt 11: The teacher (T) nominates Akari (A) to answer a word search activity while the other students (Ss) observe.]

1T: ((T writes A's name on whiteboard)) <u>How many</u> words did you get?
((looks in A's direction))

2A: (5) (A looks down at her notebook, points while counting words quietly)) Seven ((looks up at T))

3T: (7) ((T nods approval and walks over to A's desk. A leans back and speaks with classmates on her left then right. T looks down at A's word list)) (3) OK (2) ((points at A's answers)) this is <u>not</u> a word (3) ((shakes head)) this is an <u>abbreviation</u> (2) *kore wa KOTOBA JA NAI (1)* ((shakes head)) *hontou wa futatsu no kotoba* (2) P is physical (1) E is education (2) physical education (.) but PE (.) is NOT a word (2) OK 'This isn't a word, this is really TWO words'

4A: (3) ((A looks up at T, nods slowly))

5T: ((T points at next word on A's list)) Ice is OK (3) ((points at next word)) <u>what's that</u>? ((shrugs, makes quizzical facial expression))

6A: (3) ((A tilts head to side, smiles uncertainly))

7T: (2) ((T points at word again, looks at A)) <u>WHAT'S that</u>↲ (3) ((shrugs animatedly))

8A: (3) ((A answers in a small voice)) Sit ((looks down))

9T: SIT↲ ((T looks puzzled, looks around classroom and laughs)) (2) how do you <u>spell</u> SIT↲ (.) S-I-T (laughs while looking around at Ss) so that's NO (2) <u>no good</u> (1) ((shakes head, points at word on list)) this is OK (2) ((nods once, points at word)) <u>what's that</u>↲ (1) ACTUS↲ (2) what's actus↲ ((throws arms up in animated gesture)) (2) I don't know (1) ((laughs loudly)) <u>you're just making words up</u> ((laughs animatedly))

10A: (5) ((A looks up at T, then down at desk))

11T: (3) ((T places hands together in prayer position)) Now someone with some REAL words PLEASE ((looks around at Ss))

In the initial stages of the exchange (turn 1 through 3) the teacher asks Akari to indicate how many words she has identified and nods his approval when she announces her total of seven. Akari's total, higher than those of the two students who responded before her, meets with a positive teacher response and indicates to Akari and the observing students that he is pleased with her performance. As opposed to moving on to the next student, in turn 2 the teacher then begins moving towards Akari's desk which suggests that he is not just taking her word for it, but would like to confirm the number of words. Akari appears to be nervous as she can be seen physically leaning back as if to establish some additional distance between herself and the teacher, after which she turns towards the students seated on either side of her and says something inaudible. The students watch on in silence as the teacher, standing directly in front of Akari, leans forward and immediately points out an error, 'This is not a word'. In turn 3 the teacher then appears to make an effort to lessen this threat by providing an explanation in Japanese stating that *'kore wa kotoba ja nai hontou wa futatsu no kotoba'* (This isn't a word, this is really two words). The potential threat to Akari's face is partially diffused when the teacher notes that the next word on her list is permissible, 'Ice is OK'. The respite for Akari is only to be momentary as the teacher again detects and publicly announces an error at a volume clearly audible to the entire class, 'What's that↲' (turn 5). The threat to Akari's face is heightened by the teacher's perplexed tone of voice and exaggerated quizzical expression. Responding with silence and tilting her head in order to express uncertainty, Akari does not try to explain her answer, but rather attempts to defuse the situation and the threat to her face by petitioning the teacher for assistance by tilting her head to the side while smiling apprehensively (turn 6). Failing to recognise or rejecting her call for assistance, the teacher further threatens Akari's face in turn 7 when pointing at her notebook he repeats the question 'What's that?' and thereby indicates that the onus is on Akari whom he now expects to explain her work. Once again the teacher's puzzled demeanour amplifies the threat to Akari's face as it indicates that the answer is not only incorrect, but that the teacher is at a loss as to what the student has intended to communicate and has therefore elected to no longer progress with the activity without adequate clarification. In turn 8, recognising that she is required to verbally defend her work, Akari is left with no other option but to respond and in a small voice announces that the intended word is *'Sit.'* In turn 9, the teacher does not appear to be aware of or concerned about Akari's loss of face and repeats her answer, *'Sit?'* while looking comically puzzled and laughing. The threat is increased when the laughing teacher asks Akari 'How do you spell sit? S-I-T'. Laughing, the teacher looks around at the other students as if to invite them to share in the humour he sees in Akari's response. The teacher proceeds to explain that Akari's spelling is incorrect and therefore the answer is not acceptable. While the next work on Akari's list is correct, the teacher only fleetingly mentions this 'This is OK', before immediately identifying and publicly announcing the next error on her list. As if to illustrate his confusion, the teacher reads the words aloud and in doing so, once again appears to be inviting Akari's classmates to share in what he finds to be amusing at Akari's expense, 'What's that? Actus? What's actus? I don't know' (turn 9). Akari's loss of face and humiliation is complete when the teacher, as if by way of affirming the difficulty he is faced with, dramatically throws his arms up in exasperation while forcefully stating, 'You're just making words up'. Inferring that he has been wasting his time questioning Akari and that he requires help in rectifying the situation the teacher turns his attention back to the task and appeals for assistance by placing his hands in prayer position and imploring the students: 'Now someone with some real words please'.

When reflecting on this classroom exchange during retrospection, Akari indicated the depth of her frustration and humiliation when commenting *'kono sensei hontou ni kirai'* (I really hate this teacher). Akari, reacting to the loss of face that results from the embarrassment she is forced to endure in the presence of classmates, provides insight into the potential repercussions of the above exchange on her attitude towards English activities when she indignantly comments *'eigo o benkyou shitaku nai (…) kono sensei yada'* (I don't want to study English. I don't like this teacher). The comment demonstrates Akari's resistance not only to the teacher, but goes on to fortify this by means of indicating, more generally, that she does not want to study English. Providing insight into her interpretation of the exchange Akari comments *'futsuu ni ienakatta no ka na to omotta (…) kono sensei wa seito no kimochi ga zenzen wakatte nai to omou'* (I wondered why he couldn't just tell me in a normal way. I think that this teacher has no idea about how students feel). This highlights Akari's discomfort with the teacher's line of approach through bringing into focus his non-Japanese status as evidenced in his inability to react in what she views as being a normal *'futsuu'* manner. Akari's reference to the teacher's non-Japanese status implies that she feels there is a cultural gap within the classroom that distances students from the English language activities. In a sense, by focusing on cultural disparities, Akari is able to protect herself from the public loss of face she has endured by implying that it is the teacher who has failed to understand the students. In other words, by drawing on her Japanese identity as a means of rationalising the teacher's confrontational approach Akari is able to distance herself from the loss of face that occurs as a result of the exchange. Reischauer (1981, as cited in Hinenoya & Gatbonton, 2000) characterises Japanese ethnocentrism as a distinction felt by the Japanese that stresses the feelings of uniqueness and separateness from other world societies. Ethnocentrism is defined by Kalin and Berry (1994) as 'the tendency to make "we-they" distinctions, accompanied by a relatively positive evaluation of "we" and a negative evaluation of "they"'. Among other things, this is characterised by 'the tendency to judge others by the standards and values of one's own Group' (1994: 301–302). Japanese ethnocentricity rhetoric conceives the Japanese language as being central to Japanese identity and therein, the learning of English as potentially contaminating this national identity. More recently the potential implications of ethnocentrism on English language education in Japan are brought into focus by Reischauer and Jansen (1988) who state: 'Ridiculous though this may seem, there appears to be a genuine reluctance to have English very well known by many Japanese. Knowing a foreign language too well, it is feared, would erode the uniqueness of the Japanese people' (1988: 392). While the extent to which ethnocentrism is relevant to modern Japan is open to debate, the students' tendency to classify classroom experiences through 'we' Japanese versus 'they' non-Japanese illustrates that there was a perceptible tendency to seek understanding through 'Othering'.

Positive Teacher Feedback Following Correction

A final area of cultural disparity highlighted by the Japanese students as being inconsistent with Japanese classroom practices and a persistent source of teacher/student friction was the teacher's tendency to proffer positive reinforcement following error correction. Students noted that they considered upbeat feedback subsequent to an erroneous response as humiliating and consequently the teacher's approach met with vigorous student resistance. Bringing into focus the teacher's non-Japanese status, student feedback directly pointed to inconsistencies between Japanese/non-Japanese teaching practices and therein evoked alignment to a Japanese identity. While the teacher did not intend or comprehend the negative impact of what he viewed as verbal reassurance, his positive reinforcement was cited as being demeaning with feedback characterised by student Akari's comments *'nan ka yoku imi ga wakaranai shi'* (I didn't really know what he meant by it), and *'mou ochikonjau'* (I felt down) underscoring the sense of student confusion at the pairing of correction with positive feedback. For example, reflecting on a point during which the teacher corrected her answer and then commented, 'Wrong answer but you tried. Good job', Hikari commented: *'hen datta to omou (…) watashi ga machigatta toki sensei wa "good job" to itta (…) okashikatta (…) minna wa watashi no koto o mita'* (I think that was weird. When I made a mistake the teacher said good job. It was strange. Everyone looked at me). Rather than recognising the encouraging trajectory of the teacher's response as supporting her face through acknowledging the effort she has made, Hikari instead focuses on the increased peer attention and by implication, suggests that the teacher's feedback has triggered greater attention to her original error. Accordingly, Hikari's feedback suggests that she rejects the teacher's positive feedback and any face enhancing objectives that it may carry as meaningless.

Providing insight into his line of reasoning regarding corrective feedback the teacher stated, 'Many times the students are afraid of making mistakes. Basically, I deal with this by letting them know that I believe any effort is a good effort. Even if they did make a mistake I would still praise them for trying. Students love praise'. The teacher's comments disclose that he assumes that the students will inherently recognise and respond to praise in a positive way. The teacher attaches a high value to positive feedback as a means of lessening the potential threat to the students face associated with error within the classroom. The implication being here that this positive acknowledgment of effort can productively assist students in dealing with what the teacher assumes to be their fear of making mistakes as the priority attached to praise will compensate for the potential loss of face associated with error correction. Expanding on his approach to positive reinforcement the teacher explained that, 'After they (the students) are done you say, "Good job, that was really good" and encourage them. You praise them so that they look forward to that, to doing it next time'.

While the teacher's positive intentions are genuine, they are misunderstood by student Sayaka who, like her classmates, asserts that his feedback is inappropriate and moreover interpreted as being malicious. Sayaka's line of reasoning is explained when she comments *'jibun ga machigaete tadashii yatsu o itte kureta kara ii to omou kedo yoku dekita tte iwanai hou ga ii to omou (...) sore wa ijiwaru da to omou (...) sensei ga sassa to kotaereba ii'* (When I made a mistake the teacher said the correct [sentence]. I think this is good, but I didn't think he should say good job. I think that's mean. He should just hurry up and give us the answer). As opposed to positive feedback following error correction, Sayaka would prefer that the teacher simply provide the correct response promptly. In this way, the loss of face she associates with her incorrect answer can be interactionally managed by progressing through the lesson. In contrast with Sayaka and her classmates' preference for a prompt resolution through direct correction, the teacher would frequently praise students' effort and would then solicit contributions in order to identify the correct answer. This in turn resulted in frustration such as expressed by student Marin who, when praised for her effort following the correction of a mistake, commented *'shippai shita kara homete hoshiku nai (...) yokei hazukashii'* (I messed-up so I didn't want the teacher to praise me. It's even more embarrassing). Criticism of the teacher's practice of following-up on corrections with positive feedback was echoed by student Risa who after being corrected for incorrectly answering a question regarding the use of the title 'Mr.' remarked, *'"Mr." tte atteru to omotteta kara nande machigatteru to omotte (...) nan ka bikkuri shita (...) sore wa "good job" ja nai yo ne'* (I thought that 'Mr' was correct so I was wondering why it was wrong. I was surprised. [The teacher said] 'Good job' but it wasn't a good job). The teacher's approach to error correction was of importance to the students with their persuasive criticism effectively aligning them with Japanese identities which served as a platform from which to question the teacher's professional competence and intentions. Typically, this was achieved by comparing the non-Japanese teacher and the way he used positive feedback following correction, with the strategies employed by more highly regarded Japanese teachers. For example, Akari commented: *'imi wakaranakatta hen da na to omotta sensei wa yatteru koto ga wakatteru no kana'* (I didn't understand. I thought it was weird. Does the teacher know what he's doing?) and *'nihonjin no sensei wa kotae o wakaru shi setsumei mo dekiru'* (Japanese teachers understand the answers and can explain). In this way, the students' feedback reinforced an awareness of Japanese identity alignment and the assumption that this was not compatible with the practices employed by the non-Japanese teacher.

Student resistance to the teacher's tendency to offer positive feedback following error correction revealed a gap in the teacher and students' interpretation of motivations. From the students' perspective, positive feedback not only failed to restore lost face, but appears to have inadvertently heightened the threat to face by drawing further classroom attention to errors.

This was highlighted in feedback offered by a student Sayaka, in which she commented: *'sore ga gaikoku no yarikata kamo shirenai kedo watashi ni totte mo kurasu no dare ni totte mo imi ga wakaranai'* (It might be the foreign way but it doesn't make sense to me or any other student in this class). When the teacher follows correction with the comment 'Good job' another student, Marin, expressed the view that *'sensei wa machigae o mitsuketa ato ni "yoku yatta" tte homenai hou ga ii (…) kotae ga tadashii toki ni dake "yoku yatta" tte itta hou ga ii (…) machigatta toki wa homete hoshiku nai'* (The teacher shouldn't say 'good job' after finding a mistake. He should only say 'good job' when the answer is correct. I don't want to be praised when I made a mistake). The feedback indicates that Marin, rather than desiring positive teacher feedback in this situation, does not wish to be aligned with a 'good student' identity particularly as she does not feel she deserves this status. In line with Marin's feedback, Ellwood's (2008) examination of classroom identity found that students resisted or rejected student identities they associated with roles that enforced positioning they did not wish to align to. Ellwood noted that students, while appearing to align with the role of 'good student', indexed resistance to aspects of the classroom through criticism of classes and teachers during interviews. This is true of the current study in which students tended to align with teacher expectations during classroom activities, yet used retrospective sessions to signal resistance to imposed identities that they viewed as inappropriate. In the following excerpts (excerpts 12 and 13), the teacher's intention to inspire a sense of accomplishment through the acknowledgement of student effort as opposed to the accuracy of one's contributions, assumes culturally shared values that the students challenge during retrospective feedback.

[Classroom excerpt 12: The teacher (T) directs students (Ss) to construct regular plural nouns corresponding to illustrations. Students Satoko (S) and Hikari (H) are nominated to respond.

1T: ((T holds T/B up facing Ss, points to indicate series of illustrations)) One ((holds up one finger)) (1.) one brush (2) <u>four</u> ((holds up four fingers)) (1) I have (.) <u>four</u> BRUSH::ES:: ((points at second illustration)) (3) your turn ((nods towards S))

2S: ((S looks down at T/B)) (2) I have (2) five pencil cases ((cautiously looks up at T))

3T: ((T nods)) <u>Great</u> (2) alright (2) <u>five</u> pencil cas<u>es</u> ((looks around at Ss)) and (1) <u>number 3</u> (2) WHO can do <u>number 3</u>¿ (5) Hikari ((points towards H, nods, Ss look in H's direction))

4H: ((H looks at T/B)) (5) I have (4) ((small voice)) two glass ((glances up at T))

5T: ((T walks over to H's desk)) (3) Two glass:: (3) ((points at illustration in H's T/B)) five pencil cas<u>es</u> (2) two gla::ss:: ((looks at H, smiles then nods))

6H: (4) ((H looks from T down to T/B, remains silent))

7T: ((T moves hand up and down demonstrating rhythm of syllables)) Five pencil cas::ES:: (3) ((taps hand on desk to demonstrate syllable pattern)) Two glass:::ES (3)

8H: ((H glances up at T, looks down at T/B)) (3) Glass:::es

9T: ((T smiles and nods)) OK (.) two glasses (2) <u>very good</u> (1) <u>very good</u> (.) next (.) number 4

The excerpt begins with the teacher modelling the plural noun form which is the focus of the activity, 'I have four brushes' after which he directs a student to answer question 2, 'Your turn' (turn 1). Stressing the verb form through markedly increasing the volume of his voice, the teacher's scaffolding reduces the likelihood of students responding incorrectly. In this way, it appears that the teacher is aiming to institute a classroom atmosphere in which the students recognise that they are supported and therefore feel confident that they can take part with minimal apprehension. In turn 2, student Satoko's correct response 'I have five pencil cases' suggests that the preliminary modelling has been advantageous and the teacher promptly responds by affirming that her answer is accurate, 'Great' (turn 3). Maintaining the momentum of the activity, the teacher can be seen looking around the classroom so as to nominate the next student while asking 'Who can do number three?' After a brief pause during which none of the students accept the invitation to take part, the teacher nominates student Hikari thereby intimating that he considers her capable of responding. There is a sense of Hikari being thrown into the spotlight as the remaining students can be seen shifting their gaze or adjusting their seating positions in order to better look in her direction.

In turn 4, there is a protracted silence as Hikari pauses before quietly venturing the first part of her response, 'I have', then once again pauses prior to concluding 'two glass'. As opposed to definitively correcting Hikari's answer, the teacher protects her face by electing to present additional scaffolding and therein guide her towards the accurate response. In doing so the teacher repeats Hikari's response 'Two glass', and then contrasts this with the correct response tendered by her classmate, Satoko, in the previous turn 'five pencil cases'. From the teacher's perspective, it appears that this approach is intended to uphold Hikari's face in that it gives her the opportunity to arrive at the correct response and thus demonstrates to her classmates that the teacher assumes she is capable. In the teacher's own words, 'I like to guide the student towards the answer when I can. If it is just a "Yes" or "No" from me the students are going to feel nervous and less likely to try'. When Hikari remains silent (turn 6) the teacher again seeks to reduce the threat to her face when he reasserts his confidence in her ability to identify the answer through again repeating Satoko's response, 'five pencil cases'. At the same time the teacher animatedly moves his hand up and down to mark the syllables, then taps the desk to rhythmically and audibly highlight the plural form. After interpreting Hikari's silence as an indication that she is unable to answer, the teacher brings closure to the exchange by providing the answer, 'two glasses' (turn 7). Hikari, appearing uncomfortable while briefly glancing up at the teacher and then down at her desk, repeats the plural form 'glasses'. The teacher, aware of Hikari's discomfort, repeats the correct response in turn 9 and attempts to dodge further loss of face by smiling, nodding approval, and praising her effort 'very good, very good'.

During retrospection Hikari provided insight into her interpretation of the exchange commenting that, *'nihonjin no senseitachi wa sou iu koto o shinai (...) kono sensei wa takusan no machigae o mitsukete sore kara "very good" tte iu (...) machigae o mitsukete kara "very good" tte iu no wa okashii shi (...) kimochi yoku nai'* (My Japanese teachers don't do things like that. This teacher finds a lot of mistakes and then he says 'very good'. It's strange to find mistakes and then say 'very good'. I don't feel good about it). The loss of face and humiliation Hikari experiences is directly associated with being praised following her incorrect classroom contribution. From Hikari's perspective, the timing of the teacher's positive feedback renders it meaningless and even demeaning as it has come after a classroom correction that has publicly revealed she was unable to respond to the question. Moreover, Hikari's classmate Satoko had been capable of responding to the prior question with what appeared to be relative ease and this had been reinforced by the teacher's modelling of the correct response. As in Satoko's case, Hikari had been specifically nominated by the teacher presumably based on the assumption that she is capable of responding, however unlike her classmate, struggles with the task. For these reasons, the positive reinforcement offered by the teacher, while appearing to be spontaneous and somewhat perfunctory in that the teacher then quickly moves on to the next question, was perceived by the student as being situationally inappropriate and therefore may have compounded the loss of face. Hikari's reference to Japanese teaching practices insinuates that she views her non-Japanese teacher's timing when offering praise as indicating a distinct boundary between the Japanese way and the non-Japanese way of teaching and engaging students.

The teacher's positive reinforcement, while intended as an offer of redress for the potential imposition that students link with correction in the presence of classmates, has in effect amplified rather than alleviated the threat to face. Discord intimates that a lack of cultural uniformity between the discursive function of positive feedback as recognised and internalised by the students and teacher complicated the mutual management of classroom interaction. Resistance to the teacher's positive feedback following error correction is once again evidenced in the following excerpt during which students take part in an activity in which they are provided the answer and instructed to identify the corresponding question.

[Classroom excerpt 13: The teacher (T) asks students Ami (A) and Mimi (M) to identify answers to an activity while students (Ss) observe.]

1T: ((T holds up W/B, moves to centre of classroom)) Number 1 (.) how do you spell PEN¿ (2) is the *shitsumon ne* 'the questions, right!' (1) *kotae wa* 'What's the answer¿' (2) answer is P-E-N (2) how do you spell pen¿ (1) P- E-N (3) ((points to questions in W/B)) number 2¿ ((looks at Ss, nods, gestures with arm extended and palms upward to invite contributions))

2P: (14) ((Ss remain silent, look down at desks, W/Bs, fidget with pencil cases. Some whispering between Ss))

3T: ((T taps on W/B)) What's number 2¿ (2) the answer is pencil (3) ((mimes drawing a question mark)) question *wa* 'What's the QUESTION¿' (3) ((looks directly at A, nods to invite response))

4A: (4) ((A looks from W/B to T several times, reads in a quiet voice)) How do you (.) spell pencil¿ ((looks up at T))

5T: ((T shakes head from left to right)) NO (2) ((A looks down at desk)) good try though (1) different question (.) different question (3) but it's a good try though (.) good try (2) so let's have a look (nods in direction of M))

6M: (2) ((M looks at T, tilts head to side))

7T: (2) Try ((nods at M, gestures towards her with chin))

The exchange begins with the teacher modelling a correct response in which he begins by addressing potential confusion he foresees with the activity by directly outlining in the L1 Japanese which part of the response constitutes the *'shitsumon'* (question) and which part is the *'kotae'* (answer). In doing so, the teacher claims professional identity through demonstrating that he has the experience to forecast problems he expects the students will face, and the capacity to provide clarification in advance through demonstrating in English and explaining in Japanese. This line of approach pre-empts and resolves the potential threat to the students' face and thus can be interpreted as facilitating greater student participation. The projection of face is not endorsed by the students who maintain an extended silence when pressed by the teacher to attempt question number 2. In turn 3, the teacher again invites student contributions when he repeats the question, 'What's number two?' before reiterating what the expectations of the task are by identifying the answer, 'The answer is "pencil"'. The teacher then draws a large question mark in the air and restates that it is the question that needs to be identified 'question wa' (What's the question?). Nominated by the teacher who nods purposefully in her direction, student Ami appears to hesitate as she looks from her workbook to the teacher several times before quietly responding 'How do you spell pencil?' The teacher reacts definitively and swiftly by shaking his head while stating that the response is incorrect, 'No'. The loss of face on Ami's part is evident as she looks away from the teacher and down at her desk. The teacher, perhaps cognisant of Ami's loss of face, attempts to reduce this threat by noting that he recognises her effort and makes clear to the class that this is highly valued, 'But it's a good try though, good try'. The teacher's positive acknowledgement of Ami's effort does not appear to replace the discomfort she feels, but rather aligns her with a capable student identity that she reveals during retrospection as contributing to her sense of humiliation: 'homete moratte mo sensei ni kouinshou o motanakatta (…) imi nai shi ochikonjau dake (…) kou iu koto o suru no wa sensei toshite ikenai to omou' (Even though the teacher praised me it didn't impress me. It's meaningless and I just felt down. I think it's wrong for the teacher to do this).

Ami's retrospective feedback is defensive and agitated as she emphasises that teacher positive feedback is not going to alter the fact that she is not left with a good impression 'kouinshou o motanakatta' (It didn't impress me). By way of explanation, Ami argues that the positive feedback, rather than enhancing motivation, is viewed as being empty of substance and consequently undermines her face. Ami describes the teacher's approach as being 'ikenai' (not good/wrong) and distinct from what we can assume she views as being situationally appropriate. In concluding, the student intimates that she does not see any potential for modification to classroom practices and consequently must accept, though not necessarily agree with, the teaching practices employed: 'shouganai kamo shirenai' (maybe there is nothing that can be done about it). While Ami does not clarify why nothing can be done, her comparative 'we-they' narrative draws attention to the teacher's non-Japanese status which she implies is culturally incompatible with her expectations as a Japanese student. In this way, Ami claims disparity in what the teacher and Japanese students recognise as being norms of interaction associated with teacher feedback. While cross-cultural variation within the classroom is inevitable, the data illustrates that the teacher's inability to recognise and manage disparities regarding the role and timing of positive feedback left Ami feeling that redressive attempts were *'imi nai'* (meaningless). Potentially of more concern is that Ami's explicit reference to feeling *'ochikonjau'* (feel down/depressed) conveys that the teacher's well-intentioned feedback may negatively threaten her motivation to engage in classroom communication activities and potentially inhibit her ability to take risks when nominated by the teacher to contribute. In this sense, contrary to teacher intentions, verbal positive reinforcement following error appears to compound the loss of face and impact on the students' feelings toward the teacher and English activities.

During retrospection, perceptions of cross-cultural disparity are rationalised by the students through reference to how the teacher's approach to feedback fails to adhere to Japanese classroom practices and in particular, contradicts the way in which their Japanese teachers negotiate correction. At the same time, it is interesting to take into account that the students' reactions to positive teacher feedback following successful classroom contributions were overwhelmingly positive. Verbal reassurance offered in front of classmates was a source of encouragement and favourably received by students as is indicated in student Iori's comment: *'machigae nakute sensei ga yoku yatta tte hometa toki sugoku ureshikatta oo yoku dekitanda na tte kanji'* (When I didn't make a mistake and the teacher praised me and said 'Good job' I felt really reassurance. It's like 'Wow, I did a good job'). Expressing a similar point of view student Sayaka stated: *'kotaetara sensei ni "yoku yatta" tte homerare te sugoku ii kimochi ni natta (…) sensei ga nani mo machigae o mitsukenakatta kara hotto shita'* (When I answered the teacher praised me and said 'good job' and I felt great. The teacher didn't find any mistakes so it was a relief). Student feedback highlighted that the appropriateness and sincerity of the teacher's positive feedback was determined to be based on whether or not it was associated with a correct classroom contribution. In addition to positive feedback, when the teacher offered no response, the students cited his silence as equating to an affirmation of accuracy and thereby a positive evaluation. The students' ability to avoid error, coupled with the public affirmation of accuracy expressed through positive teacher feedback, resulted in a sense of accomplishment and publicly aligns the student with a competent student identity that is clear to the students and their classmates.

Implications: Blocked Japanese Identities

What emerges from the above analysis is that recurring points of disparity in the communicative strategies and practices employed within the classroom associated with classroom correction strategies and teacher feedback following points of correction, interfered with the students' alignment with Japanese identities and led to complex exchanges involving the management of face. In particular, the above practices had an alienating effect on students for the reason that they interfered with their ability to align with Japanese classroom practices and present themselves as competent and participating members of the class. In addition, the teacher's expectation of alignment with unfamiliar practices during L2 activities contributed to student assumptions of conflicting Japanese/non-Japanese identities and prompted students to seek shelter by assuming cultural otherness. In response, the students challenged the appropriateness of these unfamiliar classroom practices during retrospection primarily through describing what they viewed as being the Japanese way of doing things. In addition, students exhibited displays of resistance to teacher alignment with what they viewed as constituting 'non-Japanese' classroom practices through electing not to participate in learning activities. Understated displays of resistance to unfamiliar or objectionable teaching practices, such as those associated with error correction, were demonstrated through gesture and body language. These mild acts of resistance, while at times hidden from the teacher, were ways by which the students flaunted the conventions associated with 'good student' behaviour (Ellwood, 2008) and aligned with Japanese identities to which the teacher could not claim membership. In this way, a unified 'we-Japanese' identity was closely associated with resistance to classroom influences that were viewed as being non-Japanese.

The students' response to unfamiliar classroom practices highlights shared linguistic and cultural identities which are maintained and possibly strengthened through narratives which draw attention to face threats posed by unfamiliar L2 practices and/or classroom expectations encountered when interacting with the teacher. By framing the teacher as the cultural 'other' retrospective insights suggest that the students were distinctly aware of their Japanese identities and felt that specific features of the 'Japanese way' of doing things within the classroom deviated from the non-Japanese teacher's approach. Student opinion highlighted that what was identified by student Sayaka as the teacher's *'nihon rashiku nai'* unJapanese approach to instruction increased student sensitivity to the assumption of competing 'Japanese' and 'non-Japanese' identities. The implication that Japanese identities were under threat and needed to be protected illustrated that the students experienced a degree of friction between the constructs of nationalism and *kokusaika* (internationalisation) within the L2 classroom. Japanese identities were viewed by the students as associated with Japanese culture and values that the teacher could not, for reason of his non-Japanese status, be expected to understand. For the students, this line of reasoning aided in managing loss of face as it allowed them assert group unity, and to make sense of unfamiliar practices employed by the teacher.

Unfamiliar practices associated with classroom correction and feedback were not only viewed as potentially threatening, but also challenged the unity of the student group. For example, reflecting on the practice of having students actively take part in correcting classmates' errors student Iori stated that *'nihonjin no sensei wa watashitachi o chi-mu no you ni tsukuru kedo kono sensei wa hitori ni saseru'* (Japanese teachers make us work as a team but this teacher makes me work alone.). Sayaka spoke of her desire for the teacher to assume an approach that was *'motto nihonjin ni awasete'* (more suited to Japanese) while Marin stated *'minna ga jugyouchu ni kyousou shiteru kimochi ni naritaku nai kara guru-pu de benkyou suru hou ga suki'* (We like to work in a group because we don't like to feel that we are competing during lessons). For the students, the assumption of cultural discrepancies combined with an acute sense of frustration that they felt compelled to align intensified the desire to claim Japanese identities and resist the perceived foreign threat. These attitudes raise questions as to how one's understanding of *kokusaika* can both influence and be influenced by English activities taught by a single non-Japanese teacher who may be incorrectly assumed by students' as the bearer of non-Japanese culture.

In order to protect national identity from foreign influence a number of researchers have argued, as we suggest above, that English language curriculum within Japan, rather than facilitating the promotion of internationalisation, is geared towards instilling a sense of national identity (see Gottlieb, 2005; Hashimoto, 2009, 2011; Liddicoat, 2007; McVeigh, 2004). In other words, a nationalistic agenda is paradoxically being pursued within the classroom under the pretext of internationalisation. Liddicoat (2007) explains Japan's view of *kokusaika* as being motivated by nationalistic motives which focus on English as an instrument for promoting Japanese identity on an international platform. Kubota (1998) makes the interesting point that, 'It appears that *nihonjinron* as cultural nationalism and "English allergy" prevent a spread of English. However, the discourse of *kokusaika* which is closely affiliated with *nihonjinron* clearly represents an ideology that promotes teaching and learning English' (1998: 300–301). Kubota further notes that critics argue the concepts of homogeneity, harmony and groupism promote loyalty to the nation while the assumption of cultural uniqueness serves as 'a convenient excuse to legitimate Japan's position in the event of international political and economic conflicts' (Kubota, 1999: 20–21). In order to advance a distinctive ideological conceptualisation of Japanese identity consistent with the *nihonjinron* theories of Japaneseness English education policy is orientated towards promoting intercultural understanding of Japanese culture

(Liddicoat, 2007: 41). Liddicoat maintains that English communication ability, regarded as vital for expressing Japanese thoughts and values, is motivated by a desire to protect rather than expand cultural boundaries. Concurring with this position, Kawai (2007) argues that English language ability is promoted by the Japanese government as an instrument of internationalisation and serves Japan's national interests as a means by which Japanese people can communicate Japanese culture, values and history to the global community (2007: 49). The use of the term *kokusaika*, described by Hashimoto (2009: 22) as 'the promotion of "Japaneseness"' in the international community' is explained as a position that expresses openness to the world outside Japan in order to protect and promote Japan's uniqueness and national culture. On this argument, *kokusaika,* Japanese identity and patriotism coexist as the English language represents a means by which the Japanese can maintain identity when interacting on a global scale by articulating a Japanese worldview.

Expressing a different view of English and Japanese government policy, Kawai (2007) maintains that English is promoted in Japanese government discourse as a neutral tool of communication detached from cultural and historical contexts. This de-culturalised status effectively removes the sense of threat to Japanese identity associated with the prominent and ever-increasing position that English assumes in Japanese education and everyday life. The Japanese government's focus on English as a de-culturalised tool is viewed by Kawai as a means by which to avoid the assumed threat to Japanese culture.

> Through portraying English as a neutral, international instrument of communication, the Japanese government legitimises its promotion of English language education and its call for the Japanese people to spend time and money on mastering the language. This portrayal provides a way of rationalising the necessity to learn English without national sentiment being threatened, while simultaneously sustaining the dominant position of English. (Kawai, 2007: 50)

Nevertheless, Kawai (2007) argues that the 'public discourse differs from the governmental discourse insofar as English is portrayed not only as a tool but also as a cultural force in accordance with the essentialist view of language' (2007: 49). The researcher maintains that within public discourse, English is perceived as representing the cultures of other nations frequently perceived as being more powerful and influential than Japanese culture. Distinguishing between the government and public stance, Kawai argues that governmental discourse leads to a 'new' type of Japanese nationalism whereas public discourse results in an 'old' type of Japanese nationalism which coexists with the new nationalism. The old nationalism is described as being ethnic nationalism in that the Japanese language is essentialised as the embodiment of Japaneseness. Kawai notes that 'to establish English as an official language of Japan is unacceptable because fluency in Japanese is a potent nationalist symbol, and the Japanese who are fluent in English are therefore perceived as "less Japanese"' (2007: 49). The contentious link between Japanese identity and an international identity is underlined by McVeigh's (2002) argument that *kokusaika* is essentially a cover for nationalism. Given that explicit nationalism is not acceptable on the world stage, McVeigh maintains that internationalism serves as a cover for such sentiments by disguising the dividing and essentialising of people into national groups behind terms such as 'cross-cultural understanding' and 'world peace'. In other words, the construction of a strong Japanese identity is developed through promoting a view of 'non-Japaneseness' which highlights a distinction between Japan and the outside world. In the current study, the students' criticism of the teacher during retrospection illustrates that students regarded their Japanese identities as something which had to be protected from the intrusion of the outside world. Hashimoto's (2011) examination of English activities at the elementary school level in Japan offers insights into the students' mind-set through an examination of English language policy and curriculum implementation. According to Hashimoto:

> Japan's identity has been carefully constructed within geographical and historical boundaries, and the Japanese government is actively seeking to maintain this identity, or seeking to promote Japanese culture and traditions on Japanese terms, by undermining the position of English and refusing to accept the language as a core part of its identity. (Hashimoto, 2011: 181)

This tension between globalisation and a national identity is addressed by Kobayashi (2011) who comments that 'the modern Japanese educational context, which appears to be heading in the direction of globalisation and multiculturalism, never fails to offer conditions that foster Japanese youth's sense of Japaneseness' (2011: 10). In the same vein, Takayama (2008) maintains that 'Japan's cultural marginality relative to the West's has created among many Japanese a pressing need to reaffirm their own cultural uniqueness against the dominant western cultural force and, more specifically, against American cultural encroachment' (2008: 24). With these issues impacting the young student of English, the task of preparing Japanese students to linguistically meet new challenges in English, while at the same time preserving a sense of national identity, represents a significant challenge for educators. *Kokusaika* presents a confusing picture given that on the one hand it is presented as modern, progressive and dynamic, while on the other, it is associated with external pressure to move in a non-Japanese direction. Within the framework of *kokusaika*, Japan and a vaguely defined notion of the outside world are distinguished with the English language viewed both as the primary symbol of the world outside Japan, and as a means by which to understand it. The role of English as a means of communicating Japanese identity is noted by Liddicoat (2007) who argues, as we have indicated, that 'English language communication is constructed as a necessity for representing Japanese thoughts and values in an international area in which Japanese is not a language of international communication' (2007: 37). Reflecting on the view of English policy as divisive, Yoshino (2002) goes so far as to suggest that due to the attention to a discourse of nationalism, English teachers have focused on comparing Japan with Anglo-Saxon English speaking countries and 'have become the reproducers and transmitters of discourses of cultural difference' (2002: 142).

Accordingly, and on these arguments, one of the questions to be asked is how English teaching practices can empower students to embrace global identities while recognising and encouraging the Japanese identities that they bring to the classroom. This is particularly relevant when studying English, as its global status may on some level be perceived by students as working to suppress their native Japanese language and culture. As Kawai (2007) explains:

> English can be empowering when it is used as a common or international language for mutual understanding among people with various linguistic backgrounds. Yet the status enjoyed by English as a medium of international communication can also involve oppressive power relations between those people who acquire English as their first language and those who do not, when so called 'non-native' speakers of English are silenced (or feel silenced) because their English proficiency 'fails' to reach the level of so called 'native' speakers of English. At the same time, overstressing the oppressive dimension of English can end up intensifying parochial linguistic nationalism, for example, through a dichotomy that characterises English as 'their language' and Japanese as 'our language' (the oppressive-empowering dialectic). (Kawai, 2007: 52)

For students the English language classroom can potentially be both an inclusive and an exclusive environment. If students feel threatened this can impact on willingness to engage in classroom oral activities, reduce ability to take risks, and contribute to negative impressions of the teacher. Awareness of these issues requires teacher skill and sensitivity in order to avoid perpetuating rhetoric that assumes Japanese society and language are fundamentally incompatible with non-Japanese cultures. Moreover, students need to be encouraged to recognise that national identity does not have to equate to the rejection of perceived foreign influences. In other words, students and teachers alike need to be taught that successful international communication and cooperation can be achieved through the understanding and expression of both separateness and difference.

9 Teacher Use of L1 Japanese

Overview: L1 in the L2 Classroom

This chapter examines students' management of face at points during English activities when the teacher employed the L1 Japanese to instruct the class. Of interest here is that while retrospective feedback indicated that the use of Japanese at times aided comprehension of instructions and lesson content, students' noted that they felt threatened by the teacher's use of the L1. Among other matters, student objections to the use of Japanese were associated with the assumption that Japanese, when spoken by the teacher, was a response to the mistaken perception that students were experiencing comprehension difficulties. In other words, when the teacher employed Japanese, students interpreted this as an indication that he assumed they were unable to comprehend lesson instructions or content when delivered in English. Confirming the students suspicions, teacher interview feedback such as, 'I use Japanese to cover difficult points that come up during lessons. For the students a little Japanese help can be the difference between understanding and not understanding' underscored that the teacher's use of Japanese was indeed in part motivated by the view that students were struggling with comprehension.

Retrospective feedback draws attention to the students' attentiveness to how Japanese was being used by the teacher, and importantly for the following discussion, how this made them feel and act within the classroom. Interestingly, students indicated a general preference for the teacher to use the L2 English when instructing as he was perceived as being *'motto yasashii'* (kinder), yet at the same time remarked that they viewed the teacher's use of the L1 Japanese as increasing the comprehensibility of lesson content as it was *'wakariyasui'* (easy to understand). For example, on observing a particular point during English activities when the teacher explained in Japanese Fuuka commented, *'eigo de iu yori wakariyasui ka na (…) toki doki eigo de iwarete*

*mo minna "ee?" tte kanji no toki ga aru kara nihongo ni suru to "aa sou iu koto ka"
tte naru'* (I think it's easier to understand than when the teacher says it in
English. Sometimes when we're told in English we're all like, 'Huh?' [But)]
when it's in Japanese it's like, 'Oh, that's what it means'). Similarly, student
Kaori commented, *'sukoshi nihongo ga atta hou ga wakari yasukute ii to omou'*
(I think it's easier to understand if there is some Japanese. I think it's good).
In contrast, Kaori reflected *'sensei ga nihongo de setsumei suru to ijiwaru ku
kikoeru kara iya da'* (I don't like it when the teacher explains in Japanese
because it sounds mean). Retrospective feedback illustrates that the students'
general preference for the teacher to use the L2 was not associated with a
desire to maximise contact with the L2, but rather a desire to avoid being
aligned with a negative student identity. In other words, students' objected
to what was felt to be the implication that they lacked L2 competence,
lacked motivation, or had failed to demonstrate appropriate effort.

While observing recordings of English activities a number of students
objected to the assumption that they were experiencing difficulties and
expressed concern that the teacher was incorrectly underestimating their L2
English proficiency. For example, Ami commented: *'eigo wa sonna ni muzukashiku nai no ni sensei ga nihongo ni yakusu to watashitachi o baka da to omotte
irunda na tte omoete sukoshi kuyashikatta'* (It was kind of frustrating because
the English wasn't that difficult but when the teacher translates into
Japanese I feel like he must think we are stupid). Concurring, Hikari
reflected: *'sensei ga nihongo de hanasu to watashitachi wa rikai shitenainda to
omotte iru no ga wakaru kara sugoku iya da'* (I really don't like it when the
teacher speaks Japanese because I know it means that he thinks we don't
understand). Moreover, student feedback implied that the use of Japanese
during activities did not always serve to clarify content in the way in which
the teacher intended or believed it did. On the contrary, it was noted to give
rise to confusion as illustrated by Iori: *'sensei ga nihongo de setsumei shiyou to
suru to motto konran suru (...) hontou ni mattaku wakaranai'* (It becomes much
more confusing when the teacher tries to explain in Japanese. I really have
no idea [what he is trying to say]). Communicative ambiguity associated
with the use of the L1 not only caused confusion, but negatively affected
students participation in learning activities. Moreover, classroom recordings
reveal that with the teacher determining access and usage of both English
and Japanese in terms of directing students when to speak and monitoring
L1 use, students were restricted in their ability to indicate when L1 support
was or was not required.

In addition to communicative ambiguity stemming from the teacher's
use of the L1, data draws attention to cross-cultural misunderstandings pertaining to the illocutionary force of the teacher's Japanese, which although

unintended, compromised the students' management of face and ability to align with and enact desired identities. In particular, feedback highlighted that the non-conventional use of Japanese and the associated illocutionary force was inconsistent with the communicative strategies they associated with the role of the teacher therefore making it difficult for them to relax. For example, students Sayaka and Fuuka comment: *'sensei no nihongo no hana-shikata ga watashi o fuyukai na kimochi ni saseru'* (The way the teacher speaks Japanese makes me feel uncomfortable) and *'sensei ga nihongo de monogoto o iu to kitsuku te sensei to wa omoenai'* (When the teacher says things in Japanese it sounds so harsh that I can't think of him as the teacher). In addition, Iori's comment that *'sensei toshite no hanashikata ga wakatte nai kara nihongo o tsu-kawanai hou ga ii to omou'* (I think it would be better for him not to use Japanese because he doesn't know how teachers are supposed to talk) illustrates that the teacher's use of Japanese made it difficult for the students to acknowledge his professional identity as it inadvertently disaligned him from communicative expectations associated with the role of the teacher within the context of the classroom. The ramifications are significant as the students at times indicated feeling alienated, humiliated and even confused by the teacher's unfamiliar use of Japanese particularly when appropriate levels of formality were not achieved. Predictably, student feedback illustrates frustration at being viewed by the teacher as struggling with learning activities and a desire to be recognised as productive and proficient members of the class. The students registered their resistance to what they recognised as a negative teacher positioning through their use of language and behaviour detailed in the following discussion.

Notably, while the teacher's use of Japanese was at times threatening for students, the teacher was unaware of this threat to the students' management of face and consequently did not recognise student displays of subtle resistance. On the contrary, the teacher mistakenly assumed that his Japanese aided rapport as it impelled students to acknowledge him as being a 'teacher' as opposed to a 'foreign teacher': 'When I speak in Japanese it's a chance to connect with the students. I'm no longer the scary foreign teacher. For the students it's important to see I'm the same as their Japanese teachers. I feel like the students can move beyond appearances'. In this way, Japanese was exploited by the teacher to establish himself as a member of the group, that being a teacher viewed by the students as being of equal standing to Japanese teachers. At the same time, Japanese was viewed by the teacher as a way by which to claim solidarity with the students through demonstrating familiarity with Japanese life: 'When we talk about everyday things in Japanese they (the students) can see I know about Japanese life. It gives us a connection'. Unintended pragmatic errors are of relevance as the exploration and accounting of student feedback highlights that while the teacher thought he was promoting positive relationships and meaningful learning experiences, his at times pragmatically inappropriate Japanese unintentionally alienated the students. In these cases, L1 instruction adversely impacted on learning activities and disempowered rather than empowered students as captured in Marin's point: *'nihongo no hanashikata wa iya dashi nani ka kikareru to kowai (...) nani o ittara ii noka wakaranai'* (I don't even like the way he speaks Japanese, and when I get asked something it's scary. I don't know what to say). To recap, this chapter explores the students' management of face at points when the non-Japanese teacher's use of Japanese deviates from what the students perceive to be classroom norms. It is here that feedback brings into focus power imbalance associated with the teacher's freedom to access both Japanese and English when interacting with students. By contrast, the teacher places restrictions on the students' language use through maintaining control over if and when the L1 can be employed, the content of exchanges and pairings and groupings. Observations acquired through questionnaire feedback are viewed in order to better understand the teacher's beliefs and practices associated with L1 use in the classroom. Student attitudes towards the teacher's Japanese are examined through attention to the following three themes:

- Japanese intervention and the assumption of student L2 comprehension difficulties.
- Illocutionary force: lexical choices and discourse particles.
- Erroneous and/or ambiguous use of Japanese.

The chapter then examines the students' reaction to the teacher's ability to decide when, and for what purposes, students are permitted to use the L1 and his authority to withhold or offer L1 support. Of relevance here is the teacher's ability to control the flow of information within the classroom which places students in a vulnerable and dependent position.

Teacher View of L1 Use

Within the English language classroom in Japan it is standard for Japanese teachers to engage students in the L1 in order to explicate grammatical structures, while the non-Japanese teachers role is to maximise student exposure to 'real' English (Norman, 2008). In cases in which the teacher has autonomy to determine L1/L2 use, this decision will be influenced by an array of factors including social and cultural standards, the L2 proficiency and age of students, course objectives, the teacher's proficiency in the students' L1, and of course, the orientation of the teacher in terms of his professional position concerning mother tongue use within the classroom. Arguing that training and personal experience are the key factors shaping language teachers L1 attitudes, Mattioli (2004) advocates that 'most teachers tend to have opinions about native language use, depending largely on the way in which they have been trained and, in some cases, on their own language education' (2004: 21).

In regard to our study, the teacher noted using the L1 to translate vocabulary or grammar, check comprehension, and to teach vocabulary or grammar. In addition he indicated the use of the L1 as a means by which to speed-up instruction, explain task requirements, and to communicate and joke with students outside of class time. Offering insight into his professional position he stated: 'I guess I'm basically a believer in using the target language as much as possible. I was trained to use English to teach English because it means that there are more chances for the students to hear and use English'. As to his personal experiences as a language learner, a glimpse is offered in the comment: 'As a kid I was never interested in foreign languages. My real learning only started after coming to Japan when I found I actually needed to speak Japanese to get by. The places I did my learning were supermarkets, bus stops, taxis. Mixing with Japanese people doing daily things'. The teacher stated that within the L2 classroom he regards Japanese as a useful tool for overcoming student comprehension difficulties, however this is only after alternative approaches to promoting understanding have been exhausted: 'I try to explain in three or four different ways and demonstrate, but if they still don't understand then I explain in Japanese'. At the same time, he expressed the view that it is 'not good for students to be using Japanese' as it effectively 'defeats the purpose of the English class'. The teacher indicated that his L1 expectations are made clear at the beginning of the course and reinforced throughout. In order to foster use of the L2 the teacher further noted teaching students 'strategies to help them communicate when they don't have the level of English they need'.

The teacher's use of Japanese in aiding comprehension finds support in Krieger's (2005) work with Japanese students which argues that when students share a common language 'the teacher can exploit the linguistic homogeneity of the students as a valuable resource' (2005: 14). The point being that as a key linguistic resource the L1 can be utilised in controlled, pedagogically appropriate and concrete ways such as in comparing and contrasting L1 and L2 forms, explaining complex structures, clarifying and testing comprehension and classroom management. Rolin-Ianziti and Varshney (2008), drawing from Ellis (1988, 1994) found that teachers reasons for using the L1 include; (a) teaching the TL such as explaining grammatical structures and vocabulary, (b) organisation and management of classroom events such as providing procedural instructions, and (c) to negotiate affective aspects of classroom interaction with the students such as indexing empathy or alleviating anxiety. Moreover, the researchers' quantitative analysis found that the vast majority of students felt that the L1 facilitated their understanding and memorisation of vocabulary and the comprehension of grammatical explanations. In addition to serving pedagogical purposes, the teacher in our study indicated that he felt his ability to use Japanese provided the students with a positive model of a successful language learner and for this reason, enhanced student confidence in their ability to attain L2 competence: 'The students can see that I speak Japanese. I enjoy speaking Japanese. I think it gives them confidence. It shows them that they can learn a different language'. The assumption here being that by employing Japanese the teacher was able to adopt and communicate a stance of empathy or solidarity towards the students through connecting not as a teacher, but as a fellow language learner.

Speaking to his use of Japanese and the assumed repercussions the teacher commented: 'Obviously when you're speaking to them (students) in their own language they're more relaxed' and further explained that: 'It's like a bridge for the students. Gradually I can reduce the time I speak Japanese but it's always good to know it's there when I need to help them understand'. A controlled approach to the L1 as a temporary measure for rendering and enabling the L2 comprehensible finds support from Butzkamm (2003) who argues that 'with growing proficiency in the foreign language, the use of the MT (mother tongue) becomes largely redundant and the FL (foreign language) will stand on its own two feet' (2003: 36). In support of this position, a significant body of research argues that the L1 may indeed provide considerable cognitive rewards as well as serving communicative and social functions within L2 classrooms (see Auerbach, 1993; Butzkamm & Caldwell, 2009; Cook, 1999, 2001; Duff & Polio, 1990; Levine, 2003; Macaro, 2001; Meyer, 2008; Norman, 2008; Polio & Duff, 1994; Rolin-Ianziti & Brownlie, 2002; Turnbull & Arnett, 2002; Turnbull & Dailey-O'Cain, 2009; Wilkerson, 2008). One example of such a study is that of Alegria de la Colina and Del Pilar Garcia Mayo's (2009) examination of low proficiency EFL learners' use of the L1 in order to manage tasks and to discuss grammar and vocabulary during collaborative activities. The researchers found that the L1 provided essential cognitive support which functioned as a cognitive tool by which students could access L2 forms, focus attention, retain semantic meaning and created new meaning in the L2. Similarly, Storch and Wigglesworth's (2003) investigation of students' use of their L1 as a mediating tool in performing complex tasks concluded that the L1 enabled students to analyse language and perform tasks at a higher cognitive level than would be possible in the L2. In sum, benefits associated with the judicious use of the L1 have been found to include lowering the affective filter, making input more comprehensible, connecting with the students' identity, and creating better understand of tasks to ensure successful task completion.

Classroom excerpts in which the teacher's use of Japanese can be observed, together with student retrospective feedback regarding these specific moments, provide insight into the students' interpretations of the teacher's L1 use. Of interest here is that differences regarding interpretations of the same events reveal a gap in perceptions of how L1 use was intended by the teacher and how it was interpreted by the students. So as to understand how Japanese was being used by the teacher we now turn to a discussion of code-switching as practiced by the teacher, and interpreted by the students.

Code-Switching

Classroom recordings illustrate that when instructing the students the teacher would code-switch both isolated words or short phrases and whole clauses. Code-switching, the alternating use of two or more languages, has been defined in a number of ways. Gumperz (1982) refers to code-switching as 'the juxtaposition within the same speech exchange of passages of speech belonging to two different grammatical systems or subsystems' (1982: 59). Another approach is suggested by Cook (2001) who defines code-switching as the process of 'going from one language to the other in mid-speech when both speakers know the same languages' (2001: 83). Woolard (2004) explains code-switching as 'an individual's use of two or more language varieties in the same speech event or exchange' (2004: 73) while Hughes *et al.* (2006) propose that code-switching is the 'use of complete sentences, phrases, and borrowed words from another language' (2006: 8). As defined by Lightbown (2001), code-switching is 'the systematic alternating use of two languages or language varieties within a single conversation or utterance' (2001: 598). While explanations differ, as code-switching requires the speaker to draw from two or more languages, it can be assumed that the speaker has the capacity to select the words or phrases they will use from these languages. This differentiates code-switching from other language interaction phenomena such as lexical borrowing which is the result of lack of lexical terms in the speaker's repertoire. In other words, a speaker who code-switches is assumed to have an adequate assortment of lexical terms and phrases at their disposal and this enables the speaker to shift codes freely in different circumstances and for different reasons.

The difficulty in definitively classifying code-switching derives from the very nature of code-switching itself, which, rather than being made up of unitary and clearly identifiable phenomena, can be understood as part of a continuum. Observing that code-switching is a 'fuzzy-edged concept', Gardner-Chloros (1995) points out that 'the conventional view of code switching implies that speakers make binary choices, operating in one code or the other at any given time, when in fact code switching overlaps with other kinds of bilingual mixture, and the boundaries between them are difficult to establish' (1995: 70). The three main processes through which code-switching is performed are described by Muysken (2000) as: the insertion of material (lexical or entire constituents) from one language into the structure of another language, the alternation between structures from different languages and the congruent lexicalisation of material from different lexical inventories into a shared grammatical structure. Similarly, Poplack's (1980) typological framework identifies three different types of switching: namely tag, intersentential and extrasentential switching. Tag-switching refers to the insertion of a tag phrase from one language into an utterance from another language. As tags are subject to minimal syntactic restrictions, the assumption is that they can readily be inserted at a number of points in a monolingual utterance without violating syntactic rules. Intersentential switching occurs at a clause or sentence boundary where each clause or sentence is in one language or another, while intrasentential switching takes place within the clause or sentence and is therefore considered to be the most complex form of switching. Intrasentential, found within utterances, is thought to involve the greatest syntactic risk as the switching between languages occurs within the clause or sentence boundaries and therefore is avoided by all but the most fluent bilinguals.

For the purpose of the following discussion, code-switching is used as a broad cover term which refers to the alternate use of the target language and the native language. We adopt this rather liberal definition of code-switching for the reason that the nature of the code-switching phenomenon is not our sole interest, as we are more concerned with how the teacher's functional use of code-switching during English activities impacted on the students' management of face and alignment with desired identities. We present examples of switches of isolated words, short phrases and whole clauses, however we focus our attention primarily on the students' pragmatic interpretation of exchanges involving code-switching. The teacher, shining light on his perceptions regarding his linguistic capacity to code-switch remarked: 'I can move from English to Japanese without really thinking about it which helps keep things moving. It makes it more interesting for the students because they understand what's going on'. Intimating that the motivation behind code-switching was in part intuitive he noted 'You get a feel for what students won't understand and I can translate before this becomes a problem'.

Classroom recordings illustrated that whereas single word code-switching often appeared to be spontaneous and comfortable for the teacher, the points during which he attempted more complex translations of whole clauses from English to Japanese were both time consuming and awkward. The teacher visibly struggled as he paused frequently during the awkward process of phrasing then re-phrasing variations of the target structures. For the teacher, translation was one of many functions accomplished by code-switching and frequently reformulation was used instead of literal translation. Classroom recordings demonstrated that the teacher primarily translated whole clauses when explaining grammatical structures, items of vocabulary, or Japanese translations of short dialogues from the textbook. Below are two classroom excerpts which illustrate the code-switching practices employed:

[Classroom excerpt 14: The teacher (T) instructs students (Ss) to open their textbooks in order to carry out a short review before continuing with new content.]

(1)   ((T holds up open T/B facing Ss)) Open up guys (.) let's look at the
(2)   textbook (2) ((taps T/B)) we're doing (2) page 10 (2) we're going to
(3)   review PAGE 10 (1) then continue (1) OK ((nods)) (5) ((Ss remain silent, do
(4)   not open T/Bs)) page 10 *wa senshuu yatta kedo* (1) we're going to *sukoshi*
(5)   *fukushuu* (.) *fukushuu ne* then continue to page 11 (1) OK (6) ((Ss open
      T/Bs))
      (a) 'We did page 10 last week but we're going do a short review, review
      right!'
(6)   OK (1) OK ((looks around at Ss)) (2) please listen and repeat (1) *kurikaeshi*
      (repeat) OK ((makes speaking gesture with right hand))

In this excerpt, the teacher instructs the students in English to open their books, and as way of explanation states that, 'we're going to review page 10, then continue' (lines 2 and 3). What follows is a period of student inactivity during which a number of students can be seen looking around at classmates and/or whispering, intimating a degree of uncertainty as to what they are expected to do. After a short pause, the teacher responds to the students' indecision by providing additional instruction in Japanese, *'page 10 wa senshuu yatta kedo* we're going to do *sukoshi fukushuu ne'* (We did page 10 last week but we're going to do a short review, review right!). This additional information communicated in Japanese appears to resolve the indecision as the students can be seen turning to the correct page without delay.

In addition, the teacher's use of Japanese not only serves to reiterate what students are expected open to page 10, but also expands upon the initial English instruction by potentially clearing-up any ambiguity through directly acknowledging that this is work *'senshuu yatta kedo'* that has previously been covered in class last week. In this way the teacher provides greater detail by explaining that the task is intended to serve as a *'sukoshi fukushuu'* (short review). The students, now with what appears to be a clearer understanding of why they are being directed to turn to a completed activity in their textbooks, come across as being confident that they have not misinterpreted the teacher's instructions as they turn their attention to their textbooks.

In comparison to the relative ease with which the teacher appeared to shift between Japanese and English in the above example, points during which he directly code-switched longer sections of lesson material were punctuated by frequent pausing and rephrasing. For example, prior to the following excerpt the teacher had the students read the following dialogue from the textbook aloud:

A: Let's go to the movies on Thursday.
B: I can't. How about Friday?
A: Friday? I'm busy. How about Saturday?
B: I'm free on Saturday. What time?
A: Let's meet at 10 o'clock in the morning.
B: OK. See you then.

When the students completed reading the above dialogue, the teacher proceeded to ask: *'imi wakaru?* Do you understand?' The students did not reply and an awkwardly long silence of approximately 10 seconds ensued during which the students could be seen trying to avoid unwanted attention as they looked down at their desks appearing to shun eye contact with the teacher and classmates. Assuming that silence was an indication that the students had been unable to comprehend the material, the teacher responded by translating the dialogue into Japanese.

[Classroom excerpt 15: The teacher (T) translates dialogue following student (S) silence.]

(1)   ((T looks around at Ss)) *'imi wakaru? Do you understand?'* (10) ((S silence))
(2)   Sunday is (2) *nichiyoubi* (1) *nichiyoubi* ((looks at Ss, then down at T/B))
(3)   (3) *kaimono ikou* (2) *kaimono ikou* (2) *ka* (1) *ikimashou ne* (1) let's go (1)
(4)   *ikimashou* (.) *ne* (2) ((looks around class from left to right, nods several times,
(5)   looks down at T/B)) let's go shopping on Sunday (2) so shopping *kaimono*

(6) *ikimashou* (2) *ka* ((looks at Ss, nods)) OK⸮ ((looks at T/B)) I can't (1)
(7) how about Sunday⸮ (.) I can't (.) *watashi wa muri* (2) *ikanai* (2) yeah⸮ ((nods
(8) in direction of Ss)) (1) *watashi wa ikanai* (.) yeah⸮ ((nods at Ss, looks at
(9) T/B)) (.) how about Monday⸮ *wa* (2) *getsuyoubi* (2) *getsuyoubi iku* (3)
(10) *getsuyoubi ikimasu* (4) *getsuyoubi ikanai* (2) *ne* ((looks up at Ss))
(11) OK⸮ ((smiles and nods))

In this excerpt, representative of many points during the learning activities, the teacher initially attempts to confirm student comprehension by
asking '*imi wakaru⸮* Do you understand⸮' Based on the ensuing silence, the
teacher assumes that the students are not confident with the material and
elects to translate parts of the dialogue. While translating the teacher can
be seen frequently pausing to look in the direction of the students as if seeking to establish whether they have effectively understood his halting and
seemingly tentative translation. For example, when translating 'Let's go'
(line 3) the teacher gives the impression he is uncertain of the appropriate
Japanese verb form as he elects to present the students with several alternatives in which the conjugation of the verb '*iku*' (to go) is varied. The teacher
initially employs the volitional affirmative plain form '*ikou*' which expresses
intention before briefly pausing and adding the question denominator '*ka*'.
Once again the teacher subsequently rephrases to employ the polite volitional form '*ikimashou*' and then, appearing to have settled on this conjugation of the verb, goes on to repeat this form with the additional '*ne*' which
asks or shows agreement and reflection at the end of the phrase and thereby
implies that he is satisfied. In line 5 the teacher again adds the question
denominator '*ka*' and subsequently looks up at the students as if to ascertain
if his Japanese translations have shed light on the exchange by asking 'OK⸮'
Once again, the teacher appears uncertain of the accuracy of the initial
translation and introduces a second option, '*ikanai*' (I won't go), the negative
plain form of the verb 'to go' (iku). This approach is repeated in lines 6 to 8
during which the teacher initially translates '*I can't*' as '*ikanai*' (I won't go),
as opposed to, '*ikenai*' (I can't go). With the addition of '*muri*' (impossible)
the result is that the conjugation of the required verb form as '*muri ikanani*'
conveys the nuance, 'Impossible, I won't go!' and comes across as defiant
and combative.

The strength of the nuance, '*muri ikanani*' (Impossible, I won't go!) is
likely to be confusing and misleading for the students as it comes across as
being inappropriately confrontational, particularly as the tone conveyed by
the original text is a desire to inform and negotiate a mutually convenient
option for both parties. Appearing uncertain with the accuracy of his translation the teacher repeats '*watashi wa ikanai*' (I won't go) before seeking

confirmation from the students by means of asking *'Yeah?'* The invitation for students to confirm understanding is rendered rhetorical when the teacher swiftly moves ahead with the translation. In lines 9 and 10 the teacher again appears uncertain as to how to translate 'How about Monday?' and once again proceeds to base his translation on the verb *'iku'* (to go). The teacher begins by using the affirmative plain form, *'iku'*, however after a brief pause then changes to the polite *'ikimasu'* before then transitioning to the negative plain form *'ikanai'*. Transitioning from the plain form *'iku'* used in casual language, to the *'-masu form'* or 'polite form' and then back to the plain negative indicates that the teacher is uncertain as to how best to convey the intended meaning. After offering this selection of translations the teacher interjects with the particle *'ne'* (line 10) which, when communicated with weak stress, serves as an uncertain particle of confirmation, and then proceeds to bring his translation to a close by turning to the students seeking to confirm if they have understood, 'OK?'

Student Attitudes to Teacher's Japanese

The driving force behind the teacher's use of the L1 during learning activities was the desire to supplement L2 instruction with comprehensible L1 input. In this way, the teacher aimed to build a learning environment in which students were both willing and able to partake: 'I want the students to be able to understand because it gets them involved. If they understand then they start to join in. They feel like getting involved because they see that they can'. In line with teacher intentions, retrospective feedback offered by student Hikari illustrated that L1 support was at times welcomed, and even preferred to a monolingual approach as she felt it assisted her English comprehension and learning: *'un sono hou ga jibun de mo wakaru shi eigo bakkari yori wa unto kantan (…) imi mo wakaru kara oboeyasui to iu ka wakariyasui to omou'* (Well, that way I could even understand by myself, it's much easier than when it is only in English. I could understand the meaning as well so it's easier for me to remember, or rather, I think it's easier to understand). Hikari went on to explain that: *'eigo bakkari da to jibun de rikai dekinai tokoro ga aru kara'* (If it's only in English then there are some parts that I can't understand on my own). This view was shared by student Akari who commented that, *'nihongo de itte kureru to tasukaru'* (It helps me when he says it in Japanese) and *'nihongo wa motto tsuujiru (…) eigo wa anmari wakaranai kara'* (I understand more when it's in Japanese because I don't really understand English). The students' deduction that their understanding of English was aided by means of Japanese support was evidenced during activities such as can be seen in the following excerpt. When the students fail to begin a writing activity as instructed, the teacher employs Japanese to restate his expectations after which the students could be seen commencing the task without delay.

[Classroom excerpt 16: The teacher (T) directs students (Ss) to complete an activity in their workbooks.]

1T: ((T meanders to centre of classroom)) When you finish reading (2) I want you to write your answers in the <u>boxes</u> (6) ((picks-up W/B)) in your <u>workbooks</u> ((replaces W/B on desk, turns and moves to whiteboard, writes 'Activity 5'))

2S: ((S silence)) 8 ((Ss look around at classmates, begin to whisper among themselves))

3T: ((T looks in direction of talking Ss)) <u>Write</u> your answers in the BOX (1) ((points at instructions on whiteboard)) *kotae o <u>waku no naka</u> ni kaite* (2) *waku no NAKA ni kaite*
'Write your answers in the box, write in the box'

4S: ((Ss begin writing in W/Bs))

In turn 1, ascertaining that the students have not fully comprehended the requirements he associates with the instruction to 'Write your answers in the boxes', the teacher proceeds to make available further information by indicating that this task is to be conducted 'In your workbooks'. In addition, visual reinforcement is provided when the teacher picks-up and visibly displays the workbook after which he confirms the precise number of the activity by printing 'Activity 5' on the whiteboard in large lettering. An extended silence followed by whispered exchanges in turn 2 illustrates a persisting sense of student confusion which the teacher resolves by repeating the instruction to 'Write your answers in the box' which he immediately follows with a Japanese translation of the instruction, and to ensure compliance, reiterates the instruction. From the teacher's perspective, the outcome is both rapid and successful as the students can be seen taking up their pencils and filling out the designated area without delay. The support associated with the L1 translation at this point is further confirmed by student Miku who commented: *'nihongo de setsumei shite morau to wakaru kara ureshikatta'* (I was happy because I can understand when he explains in Japanese). For Miku, the inclusion of Japanese L1 support provided clarity, and by implication, reduced the threat to face by enabling her and her classmates to progress with the activity.

In the current observation, what is important to note is that while the use of Japanese tended to be positively received as a means of facilitating comprehension, the greater part of retrospective feedback identified elements of the teacher's Japanese use as inappropriate and causing uneasiness. The resulting threat to student face was evident in the forcefulness of student feedback such as Iori's comment, *'nihongo dato kitsuku te tsuyosugiru kara iya da'* (It's harsh and too strong if it's in Japanese so I don't like it). Reflecting on the teacher's use of Japanese, student Marin commented that it made her feel that she was being negatively appraised by the teacher: *'eigo de dekinai to omotteru'* ([The teacher] thought I couldn't do this in English.). Marin went on to explain commenting, *'nande darou (…) nan ka iya da yo ne (…) nihongo ga kitsui'* (I wonder why. Well, there's just something about it that I don't like. [The teacher's] Japanese is harsh). The retrospective views of students bring into focus the threat to face and highlight the potential difficulties students encounter when attempting to align with a competent student identity given that the teacher's use of Japanese is associated with the assumption of comprehension difficulties. In this sense, while Japanese was viewed by the students' on the one hand as aiding comprehension, students also indicated feeling that L1 support was affronting as it was associated with a negative teacher appraisal of the student and, though unintended by the teacher was employed with illocutionary force viewed as being inappropriate and threatening. Classroom recordings illustrate that the students at times reacted to the teacher's use of Japanese, when interpreted as being threatening, through electing not to participate and openly criticising the teacher during retrospective interviews for among other things, being *'hen'* (strange), *'mezurashii'* (unusual), *'kitsui'* (harsh) and *'tsuyoi'* (strong).

L1 and the Assumption of Comprehension Difficulties

Frequent points during English activities at which the teacher elected to make use of Japanese were predominantly associated with his intuitive perceptions of content difficulty and/or his discernment regarding student L2 proficiency levels. Contesting the teacher's assumptions, student retrospective feedback argued that teacher concern was often unfounded, erroneous and displayed a tendency to underestimate the students' L2 ability. This gap in teacher/student perceptions illustrates that instructional decisions taken in order to intervene or facilitate learning were not always supported by evidence or an accurate reading of the situation. The first two classroom excerpts relate to student loss of face resulting from exchanges during which the teacher assumes failure to comprehend the instructional content of activities and intervenes by providing L1 assistance. Of relevance here is that irrespective of the attempts to claim face through demonstrating command of the English content, students are rendered powerless to contest the teacher's speculation that the lesson content is beyond their L2 capabilities. In the first excerpt the teacher interjects in Japanese when the students remain unresponsive when asked to contribute their interpretations on the target phrase 'Have a snack'.

[Classroom excerpt 17: The teacher (T) employs Japanese when students (Ss) do not provide evidence of comprehension.]

(1)   ((T taps on W/B)) OK (1) number one (2) HAVE a <u>snack</u> (4) what's the meaning‹ (5)

(2)   ((T looks around class)) *dou iu imi‹*
       (a) (What does it mean‹)

(3)   3 (4) ((T transfers weight from left to right in a rocking motion)) Have a <u>snack</u> (2) *dou iu imi‹*. (5) ((S silence, T raises shoulders and looks at Ss)) ANYBODY‹ ((raises shoulders))
       (a) 'What does it mean‹'

(4)   4 ((T looks deliberately from left to right)) (5) Don't know‹ (3) ((walks around classroom)) *TABERU* (3) ((uses hand to gesture eating))
       (a) 'To eat'

(5)   5   *sunakku taberu* (2) *ne* ((T looks around at Ss, nods))
       (a) 'To eat a snack, right!'

(6)   Snack is <u>sunakku</u> (3) *aru* (2) to have (2) to eat (1) <u>*taberu*</u> (2) now you understand ((looks around at Ss)) (2) let's move on ((holds up W/B))

After introducing the target structure, 'Have a snack' (line 1) the teacher moves to involve the students by inviting them to contribute their interpretations, 'What's the meaning‹', and thereby implicitly conveys that he assumes the students have understood the phrase. When the students are unresponsive the teacher appears to make an effort to lessen the threat to face in line 2 by looking around the class while asking the question again, however this time, in Japanese, *'dou iu imi‹'* (What does it mean‹). The students once again remain silent, which prompts the teacher (line 3) to repeat the target structure 'Have a snack' and follow this directly with an invitation for students to contribute *'dou iu imi‹'* (What does it mean‹). When students again fail to respond as he intends, the teacher's discomfort is apparent as he becomes mildly agitated when asking, 'Anybody‹' while animatedly raising his shoulders. The subsequent student silence projects a threat to the teacher's face as it impugns his ability to engage the class as he intends. Shifting his approach, the teacher interprets the lack of responsiveness as equating to a lack of comprehension and modifies his tone of voice after deliberately scanning the class from left to right: 'Don't know?' (line 4). Interpreting the ensuing silence as affirmation that students are uncertain, the teacher seeks to reduce the threat to the students' face by directly providing a Japanese translation of the verb *'taberu'* (to eat). In line 5 the teacher follows this by repeating the central verb phrase *'sunakku taberu ne'* (To eat a snack, right!).

In line 5 the use of the particle *ne* functions to seek assent or confirmation from the students, thereby indicating that the teacher assumes the request for agreement to be perfunctory. Hasegawa (2010) explains that *ne* is said to be employed when 'the speaker assumes that s/he and the addressee have the same status regarding the knowledge of or belief about the piece of information being conveyed' (2010: 73). Hasegawa notes that *ne* is employed when the speaker expects the addressee to be aware of the information being communicated with functions including requests for confirmation and seeking or showing agreement. As such, the particle *ne* reflects the teacher's attitude towards the proposition, that being as a result of his L1 instruction, the students are now expected to understand the meaning of *'have a snack'*. In line 6 the teacher goes on to once again explain each of the components of the sentence by stating that: 'snack is *sunakku, aru* to have, to eat *taberu'* after which he concludes by emphatically stating 'Now you understand'. Appearing confident that his Japanese translation has cleared-up any questions the students might have, the teacher does not seek to confirm student understanding or provide time for student questions, but instead announces that he intends to *'move on'*. In this way it is clear that the teacher feels that he has provided sufficient information and projects his claim for face not by seeking ratification, but by presuming that as a skilled teacher he has achieved his objective.

While the teacher assumed that the students did not understand the target phrase, retrospective feedback provided by student Marin offers an explanation: *'wakatteru tte iitakatta'* (I wanted to say I get it) and explained *'kantan datta kara kikanakatta (...) eigo de iu "snack" wa nihongo de "sunakku" tte iu kara hotondo onaji dakara'* (I didn't ask [the teacher] because it was easy. The word 'snack' in English is said 'sunakku' in Japanese as well so it's basically the same.). Marin's comment illustrates that she regards the L1 support as being unsolicited and unnecessary and wanted to indicate that she understood *'wakatteru'* (I know). In this case the -*iru* placed after the verb in the *te* form is colloquially shortened to just *'ru'* so this is the present progressive *'wakatte iru'* which literally can be translated as 'I am understanding'. The -*te iru* form is employed by Marin to indicate that the information being communicated by the teacher has been understood by her long in advance of the teacher telling her, and by implication, is superfluous and unwelcome.

While Marin is not addressing the teacher directly, her communicative choices nevertheless demonstrate the depth of her frustration as the nuance conveyed is one of dissent and confrontation. Unable to align herself with a competent student identity, Marin takes exception to the assumption that she does not understand the lesson content despite it being within her territory. Accordingly, in framing her response, Marin indicates her objection to the unfavourable teacher positioning through pointing out that the content was *'kantan'* (easy) and did not merit teacher clarification. In addition, Marin questions the teacher's Japanese proficiency and therein expresses doubts regarding his professional credibility when she notes his failure to recognise the katakana rendering of *'sunakku'*. The student's point is valid given that the Japanese word *'sunakku'* is a commonly used loan word that has been integrated into Japanese everyday language. As loan words from English are written in katakana and tend to be closely matched to their original derivatives, she assumes the teacher will be familiar with the vocabulary. The following classroom excerpt provides a further example of a point during English activities when the teacher presumes that students have not been able to understand lesson content and elects to intervene in Japanese.

[Classroom excerpt 18: Students (Ss) repeat a textbook exchange after the teacher (T).]

1T: OK (3) so one more time (2) please <u>listen</u> and <u>repeat</u> (4) let's go to the movies on Thursday ((looks in direction of Ss, cups hand to ear to indicate listening, then moves fingers to gesture speaking))

2S: (4) ((Ss look around at classmates)) Let's go to the movies on Thursday

3T: (2) ((T nods several times, smiles, raises thumb)) I can't (1) how about Friday?

4S: (2) ((Ss look at T and/or T/Bs)) I can't (1) how about Friday?

5T: (2) ((T nods)) Sorry (.) I'm busy (.) is Saturday OK?

6S: (2) Sorry (.) I'm busy (.) is Saturday OK?

7T: (3) ((T nods)) No (.) what about <u>Sunday</u>?

8S: (2) No (.) what about <u>Sunday</u>?

9T: (1) Sure

10S: (1) Sure

11T: (.) Sounds good

12S: (.) Sounds good

13T: (3) ((T points at T/B)) All right (2) from the start (1) let's go to the movies on Thursday ((looks at Ss)) (2) *imi wakaru* ((Ss look down or at classmates)) (3) do you understand? ((T paces around classroom))

14S: (7) ((Ss look around, whisper together))

15T: Let me explain (2) so (.) Thursday is *MOKUYOUBI* (2) *mokuyoubi*
(…) *de* (1) *tsugi wa* (2) *eiga* (1) *eiga* (1) <u>movie</u> *NE*
'Next is *eiga, eiga*. This is movie, right!'

16S: ((Ss whisper with classmates))

17T: (3) *iku¿* (1) *ikanai¿* (1) *IKU DESHOU* ((nods and raises right thumb))
(1) next
'Going¿ Not going¿ Going right!'

18S: ((Ss turn and whisper with classmates))

From turns 1 through 12, the students take part in a group chorus reading
in which they repeat scripted dialogue first read by the teacher line by line. In
turn 1, the teacher begins by directing the class to 'listen and repeat' while at
the same time cupping his hand to his ear (listen) and then moving his fingers
as if speaking (repeat). The students briefly pause and can be seen looking
around at classmates, after which they hesitatingly begin to repeat the first
part of the exchange, 'Let's go to the movies on Thursday'. Responding to the
students' hesitation, the teacher vigorously nods several times, smiles, and
raises his right thumb to confirm that the students have correctly understood
the task expectations before continuing with the dialogue. In turn 4 it is apparent that the students are more confident as they repeat 'I can't how about
Friday¿' without first looking in the direction of classmates for confirmation.
While repeating the remainder of the dialogue, the volume of the students'
collective repetition increases and students can be seen looking in the direction
of the teacher as they competently repeat the exchange. Following the group
drill, the teacher shifts the focus of the activity to an examination of meaning
(turn 13) and directs the students' attention to the first phrase in the exchange,
'Let's go to the movies on Thursday *imi wakaru¿*' (Do you understand¿). The
teacher uses the unconjugated verb form *wakaru* (understand) which implies
familiarity with the students while at the same time reinforcing his status as
the authority within the classroom, and consequently, the person who retains
the position to ask questions. After once again asking in English, 'Do you
understand¿' (turn 13) there is a lengthy pause of approximately 7 seconds
during which the students can be seen uncomfortably looking around at classmates or whispering together. The extended wait implicitly reminds the students that the only person with the power to end this impasse is the teacher.
In this way, then, the potential threat to the students face is ever present in
that the students, many of whom can be seen avoiding eye contact with the
teacher, are liable to be individually nominated to respond to the question.

In turn 15, the teacher appears to have assumed that the students are
struggling with the meaning of the exchange and makes an effort to lessen
the threat to face by initiating a basic translation, 'Let me explain, so,

Thursday is mokuyoubi, mokuyoubi.' The teacher continues by stating *'tsugi wa eiga eiga* movie *ne'* (Next is *eiga, eiga*. This is movie, right!). As seen in excerpt 15, the teacher then goes on to conjugate the verb 'to go' using the affirmative plain form *'iku'* before transitioning to the negative plain form *'ikanai'*, and then the presumptive polite *'iku deshou'* (Going right!) in which *'deshou'* serves to present the proposition that the addressee will indeed go. This time, the teacher follows by nodding his head and raising his thumb while indicating it is time to move on: *'next'*. In this way, the teacher conveys to the class that he assumes his Japanese translation has bridged the gaps in comprehension, and confident that this does not require confirmation, has decided to proceed with the translation. At this point (turn 18) several students can be seen turning towards classmates and whispering amongst themselves. There is a sense of student vulnerability and powerlessness in turns 16 and 18 when the students seen to be quietly whispering with classmates, appear reluctant or unable to identify acceptable response strategies to directly express themselves. The subtle act of turning to peers, and therefore away from the teacher, insinuates that the students are united by their confusion. As Ellwood (2008) points out, 'resistive acts are often manifested through a flaunting of the conventions of "good student" physical behaviour' (2008: 545). The whispering serves as a mild resistive act in that it implies that the students have taken issue with some element of the translation or approach the teacher has taken. Shedding light on her interpretation of the exchange during retrospection, Fuuka commented: *'minna rikai shiteta no ni sensei ga yakushichatta (…) nani mo wakatte nai to omotteru mitai de youbi nan te youchien no toki ni naratta no ni shikamo sensei no yakushikata wa yoku nakatta (…) "Go" o nihongo de dou ieba ii no ka wakaranakatta'* (We understood but the teacher translated. It's like he thinks that we don't understand anything but we learnt the days of the week in kindergarten. His translation wasn't even good either. He didn't know how to say 'Go' in Japanese).

Paradoxically, Fuuka's feedback reveals that it may actually be the use of Japanese that unintentionally contributes to silencing students as it provides students with no alternative but to align with an unfavourable identity, which in turn assumes comprehension difficulties. Fuuka's reaction underscores that what the teacher views as the use of the L1 to facilitate student comprehension was in fact counterproductive as it was interpreted by Fuuka, and perhaps her classmates, as an indication that her L2 competence was being underestimated. As in the previous excerpt, the teacher's assumption that the students did not understand what appears to be relatively straightforward lesson content, is a positioning Fuuka rejects during retrospection. The threat to the student's face is heightened by the fact that she appears to be uncertain as to how to communicate to the teacher that she has understood the dialogue and does not require a translation. Without having conveyed her comprehension, Fuuka must quietly accept the teacher's evaluation that she requires L1 support in order to understand the content. Signalling her objection to the assumption that she and her classmates are unable to understand the dialogue, Fuuka suggests that the teacher is out of touch as he does not realise that learning the days of the week is content applicable to the level of *'youchien'* (kindergarten). Indeed, it is very common for kindergartens in Japan to have English language activities as part of their curriculum. Programmes frequently rely heavily on singing and chanting activities with the 'Days of the Week' song being a tried and tested favourite. The loss of face on Fuuka's part is expressed when she challenges the teacher's authority and right to be taken seriously by further questioning the integrity of the translation in describing it as being *'yoku nakatta'* (not good). This line of approach, through which Fuuka implies criticism of the teacher's performance through challenging his ability to accurately employ Japanese, is indicative of Fuuka's unhappiness with the teacher, and accordingly may be taken as evidence of Fuuka's interpreting of the above exchange as threatening her, and her classmates face.

Threatening L1 Discursive Force

Undetected by the teacher, student retrospective feedback exposed the discursive force of the teacher's Japanese as a pervasive and ongoing threat to the management of face which left students feeling both slighted and perplexed. While the teacher certainly did not intended or indeed recognise the damaging consequences of his Japanese, limitations in his pragmatic awareness of Japanese were revealed as a source of communication breakdown and more. Of note here is that cross-cultural pragmatic disparity led to a critical student appraisal of the teacher and considerably reduced student verbal contributions during English activities. Reaction to the teacher's use of Japanese is reflected in student Sayaka's comment that: *'sensei ga nihongo de hanasu to sugoku okotta you ni kikoeru kara kowai'* (It's scary because when the teacher speaks in Japanese he comes across as being angry) and Kaori's submission that *'sensei ga motto yasashii hanashikata dattara motto sanka suru kamo shirenai'* (If the teacher said things in a kinder way I would probably join in more). Issues of disparity are brought to the forefront when student reflections are juxtaposed against upbeat teacher observations in which the teacher positively evaluates the impact of his use of Japanese on student classroom performance:

You can really see the students were comfortable with the lesson and could discuss the questions. I used more Japanese today and this was the difference because it gets everyone involved. Especially the students who aren't perhaps as strong can understand. You can see it in their faces. They're more excited about joining in. Definitely not as nervous.

The teacher's assured tone when reflecting on 'when and where' he made use of Japanese affirms that he feels there has been a marked 'difference' between student involvement in today's lesson and the students classroom performance from the previous week. Of note here is that the teacher credits his use of Japanese with inspiring whole class involvement, reducing nerves, facilitating the inclusion of less proficient students, and generating enthusiasm. Contesting these claims, retrospection reveals that while the students show a degree of accommodation towards the teacher's limitations in Japanese, they are less accommodating when these divergences fail to orient to Japanese norms of classroom interaction. In particular, the student's isolated two aspects of the teacher's use of Japanese which they cited as frequently deviating from Japanese pragmatic norms as; (a) erroneous Japanese lexical choices, and (b) unfamiliar use of discourse particles. The implications are significant for as Katagiri (2007) explains, the extensive use of discourse particles is one of the most salient characteristics of spoken Japanese and therefore, a feature of spoken discourse that is ever present. Obligatory to the production of natural speech, discourse particles tend to be attached to the end of phrases and therefore are frequently termed sentence-final particles. While this is indeed the most common position, discourse particles are also found alone, at the beginning or within a phrase. Regardless of position, discourse particles serve multiple social and communicative functions including marking assertions, questions, assent and inhibition.

Apprehension regarding the teacher's lexical choices and use of discourse particles is noteworthy given that while a number of the students felt that the teacher's use of Japanese aided comprehension, this was undermined by a prevailing and intense sense of vulnerability. Accordingly, the students expressed a preference for the teacher to use the L2 as the language of instruction. For example, student Risa comments, *'eigo no toki sensei wa motto yasashiku kikoeru'* (The teacher sounds much nicer when it's in English). In addition, students indicated that the teacher's use of Japanese at times left them feeling alienated, undervalued and unable to claim autonomy and even silenced. For example, student Miu expressed the view that she would take on a non-participatory role and avoid classroom situations that could potentially lead to her drawing unwanted teacher attention in Japanese *'shizuka ni medatanai you ni suru no ga ichiban anzen (...) sou sureba sensei wa nihongo de setsumei shiyou to shinai kara'* (The safest thing to do is to stay quiet and not draw attention to yourself because then the teacher won't start explaining things in Japanese). Similarly, expressing her desire to be engaged in classroom activities yet concern as to what the teacher may say in Japanese student Iori remarked *'nihongo de setsumei suru no ga iya da (...) sanka shitai kedo sensei ga ijiwaru na koto o iu kamo shirenai kara shinpai'* (I don't like it when the teacher explains in Japanese. I want to join in but I'm worried the teacher might say something mean). The conflicted tone of the students' feedback in response to L1 use stands in stark contrast to views expressed by the teacher such as: 'Sometimes I see Japanese as the only way to really connect with students. I don't think that it's ideal for teaching, but it can be the key to getting the students to take the first step. I mean that Japanese breaks down barriers'. As a way of entry into divergent student/teacher views, we examine students' insights into their own attitudes and perceptions of the teacher's L1 use in relation to five short classroom excerpts (excerpts 19–23). These excerpts are dealt with in two sub-categories with the former set focusing on the discursive force of the teacher's L1 lexical choices, and the latter set attending to discursive force as expressed through the teacher's use of Japanese particles.

Discursive impact of lexical decisions

The following excerpts, taken from points during activities identified by students, shed light on pragmatic digressions associated with transfer of expressions from the L1. The excerpts show evidence of the students' resistance to classroom activities when the teacher's use of Japanese is interpreted as alienating and offensive. In the opening excerpt, the teacher attempts to encourage the students to partake in a word search task by emphasising that the vocabulary required is within their L2 range of competence.

[Classroom excerpt 19: The teacher (T) asks students (Ss) to contribute to a word search activity.]

((T strides to centre of classroom, stops, places hands on hips, and looks from left to right at Ss) (5) COME ON you guys (2) come on (4) you KNOW these words (2) these are EASY WORDS (.) you should try (1) eat (.) *wakaru deshou* ((looks from left to right)) (2) *shitteru deshou* (1) ten (.) WAKARU DESHOU (1) *wakaranai* (2) ten *wakaru* YEAH (.) ((nods)) ten *wakaru* (.) *shitteru* (1) ate (.) WAKARU (1) ((nods)) *shitteru* ate (.) I ate pizza (.) SHITTERU ((looks from left to right)) (1) *tabeta* (1) yeah eat (1) read (1) *yomu* (1) SHITTERU (3) WAKARU ... you know these words (2) WAKATTA (1) TRY ((paces around classroom))

The teacher purposefully moves to the centre of the classroom where he then stops, places his hands on his hips, and takes several seconds to slowly scan over the students as his head moves from left to right and back again. Stressing that he expects the students to become verbally involved in the task, the teacher is notably frustrated as he implores the class, 'Come on you guys, come on'. This line of approach emphasises that the teacher is not satisfied with the current level of student participation and therefore feels justified in admonishing the class for failing to contribute in line with his expectations, while at the same time entreating the students to correct their lack of participation by becoming involved. Following a brief pause during which the students remain silent, the teacher asserts his professional status by declaring that he judges the task requirements as being within the students L2 competence, 'you know these words'. This claim is apparent from the teacher's forthright demeanour throughout the excerpt and declaration that he views the vocabulary as essentially 'easy words'. The implication being here that the lack of student involvement is therefore unacceptable as there is no legitimate reason for the students not to take part. As a way of demonstration, the teacher proceeds to methodically identify words from the activity which he believes the students should be familiar with, 'eat', 'ten', 'ate' 'read', punctuating this list with the two commonly used Japanese verbs to describe possessing knowledge, 'wakaru' and 'shitteru' and the modal auxiliary 'deshou'. 'Deshou', while typically used to seek addressee confirmation of speaker's conjecture, is framed as a proposition and indicates that the teacher knows for fact that the students are aware of the vocabulary in question (Hayashi, 2010). The aggressive tone and escalating volume with which the verbs 'wakaru' and 'shiru' are articulated underscores the teacher's frustration, and serves to strengthen the teacher's claims that the vocabulary presented is indisputably familiar to the students. Presenting insight into the effect the teacher's endeavor to promote participation had on her, student Miku commented: 'sensei ga kodomo mitai (...) zutto "anata kore shitteru yo!" "anata kore wakaru yo!" to sakendeta (...) daremo sensei o suki ni naranai to omou (...) uzai kara (...) "damare!" tte iitakatta (...) mochiron iwanakatta kedo' (The teacher acted like a child [...] [He] kept shouting 'You know this, right! You understand this, right!' I don't think anyone is going to like him because he's annoying [...] I wanted to say 'Shut-up!', but of course I didn't.). Taking issue with the teacher's professional behaviour, Miku becomes visibly agitated as she states in no uncertain terms that she feels the teacher is conducting himself in a manner she describes as 'kodomo mitai' (like a child) and is 'uzai' (annoying). The line of questioning threatens the teacher's professional credibility given that if the students are unable to view him in his professional capacity as a teacher, then it is no longer clear what role he does serve. Further undermining the teacher's credibility, Miku draws attention to what she views as being the futility of his approach by noting that it is not only unconstructive, but will also negatively impact his standing with the students who may find him to be *'uzai'* (annoying). Miku makes a point of following-up her condemnation of the teacher by noting that she would like to tell him to *'damare!'* (Shut-up!) yet is cautious to stress that while entertaining this option, she of course did not exhibit such a confrontational line. Miku does not intend to overtly confront the teacher, yet this does not mean that she is without recourse for she explicitly later states that she will no longer be taking part in the speaking activity: *'kaiwa ni hairou tomo shinai'* (I'm not even going to try to join in the conversation). Non-participation allows Miku not only to retain control over her actions, but also to extend a measure of influence over the teacher's ability to manage the activity in the way in which he intends. The implication here being that Miku regards her autonomy as being of higher importance than a potentially negative teacher evaluation. Miku's reaction was shared by a number of her classmates who could be seen expressing subtle forms of resistance such as appearing uninterested, yawning and slouching on desks.

What is of importance to note here is that the teacher does not appear to employ any Japanese word or structure that alone would be considered overtly offensive or threatening. Rather, as Miku indicates, of consequence is the repetitive use of the Japanese verbs *'shiru'* and *'wakaru'* which the student equates to the teacher *'sakendetara'* (shouting). While classroom recordings reveal that the teacher did not appear to be shouting at the students, Miku's feedback serves as a poignant reminder that she is involved in a process of negotiation and renegotiation of face based on developing perceptions of evolving factors and influences associated with the use and interpretation of language. In this sense, the threat to face Miku associates with the teacher's use of the L1, namely repetition of the phrase *'anata kore shitteru yo!' 'anata kore wakaru yo!'* (You know this, right! You understand this, right!) accentuates that the L1, while perceived by the teacher as a tool for generating participation, can inadvertently provoke a defensive student reaction. In short, counter to advocating and facilitating input, this may ultimately lead to students resisting participation.

Commonly used in spoken Japanese, the verb *shiru* can be translated in English as 'to learn/to know/to find out' and the verb *wakaru* as 'to be clear/to be understood/to understand' (Manita & Blagdon, 2010: 21). Expressing the cognitive process of possessing knowledge, the researchers explain that while the two give the impression of being very similar and are frequently employed in similar situations, there are distinct differences. The transitive verb *shiru* expresses the future possession of knowledge and refers to something that the speaker was not conscious of entering his consciousness from outside such through information, experience and learning. *Wakaru*, a potential verb, expresses the notion of something that has become clear in a speaker's mind and 'represents an event that is not controllable by the speaker' (Miura, 1983: 210–211). Sadler (2010) drawing on Kato (2002) explains that 'while both *wakaru* and *shiru* express the possession of information, *wakaru* is associated with the process of acquiring information, while *shiru* is related to the point-in time when the information is acquired' (2002: 112). Stressing that a speakers' lexical choice of *wakaru* or *shiru* is not absolute, Sadler notes that verb selection is 'susceptible to discourse-pragmatic meanings/usages' as they 'are expressions of position and attitude that are relevant both to individual speakers (i.e. subjective uses) and to relational activities among participants (i.e. intersubjective uses)' (2002: 111). On this basis, Sadler proposes that the use of *wakaru* can be understood as experiencer perspective associated with speaker empathy, involvement, directness, and immediacy, whereas the use of *shiru* can be understood as observer perspective associated with features such as speaker detachment and indirectness (2002: 126). On this basis, it is assumed that the speaker will select the appropriate verb based on his attitudes toward the content being communicated and the knowledge base he assumes his interlocutors to have regarding the specific content being addressed.

The potential for miscommunication is evident in the above excerpt during which the teacher exhibits a tendency to use the verbs interchangeably. Addressing this problem, Lee (2006: 196) points out that they are not in fact interchangeable, rather they are dictated by the individual's territory of information. Lee explains that if the speaker does not have access to the hearer's territory of information, it is safer to avoid imposition and threat to face through the form *shitteru* (to know). On the other hand, if the speaker assumes the hearer to be aware of the information being communicated then *wakaru* (to understand) in an interrogative sentence structure is the appropriate form (2006: 201). Based on Lee's argument, if the teacher assumes that the information he has requested is within the students territory, *wakaru* would be the most appropriate choice; if, however, the teacher does not assume that the students have this information, *shitteru* would be more appropriate. As the speaker has the ability to manipulate the territory boundary through verb selection, the students will assume that the teacher's preference reflects his attitudes to whether the requested information is or is not within the students' territory, and moreover, whether he empathises with students or desires to create observer distance.

Given the teacher's Japanese in the above excerpt and throughout the recordings does not follow a discernible pattern in regard to *wakaru* and *shiru*, Miku indicates feeling resentful as expressed in her stinging response: *'damare!' 'tte iitakatta'* (I wanted to say 'Shut-up!'). In this case, the teacher's departure from expected Japanese pragmatic norms influences the students' ability to uphold face as it contradicts student assumptions regarding the role and rank of the teacher, therein the students' facility to position themselves in the customary student role. The bearing of pragmatic inconsistency on classroom communication is well expressed by LoCastro (2003: 231) who makes the point that, 'grammatical errors made by a NNS may be forgiven, attributed to a low proficiency in the target language. However, pragmatic failure is less frequently explained away'. Miku's reaction indicates that she has not made special allowances for digressions in the pragmatic force of the teacher's Japanese based on his non-Japanese status or views of his Japanese aptitude. As the teacher's use of *wakaru* and *shiru* is not recognised as an error in grammar, it is understandable that Miku's attention is fixed on the content of what is being communicated which she assumes to be controlled and deliberate. In the following excerpt the teacher moves among students checking responses to a homework activity.

[Classroom excerpt 20: The teacher (T) moves among the students (Ss) stopping to check Marin (M) and Risa's (R) homework.]

1T: Homework everyone ((T moves to centre of classroom, looks around at Ss)) (3) books (6) ((Ss take out books, confer with classmates. T moves over to M's desk. M glances up at T several times, then quickly looks away. T leans forward)) HOMEWORK (2) did you do your homework‽ ((M looks at T, leans back))

2M: (2) U::n:: (nods) yes ((M places hand on her homework, lifts book up)) 'Yes'

3T: (3) ((T takes W/B, corrects with red pen, nods, and places on M's desk)) (3) ((moves to next student)) Good job ((R glances up at T then down at W/B)) (4) homework (3) did you do your homework‽ ((looks down at R's W/B)) ((2)) no homework here ((raises eyebrows))

4R: (3) ((R slowly looks up at T, smiles and tilts head)) (2) *hai* (3) ((looks down)) *wakaranakatta* ((shuffles papers)) 'Yes. I didn't understand'

5T: (4) ((R looks up, T mimics R's tone of voice and tilts head)) *wakaranakatta‽* (2) ((R smiles)) *nande‽* ((R appears surprised, raises eyebrows, looks down)) 'You didn't understand. Why‽'

6R: (5) ((R looks away from T in direction of classmates))

7T: ((T looks at R and shrugs)) (2) *wakaranakatta‽* (2) ((leans forward over desk to look at R's W/B)) *nande‽*

8R: (3) ((R looks in direction of classmates and laughs uneasily))

9T: (2) ((T shrugs, moves away while shaking head))

In turn 1 the teacher's instruction 'Homework everyone. Books!' results in a rapid shift as the calm and composed classroom atmosphere gives way to rapid activity during which students can be observed taking out books, flipping through pages and hastily conferring with classmates. In the hustle of activity the teacher moves from the centre of the classroom directly towards visibly nervous student Marin's desk. Marin can be seen furtively glancing up at the teacher several times before shifting her line of gaze away from the teacher in the direction of a classmate. The teacher, standing directly in front of Marin, reacts to her avoidance and detached manner by imposingly leaning forward over her desk and directly asking 'Homework, did you do your homework?' The physical proximity appears to make Marin uncomfortable which she addresses by leaning back on her chair while at the same time confirming *'Un'* (Yes) which she follows with 'Yes'. Anticipating that the teacher will want evidence that the activity has been completed, Marin looks down at her desk, places her hand on her workbook, and then lifts it up slightly. The teacher takes the workbook, corrects the homework, and indicates that he is satisfied with a crisp nod before placing it on Marin's desk and moving in the direction of the next student while offering a belated and seemingly perfunctory 'Good job'. Student, Risa appears anxious as she glances up and then down at her workbook as the teacher once again seeks verification as to whether the homework activity has been completed: 'Did you do your homework?', before observing that there is 'no homework here'. In turn 4, Risa appears tense as she cautiously raises her eyes to meet the teacher's before pausing, and then indicating that she has not finished the homework *'hai'* (Yes). Risa then breaks eye contact with the teacher and looks down at her desk while by way of explanation stating that she did not understsand, *'wakaranakatta'* and then proceeds to uneasily shuffle her notes. By announcing that she has not understood the homework, *'wakaranakatta'* (I didn't understand it), as opposed to *'yaranakatta'* (I didn't do it), Risa is projecting a claim for face in the sense that while unable to complete the task, she has nonetheless attempted to do the homework activity. This is made clear, and thereby her loss of face is foregrounded when Risa, upon viewing this excerpt states: *'sensei wa watashi ga nani mo shinakatta mitai na kanji de itta kara hazukashikatta'* (I felt embarrassed because the teacher made it sound like I didn't do anything). Risa's insight into how the teacher's reaction involves a threat to face in that impugns her ability to demonstrate the effort she has put into the task, brings into focus the fact that she appears to have no recourse other than to quietly accept this critical teacher evaluation.

The threat to face is elevated when the teacher remains in place and silently waits until Risa, conscious that the impasse indicates that the exchange has not been concluded, again looks up at the teacher. The teacher blocks Risa's claim for face in turn 5 by mockingly challenging the credibility of her justification for not having completed the task through mimicking her claim of not having understood, *'wakaranakattaↄ'* (You didn't understandↄ). The teacher's mimicking tone of voice and joking manner appear to be intended to generate a humorous reaction, however there is a striking shift when the teacher follows-up by forcefully indicating that he would like an explanation *'nandeↄ'* (Whyↄ). Risa's stunned facial expression, concomitant body language, and refocusing of her gaze away from the teacher and down at her desk expose her discomfort with the situation. The teacher's line of questioning implies criticism of Risa's effort through declaring, in the presence of her peers, that the task should have been within her L2 field of knowledge. As he does not appear to regard the task as being overly complex, the teacher arguably feels justified in pressing Risa for an explanation which he does again in turn 7 asks, *'wakaranakattaↄ nandeↄ'* (You didn't understandↄ Whyↄ). Perhaps threatened by the teacher's continued attention, the public nature of the exchange and the fact that the teacher appears to be intent on obtaining some kind of account, Risa appears to be at a loss as to how to respond. She registers her embarrassment and subtle resistance to the teacher's demand for an explanation, by turning in the direction of her peers, smiling and uneasily laughing (turn 8). In contrast to Risa's attempt to diffuse the situation, the teacher becomes progressively agitated by what he views as Risa's attempt to laugh at the situation and makes the point that he is not impressed by irritably shrugging, turning and moving away while shaking his head.

While Risa can be observed laughing at the situation, it is also clear that she has lost face through this incident, as her inability to finish the task has been humiliatingly and highly visibly interpreted as constituting a lack of effort: *'kowai to omotta (…) mou chotto yasashiku oshieta hou ga ii kana (…) yasashiku shite hoshii'* (I thought he was scary. I think it would be better if he taught us in a kinder way. I want him to be kind). The force of the Japanese appears to have impacted on the student's view of the teacher, however her disapproval is tempered by criticism punctuated with the doubt marker, *'kana'*. The use of the *kana* form implies Risa's uncertainty regarding the accuracy of her suggestion and consequently frames her approach as critical, without directly going so far as to state that the teacher's *'less-kind'* approach to instruction is incorrect. The doubt marker is self-addressed and does not seek or require confirmation, yet moderates the assertiveness of the claims. Matsugu's (2005) examination of *kana* observes that among other things, Japanese speakers systematically employ *kana* 'to downplay their previous statements or to reduce the force with which they assert thoughts such as disagreement' and therein mitigate preceding information presented at the sentence level, and thoughts either directly or indirectly advanced earlier (2005: 429). Risa's mitigated criticism denotes a reluctance to criticise the teacher by framing her thoughts merely as constituting a suggestion and thereby does not directly challenge the status of the teacher. Nevertheless, this mild form of resistance illustrates Risa's desire to evade an imposed identity she views as being associated with a poor student performance.

Discursive force of discourse particles

The second area of examination to emerge from students' feedback regarding the discursive force of Japanese as employed by the teacher relates to the use of Japanese discourse particles. Referred to by Maynard (1990) as verbal social packaging, Janes (2000) informs that particles demonstrate 'the speaker's involvement in the conversation and his/her concern for and sensitivity towards the needs of the hearer' (1990: 1824). As way of explanation, Janes (2000) found that the use of Japanese particles varies according to the motivation for style shift and the attitude the speaker wishes to convey during interaction. For example, a speaker may elect to give the interlocutor options by using the interactional particle *ne* while at other times seeking distance by using the particle *yo* which functions as an intensifier. Janes found that style shifts motivated by negative politeness are characterised by particles that provide the interlocutor with options, while at other times style shifts appear to be 'motivated by a conflict between the preferred style and the particle chosen' (2000: 1824). On the basis of these findings Janes hypothesises that for the student of Japanese, understanding particles will facilitate one's ability to interpret speaker attitudes, express attitudes appropriately, and avoid cross-cultural misunderstanding (2000: 1850).

The intentional and skilled manipulation of particles is a tool by which Japanese speakers convey meaning, and consequently this same tool when incorrectly applied by a NS teacher can unintentionally align students with identities that they may find objectionable. In short, the use of particles can function to emphasise inferiority and reduce the students' ability to voice their own opinions by assuming or demanding compliance. Whereas the conventional use of Japanese particles by the students embodies assumptions as to status, formality, power and distance, the teacher's tendency to use particles interchangeably and seemingly randomly in both English and Japanese contributed to conveying inappropriate linguistic force. While the frequency of the teacher's use of particles is on one level consistent with spoken Japanese (see Maynard, 1990), his unfamiliar selection and application of particles contributed to student feelings of anxiety. Acknowledging the key role discourse particles play in Japanese communication, the subsequent excerpts highlight the potential for socio-pragmatic failure when the teacher's use of particles diverges from the students' expectations pertaining to the context of the classroom and respective teacher/student roles.

Classroom recordings demonstrate that the particles *ne, yo* and *deshou* were frequently, almost habitually, added to the end of sentences by the teacher irrespective of whether he was communicating in English or Japanese. In defense of the teacher, it should be noted that omitting discourse particles expressions that are in many cases considered obligatory in interactions, makes utterances less interactive (see Hasegawa, 2010; Katagiri, 2007). Nevertheless, of relevance here is that the teacher's use of Japanese particles, while appearing to be random and non-confrontational, was repeatedly identified in student retrospection with the loss of face. In short, unbeknownst to the teacher, his inadvertent deviation from Japanese linguistics practices impacted classroom rank, roles and practices. The point here being that there was a direct bearing on student attitudes which negatively filtered through to classroom participation. In the first excerpt the students take part in a pair work exchange with the teacher during which the teacher points out classroom objects and directs students to identify the corresponding English word.

[Classroom excerpt 21: The teacher (T) asks Marin (M) to identify the English names of specific objects.]

1T: ((T points to clock)) What is THIS¿
2M: (2) ((M looks in direction of classroom clock)) It's a clock ((looks up at T))
3T: (2) ((T nods, then points at bookcase)) What is this¿
4M: (3) ((M looks in direction of bookcase)) It's a <u>bookcase</u> ((looks at T))
5T: ((T looks around classroom)) (5) ((points to exposed beam in classroom ceiling)) What is this¿
6M: (6) ((M remains silent, looks around at classmates))
7T: ((T points at beam then M)) <u>What's this¿</u>
8M: ((M looks up at T)) (6) Wood ((glances at classmates))
9T: (2) <u>No</u> (1) ((T shakes head, looks up at ceiling)) <u>What's this¿</u> ((points at beam))
10M: (5) ((M looks down at desk and in soft voice)) Tree
11T: <u>NO</u> (2) what is THIS¿ ((T shakes head, points at beam)) (2) because <u>everything is wood</u> *NE* (2) it's <u>not</u> wood *DESHOU* (1) NOT TREE *DESHOU* (2) it is wood (.) *kedo* ((points towards classroom door)) it's a door *deshou* (1) so what is this¿ (2) what is this¿ *NE* (2) do you

know‹ (3) <u>you don't know *ne*</u> (.) this is a BEAM *deshou* (1) B-E-A-M
(1) *NE*

12M: ((M nods. T turns, meanders to front of classroom. M raises
eyebrows, shrugs in direction of classmates. M mimics T by
pointing at beam while silently mouthing 'B-E-A-M *NE'*. Ss smile
and stifle laughter.))

Asked 'What is this‹' student Marin appears to be well within her area of
knowledge as she fixes her gaze on the object being referred to and responds
in a assured voice 'It's a clock' (turn 2). Marin's confidence is proven to be
warranted when the teacher crisply nods confirmation, then swiftly identifies the next classroom object again asking 'What is this‹' Once more Marin
is able to identify the object 'It's a bookcase' and is poised as she looks directly
at the teacher and waits for confirmation (turn 4). Accuracy is verified when
the teacher proceeds to look around the classroom in order to identify a further classroom item. In search of a greater challenge the teacher takes several
seconds to identify a classroom object and settles on what appears to be a
particularly obscure choice, an exposed ceiling beam. Marin is hesitant as she
takes some time to ponder the object before responding 'wood' in a softly
spoken and barely audible voice (turn 8). The teacher rejects the response by
stating 'No' (turn 9), and then, without providing any additional instruction
that may assist, immediately asks Marin to identify the object 'What's this‹'
The transformation is rapid as Marin, now appearing self-conscious and
uncertain, pauses as she shifts her gaze away from the teacher and down at
her desk as she whispers 'tree' (turn 10). The threat to Marin's face is amplified when the teacher again rejects her attempted response with a clear-cut
'No', then as opposed to providing the answer he requires, proceeds to explain
why Marin's choice of wood and tree do not qualify as being correct 'It's not
wood *deshou* (right) not tree *deshou* (right) it is wood *kedo* (but) (pointing at
wooden classroom door) it's a door *deshou* (right!)'. In this rationalisation, the
teacher attempts to clarify by guiding the student's attention in the direction
of the classroom door in order to stress that it is neither referred to as 'wood'
nor 'tree', but a 'door'. Along these lines, the teacher concludes his turn by
forcefully stating that 'This is a beam *deshou* (right) B-E-A-M *ne* (right!)' (turn
11). Marin nods to express comprehension (turn 12), yet once the teacher
turns, can be observed looking over at her classmates and comically raising
her eyebrows, shrugging, and silently mimicking the teacher talking. Marin's
classmates appear to empathise with her amusing display of confusion and
can be seen smiling and stifling laughter as they watch her comical performance. This interplay, reserved exclusively for the students, establishes
boundaries between the students and the teacher through the indexing of the

inner-group *uchi*, and outer-group *soto*, positioning. The *uchi-soto* distinction Marin draws ridicules the teacher and therein enables her to mitigate loss of face through invoking intimacy with her classmates while simultaneously accentuating that the teacher does not share this affiliation.

Following routine classroom vocabulary 'clock' and 'bookcase', the teacher's unusual choice of the somewhat obscure term 'beam' was noted by student Marin who commented: *'nihongo de nani ka mo shiranai no ni'* (I didn't even know what it is in Japanese) and further remarked *'beam deshou!' 'beam deshou!' 'beam ne!' 'no iikata ga kirai (…) nan ka uzai'* (I didn't like the way he said 'It's beam, right!', 'It's beam, right!', 'It's beam, right!' Well, it's annoying [the way the teacher says it]). Revealing that she assumed the teacher's motivations may not necessarily have been positive, Marin speculates: *'nantonaku muzukashii no o tokidoki dashitai mitai (…) machigaete hoshii mitai'* (It's kind of like he sometimes wants to give us a difficult question. It's like he wants us to make a mistake). In the above excerpt the threat to Marin's face is increased by the teacher's excessive use of discourse particles *'deshou'* and *'ne'* as they delineate boundaries in terms of both classroom status and subject knowledge implying that the teacher's line of reasoning is not only clear, but should also be evident to Marin. The particle *ne* can be regarded as a particle of confirmation and shared knowledge and therefore presupposing that information falls within the addressee's, in this case the student's territory (see Hasegawa, 2010; Janes, 2000; Kamio, 1994; Katagiri, 2007). The particle serves as a request for confirmation or agreement (Makino & Tsutsui, 1986) and consequently irrespective of whether Marin has or has not understood the teacher's explanation, she is compelled to express her agreement and acceptance as to how wood, tree and beam have been differentiated.

Uncertainty regarding the teacher's use of Japanese discourse particles and the suggestion that the use of *yo, ne* and *deshou* was not only unconventional, but also represented a threat to face was evident in student Akari's comment: *'sensei ga yoku nihongo o hanasu toki "deshou" "ne" "yo" tte itte hanashikata ga kitsuku kanjiru'* (When the teacher speaks Japanese he often says *'deshou', 'ne', 'yo'* and the way he says them sounds harsh). The implication being that the teacher's use of particles not only threatens face by conveying that the instructional content should be comprehensible, but also plays a role in the construction of student identities in that it forces students to align with an identity that meets the teacher's expectations rather than the students' needs. As the particle *ne* indicates that the teacher's analysis falls into both teacher and students' territory, it was at times difficult for students to express comprehension difficulties or to seek teacher assistance as is noted in Akari's feedback: *'sensei wa "deshou" toka "ne" o tsukatte atarimae no you ni hanasu kara wakaranakute mo kikenai to omou'* (The teacher uses words like *'deshou'* and *'ne'* and speaks as if it [the answer] is obvious. So even if I don't know I feel like I can't ask). In effect, the students are being told that they should catch on, and therefore to request additional instruction is to publicly indicate one's failure to acquire or perform as expected by the teacher. This is supported by classroom recordings which highlight that the students played the role of the 'good student' when interacting with the teacher by seeking to express comprehension. When the teacher turned away, however, face threat was evident in the student's body language such as overt gestures including the shrugging of shoulders, exaggerated expressions of confusion, and whispering between classmates. The following excerpt in which students practice the present continuous verb form once again illustrates face loss associated with the teacher's use of Japanese particles.

[Classroom excerpt 22: The teacher (T) reviews the present continuous verb form.]

So here we have ((T points at T/B)) (2) have a snack (1) *deshou* (.) exercise *ne* (1) etcetera (1) so number one *ne* (1) have a <u>snack *ne*</u> (1) *sunakku taberu ne* (1) *otoko dakara* HE <u>*deshou*</u> (1) he is have a snack *ja nakute* (1) *suru toki ni wa* (.) ING *ne* (.) ING *yo* (1) he is having (.) having a snack *taberu tabeteru* (1) number two (.) <u>*futari deshou*</u> (1) they (.) *toriaezu* LISTEN CAREFULLY (.) <u>*kore yo*</u>! ((looks around at Ss, nods)

So here we have, 'Have a snack', right 'Exercise' right, etcetera. So number one OK, 'Have a snack' right! 'Have a snack' right! He's male, so it's 'he', right! It's not, 'He is have a snack.' When it's at the time (we add) ING right! I tell you it's ING right! 'He is having, having a snack.' Eat, eating. Number two. There are two (people) right! (Therefore it's) 'they'! For now listen carefully to this! I tell you this is it!

Shifting between Japanese and English, the grammatical focus of the exercise is outlined by the teacher and punctuated throughout with the discourse particles *yo, ne* and *deshou* making it appear he is both assertive and confident. Japanese is used by the teacher to direct the students' attention to the verb form *'taberu'* (to have/to eat) and to the accompanying pronoun 'He': *'otoko dakara* 'he' *deshou'* (He's male, so it's 'He', right!). Claiming status associated with his experience and professional competence, the teacher employs a mix of Japanese and English in order to preempt what he views as potential student confusion with the verb form by demonstrating an incorrect response *'He is have a snack ja nakute'* (It's not, 'He is have a snack'), after which he explains in Japanese that conjugating the verb through adding 'ING' is required when *'suru toki ni wa'* ([the action is performed] at the time).

The teacher concludes by providing an example of a correct response 'He is having, having a snack', classroom recordings illustrate that following the teacher's explanation the students were indeed able to smoothly perform the speaking activity using the present continuous verb form. While the apparent ease with which the students were able to complete the spoken drill illustrates that the teacher's instruction was indeed beneficial in terms of achieving the teaching/learning objectives and facilitating student participation, it is interesting to note that student Miu, while able to complete the task, felt negatively about this exchange. Specifically, Miu noted that the discursive force of the teacher's explanation was threatening and, by implication, overshadowed her feelings of accomplishment at having successfully partaken in the drill. In Miu's words, *'sensei wa kizuite inai no ka yoku wakatte inai no ka (...) okotte iru ka no you ni kikoeru "nantoka ne" to ka "nantoka deshou" un sou iu kotoba zukai'* (I don't know if the teacher hasn't realised or he doesn't know, but it sounds like he's angry or something. Like when he says, 'It's this! It's this, right!' Yeah, words used like that).

Discourse particles *ne* and *yo* appear primarily in spoken Japanese and convey the speaker's position towards the content of the information being communicated as well as the social relationship between the speaker and the hearer (Hasegawa, 2010). While *ne* suggests that interlocutors share common knowledge and agreement, *yo* implies that the addressee may not be aware of some information. Hasegawa explains that *yo* tends to be understood as indicating 'the speaker's assumption that s/he and the addressee possess variant cognitive statuses regarding the information at hand' (2010: 77). In this way, *ne* and *yo* designate different attitudes of the speaker toward the content of an utterance (Katagiri, 2007). Outlining the communicative functions of *ne* and *yo,* Katagiri maintains that while *yo* is used to present information accepted by the speaker, *ne* expresses information that has not yet been thoroughly accepted. Based on this position, *ne* and *yo* indicate the speaker's degree of acceptance/nonacceptance regarding the information expressed and allows the addressee to determine the acceptability of the information presented (2007: 1317). According to Kamio (1994), *ne* is used when the information falls within the addressee's territory whereas *yo* is used when it falls within the speaker's territory. Izuhara (2003) explains *ne* and *yo* as serving to persuade the addressee to accept the same cognitive state as that of the speaker, however points out that this is achieved in different ways. Izuhara clarifies that *yo* has three kinds of usages: (1) to appeal to the listener's perception/recognition and persuade him/her to take an action, (2) to try to correct the listener's perception/recognition, and (3) to urge the listener to accept the speaker's perception/recognition. In all cases, *yo* is employed to modify the addressee's cognition through asserting the speaker's own position.

While discourse particles cannot accurately be defined outside their specific discursive event and context, *yo*, often described as a 'verbal exclamation point', is typically employed to express a strong conviction about something, and for this reason can come across as being confrontational and should accordingly be carefully employed (see Hasegawa, 2010; Izuhara, 2003; Janes, 2000; Katagiri, 2007). In the above excerpt, the use of the particle *yo*, accompanied with falling intonation, intimates authority and a confidence that the position the speaker (in this case the teacher) asserts will bring about compliance from the student. In the retrospective feedback above, it appears that Miu is inclined to believe that the illocutionary force of the teacher's Japanese is unintentional: *'kizuite inai no ka yoku wakatte inai no ka'* (I don't know if the teacher hasn't realised or he doesn't know). Nonetheless, this does not diminish the loss of face she feels or for that matter temper her desire to directly address her concerns during retrospection as she must still deal with the fact that the teacher's Japanese comes across as *'nan ka okotte iru ka no you ni kikoeru'* (It sounds like he's angry or something). The perception of the teacher as being angry, combined with the assumption that student comprehension should be achieved, places the student in a vulnerable and awkward position. While discourse particles are central to dialogue coordination, for Miu, the teacher's unfamiliar use of particles threatens her face in that it has left her feeling reluctant to express comprehension difficulties and therefore less able to proactively request solutions when seeking to negotiate comprehension challenges that occur during English activities. Miu's ability to manage face is compromised by the teacher's failure to uphold social distance associated with her rights as the listener by requiring alignment through his use of particles. The teacher's use of the particles *ne* and *deshou* are once again referred to as threatening by students subsequent to viewing the following short classroom exchange.

[Classroom excerpt 23: Students (Ss) participate in a group spelling task. When Akane (A) is unable to answer Mimi's (M) question the teacher (T) intervenes.]

1M: ((M turns to A seated next to her)) How do you spell watch؟
2A: (4) ((A looks at M, raises eyebrows and tilts head))
3T: (5) ((T looks at A)) (2) *dakara sakki* (.) ABC *hatsuon yatta ne* (2) ((looks around at Ss, extends arms out from body with palms faced upward)) because *moshi* (.) ABC *hatsuon zenbu oboeteru* (1) *nandemo kakeru* (.) you can write any word *DESHOU* (1) so watch *ne* (.) watch (.) W *NE* (.) alright LISTEN *NE* (.) watch *ne* (.) W *deshou* (.) *WAKATTA* ((A looks down at desk))

'How do you spell "watch"? "Watch". That's why we just worked through the pronunciation of the alphabet. Because if you remember the pronunciation of the letters in the alphabet, you can write anything, right! You can write any word! So for "watch", "watch", right! There is a W, right! Alright listen! "Watch", right! There's a W, right! Got it!'

The interactional style conveyed by the teacher implies that the content should be comprehensible and assumes that the class has been incapable of grasping this. Here the teacher's use of *deshou* functions on a discursive level to reinforce the notion that the teacher and students are inherently unequal and that the teacher is the holder of knowledge. The power imbalance threatens the students' face in that the students, while required to take on an active and vocal classroom role, are addressed in a way that makes participation threatening. In addition, the frequent use of particle *ne,* marked with falling intonation, punctuates the teacher's explanation and conveys that he believes that his cognitive stance regarding pronunciation will be shared by the students. Explaining that falling intonation expresses a non-committed assertion, Katagiri (2007) argues that 'the "non-committal assertion" use of "ne" can often make a strong assertion, despite its non-committal nature' due to the suggestion that there is 'an external source of information' (2007: 1322). The point being that the speaker implies a higher authority and therein assumes justification in denying potential challenges to these assertions. Student Akane's candid reflections shed insight into how she felt at the time of the above exchange: *'nande "ne" "ne" "deshou" "deshou" iu no (…) nan ka machigae-chatta kara hazukashikatta'* (Why does he say *'ne' 'ne' 'deshou' 'deshou'* (Right! Right!) Well, I made a mistake so I was embarrassed). As Akane's sense of embarrassment illustrates, the tone of the instruction is interpreted as a criticism, albeit inappropriate, of her failure to spell 'watch'. Identifying the teacher's use of Japanese as a source of friction, Akane further comments, *'sensei no iikata wa kibishisugiru (…) sugoi hen datta'* (The teacher's way of speaking is too harsh. It was really strange.). In this way the teacher's use of Japanese both creates and exposes a gap between his positive intentions to establish a supportive classroom environment, and the atmosphere that is manifested as a result of unintended L1 force brought about in part by the use of discourse particles. Communication breakdown is all the more difficult for the teacher to address given that he assumed the students were empowered and felt valued by the way in which he interacted with them within the classroom: 'It's important being respectful to the student, not looking down on the student or saying "I'm the teacher! You're the students!" but saying that we're two people. Let's communicate on an equal even plane'. The position expressed by the teacher emphasises his desire to communicate on an 'even plane' and perhaps avoid more traditional teacher/student delineations of rank and role. In addition, it is important to note that the teacher did not feel that his L1 use impacted his relationship with the students: 'They know that I can speak Japanese so I don't think it's really an issue to them. I think these days most students kind of expect you to speak Japanese because a lot of foreigners do speak Japanese now. I don't think it changes how they view me as the teacher'.

While the teacher's observations regarding the Japanese proficiency of non-Japanese residents within Japan does to some extent reflect the current climate, the potential for inappropriate use of the L1 to unintentionally convey attitudes that do not accurately reflect those held by the speaker is a source of cross-cultural misunderstanding. As illustrated above, while the teacher did not view his use of Japanese as registering a specific attitude, feedback demonstrated that it frequently distanced students. In particular, intonational patterns and the over-use or inappropriate use of the discourse particles *ne, yo* and *deshou* were interpreted negatively by the students and made it difficult for students and teacher to 'communicate on an equal, even plane'. The cross-cultural conflict pertaining to inappropriate discursive force, while likely the result of the teacher's Japanese limitations rather than a deliberate attempt to offend, is effectively a moot point for the students as the damage is equivalent. In short, the student is left feeling discouraged, embarrassed and reluctant to participate. This is perhaps most clearly reflected in student preferences for the teacher to instruct in English such as shared by student Sayaka: *'nihongo o hanasu to kowaku nacchau (…) wakaranai mama demo ii kara eigo de hanashite hoshii'* (I get scared when he speaks Japanese. I would prefer the teacher to speak in English even if I still don't understand). Of interest here is that the student would rather forgo L1 support and contend with any resulting comprehension difficulties than have to deal with the threat and criticism associated with the teacher's use of Japanese. As such, the feedback draws attention to the potential implications of cross-cultural pragmatic failure on student attitudes and language acquisition.

Ambiguity and Erroneous L1 Practices

The focus of the third area of teacher L1 use centres on the impact of erroneous or ambiguous Japanese lexical choices and the impact on student alignment with positive identities. For example student Ami, in a comment reflective of those contributed by a number of the students questioned: *'nante itterundaro tte wakaranai toki kekkou atte rikai suru no ni kekkou jikan kakaru'* (There were quite a few times I didn't understand what he was saying. It took quite a long time for me to catch on). In this way, feedback illustrated that contrary to the teacher's positive assessment of his L1 support on learning, the inaccurate use of Japanese frequently interfered with comprehension and even undermined student confidence and ability to engage in speaking tasks. In light of the interview data, I argue that the erroneous use of Japanese, while seemingly unknown to the teacher, at times threatened the students' ability to display their L2 competence as they intended to. As a result, students were frequently unable to claim recognition as competent and engaged members of the classroom as the teacher assumed that they had failed to understand content or to comply with his instructions. Moreover, a tendency for students to rely on silence, a trait identified in Nakane's (2003) research into Japanese students' silence and politeness orientations, leads to a positioning by the teacher that appears based primarily on stereotypes rather than an accurate depiction of the students' involvement.

The following excerpt illustrates how the student's reluctance to seek clarification when negotiating the teacher's ambiguous Japanese instructions results in a less competent identity being assigned as the teacher assumes failure to comprehend L2 content. In this way, the student's desire to avoid threatening the teacher's face by concealing confusion effectively upheld the teacher's face at the expense of the student's own desire to maintain face and align with a competent student identity. Furthermore, what appeared to be a lack of engagement resulted in the teacher not only aligning the student with a less capable identity, but more importantly, assuming a general reluctance to comply with instruction. The result being that the student was aligned with a defiant identity as implied in the comment: 'It's very clear when students don't want to join in. I think it's an attitude issue. You have to want to join in but in some cases it doesn't feel like the students are here because they want to be'. Within the following excerpt, the student Shusei appears hesitant to speak out and seek confirmation when the teacher's Japanese instructions fail to accurately express the task requirements.

[Classroom excerpt 24: The teacher (T) asks Shusei (S) to select a number from between 1 and 20 in order to fill out a bingo grid.]

1T: ((T moves around classroom, stops and looks at S's W/B)) Choose a number between 1 and 20 (1) *ichi kara nijuu made* (2) *docchi demo ii yo* ((smiles, nods, hastily steps back toward centre of classroom)) 'From 1 to 20. Either one (of the two) is fine'

2S: (5) ((S looks at T, tilts head to side)) (2) ((leans back))

3T: (6) ((T raises shoulders, moves hastily towards S's desk, leans over desk and points at activity in S's W/B, S looks down)) <u>Between 1 and 20</u> (1) *ichi kara* (.) *nijuu made* (1) <u>*docchi demo ii yo*</u>

'From 1 to 20, either one (of the two) is fine'

4S: (4) ((S looks up at T, tilts head, glances at classmates then looks down at desk)

5T: (3) ((T drums fingers on S's desk loudly, points at W/B)) Write it HERE ((taps S's W/B))

6S: (6) ((S looks down, does not write))

7T: (4) ((T turns and paces to centre of classroom, stops and points at S)) *HAYAKU SHITE* (2) *hayaku shite* 'Do it quickly! Do it quickly!'

8: ((S looks down, Ss begin whispering among themselves))

The exchange commences when the teacher instructs Shusei, described by a classmate as being a *hazukashigariya* (shy person), to 'Choose a number between 1 and 20' in English then Japanese. Giving the appearance that he is confident task requirements have been effectively communicated and understood, the teacher briefly smiles, offers a decisive nod, and then proceeds to take several brisk steps toward the centre of the classroom. The teacher's assumption that the student should now be able to perform the seemingly simple task is challenged when Shusei, rhythmically twirling his pencil in his fingers, silently looks up at the teacher and tilts his head to the side. Having assumed that he has projected uncertainty and registered an appeal for assistance, Shusei proceeds to lean back and wait for teacher intervention. After a short period of indecision (turn 3), the teacher appears confused by Shusei's lack of visible activity and distinctly raises his shoulders after which he swiftly moves in the direction of the student's desk. Shusei's appeal for assistance appears to have gone unnoticed by the teacher who forcefully repeats part of the initial instruction 'between 1 and 20 *ichi kara nijuu made docchi demo ii yo*' (From 1 to 20. Either one [of the two] is fine).

Shusei, given the same directive, remains unable to resolve what is expected and this time, appearing embarrassed, sheepishly looks up at the teacher and tilts his head to once again assert his confusion. Visibly anxious, Shusei turns his line of gaze away from the teacher, glances at his classmates and then looks down at his desk. The threat to Shusei's face is elevated when the teacher, signalling his frustration at what he views to be Shusei's lack of responsiveness, reacts by drumming his fingers rapidly on his desk which he breaks-off by abrasively tapping his index finger on the area in the workbook where the number is to be written: 'Write it here' (turn 5). When this fails to bring about the desired response, the teacher, whose tone of voice again betrays his impatience, twice orders Shusei to complete the task *'hayaku shite hayaku shite'* (Do it quickly! Do it quickly!) The force of the demand implies that the teacher assumes Shusei has been deliberately avoiding participation and therefore he appears to feel it appropriate to align Shusei with a negative, non-participatory identity which requires aggressive intervention in order to negotiate. In turn 8, Shusei retreats by fixing his gaze down at the desk while his classmates, indexing criticism of the teacher's approach, can be observed whispering about the exchange and criticising the teacher at a volume that while hushed, was distinctly audible.

During retrospection, one of Shusei's classmates, Ami, appearing disturbed at the exchange, elected to voice her opposition to the teacher's negative appraisal of Shusei stating:

docchi ga ii tte itteru kara Shusei-kun ga wakaranakatta to omou (…) nani ka kara nani ka no aida de dore ga ii tte kikeba ii kedo kore ka kore docchi da to nan ka hitotsu dake mitai na (…) yoku wakaranai (…) kawaisou datta

I think that Shusei didn't understand because (the teacher) asked, 'docchi?' (= which one of two options). It would be fine if (the teacher) asked 'dore?' (= which one out of a range of numbers) between this and 'that?' But if (the teacher asks) 'docchi?' It's which one, this or that, well, it's like (Shusei had to choose) one (of two options). I felt sorry for him (Shusei)

Ami's feedback highlights the L2 ambiguity of the teacher's instruction and contradicts the implication that Shusei's lack of responsiveness represented inadequate effort or commitment. What is important to note is that the fellow student, while perhaps feeling powerless to support Shusei at the time of the activity, defends him vigorously during the retrospective interview. Determining that the problem is due to the teacher's errant Japanese, Ami points out that the threat to Shusei's face is born from confusion stemming from the incorrect use of the expression *docchi* (which one of two options) as opposed to *dore* (which one among more than three options). It is how many choices the teacher suggests are offered that matters here rather than how many numbers Shusei was supposed to select. The confusion caused by the teacher's (mis)use of *'docchi'* resulted in Shusei's uncertainty as to whether he should choose either the number 1 or 20 given that *docchi* implies two choices are available, or he could pick any number between 1 and 20 given that *dore* implies three choices or more are available. The excerpt illustrates that once the teacher fails to correctly deduce the student's requests for assistance; Shusei effectively has no recourse and is forced to silently accept a negative non-compliant positioning. Although Ami states that she assumes the problem is related to the teacher's Japanese limitations and provides an explanation, this does not excuse the fact that Shusei has been unfairly and inappropriately humiliated. Aligning with her classmate, Ami goes on record during retrospection as sympathising with Shusei's predicament through critically expressing her interpretation of the teacher's conduct when she states: *'kawaisou datta'* (I felt sorry for him).

While the teacher's basic command of Japanese arguably provides Shusei and his classmates with the opportunity to request confirmation in Japanese, retrospection indicates that students at times viewed this as escalating the threat to face. An active concern for the students appears to relate to their identity within the group and a desire not to hold back peers, as is illustrated in feedback such as that offered by student Kaori who commented: *'susumi ga osoku naru kara shitsumon suru no wa yoku nai (…) tada kiiteru dake no hou ga ii'* (It's not good to ask questions because it slows everyone down. It would be better to just listen). The implication being here that an individual request for clarification may draw attention away from the lesson and impede class progress. These findings echo feedback discussed by Murata (2011) in which Japanese students were found to experience greater difficulty than British students when giving opinions and asking questions. Murata noted that while Japanese students recognised asking questions or giving opinions as important, factors such as attention to maintaining public image and consideration for lesson flow and peers were more highly prioritised. Moreover, Murata notes that Japanese students interpret asking questions as depriving 'fellow students of the opportunity to listen to lectures or receive the maximum information available within a designated period' (2011: 15). This position is consistent with Aspinall's (2006) research findings which maintain that one of the primary factors constraining Japanese students in class is an egalitarian approach to education cited as a barrier to fostering able students, as well as inhibiting students with learning difficulties. The basic argument here being that Japanese students consider group needs above those of the individual. While variation in how the group and individual needs are prioritised is inevitable, what is apparent in the above feedback is that student Kaori and a number of her classmates specifically noted they were concerned that seeking the teacher's assistance would interfere with the progress of classmates.

The submission that students felt requests for individual clarification impinged on classmates' access to the teacher were cited in student Sayaka's comment: *'yoku wakaranakatta jugyou no susumi o osoku shitaku nai kara nani mo kikitakunakatta (…) nan ka watashi wa sensei ga itte hoshii koto o iwanakucha ikenai kimochi ni natta (…) mattaku imi ga wakaranakatta'* (I didn't really understand. I didn't want to slow the lesson down so I didn't want to ask [the teacher] anything. I felt like I had to say what the teacher wanted me to say. I didn't have a clue at all). Both Kaori and Sayaka's feedback intimates that the students do not wish to challenge their legitimacy within the group by contradicting acts associated with a 'good classmate' identity. Accordingly, the students have avoided requests for individualised attention and elected to conceal comprehension difficulties in preference to inconveniencing peers or potentially acquiring a negative teacher appraisal. The desire to evade excessive teacher attention, even if this resulted in diminished comprehension, was evidenced in Saori's comment, *'minna imi ga wakannai toki wa tada unazuku dake de nani mo shitsumon shiyou to shinai de tada unazuku dake'* (Everyone just nods and doesn't ask any questions when we don't understand, we just nod). In this way, the class aligned with what they recognised as constituting a 'good student' identity while maintaining face by displaying behaviours they assumed the teacher would associate with a competent student performance.

The above excerpts illustrate that the teacher's assumption that the use of the L1 enables students to overcome comprehension difficulties, may inadvertently force students to play an 'enlightened role' that does not accurately reflect their status in relation to classroom content. Moreover, sensitivity to the teacher's status as the expert within the classroom may at times make it difficult for students to seek clarification, particularly when the teacher is communicating in the L1 and assumes comprehension has been facilitated. In these cases, to indicate confusion can be viewed as inappropriate and as constituting a risk as it ultimately draws attention to the fact that the teacher's L1 explanation has not been satisfactory. The students' apprehension towards seeking additional teacher support when uncertain reinforced that they were acutely conscious of avoiding individualised teacher attention within the L2 classroom. Candid feedback revealed that students' self-preservation of face was closely associated with identifying with the group, even if that meant reconciling oneself to less than perfect comprehension of lesson content. For example, asked whether she considered asking the teacher for assistance when uncertain of task requirements, student Akari commented that she did not because it would be *'mendokusai'* (troublesome) and as way of explanation noted *'zenbu eigo de ie tte iwaresou'* ([The teacher] would probably tell me to say it all in English). These attitudes and beliefs point to the students' desire to avoid imposition and to preserve face, even though students were aware that this would potentially lead to a negative teacher evaluation.

Teacher as Holder of Knowledge

A final area of interest that arises from retrospective feedback regarding the teacher's use of Japanese is the implication that Japanese L1 support was at times viewed by students as being deliberately and unfairly withheld. In other words, as the teacher has a degree of proficiency in Japanese, it was not always clear to the students why he was at times willing to provide L1 support, and yet at other times appeared reluctant to offer L1 instruction particularly when students felt this could facilitate comprehension. Student feedback illustrated that the teacher's tendency to control and dictate the flow of L1 information within the classroom frequently positioned the students as vulnerable, and dependent on Japanese support that was controlled by impulse rather than a discernible pattern. The view that the teacher was at times unnecessarily withholding L1 support was referred to in retrospective feedback such as Hiroki's comment: *'wakannai nara sensei ga mou oshiete hoshii* (...) *itsu made mo kiite nai de'* (If I don't understand, then I want the teacher to tell me, not go on forever asking questions), and Iori's view that, *'zutto kiiteru yori itte kureta hou ga raku da to omou'* (Rather than continually asking I think it's easier to just tell us). Student Miu expressed the sentiment that this was not only deliberate, but cynically mused: *'sensei wa tada ijiwaru suru tame ni nihongo o tsukatte inai you ni kanjiru* (...) *nihongo de hanaseba kantan datte wakaru'* (I feel like the teacher doesn't use Japanese just to be mean to us. We know that it would be easy for us if he spoke in Japanese).

Within the classroom, Chávez (2007) makes the point that 'teacher talk' tends to dominate 'student talk' both in quantity and in quality. Moreover, the teacher tends to have the authority to claim special speaking rights while the students 'adhere to or at least notice as preferred certain language-use practices' (2007: 163). Along these lines, student feedback illustrates that the teacher's ability to withhold or grant comprehension reinforced traditional notions of teacher/student power imbalance through keeping the vulnerability of the students at the forefront. In this way, supported by the order of status and role within the classroom, the teacher used his position to control what was communicated to students and when through a seemingly random approach to L1 support. Apart from being cited by students as arbitrary, the withholding of L1 support drew attention to the students' distinct lack of L2 discursive strategies by which they could actively seek comprehension when L1 support was not forthcoming. Illustrating this sense of powerlessness, student Kotomi commented, *'jibun de eigo o hanasenai kara tada soko de suwatte matsu shika nai'* (I just had to sit there and wait because I don't speak English). The student views are supported by Scott and de la Fuente's (2008) observation that students not permitted to use the L1 during grammar peer activities displayed reduced and fragmented levels of interaction. The researchers theorised that when students were 'forbidden to use the L1, their two languages compete, causing frustration and cognitive strain' (2008: 110). As the teacher was viewed as being capable of speaking a degree of Japanese, when L1 support was not in the offing, students expressed irritation illustrated when student Hikari irritably questioned *'nande eigo dake na no'* (Why only English?). The following exchange was cited by the participating student as a point at which she felt the teacher was inappropriately withholding L1 support.

[Classroom excerpt 25: After the teacher (T) nominates students (Ss) to read a short dialogue Miu (M) consults Risa (R).]

1T: Number 1 ((T points at himself)) (.) number 2 ((points at M)) (.) number 3 ((points at R))

2M: ((M turns and consults R while looking at T/B))

3T: ((T moves over to M)) You are ((points at M's T/B)) yeah (1) you are HERE ((taps fingers on T/B)) this girl (.) OK

4M: ((M turns to R, quietly converses while pointing at T/B)) (6)

5T: ((T begins to read role from T/B)) All right (.) let's go to the museum on Friday (2) ((gestures toward M with hand for her to continue reading))

6M: (2) ((M glances up at T then R)) I can't (.) how about Saturday? ((small voice)) (5) ((looks up at T))

7T: ((T moves over to M's desk)) That's YOU ((taps on T/B))

8M: (2) *KOKO?* ((looks up at T while pointing at text. Ss look over at M))
'Here?'

9T: NO (1) you are this woman (.) *NE* (1) I'm <u>number 1</u> ((points at himself)) (2) <u>you</u> are <u>number 2</u> ((points at M) (.) and you are <u>number 3</u> ((points at R))

10R: (2) ((R reads from T/B)) I'm sorry (.) I'm busy (1) is Sunday OK?

11M: ((Inaudible))

12T: (3) ((T laughs)) NO NO NO (1) try again ((laughs, looks around at Ss and shrugs shoulders))

13M: ((M consults R))

The excerpt illustrates a number of key points in that it highlights the student's struggle to understand task requirements, the teacher's failure to clarify this misunderstanding and the student's reliance on classmate support. In turn 1, the teacher nominates students to take part in a small group reading task. The student, Miu, uncertain as to the role she is to read, consults a classmate sitting next to her while pointing at the dialogue in her textbook (turn 2). In turn 3, the teacher who is in close physical proximity, intervenes by reaffirming the role she is to read, 'Yeah, you are here, this girl.

OK!' However, the teacher's explanation has clearly not abated Miu's uncertainty, and she once again hastily seeks clarification from her classmate in turn 4. The teacher sanctions a short pause during which he flicks through his textbook allowing time for Miu and Risa to confer the task requirements. In turn 5, the teacher, determining that Miu and classmate Risa have had ample time and adequate instruction, initiates the exchange by interjecting 'All right'. In turn 6, while still appearing uncertain, Miu, glances up anxiously at the teacher then across at Risa as she attempts to identify and read her part rather than hold up progression of the activity. After reading (turn 6) and omitting part of the exchange, Miu's face is threatened as an uncomfortable silence envelopes the classroom. Miu's loss of face is compounded when the teacher moves forward in turn 7 and impatiently taps her textbook while stating, 'That's you' indicating that she is yet to finish reading her role and is by implication, responsible for the holdup.

In turn 8, Miu, appearing aggravated at the implication she should have understand the task requirements, looks up directly at the teacher and elects to address the implied criticism through requesting confirmation in Japanese. Her classmates appear caught by surprise and can be observed looking over as Miu, in an unexpectedly loud voice, uses the Japanese demonstrative pronoun *'koko'* (Here?) while pointing at the dialogue in her textbook in an attempt to pinpoint the precise area she is to read. Miu frames the request by omitting the copula *desu* and question denominator *ka*, which presents as informal when interacting with the teacher and implies that he shares responsibility for her inability to take part in the exchange in the manner she would like. Socio-linguistic speech-level markers, the *desu/masu* and plain form are chiefly used in clause-final positions. The *desu* is used in nominal endings while the *masu* is used in verbal endings (see Maynard, 1991). In contrast, the plain form is regarded as an informal speech-level marker. The *desu/masu* and plain forms index the speaker's affective attitudes towards the addressee such as stance on formality and is dependent on static contextual features such as social status or age (see Niyekawa, 1991). Miu's zero particle choice registers as a sign to her classmates that she is irritated by the lack of clear direction, and consequently does not feel the necessity to endorse the teacher's face, as would be consistent with his status as authority within the classroom. In this way Miu indexes her stance and manages her loss of face by making sure her peers are aware that she cannot follow the teacher's directions, and that she believes the fault to lie with the teacher's insufficient description of task requirements.

Providing insight into her views of this classroom exchange, Miu commented: *'eigo de wakaranai toki wakaru you ni shite hoshii* (...) *nihongo nara wakaru'* (When I don't understand in English, I want the teacher to make it clear for me. If it's in Japanese I can understand). The student went on to further explain: *'shippai shita toki minna ga miteta kara sugoi hazukashikatta (...) sensei ga chanto setsumei shite kurenakatta kara'* (When I made a mistake everyone was watching me so I was really embarrassed. It was because the teacher didn't explain clearly). Miu's expectation that the teacher will clarify the task in greater detail is consistent with research findings which argue that within Japanese schools the role of the teacher tends to be associated primarily with the transmission of knowledge, while the student is expected to receive this knowledge without question (Nakane, 2006; Yoneyama, 1999). Moreover, Miu notes that as the teacher has frequently and publicly engaged the students in Japanese at other points during learning activities, it is not clear why he has not provided the same support at this time, *'sensei ga hanashitai toki dake nihongo o hanasu no wa fukouhei da to omou'* (I don't think it's fair the way the teacher speaks Japanese only when he feels like it). Not only is her face threatened by the teacher's refusal to provide L1 direction, but the obligatory *ne* (turn 9) 'You are this woman *ne*' functions to seek assent and assumes that Miu should be aware of the information and capable of understanding the direction that has been provided. In turn 12, the teacher laughs when Miu is once again unable to complete the task as expected, and this time, moves to convey his bewilderment with the rest of the student as he looks around the classroom while shrugging. Miu, having lost face through this incident, reacts by asserting her resistance through turning away from the teacher and seeking student rather than teacher assistance when she visibly turns to Risa and begins talking. From Miu's perspective, the teacher has the ability to grant comprehension of lesson content, and therefore not to do so is viewed suspiciously. Irrespective of whether or not holding back information is a justifiable teaching technique, what is clear is that at times the students found the teacher's refusal to convey relevant subject matter difficult to rationalise. The teacher's ability to choose whether or not to withhold the L1 thus involves a threat to the students' face in that it impugned their ability to engage in activities and to control their own participation. As noted, ultimately, this brings into focus the power imbalance within the classroom and the status of the students who, unable to voice their concerns with the teacher, must take a 'wait and see' approach.

Implications: L1 Use within the L2 Classroom

Throughout the period of observation, the timing of the teacher's use of Japanese was directly associated with his belief that students were unable or struggling to comprehend instruction in English. While opposed to students employing Japanese, the teacher stated that he viewed his use of the L1 as critical to facilitating comprehension, encouraging participation, and establishing a psychological comfort zone for students. Expressing a markedly different interpretation of classroom interaction, the students objected to the teacher's erroneous use of the L1, inappropriate management of linguistic force and social aspects associated with L1 particles, and the teacher's power to choose whether or not to provide L1 support. Recognising the teacher's L1 support as an indication that he assumed they were unable to comprehend L2 lesson content, the students expressed frustration particularly when learning activities were within their L2 level of competence. At other times, issues of access surfaced as a threat to students face particularly when students felt they were being denied access to L1 support for reasons that were not obvious to them. In other words, the teacher's authority and ability to control the use and flow of Japanese support offered to the students within the classroom at times positioned the students as being overly dependent on the teacher. Of significance here is that attitudes towards the teacher's use of Japanese within the classroom underscore that the students, irrespective of their young age, are inherently complex, multilayered beings who attach great significance to the role of their L1 and the cultural and social elements it embodies in relation to the management of face and alignment with identities.

While the students noted that they had reservations about the teacher's use of Japanese, interview data highlighted that the teacher viewed his ability to utilise Japanese as a means by which he could achieve positive outcomes such as facilitate student comprehension of lesson content, confirm understanding and make productive use of limited lesson time. In addition, the teacher indicated that he believed the L1 was a means by which he could make students feel comfortable, develop rapport with the class, and demonstrate to the students that he was no different from the Japanese teachers they have studied with. This disparity in student/teacher views is of interest as there is a tendency to assume that students, particularly at lower proficiency levels, will need and welcome support in their native language (Chávez, 2006). While students noted that the L1 when employed by the teacher did at times aid comprehension, their reactions were predominantly critical and underscored that L1 use tended to impede, rather than encourage, student participation. In short, the potential benefits of increased understanding associated with the L1 were nullified by the unintended threat to face associated with what the students cited as being non-standard Japanese communicative practices.

Debate as to the potential roles the L1 can best serve within the L2 classroom is of importance for teachers and continues to generate substantial interest and controversy in the field of L2 acquisition. Traditionally, anti-L1 attitudes have tended to dominate teaching pedagogy based principally on the assumption that student exposure to, and acquisition of the L2, decreases if the L1 is featured. This rationale is succinctly explained by Auerbach (1993) as derived from the basic premise that 'the more students are exposed to English, the more quickly they will learn; as they hear and use English, they will internalize it to begin to think in English; the only way they will learn it is if they are forced to use it' (1993: 14–15). Auerbach makes the point that 'the English-only axiom is so strong that ... teachers assigned a negative value to "lapses" into the L1, seeing them as failures or aberrations, a cause for guilt' (1993: 13). In recent years, there has been a pronounced shift in attitudes propelled by growing evidence that the L1 has been an overlooked or undervalued teaching/learning resource.

Macaro (2001: 535) outlines three positions to make sense of various stated beliefs regarding teacher's use of the students' L1. The Virtual Position states that the classroom is the virtual target country and consequently the aim of the classroom is the total, or near-total, exclusion of the L1. The Maximal Position forwards the belief that because there is no pedagogical value in L1 use, teachers try to employ the L2 maximally as the language of instruction. The Optimal Position suggests that some aspects of learning may actually be enhanced by the use of the L1. It is this Optimal Position which speaks to a fundamental shift in attitudes towards the L1 as a tool for instruction as researchers and educators scramble to identify how to effectively harness the L1 in order to bring about positive learning outcomes. Among other things, research targeting this middle-ground position has demonstrated that the judicious use of the L1 carries benefits associated with making input more salient and comprehensible, and lowering the affective filter (Auerbach, 1993; Cook, 1999, 2001; Crichton, 2009; Duff & Polio, 1990; Levine, 2003; Polio & Duff, 1994; Rolin-Ianziti & Brownlie, 2002; Turnbull & Arnett, 2002; Wilkerson, 2008). Advancing an increased role for the L1, Butzkamm (2003) refers to the mother tongue as a language acquisition support system which he characterises as 'the greatest asset that people bring to the task of foreign language learning' (2003: 29). Challenging monolingual teaching approaches, Butzkamm looks to new teaching methodologies and materials as a way to embrace the use of the mother tongue within the language classroom. As a first step, a key priority is to identify when the L1 can be effectively employed within the classroom in pedagogically beneficial ways. Speaking to this issue Krieger (2005) argue that the teacher should attempt to 'preempt L1 usage that does not serve some purpose by making absolutely clear what constitutes acceptable L1 usage and what does not' (2005: 14). The point being that the L1 is viewed as a tool that needs to be consciously and thoughtfully employed by the teacher and students in a controlled and pedagogically beneficial way in order to be of advantage.

Within the context of this investigation, the teacher's use of Japanese, while well intentioned, on occasion created a dilemma for students, who resisted, rejected, and at times aligned with identities imposed by the teacher. What is clear is that the L1 is an intrinsic part of the students' identities and its use by NNS teachers needs to be approached with due consideration. Identities imposed by the teacher were at times in conflict with those identities sought by students, in turn contributing to ongoing tensions in the management of face. While a definitive answer regarding L1 use has not been, and is unlikely to be, universally embraced, there are key questions which warrant extensive exploration within the research community and consideration by teachers working in the classroom. These relate to pedagogical issues involving the role and frequency of the L1 in L2 acquisition with students at different L2 proficiency levels and from different socio-cultural and linguistic backgrounds. Moreover, in order to avoid some instances of cross-cultural misunderstanding, the discussion needs to be broadened to include cross-cultural concerns through promoting awareness of how interpersonal relationships are influenced by L1 use. A final consideration is that as formal teacher training in students L1 is often limited, an accurate awareness of one's competency is an important consideration for teachers when assessing if, when and how to employ the mother tongue.

10 The Right to Silence: Silence as an Act of Identity

Overview: Classroom Silence

> *It used to be customary to write about silence beginning with a bit of a lament that it was a 'neglected' or 'undervalued' area of sociolinguistics, discourse analysis and other related disciplines. This is no longer necessary nor possible.*
>
> (Jaworski, 2005: 1)

This chapter examines the students' management of face as revealed through acts of student silence, instances of which were frequently observed during the English activities. Students' silence, particularly at points when invited to contribute responses, were cited as a source of frustration by the teacher who could be observed admonishing the 'silent' student. The teacher's negative appraisal of student silence was reflected in comments such as: 'It's so frustrating when nobody says anything' and 'if you're not prepared to speak you need to think about why you are here'. The forceful and confronting intervention employed underscored that silence was critically associated with a poor classroom performance and failure to contribute in the way the teacher expected or desired. Frequent communication breakdown resulted from misunderstandings based on differences in teacher/student tolerance of silence, assumptions regarding the role of silence, and variation in interpretations of silence. Of note here is that the teacher assumed silence signaled objectionable student traits such as insufficient motivation, disinterest in specific activities, limited L2 competence and a lack of confidence. While silence was often viewed by the teacher as a cover for academic limitations, this is not uncommon given that while silence is recognised as a powerful communicative tool, within communication in general 'silence is construed negatively while talk is construed positively' (Jaworski & Sachdev, 2004: 231). The tendency to assign specific meanings to silence within communicative exchanges is explained by Spencer-Oatey and Xing (2005) as follows:

> When people perceive silence (i.e. when an interlocutor is unexpectedly physically, informationally and/or participatorily silent), people typically try to interpret the silence. This is because the silence is perceived to be relevant, with a communicative import that needs to be figured out. So people try to work out if there was an informative intent (i.e. does the silence have a pragmatic meaning, such as 'I disagree with you' or 'I'm angry with you') and if so, what it was, and whether or not the 'silent' person was deliberately trying to communicate this. (Spencer-Oatey & Xing, 2005: 57–58)

Spencer-Oatey and Xing make the point that as perceptions of silence are intrinsically determined by an individual's expectations, it is necessary to examine the 'conventions/norms associated with the communicative event as to who is permitted to speak, and when' (2005: 57). The point being that silence is not universally quantifiable, but rather needs to be examined through close attention to the interlocutors' perspectives through taking in account cultural, social and linguistic factors relevant to the exchange.

In the current study, student feedback articulates ways in which teacher and student expectations regarding talk and silence diverge while illustrating that the students were keenly aware that they were being negatively evaluated when silent during English activities. Challenging this critical appraisal, a number of students' directly noted that because they may not have been verbally engaged did not mean that they were not actively engaged in the learning activities. In contrast with the teacher's critical view of student silence, the students recognised silence as being an interactive, expressive and acceptable form of communication. The argument that Japanese society has a high tolerance for silence and that silence serves a diverse array of communicative functions has been well documented (see Biggs, 1994, 1998, 1999; Liu, 2002; Nakane, 2005, 2006; Wong, 2003, 2010). Accordingly, it comes as no surprise that student feedback illustrated that teacher intervention which directly or indirectly implied that silence was undesirable was difficult for students to reconcile with their expectations of classroom behaviour. Responding to the teacher's negative evaluation of silence student Mayuko commented 'watashitachi wa itsumo doori ni shite ite nani mo warui koto o shite inai no ni nande sensei wa sonna ni okoru no ka ga wakaranakatta (...) itsumo hanashite ite hoshikatta' (We were being the same as usual and we weren't doing anything wrong. I really didn't get why the teacher was getting so angry. He always wanted us to talk). Similarly, shedding light on her reaction to the implication that silence violated unspoken classroom standards expected by the teacher Megumi commented: *'nani mo itte nai to sensei wa yarou to shitenainda na to omou no ga wakaru (...) demo sou ja nai'* (I know that when I don't say anything the teacher thinks I'm not trying. But that's not right). The feeling that failure to verbally engage in activities would result in a negative teacher evaluation was also expressed by Sayaka, who commented: *'nani ka iwanakya (...) nan ka itsumo puressha-kanjiru'* (I have to say something [...] well, I always feel pressure). The implications are important given that while students sought to align themselves with what they regarded as constituting a standard classroom performance, namely the use of silence as an interactive tool, their communicative preferences were repeatedly blocked. In sum, the teacher's tendency to paint a picture of the students as unwilling or academically challenged, based on negative perceptions of silence, represents a failure to acknowledge the non-verbal communication strategies employed by the students.

The teacher's verbal intervention during student silence, while not intended to threaten the students' face, negatively influenced the students' attitudes towards the teacher, while also affecting the students' willingness to participate in L2 classroom activities. The students' insights into what they were thinking during points of classroom silence underscore that silence represents a complex and diverse communication tool influenced by a range of contextual and socio-cultural factors. In other words, for the Japanese students the absence of talk was not viewed as the absence of communication. On the contrary, silence was employed as a communicative tool with specific objectives that were overlooked, or misinterpreted by the teacher. Relevant to the following analysis is the divergence between the students' and their teacher's interpretation of what constitutes silence, and the appropriateness of silence within the context of the classroom. In order to build an understanding of silence that speaks to the concerns of the students we overview silence in communication and interactive applications within the Japanese classroom. We then present a description of the teacher's interpretation of classroom silence. Student retrospective comments draw attention to four distinct functions of silence which are discussed in turn; (a) fear of failure, (b) L2 limitations, (c) *aizuchi* (backchannels), and (d) processing time. While these functions are interconnected, they are individually discussed as these key functions provide insights into critical aspects of the students' negotiation of face and the enactment of identities within the classroom.

The multilayered nature of identity as revealed through student silence underscores how students routinely construct and enact new selves which are not always recognised by the teacher. In this sense, silence exposes cross-cultural disparities in the management of face and illustrates how the students attempt to employ patterns of language behaviour in line with what they regard as being classroom norms, even when the identities enacted through silence are not recognised or even rejected by the teacher. The teacher's opposition to silence is relevant to student classroom involvement given that rather than encouraging participation and speeding-up learning activities as intended, intervention frequently impeded lesson progression and left students feeling agitated.

Silence in Communication

The view that silence impedes interaction and is fundamentally a form of anti-social behaviour has been discredited by compelling evidence that people from different cultures value and use silence as an essential tool for communication (see Jaworski, 2005; Jaworski & Sachdev, 2004; Sifianou, 1992, 1995, 1997). Growing awareness that socio-cultural conventions and expectations impact upon perceptions of silence, pragmatic interpretations and evaluative reactions has generated interest in understanding the communicative intentions of silence. Given that situational and cultural variables inform the many forms silence takes, it is crucial that interpretations of silence both across and within languages and cultures attend to different standards, values and expectations. Failure to appropriately contextualise silence can potentially lead to misunderstanding or misinterpretation as noted by Spencer-Oatey and Xing (2005) who make the point that complications can arise in the analyses of silence for the reason that 'differing conventions and expectations at the group level may impact upon people's perceptions of silence, pragmatic interpretations and evaluative reactions at the individual level' (2005: 58). The researchers surmise that mismatches in expectations can result in subjective feelings of 'uncomfortable silence' and may 'lead people to feel they have been "forced" into silence or have not been "allowed" to be "silent"' (2005: 55).

Supporting the position that 'silence has many faces' Jaworski (1993: 24) emphasises that silence should not be characterised as simply the absence of talk. On the contrary, Jaworski argues that a multitude of meanings and functions are served by interactive silence in different cultural contexts and in all of life's interpersonal communicative situations. Embracing a position that views interaction as structured as much by silence as it is by speech, Jaworski (2005) notes that since Tannen and Saville-Troike's 1985 publication, the examination of silence has gained mainstream status as researchers probe issues such as disparity in the use and interpretations of silence in interaction (1985: 1). Diverse manifestations of silence draw attention to the different ways in which talk and silence are juxtaposed both intentionally and unintentionally, and consequently Jaworski and Sachdev (2004) stress that 'talk and silence are not absolute categories with clear boundaries' (2004: 231). This point is raised by Spencer-Oatey (2005) who argues the need to address the complexity of silence through multiple perspectives in order to account for various manifestations, expectations and subjective feelings. Specifically, the researcher suggests attention to the manifestations of silence, contextual influences on silence, pragmatic interpretations of silence and evaluative reactions to silence (2005: 56). Emphasising that silence in cross-cultural interaction is not only context-dependent but also carries socio-culturally defined uses, Nakane (2005) makes argues that it is necessary to understand how language proficiency and culture-specific communicative styles contribute to silence in cross-cultural communication (2005: 96).

In the following discussion, we use the term 'interactive silence' to refer to the Japanese students' intentional and/or unintentional use of silence as a non-verbal means of communication. Kurzon's (1995: 65) unintentional versus intentional silence model differentiates between 'I can't tell you (because I don't know)' responses and 'I will not tell you (because I don't want to)' or 'I must/may not respond' (because I do not have permission). According to Kurzon's model, intentional silence represents a deliberate strategy to save face while unintentional silence results from anxiety, embarrassment or panic. In other words, intentional silence serves as a conscious decision or refusal to interact, while unintentional silence is an indication of one's inability to communicate or inhibitions that psychologically prevent verbal interaction. It is important to note that silence does not have to be classified as either intentional or unintentional as transitions between the two are possible (Kurzon, 2007). It is here that we turn to our attention to how silence is employed and interpreted in order to achieve specific communicative goals in the Japanese language and English classroom through attention to social and cultural contextual factors. The point being that through understanding socio-cultural attitudes towards the communicative functions of silence it is possible to gain insights into both what is said, and what is left unsaid during cross-cultural communication.

Silence and the Japanese Classroom

The prevalence of silence in the Japanese language is illustrated in Nakane's (2006) examination of silence and politeness in intercultural communication during university seminars, which found that Japanese university students employed silence with far greater frequency than did Australian students. With respect to interpretations of silence, Wong (2003), comparing Japanese and British respondents, demonstrated that Japanese overwhelmingly agreed that silence was an important means of expressing themselves leading the researcher to conclude that 'saying nothing as a form of self-expression is particularly prevalent amongst Japanese' (2003: 131). The potential for misunderstanding or misjudging communicative intentions informing silence is underscored in research such as Kato's (2000) examination of cultural differences in learning styles between Australian exchange students in Japan and their Japanese counterparts in Australia. While both groups recognised Japanese students as tending to remain silent in class the Australian students interpreted this silence as an indication of immaturity associated with perceived failure to express opinions, whereas the Japanese students viewed the Australian students' verbosity as a sign of immaturity as students 'always express clearly what they want' (2000: 63). Kato surmises that the Japanese and Australian students' views illustrate that they do not share common socio-cultural premises from which their interpretations of silence emerge.

Classroom implications associated with disparity in socio-cultural premises are underscored in Nakane's (2005) examination of Japanese students' participation during university tutorials in Australia. Drawing on data collected from interviews with non-Japanese teachers working with Japanese students, Nakane illustrates that silence has a subtle effect on misunderstanding or miscommunication such as when Japanese students are nominated to participate. Nomination was found to trigger further silence which lecturers mistakenly interpreted as a missed opportunity or request for support. Responding to Japanese students' silence, non-Japanese peers or the lecturers were found to take over the floor from the Japanese students, which inevitably silenced Japanese students (2005: 94). The issue being that Japanese speakers silence was mistaken for the absence of communication. Calling attention to disparity in teacher/student perspectives, Wong's (2003) questionnaire survey found that Japanese students at times employed silence when they, in fact, wished to be nominated to speak in formal situations such as the classroom. It is deemed unlikely, unless highly familiar with Japanese silence orientations, that the teacher will recognise and respond to this application of silence through inviting participation. In addition, Wong found that Japanese students at times elected to remain silent when they felt their opinions contradicted a generally held opinion (2003: 135).

In our research, the relationship between silence and nomination strategies was evident in feedback such as student Kaori's comment: *'hitori ni kiita hou ga ii to omoimasu* (…) *minna ni kiku to ienai* (…) *mawari no hito o kizukatte ienaku nacchau kara itte to iwareru to futsuu ni ieru'* (I think it's best to ask one student. If he asks everyone we can't answer. You can't answer because you consider the feelings of the people around you. If you're told to answer you can simply say it without worrying about others' feelings). Providing insight into how she felt the situation could be more efficiently handled, Kaori went on to note that *'itte tte sasareta hou ga sumu-zu ni ieru'* (It would be smoother if [the teacher)] chose someone to answer). Articulating a similar point of view, student Iori explains that although she felt capable of participating when the teacher sought volunteers, she did not contribute as she had not been directly instructed or invited to: *'sono toki tte wakattete mo kotaeyou to wa omowanai* (…) *wakatteta kedo sashite kurenai to kotaerarenai'* (At that time, even if I knew, I wouldn't consider answering. I knew [the answer], but unless I'm chosen I can't answer).

The following analysis underscores that classroom silence is viewed by the Japanese students not only as acceptable classroom behaviour, but also as an interactive communication strategy which functions in a diverse range of ways to both maintain the students face, and to uphold the face of the teacher. The ensuing discussion maintains that while socio-cultural factors influence both the uses and interpretations of silence within the classroom, this does not mean that 'Western' and 'Asian' cultures are categorically opposed in their respective views of silence. Speaking to this issue, Nakane (2005), while acknowledging that different cultures have different ways of valuing and using silence as a tool of communication in varied situations, makes the important point that 'rather than dichotomising East and West in their orientations to silence and talk, it is important to explain what variables are in play to what degree and why in the negotiation of participation' (2005: 95). Concurring with this position, the following analysis seeks to understand silence in terms of the variables that are in play through examining the immediate factors that influence interaction within the specific classroom context in which it occurs and as interpreted by the participants.

Teacher Response to Student Silence

Silence may at times present a valid obstacle to the teacher as is underscored by Tsui (1996) who argues that 'although one should avoid making the sweeping generalisations that talking equals learning, and forcing students to participate when they are not ready, one cannot deny that participation is very important in language learning' (1996: 145). For teachers, student silence can be ambiguous and potentially discomforting as it raises questions such as: 'Do the students understand?', 'How can I tell if learning is taking place?', 'Are the students enjoying the activities?' and 'How can I involve the students?' Nakane (2005) posits that one of the problems with Japanese student silence is that it can be difficult for the teacher to determine if silence is the 'result of linguistic problems and/or cognitive processing time, lack of comprehension, or an indirect signal of lack of confidence or lack of ideas' (2005: 94). In the current study, interview feedback, viewed in combination with classroom interaction, demonstrates that from the teacher's perspective student silence was viewed as an impediment to learning and had to be limited, or if possible, eradicated from the classroom. When a student was silent, irrespective of whether deemed intentional or unintentional, the teacher referred to this as negatively impacting on the atmosphere of the classroom, obstructing interaction, and as interfering with the flow of learning activities: 'You can't communicate if you're no prepared to say anything. Staying silent doesn't get through the lesson and it doesn't lead to learning. It creates a really apathetic atmosphere'. Suggesting that there are two culturally informed motivations for Japanese students' silence, the teacher explicitly cited the students' desire to avoid mistakes, and a lack of interest in participating: 'I think it's a Japanese cultural thing. Basically if you don't say anything you can't make a mistake. Students wait for another student to answer because it's safer. Then there are those students who stay silent because they can't be bothered. No interest in being in class or what they're going to learn'. The position that silence is associated with fear of failure finds support in Nakane's 2006 examination which found that Japanese student silence was interpreted by Australian lecturers as 'a negative indicator of academic competence' (2006: 1831). Of note here is that silent student responses were perceived by teachers as interfering with learning and consequently resulted in an unfavorable evaluative reaction. While Australian lecturers regarded silence as a threat to face and as a practice to be avoided, Nakane maintains that the avoidance of talk by Japanese students within the classroom functions to reduce the threat to one's face. Essentially, if the student elects to avoid a verbal contribution, then the student is able to control and ultimately avert any possibility that his contribution may be incorrect. Similarly, the teacher's interpretation of silence is consistent with Murata's (2011) research which highlights that one of the primary factors constraining Japanese students in class is the priority attached to accuracy. Murata hypothesises that this attention to accuracy is the result of the priority attached to the acquirement of factual knowledge within the Japanese education system.

Arguably of greater consequence to the students, the teacher identifies a second motivation for student silence as being an intentional lack of interest and/or motivation as expressed in criticism such as 'I can't make them (students) speak. You have to want to become involved. Basically I believe it's the students' responsibility to participate and embrace a positive attitude. I can encourage them but they still have to choose whether to join in'. The implication here being that irrespective of the students' actual communicative intent, the silent student will be negatively evaluated as inappropriately exhibiting non-participatory and anti-social behaviour. Drawing attention to disparity regarding interpretations of student classroom participation, Nakane (2006) surmises that 'The ideologies and theories of education in Australia encourage student centred classroom practice' and as a result, 'classroom participation is often given weight as part of assessment, and active participation may be considered as engagement and willingness to learn' (2006: 1819). Elaborating, Nakane explains that silence is viewed as a potential barrier to learning with non-Japanese teachers' assuming that 'unless the "barrier" is broken by either the student or the lecturer, the negative consequences of silence will remain' (2006: 1830). The teacher in our study, underscoring his opposition to student silences, further commented: 'I put time into getting the students talking. It is not a good situation when the class is silent. Students have to speak English if they are going to learn'. With the focus on eliciting verbal contributions, the periods of silence that punctuated learning activities challenged the teacher's face claims as among other things, they were interpreted as directly interfering with his ability to engage the class, progress with the lesson and confirm comprehension.

In our study, the teacher provided insight into his approach to silence in the classroom noting: 'I try to get them (students) to join in, but if they are having trouble or are too shy then I just move on to the next student otherwise you end up doing nothing for a long time'. Clarifying this routine the teacher stated, 'You've got to move on. Other students who do know the answers and want to join in are waiting'. Speculating that there are students who 'know the answers' and 'want to join in', the teacher's direct and authoritative tone during intervention does not seek to minimise imposition or loss of face. Intervention practices underscore the power imbalance between teacher and student for as Pavlidou (2001) notes, while the teacher can ignore a student who desires to partake, 'a student could not simply remain silent if selected by the teacher as the next speaker, at least not without severe consequences' (2001: 107). The implication here being that teachers are inclined to neglect negative face wants, while placing greater emphasis on their students' positive face. The following classroom excerpt illustrates a point during English activities when the teacher intervened following student silence.

[Classroom excerpt 26: When students (Ss) do not respond to the teacher's (T) request for responses Minori (M) is nominated.]

1T: When do you exercise‿ ((T looks around at Ss, gestures with palms upward and fingers curling inward))

2S: (7) ((Ss look at T and/or down in silence))

3T: ((T looks at Ss from left to right)) WHEN‿ (8) ((looks around at Ss, rubs hands together, paces across classroom, shrugs)) in the <u>morning</u>‿ ((stops in centre of classroom, folds arms, looks around at Ss))

4S: (6) ((Ss look down at desks and/or at classmates))

5T: ((T claps hands together quickly, Ss look up at T)) (3) In the morning‿ ((looks around at Ss))

6S: (8) ((Ss look down in silence, look through books/pencil cases, furtively glance up at T))

7T: ((T moves to his desk, drums fingers on desk several times)) <u>Come on</u> (2) ((walks to M, M looks up at T)) when do you exercise‿ ((extends hand))

8M: (2) ((M looks up at T)) In the morning ((looks down))

When seeking student contributions to the opening question 'When do you exercise‿' (turn 1) the teacher appeals for self-selection by means of looking around at the students while dynamically gesturing with his palms faced upward and fingers curling inward in a beckoning motion. The protracted student silence which ensues is interrupted by the teacher who, appearing to deduce that comprehension is not the issue, elects to again call for student participation by demanding, 'When‿' (turn 2). Assuming that student silence is viewed as a behaviour the students will recognise as being inappropriate within the classroom, the invitation is visibly more urgent as the teacher adopts a serious countenance and markedly harsher tone of voice. Waiting for a response, the teacher is clearly frustrated as he rubs his hands together, paces across the classroom and perceptibly shrugs his shoulders. At the same time, the threat to student face is minimised when the teacher moves to model the type of response he desires, 'In the morning‿' Believing that the students have sufficient scaffolding to respond, the teacher then moves to position himself in the centre of the classroom, folds his arms and looks around at the students expectantly (turn 3). When a lengthy silence implies that a student response will not be forthcoming the teacher, without warning, abruptly claps his hands together in rapid succession as if intent on waking his 'sleeping students'. The stunned students immediately look in the direction of the teacher, who exploiting this class attention, proceeds to once more ask, 'In the morning?' (turn 5). In turn 6, the students do not respond in the way in which the teacher expects or wants and can be seen looking down at their desks, through their pencil cases, or furtively stealing glances at the teacher. The teacher moves back toward his desk and impatiently drums his fingers while assuming an imploring tone as he asks 'Come on'. After a brief pause the teacher abandons this approach and proceeds to move in the direction of student, Minori. Stopping directly in front of Minori's desk, the teacher asks 'When do you exercise?' and extends his hand toward her in a gesture which removes any doubt that he is in fact nominating her and this is non-negotiable (turn 7). Minori looks up at the teacher and promptly responds correctly and seemingly without hesitation, 'In the morning' (turn 8), after which her gaze shifts down towards her desk.

Shedding light on his interpretation of this exchange, the teacher commented, 'I want the students to try. Nothing happens if no one's prepared to take a chance. You don't have to be afraid of making mistakes'. These comments are consistent with the teacher's approach throughout the above exchange during which intervention focuses on the transformation of classroom behaviour in order to increase student verbal participation. Nakane (2005) makes the point that the study of Asian students' silence has tended to focus on exploring why students are silent, and how 'this "problem" of lack of participation can be alleviated' (2005: 76). The researcher makes the point that as students' silence has typically been attributed to socio-cultural factors, the basic premise behind this reasoning and approach to intervention is the assumption that Japanese student silence is a classroom behaviour that is non-desirable and should be corrected. In the excerpt, the teacher assumes that what he views as being a lack of student compliance during the activity is chiefly associated with fear of error. The implication being that student silence was viewed as a face-saving strategy which reflected the students' tendency to avoid risks associated with potential public failure. As the task was not determined as being beyond the students L2 competence, students who remained silent and did not participate in the way desired were negatively viewed as falling short of a 'good student' performance. In terms of student identity, this has significant implications as the focus on bringing about cultural adaption represents the forced alignment with an identity not necessarily valued or desired by the students. In addition, the teacher forms an evaluative judgment of the 'silent students' based on the degree to which they align with a role that demands a reduced and restricted range of applications of interactive silence in favour of increased verbal participation.

Classroom Silence from the Students' Perspective

The teacher's assumption that silence failed to facilitate communication and constituted the deliberate avoidance of talk was rejected by the students as being both unmerited and inaccurate. On the contrary, data sources illustrated that the Japanese students' viewed silence as a normative classroom non-verbal form of communication. Accordingly, the teacher's implication that silence violated appropriate behaviour threatened the students face as is illustrated in the comments offered by students Iori and Sayaka when viewing periods of classroom silence: *'sensei wa nani ka itte hoshii to omotteru tte wakaru kara puressha-o kanjiru'* (I felt pressure because I knew that the teacher wanted me to say something) and *'nani ka kotae nai to isshoukenmei yatteru tte omotte kurenai'* (I have to answer otherwise [the teacher] won't think I'm doing my best). Compelled to verbally contribute in order to align with what the teacher accepted as being competent identities, the students felt obliged to embrace patterns of language use that they did not always favour.

The students' views parallel the findings in Jaworski and Sachdev's (1998) examination of classroom silence with students in three schools in Wales which corroborates earlier ethnographic findings that student silence is associated with the institutionalised power imbalance that exists between teachers and students. The point being that the teacher maintains control of discourse and speaking rights and therefore has the authority to nominate students to speak or demand silence. Among other things, the researchers found that the students regarded silence as being more important for learning than teachers did, and that teacher expectations for students to be verbally active can be a source of anxiety and conflict for students (1998: 284). Within our study, the issue of control surfaces in feedback such as student Marin's comment: *'nani mo iitaku nai toki demo nani ka iwanakya ikenai tte kanjiru'* (It feels like I have to say something even when I don't want to). Marin's feedback illustrates that not only was there confrontation in students' and teachers' values and assumptions regarding verbal contributions, but also that the teacher's intervention may have inadvertently perpetuated classroom silence by increasing acts of student resistance to the tasks. Moreover, teacher intervention challenged the positive value students wanted to claim by implying that the students were engaged in inappropriate classroom behaviour and not be recognised as 'good students' unless willing to embrace a vocal classroom role.

Student feedback such as Risa's comment *'nani mo iwanai hou ga kiraku de ii'* (I felt more comfortable not saying anything) confirms that at times silence was favoured by the students, and by implication, recognised by students as aligned with standard classroom behaviour. Moreover, although negatively interpreted by the teacher, silence was positively viewed by students as a facilitative device and for the most part, did not denote resistance to classroom practices introduced by the teacher. On the contrary, Akari's comment 'kikinagara dou sureba ii ka kangaeteta' (I was listening and thinking about what to do) and 'ganbattetanda kedo sensei wa kizuite kurenakatta' (I was doing my best but the teacher didn't realise) illustrate that she was actively engaged and on task yet correctly ascertained that this was not accepted by the teacher whose critical interpretation of nonverbal student participation was all too evident. Student retrospection demonstrates that while silence was in fact at times a precursor to comprehension difficulties, as assumed by the teacher, this was far from being the case during all or indeed most classroom activities. In contrast, students' retrospective feedback indicated that during silent periods they were typically absorbing and organising lesson content and consistently formulating oral responses. At other moments, students indicated that they had in fact communicated a response embedded in their silence, however the teacher had failed to recognise, permit or had misunderstood the intended message. Recurring disparity in the use and interpretation of silence impacted on the negotiation of face as the students' face claims were time and again not appraised in line with their communicative intentions or assumptions as to how they desired to be viewed by the teacher. The following four functions identified within students' retrospective interviews are the focus of the following analysis as they generate insights into silence orientations and the negotiation of face and enactment of identities from the students' perspective.

- Silence and fear of failure: Student fear of responding incorrectly.
- Silence and L2 limitations: Silence as a response to limitations in English response options.
- Silence and *aizuchi* (backchannel) communication strategies: Non-verbal and verbal communication cues employed by students.
- Silence and processing time: Variation in teacher/student assumptions regarding the amount of time required for processing lesson content.

These four key functions of silence, discussed one by one in the subsequent section, illustrate that while silence communicates information, this message does not always correspond to the interpretation rendered by the teacher. Of significance here is that the students' silence raises issues of cross-cultural pragmatic discrepancies that focus attention on the students' views regarding their right to silence in the construction of identities. This is particularly relevant as a number of the identities revealed through silence are not recognised or are even disallowed by the teacher during English activities. Within the following analysis not all of the silences observed during classroom learning activities were intentional or strategic. In addition, it was not always possible, even with the aid of retrospection, to determine the students' intentions during periods of silence. While students' motivations for silence differed according to factors such as the task and levels of English proficiency, the teacher did not have access to this information and therefore intervened in a way he intuitively felt to be appropriate. The result being that the students, at times viewed by the teacher to be non-participatory, were often silenced rather than silent.

Silence and Fear of Failure

Japanese students' silence during learning activities was in part rationalised by the teacher as constituting a cultural predisposition towards risk avoidance and non-participation.

> Most Japanese students aren't risk takers. Basically students are afraid of making mistakes so they don't say anything. Then there's no risk of messing-up. For the students it is much easier to watch than risk getting involved. For teachers working in Japan it's a challenge to get students involved because you have to encourage them to take risks rather than watch silently.

In some measure, this position was supported by student retrospective data which identified concern that making mistakes in the presence of the teacher and peers would equate to alignment with a less competent student identity. Exemplifying this sentiment, student Ami discloses, *'minna no mae de machigaeru no ga kowakatta kara amari nani mo iitaku nakatta'* (I didn't really want to say anything because I was afraid of making a mistake in front of everyone) while classmate Miu voiced similar concerns: *'shitsumon wa rikai dekita kedo machigaeru no ga kowakatta kara nani mo iwanakatta'* (I could understand the question but I was afraid of making a mistake so I didn't say anything). This function of silence as an intentional strategy by which to avoid loss of face assumed to be associated with an errant classroom contribution finds support in Aspinall's (2006) examination of Japanese in learning environments, which hypothesises that societal and cultural influences may hinder effective English language teaching and learning of communicative English skills. Among other things, Aspinall argues that the notion that there is one 'correct' answer or way to respond to a teacher's question interferes with students' willingness to express themselves freely and consequently impedes the development of communication skills. In the ensuing analysis, three classroom excerpts illustrate functions of student silence and the relationship to student fear of failure. The first excerpt illustrates a point during which student silence follows the teacher's request for voluntary student contributions to an activity.

[Classroom excerpt 27: When the teacher's (T) request for student (S) contributions to a pronunciation activity meets with silence student Hikari (H) is nominated to respond.]

1T: ((T holds up T/B facing Ss, points to target activity, taps with hand)) OK (.) we're looking at short vowels (3) what's a SHORT VOWEL↗ ((looks around at Ss, raises shoulders))

2S: (7) ((Ss look around at classmates))

3T: ((T raises shoulders, palms facing upward, shifts weight in animated rocking motion form left to right leg)) Anybody↗ (2) anybody↗ (3) ((looks around at Ss)) anybody↗ ((holds out right hand, curls fingers inward to invite response))

4S: (11) ((S silence))

5T: ((T points in direction of Ss seated on left of classroom)) (3) What's a vowel↗ ((Ss look down at desks, and/or whispering together, T smiles)) (4) ANYBODY↗ ((raises eyebrows, furrows forehead)) (6) ((clicks fingers together rapidly))

6S: (9) ((Ss look at each other, whispering))

7T: ((T moves over to H, H looks up) Don't know↗ (6) ((H remains silent, T looks down, shakes head, points to group of Ss on H's left)) do you guys know↗ ((raises eyebrows)) (3) what's a VOWEL↗ (5) ((turns toward whiteboard, picks-up marker))

8S: (6) ((S silence))

9T: ((T writes on whiteboard in large letters)) *BOIN* (1) in Japanese we say *BOIN*
'Vowel. In Japanese we say *boin*'

In turn 1 the teacher extends his index finger and taps his hand drawing student attention to a specific point in the textbook while verbally directing the students to the activity by announcing 'OK. We're looking at short vowels'. After a brief pause, the teacher assumes the class is orientated to the task and promptly invites contributions: 'What's a short vowel?' When student responses are not forthcoming the teacher is perceptibly uncomfortable as evidenced by his perplexed facial expression, concomitant shrug of his shoulders, and impatient rocking motion as he transfers his weight from left to right. Scanning the classroom attempting to inspire verbal participation, the teacher invites contributions by three times appealing for assistance: 'Anybody? Anybody? Anybody?' Pausing briefly between invitations, the teacher proceeds to extend his right hand, while animatedly curling his fingers inward in a gesture that emphatically invites contributions (turn 3). By way of accentuating that the contributions of 'anybody' willing to engage will be welcomed, the teacher seeks to reduce the potential threat to the students face through affirming that he prioritises access to the answer and consequently, is unconcerned as to which student elects to provide this information. In addition, the teacher endeavours to lessen the threat to face by smiling encouragingly, furrowing his forehead, and markedly modifying his tone of voice when again inviting 'Anybody?' (turn 5). The distinctly higher pitch of the request conveys that the teacher is pleading for contributions, without which he will be unable to progress with the activity in the way in which he desires. When this appeal for student involvement fails to generate what he deems a satisfactory student response, the teacher shifts tactics as he clicks his fingers together in rapid succession as if to denote the speed with which he expects class contributions to flow. The teacher's face is threatened when this demand for verbal engagement is again rejected and instead, met with student silence and whispered exchanges (turn 6). In turn 7, rather than directing his question to the entire class, the teacher focuses his attention on an individual student, Hikari, asking: 'Don't know?' When Hikari remains silent the teacher does not attempt to conceal his frustration as he abruptly shifts his gaze in the direction of the floor and categorically marks his dissatisfaction by shaking his head from left to right. Disclosing that he does not believe Hikari capable of responding and is no longer prepared to delay, the teacher turns his attention to a group of students seated close by: 'Do you guys know? What's a vowel?' After several seconds the teacher, having abandoned his pursuit of a student response, turns and moves toward the whiteboard. Picking up a whiteboard marker, the teacher writes B-O-I-N in conspicuously large letters and subsequently underlines them while simultaneously saying: *'boin,* in Japanese we say *boin'* (Vowel. In Japanese we say *boin*).

On viewing this classroom exchange retrospectively, student Hikari commented, *'jibun kara kotae you to omotta (…) nantonaku iu koto wakatteta kedo jishin ga nakute kowakatta'* (I thought about answering myself. I kind of knew what to say but I didn't really have any confidence. I was scared). While Hikari expresses an understanding of what a vowel is and weighs up whether or not to venture a response, she ultimately elects to remain silent citing a lack of confidence *'jishin ga nakute'* and a sense of being scared *'kowakatta'*. For Hikari, a readily accessible approach to moderating this potential threat to face is to remain silent. Hikari's course of action finds support in silence and speech research as documented by Nakane (2006), which illustrates that Japanese students orient towards negative politeness in classroom interaction, a factor which can result in more extensive use of silence following nomination. Nakane makes the point that the 'fear of face loss is partly due to perceptions of one's own insufficient language proficiency' (2006: 1817) and in regard to self-selection, the 'avoidance of voluntary participation can be a way of maintaining positive face of the self' (2006: 1831). Illustrating the potential for divergence in cultural perceptions of classroom participation, Cutrone (2009) suggests the notion that language learning requires aggressive students to individually volunteer is a reflection of Western ethnocentrism (2009: 60). While the implication that Western cultures share definitive behaviours represents a narrow and limited view of Western socio-cultural diversity, it does raise an interesting point regarding potential variation in general expectations of student performance within the classroom. For example, suggesting that the silence orientations of Japanese are influenced by cultural and social perceptions of appropriateness rather than representing a feature of the linguistic system, Murata (1994) argues that Japanese students are more likely to remain silent and less inclined to initiate interruptions than English speakers when interacting not only in Japanese, but also in English. In the above excerpt, Hikari's reflections illustrate that she second guesses herself, and that this doubt ultimately determines her course of action. Arguably what is of greater significance is that when weighed against the benefits she associates with a correct classroom response, Hikari's decision to stay silent intimates that she does not believe that the potential advantages compensate for the possible loss of face associated with an unsuccessful classroom contribution. In the end, the loss of face Hikari associates with an incorrect response determines how she chooses to involve herself during English activities and to conduct herself within the classroom.

Concern that an incorrect English contribution may undermine face claims illustrates that fear of failure, even during tasks that may not appear to be of high evaluative significance, is a potential concern for Japanese students. Along these lines, Nakane (2006) hypothesises that Japanese students draw on silence as a self face-saving strategy as opposed to a politeness strategy intended to save the addressee's face. The researcher's premise being that disparities in interpretations of the threat associated with classroom contributions may be the result of differences in educational practices and ideology. The central claim being that Japanese students are taught to value correctness of the end product over the process of learning. As way of demonstration, Nakane argues that within the Australian university context critical thinking is valued and 'expressing critical views or disagreement with classmates or the lecturer is regarded as a sign of engagement and enthusiasm in learning as well as a way of showing academic competence' (2006: 1821). In the context of the above excerpt, the Japanese students attempt to align with what they view as being a 'good student' identity by embracing silence as a means of reducing risk to face. In contrast, through prioritising student responses the teacher distinctly expresses the high value he associates with verbal participation, and therein, the potential alignment with a 'good student' identity. In the subsequent excerpt students are asked to respond to questions with the aid of a series of illustrations from their textbooks. When the class remains silent the teacher assumes that there is a problem with comprehension.

[Classroom excerpt 28: Marin (M) is nominated after the teacher's (T) request for student (S) contributions meets with silence.]

1T: ((T moves to centre of classroom)) Let's begin guys (2) number 1 (2) look at your books not me ((holds up T/B)) she has (1) WHAT does she have¿ ((taps T/B)) (2) she has (1) go ahead and count (2) ((points at illustration in T/B)) (3) ONE TWO three four five (.) SIX (2) super EASY for you guys ((looks at Ss and smiles)) (2) SIX CLOCKS (2) ((places T/B on desk, holds two fingers up, shifts gaze to Ss)) OK (1) number 2 (2) what's the answer¿ ((paces back and forth looking at Ss))

2S: (12) ((Ss look down at T/Bs, fidget with pencil cases))

3T: ((T looks around at Ss, raises shoulders with palms faced upward)) How about it¿ (3) number 2¿ (1) anybody¿ (2) ANYBODY¿ ((walks around classroom, looks at Ss in turn, holds up right hand, palm upward, curls fingers inward))

4S: (13) ((Ss look down at T/Bs and/or classmates))

5T: ((T moves to front centre of classroom, points towards M)) What's the answer¿ (6) ((M looks at T/B, then T, then classmates)) THE ANSWER¿ ((claps hands together loudly)) (3) the answer¿ ((moves to M's desk))

6M: ((M looks up at T, T nods at M)) (6) I have ((glances between T and T/B several times)) (3) five watch ((looks up at T))

7T: (3) ((T leans forward)) I have five watch¿ (2) watch (1) WHAT¿ (2) five (.) *NANI* (1) watch::: ¿ (1) five¿ ((makes circular motion with hands))

8M: (5) ((M looks from T/B to classmates several times)) Watches ((M looks down))

9T: (2) Watches (1) GOOD (2) ((nods, moves to centre of classroom)) how do you spell watches¿ (2) W-A-T-C-H-E-S *ne* (2) now for number 3 (3) ANYBODY ((looks from left to right at Ss))

In turn 1, subsequent to demonstrating the answer to the first question and noting that he regards the activity as being 'super easy for you guys', the teacher holds up two fingers and proceeds to scan the classroom while asking the students 'Number 2. What's the answer?' The students, appearing to avoid eye contact with the teacher, look down at their desks, through textbooks, or fidget with pencil cases. When verbal contributions are not in the offing the teacher attempts to break the stalemate by inviting 'How about it? Number 2? Anybody? Anybody?' This appeal for verbal engagement is reinforced when the teacher commences pacing around the classroom and directly soliciting participation by means of looking at the students in turn, extending his right hand, and curling his fingers inward (turn 3). The question being asked is one to which the teacher knows the answer and thus tests student knowledge of lesson content in addition to capacity to exhibit classroom participatory behaviour he values. In the teacher's own words: 'I appreciate when the students are willing to speak out and have a try. It makes a difference because it doesn't only help the student speaking, but it sends a clear message to all the others. To learn you have to get involved'. From the students' perspective, declining the invitation to participate is not discourteous, and moreover, potentially carries the benefit of circumventing unwanted attention allowing for the mitigation of potential threat to face. The enduring silence is eventually checked when the teacher gestures towards student Marin (turn 5), and thus in effect obliges her to respond. The threat to Marin's face is evident when she sheepishly looks up from her book, to the teacher, then back and forth to a number of her classmates. The teacher reiterates that he requires 'The answer?', and crisply claps his hands together to designate that he expects a prompt response. In turn 6, Marin, repeatedly shifting her line of gaze between her textbook and the teacher, proceeds to answer the question in a hushed and seemingly apprehensive voice. Under close observation of her watchful classmates, the threat to Marin's face is compounded when without delay, the teacher draws attention to her omission of the plural form through repeating her response with marked rising intonation: 'I have five watch?' (turn 7). The loss of face is protracted when, in preference to correcting the error, the teacher indicates that he expects Marin to reconsider her response by asking 'Watch what? Five "nani" watch. Five?' Indicating that he assumes adequate scaffolding has been offered for Marin to formulate the response he requires, the teacher proceeds to make a circular motion with his hands expressing his desire for her to continue, take over the turn, and see it through to completion. Marin, with her gaze shifting between her textbook and classmates, remains silent for a number of seconds before quietly responding with the correct answer 'watches'. Confirming the accuracy of Marin's response to be 'good', the teacher spells the plural form 'W-A-T-C-H-E-S *ne*' (W-A-T-C-H-E-S right!) and swiftly turns his attention to the next question 'Now for number 3. Anybody⸮'

Reflecting on this classroom exchange retrospectively, Marin commented: *'kotae ga wakaru hito iru kara jibun wa baka da to omowaretaku nai (…) kurasu no minna ga wakatte ite jibun dake ga wakaranai toki baka da tte kanjiru'* (There are some students who know the answer, so I don't want to look like I'm stupid. I feel stupid when everyone else in the class knows and I'm the only one who doesn't get it). Marin's feedback conveys that an incorrect response is viewed as having implications in terms of not only relational aspects of identity, but also in how she perceives herself. In other words, her silence is associated with her desire not to be thought of as being stupid *'baka da to omowaretaku nai'* by the teacher or her peers. The exchange represents a threat to Marin's face in that she feels it may expose and publicise her L2 limitations in a situation in which she assumes there will be members of the class capable of providing the response the teacher seeks. This implication here being that Marin assumes her classroom performance is being evaluated and compared with that of her classmates. This issue is raised by Cutrone (2009), who notes that the Japanese school system places substantial emphasis on the evaluation paradigm. Cutrone surmises that fear of failure associated with evaluation may explain Japanese students' reluctance to speak. Marin's retrospective insight is consistent with the feelings of embarrassment experienced in the following classroom exchange during which students are instructed to construct sentences using verb cues and illustrations.

[Classroom excerpt 29: The teacher (T) nominates Reika (R) to construct a sentence.]

1T: ((T points at R)) Can you use (1) DOES⸮ ((steps toward R's desk))

2R: (2) ((T gestures with hands for R to commence)) She does (1) game⸮ ((R looks up at T, tilts head to side))

3T: (2) ((T cocks head to side)) Hm::⸮ (1) she does game (1) is a <u>little strange</u> ((smiles, scratches head))

4R: (6) ((R points at T/B, looks up at T)) *KORE⸮* 'Is it this⸮'

5T: (2) ((T looks at R, moves towards her desk, leans forward to look at T/B, nods) Yes (.) you can use that ((points to an illustration of a child doing homework, nods)) (1) that's OK ((takes several steps back from desk))

6R: (8) ((R remains silent))

7T: (T places hands on desk) *nan de mo ii* (.) but (2) *bunpou MACHIGAE NAI DE* (2) she <u>does game</u> is a little STRANGE (1) *NE* ((paces around classroom))
'Anything is fine, but don't make a mistake with the grammar. She does game is a little strange, right!'

8R: (27) ((R remains silent))

9T: ((T meanders to centre of classroom)) I'll give you a <u>hint</u> (2) ((looks from left to right)) she plays games (3) that sounds right ((holds thumb up)) (1) now (2) how about <u>homework</u> ((raises shoulders)) (3) PLAYS HOMEWORK¿ (2) ((shakes head)) plays homework¿ ((steps toward whiteboard)) what verb goes with homework ((draws large question mark on whiteboard))

The student, Reika, begins by promptly responding to the teacher's request to use the verb 'does' in constructing a sentence (turn 2) and in doing so makes a claim for face by demonstrating to the teacher and her classmates that she has understood the classroom material and is both capable of, and prepared to, respond. At the same time, Reika's uncertainty, and thereby the potential threat to her face, is revealed through her rising intonation 'She does game¿', and manner in which she can be observed uneasily looking up at the teacher, tilting her head to the side, and waiting for verification as to the accuracy of her response (turn 2). The threat to face is magnified when the teacher, mimicking Reika's uncertainty, adopts a quizzical expression and cocks his head as he asks 'Hm ... ¿ She does game is a little strange' after which he scratches his head and smiles broadly implying that he expects Reika may detect her error and therefore share in the joke. In this brief moment the teacher blocks Reika's face claims and, as her classmates watch on, undermines Reika's attempt to align with a competent student identity. The threat to Reika's face that occasions the teacher's repetition and rejection of her response is bluntly revealed when Reika (turn 4), electing not to mask her frustration, pauses to check her textbook, points at the activity in her textbook, looks directly at the teacher, and irately snaps in a strikingly loud tone: *'kore¿'* (Is it this¿).

Reika's direct attempt to confirm the task requirements not only reveals her irritation at being mimicked in a highly visible manner, but also implies that she has been improperly disadvantaged by a lack of information pertaining to the specific nature of the task. In turn 5 the teacher, appearing to recognise the unguarded animosity in Reika's demand for clarification, comes across as somewhat stunned as he hastily moves forward in order to clarify whether Reika has located the correct point, and in a markedly softer tone of voice confirms 'Yes, you can use that. That's OK'. What may be lost on the teacher however is the way in which Reika has framed her question *'kore¿'*

(Is it this¿). Reika's omission of the copula *desu* and the question particle *ka* is described by Manita and Blagdon (2010) as being direct and conveying a sense of arrogance. The *desu/masu* form is employed to express formality when 'speaking to a stranger, a non-intimate equal, or an out-group member, as well as to someone older or higher in status than oneself' (Niyekawa, 1991: 40). In contrast, the plain form is used when interacting with someone close to show informality and is therefore employed 'only within the family and among intimate equals as the style of "intimacy", or in speaking to someone clearly younger or lower in status within a hierarchical group as the style of "condescension"' (Niyekawa, 1991: 39). Consequently, while the copula + *ka* may be omitted in colloquial speech between 'equals', Reika's choice of expression fails to invoke normative constraints on student behaviour as it undermines the rank of the teacher within the classroom. In this way, Reika's discursive challenge to the teacher's face embodied in the implication that she has not been provided with significant task information, provides her with an avenue to restore face. Reika is able to index to her peers her resistance to the negative teacher positioning without necessarily letting the teacher understand fully the implications of the interaction. As well as functioning as a mild form of resistance, this enables Reika to establish solidarity with peers who are included as the 'in-group' witnesses to her irritation.

In turn 6, Reika, apparently still uncertain, withdraws until the teacher intervenes in turn 7 by indicating that she is free to answer as she sees fit, *'nan de mo ii'* (anything is fine), however firmly cautions that she should not make a mistake with her grammar *'bunpou machigae nai de'*. The threat to Reika's face embedded in the teacher's warning that he expects a grammatically accurate response is further heightened when he again reminds her, and the class, that the previous contribution was a *'little strange "ne"'* (little strange right!). Her confidence undermined, this reiteration effectively silences Reika as it reinforces the possibility that she may again make an error or publicly say something 'a little strange'. The mixed message communicated by the teacher implies that while Reika is free to construct her own response, she should be especially cautious of making grammatical errors as she is ultimately going to be evaluated according to the grammatical accuracy of her response. The threat to Reika's face is evident in the protracted and uncomfortable silence which follows (turn 8) which leaves the teacher with no other recourse than to provide greater detail as to the grammatical requirements of the task.

Providing insight into her interpretation of the above, Reika commented: *'mou iya da dou sureba ii* (...) *nagaku tomadotteta are wa hazukashikatta nan ka machigattara dou shiyou tte omou sugoku kowaku kanjiru tasuke o matteta'* (I can't take this. What should I do¿ I was confused for a long time. That was embarrassing. I kind of feel like, 'What will I do if I make a mistake¿' and it makes me feel really scared. I was waiting for help). Reika's loss of face lies in part in the mismatch between teacher/student interpretations of the magnitude of classroom error and is compounded by the discursive force of the teacher's Japanese intervention. In such, Reika's silence is motivated by the desire to protect her positive face and her desire to be understood and approved of by the teacher. When her initial response is cited as being inaccurate, Reika assumes that the teacher will take control and provide support: *'tasuke o matteta'* (I was waiting for help). Reika's silence does not necessarily represent an inability to respond, but in part reflects her assumption that the teacher is obliged to provide specific corrective feedback. Reika's strategy is a reasonable course of action when considered within the context of Japanese classroom hierarchy which acknowledges the teacher's role as being that of expert informer. For example, commenting on pragmatic failure attributable to the disparities of politeness orientations, Nakane (2006) suggests that 'academic achievement seems to be sacrificed to some degree by Japanese students for the sake of facesaving' (2006: 1820). Potential conflict is evident when Reika, finding that teacher support is not forthcoming in the manner in which she expects, remarks *'dou sureba ii'* (What should I do?).

Throughout English activities, even when directly nominated by the teacher in front of classmates, silence was engaged as an 'off-record' politeness strategy by students in order to avoid the threat to face associated with an incorrect contribution. In this way, silence empowered the students in that it provided an accessible means by which students could independently manage face. By withholding comment, students could avoid unfavorable alignment associated with a potentially negative comparison with classmates or a failure to succeed at a supposedly achievable L2 level. For example, following an extended classroom silence, student Miho noted that while she had been able to comprehend task requirements and identify the answer, she nevertheless elected to withhold a response, *'kono toki mo kotae ga wakatteta (…) kotaerarenai wake dewa nakatta'* (At this time I also knew what the answer was. It wasn't that I couldn't answer). While this use of silence is by no means limited to Japanese students, the message conveyed in the students' silence intimates that the risk of failure is seen to outweigh the potential benefits to face that may result from a positive teacher evaluation.

Silence and L2 Limitations

Throughout English activities, silence was recurrently employed with the intention of protecting face when students deemed limitations in their L2 competence would negatively impact on how they were evaluated by the teacher.

In addition, silence was strategically engaged in response to points at which students felt that the discursive options available did not accurately allow them to express themselves. For example, students at times remained silent in situations when the teacher simplified or reduced available response options to questions such as: 'Can you play the piano?' Instructed to answer either 'Yes, I can', or 'No, I can't', students at times elected to remain silent if the response options were not an accurate representation of how they assessed their ability. For example, for students who played the piano, a definitive 'Yes' was associated with a brash claim of competence, while to answer 'No' was viewed as being dishonest. In these cases, although aware of the priority the teacher attached to vocal participation, students resisted aligning with the teacher's notion of a 'good student' identity if it failed to meet with the identities they valued and desired to enact. The following two classroom excerpts demonstrate the strategic use of silence and student reflections on these points.

[Classroom excerpt 30: The teacher (T) asks Marin (M) then Satoko (S) to indicate if they can count from 1 to 100.]

1T: ((T turns to M)) Can you count from 1 to 100?
2M: ((M looks up at the ceiling)) (8) ((T claps hands together. M looks at T)) (2) *tochuu made*
'Part of the way'
3T: ((T steps towards M)) Can you count from 1 to 100? (2) YES or NO?
4M: (6) ((M remains silent, looks around at classmates))
5T: ((T gestures for M to respond moving hands rapidly in circular motion))
6M: (8) No ((glances up at T, then turns head away))
7T: (2) ((T looks at S, gestures with chin)) Can you COUNT from 1 to 100?
8S: (11) ((shrugs))
9T: ((T shrugs shoulders, motions towards S with chin)) YES (1) NO ((tilts head to side))

When the teacher asks student Marin: 'Can you count from 1 to 100?' she initially pauses and looks up at the ceiling appearing to contemplate her response. Reacting to Marin's silence, the teacher abruptly claps his hands together at which a startled Marin refocuses her gaze on the teacher, then pauses briefly before decisively responding in Japanese, *'tochuu made'* (part of the way). The response, as a reflection on how she judges her ability to carry out the task, allows Marin to maintain face in that it indicates that she is partially capable of carrying out the task. In addition, her response offers protection from threat to face by illustrating that Marin maintains a degree of doubt as to her ability and, as a consequence, is unlikely to be asked by the teacher to demonstrate if she can in fact back up her claims. The partial confirmation of competence permits Marin to maintain Japanese behavioural conventions by understating her ability and thereby aligning herself with peers through exhibiting reserved confidence. At the same time, Marin claims credibility as a 'good student' by appealing for teacher approval by stressing she has attained a measure of competence. In turn 3, Marin's face claims are blocked by the teacher who rejects what he infers is an evasive response through repeating the initial question and this time, stipulating that he will only accept a definitive 'Yes or No' response. This 'Yes or No' condition threatens Marin's face as it not only implies that she will be judged as being capable or incapable, but also puts her in a position where she has to declare her capability in the presence of peers. The threat to Marin's face is evident in the ensuing silence during which Marin looks around at her classmates appearing confused by the teacher's demand for an answer (turn 4) before airing on the side of caution and responding, 'No' (turn 6). Marin's frustration is apparent in the way she cuts off her line of gaze from the teacher. Rather than claim face through responding in the affirmative, Marin resists aligning with a competent student identity and elects to abandon her face claims. Assuming that he has enabled her to arrive at an accurate and definitive response, the teacher no longer sees any need in questioning Marin and goes on to direct the same question to another member of the class (turn 7). During retrospection Marin provided insights into her thoughts regarding the exchange and the limitations in response strategies made available commenting that: *'shitsumon no imi wa rikai dekita kedo dou yatte kotaereba ii no ka wakaranakatta (…) sentakushi ni tadashii mono ga nakatta (…) sensei wa "Yes" ka "No" ka kiite ita kedo "Yes" demo nakute "No" demo nai'* (I could understand the question but I didn't know how to answer. There were no choices that were right. Although the teacher was asking 'Yes' or 'No' the answer was neither 'Yes' nor 'No'). The teacher's insistence that Marin directly and publicly indicate whether she is capable of carrying out the task infringe on classroom expectations that tend to side with self-deprecation. Limited to either a definitive 'Yes or No', Marin points out that she has understood the question yet cannot comfortably respond and consequently elects to respond through silence. The teacher implies that providing a one word answer, 'Yes or No', is a simple and undemanding request, however from Marin's perspective, this constraint denies her the opportunity to truthfully state what she believes to be her capacity to perform the task and to have this accepted. In this sense, the imposed limitations impede Marin's face claims as she is prevented from discursively contributing to the activity in an accurate and meaningful way.

Retrospective data illustrated that silence was a communicative strategy at times employed when freedom to respond was constrained, or when the correct form of response could not be readily identified. This is of significance given that while the teacher inferred that silence was motivated by fear of failure, a number of students noted their desire to verbally engage and expressed disappointment when they felt powerless to align with a positive identity through demonstrating L2 competence or contributing to activities. For example, when unable to answer a teacher initiated question in the manner in which she desired to, student Ami commented: *'wakatta kedo kantanna kotoba ga omoitsukanakatta kara nani mo ienakute gakkari shita (...) wakatteta kara sensei ni mo watashi wa wakatteru to shitte moraitakatta'* (I understood but I couldn't think of an easy word and couldn't say anything so I was disappointed. I understood so I wanted the teacher to know that I understood). Ami assumes that her failure to verbally respond will be interpreted by the teacher as an inability to understand the question and feels *'gakkari'* (disappointed) that she incapable of addressing this loss of face. Similarly, the loss of face student Akari associates with not being able to respond as she would like to is underlined in her frustration when she comments: *'watashi wa kotaetai to omotte ita (...) kotae ga wakatta kedo hontou ni dou yatte setsumeisureba ii ka wakannakatta (...) chou iraira shita'* (I felt like I wanted to answer. I knew what the answer was but I really didn't know how to explain it. I felt really frustrated). These comments in turn illustrate that the students felt that they did not have the L2 linguistic proficiency required to respond accurately or identify possible discursive alternatives. Without effective discursive strategies to express themselves, the students were unable to seek teacher support and therefore watched on in silence and frustration as their lack of verbal engagement was interpreted by the teacher as deficient comprehension and non-participation. It is worth noting that while students recognised silence as an acceptable and interactive form of expression within the classroom, they nevertheless expressed frustration and disappointment at points when L2 limitations forced them to abandon verbal contributions. In the following exchange a student is asked to read from her textbook and following several short unsuccessful attempts, withdraws into silence.

[Classroom excerpt 31: The teacher (T) asks Sayaka (S) then Miku (M) to read from the textbook.]

1T: OK ((T points at T/B)) so:: (1) let's look at the next part (2) <u>number one</u> ((moves over to S, points at T/B reading activity)) can you read¿ (2) what does (.) <u>this</u> say¿ ((leans over desk, points at T/B activity))

2S: ((S glances at T, looks down at T/B)) (5) Lo:: (4) loo (2) looking (1) look (2) at (.) the (2) te (3) ((glances up at T, then down at T/B)) te (15)

3T: ((T rocks from left to right foot several times)) *yomemasu ka¿* (2) *yomemasu ka¿ (.) yomenai¿* (1) *YOMENAI¿* ((looks down at S)) 'Can you read it¿ No¿ Can you read it¿ Can't read it¿ Can't read it¿'

4R: ((S looks at T/B)) (7)

5T: ((T strides toward M)) (3) Can you read it¿ (2) *YOMEMASU KA¿* 'Can you read it¿'

6M: (3) ((M nods, quiet voice)) Look at the ten boys and girls (1) look at them playing (.) in the snow (2) they are (.) having fun (1) together ((looks up at T))

In turn 1, the teacher moves over to student Sayaka, and asks her to read from the textbook as the class watches on in silence. Sayaka, under pressure to perform, initiates a cautious response as she phonetically feels her way through the textbook passage, 'Lo, loo, looking, look at the te' before appearing confused and falling silent (turn 2). The loss of face associated with her abandoned response is compounded when the teacher, impatiently rocking back and forth, abruptly inquires in Japanese if Sayaka can or cannot read the passage, *'yomemasu ka¿ yomemasu ka¿ yomenai¿ yomenai¿'* (Can you read it¿ Can you read it¿ Can't read it¿ Can't read it¿). Sayaka's silence leads the teacher to believe that she cannot read the passage, and perhaps assuming that he is saving her further embarrassment, elects to progress by redirecting his question to Miku who while appearing reluctant, subsequently goes on to smoothly read the passage 'Look at the ten boys and girls. Look at them playing in the snow. They are having fun together'. Reflecting on this exchange during retrospection, Sayaka commented: *'sono gurai yomeru kedo tochuu de tomacchatta kara sugoi zannen datta'* (I can read that kind of thing but I stopped midway through so I was really disappointed). An examination of Japanese students' attitudes towards classroom tasks and activities conducted by Dwyer and Heller-Murphy (1996) in their ESL classrooms in the UK found that while students were frustrated by not speaking in class, they did not necessarily find this uncomfortable. Identifying a gap in teacher/ student perceptions of silence, the researchers suggest that 'One learning style to which teachers may need to adapt is silence in the speaking class' (1996: 51). In the above feedback, Sayaka's loss of face occurs because she has not been able to contribute to the task and claim face in line with her intentions or how she perceives her level of ability. While she is clearly disappointed, perhaps the most critical point is that she is compelled to accept a negative teacher evaluation and watch on as the teacher seeks out a member of the class considered more capable of responding.

Silence and *Aizuchi*: Backchannels

During retrospective feedback, students stated that they were frustrated when rebuked by the teacher for failing to verbally contribute to learning activities principally when they indicated that they had in fact communicated responses. Among other things, this gap in student/teacher perceptions of silence as a tool to communicate versus silence as the absence of communication, revealed different interpretations and attitudes pertaining to the Japanese students' extensive use of *aizuchi* (backchannels) and nodding. The issue here being that students who were not always verbally participating in the ways expected by the teacher were observed in class recordings actively and recurrently employing *aizuchi* strategies along with nodding. The term *aizuchi* is derived from the rhythmic hammering of blacksmith and apprentice as they fashion the blade for a sword. Collaborating to forge the blade, the master establishes and maintains the hammering pace as the apprentice follows the lead in alternate turns. Reflecting this rhythmical alternation of blows, the interjection of *aizuchi* during interaction maintains the flow of an exchange by confirming the interest and involvement of the listener, and thereby encouraging the speaker to continue. Miyata and Nisisawa (2007) explain that 'by giving feedback signals, the listener backs up the speaker not only by signalling understanding, but also by indirectly granting the speaker the right to go on talking by defining himself as a listener' (2007: 1256). In this way, *aizuchi* and nodding are engaged by interlocutors in a collaborative negotiation which upholds the efficient transition of the floor in a socially positive manner (Kogure, 2007: 1288).

Two types of *aizuchi* outlined by Miyata and Nisisawa (2007) are utterance-internal, which signal continuation and understanding but never agreement or empathy, and utterance-final, which are comparable to English backchannel signals similar to 'I see' or 'really' (2007: 1255). The researchers explain that an *aizuchi* exchange contains a 'complementary pair of the aizuchi invitation by the speaker and the actual aizuchi delivered by the listener' (2007: 1255). A useful model for understanding specific *aizuchi* is offered by Iwasaki (1997) who defines three types of *aizuchi*: non-lexical, phrasal, and substantive: (1) non-lexical *aizuchi* refer to a closed set of short sounds with little or no referential meaning such as *ee, soo, aa*; (2) phrasal *aizuchi* are stereotypic expressions with meaning such as *naruhodo* and *uso*; and (3) substantive *aizuchi* are an open class of expressions with full referential content (1997: 666). Based on Iwasaki's categories, non-lexical backchannels tend to be treated as continuers while phrasal and substantive backchannels are interpreted as reactive backchannels. Similarly, Horiguchi (1997) classifies *aizuchi* into three types: (1) a fixed set of short expressions called *aizuchi-shi* which include *hai, ee, hoo, fuun, hee, soo desu ne, naruhodo,* and *honto;* (2) a repetition; and (3) a short reformulation of the preceding utterance. In addition to being markedly different from English short utterances in terms of pervasiveness, variety and placement (Maynard, 1986), Kita and Ide (2007) make the point that while backchannels and nodding in English typically indicate that the listener shares the speaker's evaluative stance on an event or situation, during Japanese interaction the coordination of nods, *aizuchi*, and cues that elicit them do not rely on the content of conversation. As *aizuchi* are not mediated by the content of an exchange, during interaction in Japanese, *aizuchi* perform as supportive behaviours by which a listener and speaker unite to mutually coordinate the flow of conversation (see LoCastro, 1987; Mizutani, 1983 for a list of *aizuchi*).

Maynard (1993a) outlines six primary functions of *aizuchi* as being: (1) continuer; (2) display of understanding of content; (3) support and empathy toward the speaker; (4) agreement; (5) strong emotional response; and (6) minor additions, corrections, or requests for information. These functional categories of *aizuchi* closely reflect those proposed by Horiguchi (1988) which include: (1) display of listening; (2) display of understanding; (3) display of agreement; (4) display of disagreement; and (5) expression of emotion. While commonly explained as verbal and non-verbal responses and/or reactions that a listener proffers the speaker during interaction (Cutrone, 2011), *aizuchi* can also be employed by the turn-holder to elicit further *azuchi* from the listener during the loop sequence (Kita & Ide, 2007). The loop sequence, in which short verbal and non-verbal exchanges are collaboratively interwoven by speaker and listener, is explained by Iwasaki (1997) as 'a turn-taking pattern consisting of a consecutive backchannel and back-backchannel expressions, produced by different speakers' (1997: 673). As Ike (2010) points out, 'there are multiple exchanges of backchannels and short backchannel-like utterances' (2010: 211) traded throughout the course of the loop sequence which serve to uphold interaction through performing key functions including continuer, showing acknowledgement, agreement, judgment and emotional reaction while simultaneously expressing the desired attitudinal stance toward the speaker (2010: 206). Illustrating the pervasiveness of *aizuchi*, Mizutani (1988) notes the frequency with which Japanese speakers employ *aizuchi* as being approximately 15 to 20 times per minute on average with approximately 30% of the backchannels initiated by the speaker's head movement (Maynard, 1987, 1990, 1997). Cross-cultural comparisons illustrate that the frequency of backchannels in Japanese conversation is significantly higher than recorded in both American and British English (Cutrone, 2005; Maynard, 1986, 1990, 1993a, 1997).

Comparisons of Japanese speakers' L1 and L2 backchannel behaviour with that of NSs of English demonstrate that whether speaking English or Japanese, Japanese tend to backchannel more frequently than L1 English speakers (Maynard, 1986, 1990). Similarly, various functions of head movement frequently observed in *aizuchi* are employed by Japanese speakers of English (Ike, 2010; Maynard, 1987; Szatrowski, 2000, 2003). These findings are supported by Ike's (2010) examination of narrative-style dyadic conversations produced by proficient Japanese English speakers, during which a total of 1065 backchannel instances were identified and examined for frequency, types and discourse contexts. Ike reported that Japanese English speakers used almost twice as many backchannels as Australian English speakers for the same amount of information, producing approximately one backchannel every 6.5 words in comparison to Australian English speakers 12.7 words. While research examining backchannels as they relate to politeness and face theory is still in its infancy (Cutrone, 2011), the high level of interest in the frequency, form, function, and timing of *aizuchi* reflects agreement in the research community that *aizuchi* represent an important communicative tool for Japanese speakers. Calling for greater attention to *aizuchi*, Ike (2010) surmises that *aizuchi* backchannel behaviour 'is a distinctive feature of Japanese English which should be properly recognised by Japanese speakers of English and speakers of other varieties of English in order to have successful cross-cultural communication' (2010: 205). The point being that backchannel behaviour, both employed in Japanese and transferred into Japanese English, contains cultural value and social customs employed extensively in order to manage discourse and uphold affective bonds between interlocutors.

Holding that *aizuchi*, verbal and non-verbal, constitute a unique and important feature of Japanese communication, the following analysis explores the students' use of *aizuchi*, and reaction to the teacher's implication that *aizuchi* equated to speaker silence. *Aizuchi* are discussed through contemplation of the Japanese students intended communicative functions and how cross-cultural pragmatic conflict threatens the management of face and impacts on the enactment of identity. Student feedback such as expressed in Iori's remark: *'nande watashi ga kotaete iru toki ni shikato shiteta no ka wakannai'* (I don't know why [the teacher] ignored me when I was answering) illustrates that the students expected *aizuchi* cues would be recognised by the teacher both in form and communicative intent. The teacher's failure to acknowledge *aizuchi* as a valid form of classroom discursive participation threatened the students face and resulted in the rejection of attempts to align with a 'good student' identity; in other words, students were positioned as failing to behave in accordance with a normative classroom identity as defined by the teacher. Accordingly, the students' frequent use of *aizuchi* responses resulted in a situation in which students felt that their projected claims for face as engaged and responsive students were blocked by the teacher's insistence on verbal participation as constituting the classroom standard.

Students expressed perceptible frustration that their use of *aizuchi* resulted in alignment with distinctly negative identities such as less capable, non-participatory, uncooperative and/or reticent. The rejection of these identities and the desire to be positioned in line with how they perceived their performance was expressed in student Ami's comment, *'itsumo no you ni "un" tte itteru kanji datta (…) hanasanai to kotae da to mitomete kurenai'* (It's like we were saying 'Un' [nods to indicate 'Yes'] like we usually do. [The teacher] won't accept an answer unless it's spoken.). Similarly, identifying discrepancies in teacher/student expectations regarding an appropriate classroom response and the use of head movement, Iori commented, *'futsuu ni unazuite ita kedo sensei wa "OK" to kotaete hoshikatta'* (I was nodding [to indicate 'Yes'] as usual but the teacher wanted me to answer 'OK'). Nodding, a distinctive and prevalent form of *aizuchi* referred to by Ike (2010) as an influential and multifunctional backchannel cue, was frequently used by students to engage in interaction and to establish rapport with the interlocutor. The students' awareness that *aizuchi* use, verbal and non-verbal, was a discouraged form of communication within the L2 classroom fuelled acts of classroom resistance expressed through deliberate avoidance of participation. In short, contrary to the teacher's stance, the students did not differentiate between *aizuchi* and spoken language when communicating meaning and consequently, found this unfamiliar distinction a threat to their standard forms of communication.

The following two classroom excerpts, examined with the aid of students' retrospective feedback, illustrate the gap between teacher and student perceptions of *aizuchi* as an acceptable form of classroom participation. Excerpt 32, a continuation of excerpt 30, traces an exchange during which students are asked in turn to indicate if they can count from 1 to 100:

[Classroom excerpt 32: The teacher (T) asks Kaori (K) to indicate if she can count from 1 to 100.]

1T: ((T points at K)) OK (1) next (1) can you count from 1 to 100₹

2K: (2) *u::n* :((nods))
‘Yes’

3T: (5) ((T moves toward K)) Can you₹ ((raises shoulder)) (2) ((K glances at classmates, then looks up at T))

4K: (6) ((K looks at classmates, looks up at T, nods)) *u::n*
‘Yes’

5T: (6) ((T looks at K, takes step forward)) Is that YES or NO⸮ ((looks around at Ss, shrugs, quizzical expression))

6K: (8) U::n ((T frowns, places hands on hips)) (5) yes ((K looks at T then down and shuffles through notes)) 'Yes'

7T: ((T folds arms, moves directly in front of K, taps desk with hand)) (3) Do you <u>understand the question</u>⸮ (1) *ima no shitsumon <u>wakarimashita ka</u>⸮* 'Did you understand this question⸮'

8K: (6) ((K looks at classmates, then up at T)) (1) Yes ((T shrugs, furrows forehead, turns away))

Throughout the exchange, the teacher's approach demonstrates that he will only recognise a verbal response from Kaori as a legitimate indication as to whether she can count from one to one hundred. The teacher reacts to Kaori's use of *aizuchi 'un'* (Yes) (turns 2 and 4) by demanding she provide verbal clarification: 'Can you⸮' (turn 3) and 'Is that Yes or No⸮' (turn 5) which inadvertently sparks a stumbling exchange scattered with drawn-out silences. The insistence that Kaori respond verbally, coupled with the teacher's progressively frustrated tone of voice and patently agitated body language threatens Kaori's face as she struggles to identify how she is expected to respond. At the same time, the teacher's inability to effectively manage the exchange in order to bring about the desired level of participation is compromised by his lack of awareness of, and/or reluctance to acknowledge Kaori's *aizuchi*. Having ascertained that *'un'* (Yes) and simultaneous nodding will not be permitted by the teacher as valid affirmation of her ability to count to one hundred, Kaori attempts to diffuse the threat to her face by aligning with the teacher's expectations which she does by responding 'Yes' (turn 6). As opposed to accepting Kaori's English verification of ability as reliable, the teacher folds his arms, moves directly in front of Kaori's desk, and briefly pauses before fixing his gaze on her, tapping her desk and skeptically querying *'Do you understand the question⸮ Ima no shitsumon wakarimashita ka⸮'* (Did you understand this question⸮). Through casting doubt on Kaori's comprehension the teacher brazenly threatens her face by overtly insinuating that he does not value her affirmative *'Yes'* as an accurate or truthful response. The implication being here is that Kaori's response is intended to placate the teacher and bring a swift conclusion to the exchange. Visibly confused, Kaori looks around at classmates, then up at teacher before reaffirming 'Yes', to which the teacher distrustfully shrugs, visibly furrows his forehead, and turns his back on the student.

Discussing the students use of *aizuchi* during learning activities the teacher remarked, 'I want the students to actually say something and not just make sounds or nod. That's not an answer. It doesn't tell me anything. I expect an answer. It's important that students learn this'. The teacher's rejection of *aizuchi* as a legitimate interactional strategy precludes the students from demonstrating English proficiency and engaging in classroom activities in a manner they judge to be relevant. This is evident in the above excerpt during which the use of the *aizuchi* 'un' (Yes) while nodding is intended by Kaori to serve as a transparent indication that she believes she is capable of counting to one hundred, while at the same time serving to give the floor back to the teacher. The teacher's failure to acknowledge or respond to Kaori's confirmation results in the collapse of the communicative loop sequence and is evidently perplexing for Kaori particularly as she has clearly indicated her ability to perform the task not once, but three times (turns 2, 4 and 6). During retrospection Kaori provided insight into how she felt at the time commenting: *'are kowakatta (...) kotaeteta no ni onaji shitsumon o nan kai mo kiite kita'* (That was scary. I answered but the teacher kept asking the same question). Mirroring Kaori's sentiment, concern that the teacher unfairly failed to endorse *aizuchi* and nodding was expressed by other students including Reika who commented, *'jibun no ban ni natta toki wa sugoku kinchou suru (...) kubi kashigete wakaranai koto o tsutaeyou to shita kedo sensei wa kizukanakatta mitai'* (When it was my turn I felt really nervous. I tilted my head to show that I didn't understand but the teacher didn't seem to realise). Kaori and Reika's frustration finds support in classroom silence research conducted by Nakane (2006) which points out that communication within the Japanese classroom does not rely on students providing verbal confirmation to indicate learning goals have been achieved. In the above excerpt, *aizuchi* feedback signals are employed by the student in order to support the teacher by signalling understanding and what Miyata and Nisisawa (2007) describe as 'indirectly granting the speaker the right to go on talking by defining himself as a listener' (2007: 1256). The loop-sequence however, breaks down when the teacher fails to acknowledge the students active participation in the exchange. The teacher's view that student communication through making 'sounds or nodd(ing)' does not constitute a response as it fails to communicate relevant information such as whether comprehension has been achieved, underscores the potential for the teacher to unintentionally threaten student face and the possibility for communication breakdown in cross-cultural exchanges.

Head movements, used both alone and with verbal *aizuchi*, are used by student Kaori and her classmates at grammatical conclusion points and intonation boundaries in order to develop the interaction. This role of nodding finds support in Maynard's (1993b) analyses of the frequency and functions of speaker and listener nods in Japanese which outlines functions as emphasising message, showing clause boundaries and signalling turn-end or turn-claims. Of importance here is that the multifunctional use of nods as employed throughout the loop sequence, both with and without verbal *aizuchi*, demonstrates that the listener is engaged and actively seeks to establish positive rapport with the interlocutor. Nods, produced both with and without verbal *aizuchi*, frequently occur during the loop sequence in Japanese conversation underscoring that silence is not void of meaning, but rather serves to maintain interaction through demonstrating the participants' collaborative stance (Kogure, 2007). The above excerpt illustrates that the teacher is unable or unwilling to recognise Kaori's nodding and verbal confirmation *'un'* (Yes) as an expression of affirmation. Contrary to student expectations, the teacher reacts to non-verbal communication strategies through blocking *aizuchi* until students proffered oral responses. The tendency for L2 speakers of Japanese to misinterpret the functions of *aizuchi* is illustrated in Ishida's (2006) examination of Japanese NSs and learners of Japanese knowledge of *'un'* which revealed differences in perceptions and interpretations of the communicative functions of *'un'* as causing misunderstanding. To illustrate, the researcher noted that the learners of Japanese preferred specific verbal expressions to illustrate attentiveness and responded critically to the use of *aizuchi* '"he just said *uun* or just nodded," "he didn't say "oh that's not good" or …he was just nodding,' and 'he like sort of nodding and stuff. But he didn't seem to be saying a lot' (2006: 1972). In the following classroom exchange, the teacher asks a student to confirm whether she has understood an exercise from the textbook and refuses to recognise nodding as permissible verification.

[Classroom excerpt 33: The teacher (T) asks Miu (M) to indicate whether she understands.]

1T: ((T holds up T/B)) She <u>does</u> homework (2) he <u>watches</u> TV (2) she <u>practices</u> the piano (2) he <u>plays</u> games (2) ((looks at M, gestures toward her by raising chin)) do you understand⸮

2M: (1) ((M nods))

3T: (5) ((T places hand on hips)) Do (1) you (1) <u>under::stand</u>⸮ ((raises shoulders, extends arms out from body with palms faced upward))

4M: (4) ((M looks up at T, nods))

5T: (2) ((T folds arms in front of body)) OK⸮ (1) OK⸮ (4) ((moves towards M, stronger tone)) what is that⸮ (1) is that OK⸮

6M: (3) ((M looks up at T, tilts head to side)) (5) OK ((looks down at desk))

The excerpt commences when the teacher, referring to a series of text-book illustrations from which he forms model structures such as 'She does homework. He watches TV', seeks to establish whether student Miu has understood the activity 'Do you understand?' Appearing poised and confi-dent, in turn 2 Miu meets the teacher's eyes and almost immediately nods to indicate that she can follow the lesson content. In turn 3, dismissing Miu's non-verbal confirmation proffered through nodding, the teacher radically lowers the tone of his voice and proceeds to slowly restate the question paus-ing distinctly between each word 'Do you understand?' (turn 3). Visibly apprehensive, in turn 4 Miu takes several seconds before again nodding in response to the teacher's further request for verification of comprehension. In turn 5, the teacher's serious countenance represents a clear threat to Miu's face as he communicates his displeasure by demanding, 'OK? OK?' After a brief pause the teacher follows-up by once again demanding clarification in a markedly stronger tone 'What is that? Is that OK?' Miu's discomfort is apparent as she reacts to the loss of face through tilting her head to the side in an expression of confusion, before timidly submitting to the teacher's demands when she quietly responds 'OK' after which she shifts her gaze away from the teacher and down at her desk (turn 6). While Miu assumes that she has confirmed her comprehension through nodding, her non-verbal participation is interpreted by the teacher not only as discourteous, but also as complicating efforts to confirm comprehension and to progress with the lesson. During retrospection Miu expressed her views as follows: *'futsuu ni "un" to yutteru no ni nan ka "OK" tte yutte kara wakatte kureta (…) ikinari "yutte" mitai na kanji dakara "OK" tte itta (…) unazuiteru (…) sensei wa "OK" tte kaeshite hoshikatta'* (I was saying *'un'* [Yes] as usual but it was only when I said 'OK' that [the teacher] understood. All of a sudden he was like, 'Say it! Say it!' So I said 'OK'. I was nodding [to indicate 'Yes'], [but] the teacher wanted me to answer 'OK').

Miu expresses confusion that her answer is unceremoniously rejected given that she has responded in what she terms a usual *'futsuu'* manner through *'unazuite'* (nodding) and verbal *aizuchi 'un to yutteru'* (I was saying *'un'* [Yes] as usual). Predictably, the teacher's demand for verbal confirmation is interpreted by Miu as being *'ikinari'* (sudden) and unexpected given that *aizu-chi* are frequently employed to articulate comprehension. As noted by Iwasaki (1997), 'Many non-lexical backchannels (e.g. *nn, ee, hai*) are used as an affir-mative answer token (i.e. "yes") and inherently carry a property of the second pair-part' (1997: 667). Iwasaki makes the point that non-lexical *aizuchi* func-tion as an affirmative answer token and consequently the floor-holding speaker, in this case the teacher, is expected to continue without directly responding to it (1997: 667). The above excerpt illustrates the power imbalance embodied in what Miu refers to as the teacher's demand to *'ikinari "yutte" mitai na kanji'* (All of a sudden [the teacher] was like, 'Say it! Say it!'). While the classroom excerpt reveals that *'yutte'* ('Say it! Say it!') was not the precise expression the teacher employed, this was nevertheless how the exchange was interpreted by Miu who felt she had no option but to respond in accordance with these demands. *Aizuchi* were in the teacher's view, not an acceptable form of participation, and resulted in a demand for oral participation that imposed restrictions on student freedom to interact in the way in which they are accustomed to within the classroom.

A central issue was not only the teacher's rejection of *aizuchi* as an acceptable form of classroom communication, but also his failure to acknowledge that *aizuchi* use marked the high value students' attached to upholding the teacher's face. This was reflected in feedback such as when student Fuuka, following an extended period of classroom silence during which the teacher struggled to encourage student participation commented: *'nani ka hannou shite agenai to na mitaini omotte unazuku ka kubi kashigeru ka nan ka jesucha-shinai to'* (I felt like I had to give some kind of response, maybe nod my head, or tilt my head or some kind of gesture or something) and further explains that if she does not that it may pose a problem for the teacher *'komacchattari suru kana'*. Fuuka, viewing student non-participation as generating a potential threat to the teacher's role and rank within the classroom actively engages through *'unazuku'* (nodding in assent), *'kubi kashigeru'* (tilting her head to the side to demonstrate uncertainty) and *'jesucha-'* (gesture) in order to uphold the teacher's face through demonstrating her participation. Not only does this register her support directly to the teacher, but also serves to convey to her peers a message that promotes involvement. . In short, through *aizuchi* Fuuka fills the void signalling support and empathy however, *aizuchi* are not truly effective as these intentions are not evident to the teacher.

As noted, the coordination of nods and *aizuchi* in Japanese interaction is, among other things, viewed as being a standard communicative strategy by which to uphold the exchange, support the speaker, and contribute to a positive social bond between interlocutors (Ishida, 2006; Iwasaki, 1997; Kita & Ide, 2007; Kogure, 2007). In this way, students present themselves in the language classroom through the use of *aizuchi* and nodding as a means of establishing what they view as being normative classroom roles in line with Japanese communication practices. The use of *aizuchi* within the loop sequence was either not recognised or disallowed by the teacher, resulting in a challenge to the students' capacity to align with a 'good student' identity and uphold mutual face through rejection of the students' attempts to embrace Japanese communicative strategies and to build affective bonds with the teacher.

Silence and Processing Time

The final area of silence related identity to emerge from student retrospective feedback as important to the management of student face concerns disparity between teacher/student interpretations of processing time. Specifically, students highlighted conflicting assumptions as to what constituted a reasonable allocation of time for processing information prior to the student verbally responding. Classroom recordings demonstrated that during periods of student silence the teacher repeatedly directed students in both Japanese and English to work quickly, 'Come-on hayaku quickly'. This was of consequence as students directly noted that untimely teacher intervention interfered with their capacity to respond to questions as desired and triggered silence – the very behaviour the caution was intended to correct. Students objected to being rushed and condemned, albeit during retrospective interviews, the teacher's assumption that time spent in thought indicated a lack of competence or willingness to participate as illustrated in feedback such as, *'sensei ni sonna ni isogasaretaku nai'* (I didn't want the teacher to hurry me so much), *'zutto asetteru kanji datta'* (The whole time I felt rushed) and *'jikan ga nai toki dou sureba ii no?'* (What am I going to do when I don't have time?). Conflicting teacher/student views towards the appropriate allocation of time represents a threat to identity construction and enactment given that teacher rejection of silence; (a) was interpreted as a criticism of normative classroom behaviour, (b) underlined the power differential that exists between the teacher and students, (c) prevented students from aligning with the performance of a 'good student'.

Student silence occurred primarily at the margins of speakers' turns – from the end of the teacher's turn and the onset of the student's part. Of significance here is that these switching pauses revealed inconsistencies in perceptions of response times with ensuing teacher intervention triggering communication breakdown. In the following classroom excerpts (excerpts 34, 35 and 36) the teacher assumes response time related silence represents student inability and reticence. Students, powerless to reject this critical alignment during classroom activities, were alert to the teacher's acts of positioning and voiced their frustration during retrospective interviews. In the first classroom excerpt, the teacher admonishes students when they take longer than expected to provide answers to a homework task.

[Classroom excerpt 34: The teacher (T) instructs Kaori (K) and Iori (I) to share their responses to a word search activity.]

1T: ((T points towards K)) What's your word? ((clicks fingers rapidly)) (2) QUICKLY

2K: (4) ((K glances up at T, looks down at W/B)) Challenge

3T: ((T nods and smiles)) (1) <u>Challenge</u> ((points at I, makes circular movement with hands))

4I: ((I looks down at W/B, then up at T)) (5) Alphabet

5T: (1) ((T nods)) Alphabet (1) ((turns towards K, clicks fingers, points at K) how many letters are in <u>challenge</u>? (3) ((makes rapid circular motion with hands)) how many letters? (1) C-H-A-L ((points towards K, K looks at W/B)) (2) ((T clicks fingers, points at I)) alphabet (1) how many?

6K/I: (5) ((K/I look down at W/Bs))

7T: HOW MANY letters in alphabet? (2) HOW MANY letters are in challenge? (4) ((points toward K then I with marker, shakes marker up and down rapidly)) (3) <u>quickly</u>

8K/I: (6) ((K/I glance at each other, write in notebooks))

9T: ((T taps marker against palm of hand)) Quick, quick, quick (2) QUICK (3)

10K/I: (7) ((K/I glance at each other, tilt heads, look at notebooks))

11T: ((T points at K/I with whiteboard marker)) QUICK (10) which one wins (.) alphabet (.) or challenge? (1) <u>which one is longer</u>? (2) ((looks at K/I, shrugs shoulders, shakes head)) (3) WELL ((moves toward whiteboard)) (2) looks like I'll have to do it ((writes 'challenge' and 'alphabet' on whiteboard))

In turn 1, the teacher asks student Kaori, to share the English word she has identified as containing the maximum number of alphabet letters 'What's your word?' and pauses momentarily for a response after which he abruptly demands *'Quickly'*. Appearing flustered by the implication that she has taken an excessive amount of time, Kaori glances up at the teacher with a confused expression, then shifts her attention back to her notebook to scan her work before responding 'Challenge' (turn 2). The threat to Kaori's face is in part mitigated when the teacher nods in confirmation and directs his focus on the next student, Iori, who takes approximately the same amount of time prior to tendering her response 'Alphabet' (turn 4). Through nodding his endorsement while verbally restating Iori's response 'Alphabet', the teacher expresses his approval, and then swiftly shifts his attention to establishing how many letters are in both words: 'How many letters are in challenge? How many letters? C-H-A-L? Alphabet. How many (letters are there)? (turn 5). The teacher's demand for a rapid student response is expressed through the urgency expressed in his voice and accompanying body language which is punctuated by vigorous circular motioning with his hands. When the students fail to respond in the time frame the teacher demands, he hastily intervenes restating the questions 'How many letters in alphabet? How many letters are in challenge?' and further conveys a sense of urgency by shaking the whiteboard marker in the direction of the students while stipulating they respond 'quickly' (turn 7). In turn 8, the students momentarily glance at each other before hastily turning their attention to their notebooks during which time the teacher continues to tap the whiteboard marker against the palm of his hand while in rapid succession stating 'Quick, quick quick! Quick!' (turn 9). The students are visibly uncomfortable as they glance back and forth between themselves, tilting their heads, while referring to their notebooks (turn 10) which further results in a final teacher demand for the students to be 'quick' (turn 11). The line of approach the teacher takes communicates that he assumes the students are capable of carrying out the task of identifying how many letters are in each word within the time frame he allocates. What is important to note here is that precise time requirements are at no point explicitly outlined, and, consequently, the students are expected to embrace time restraints that are not revealed and recognise the need for urgency that is not obvious or explained. The exchange concludes with the teacher determining that sufficient time has been allocated and therefore determining to take over the activity, and write both words on the whiteboard: 'Well, looks like I'll have to do it'.

The threat to student face entailed in the demand to work within a predetermined yet unspecified timeframe is evidenced in student Kaori's comment: '*"Quick quick quick quick" tte iu kara minna asette minna ga "eh" mitai na kanji (…) asetta kara osoku natta'* ([The teacher] said, 'Quick, quick, quick, quick' so we all kind of rushed. We were all like 'Huh? What?' I panicked so this slowed me down). The notion that insufficient allowances for time impeded effective participation was similarly echoed by student Fuuka who, after being directed by the teacher to work quickly, remarked: *'asecchau (…) kotaeru mae ni motto yukkuri kangaetai'* (I felt rushed. I want to take my time to think before I answer). Reflecting on a point at which she was instructed by the teacher to work quickly student Miu states *'minna maji de aseru (…) chotto matte tte kanji'* (Everybody really panicked. It's like hold on there). The teacher's untimely and often forceful intervention created apprehension which impacted on the students' facility to perform tasks through blocking their capacity to demonstrate engagement and ably partake. In short, the students' ability to express their thoughts is taken away.

Nakane's (2005) case study of Japanese students found that student silence functioned as a politeness strategy, an indication of cognitive processing time, and a feature of the students' interactive style. Based on student feedback, Nakane hypothesises that pauses are due to gaps in socio-cultural norms associated with turn-taking such as normative rapidity of turn-taking or tolerance.

The impact of timing and different levels of tolerance has been evidenced in early research such as Rowe's (1974) six year investigation of 'wait-time' on the development of language and logic in children taking part in elementary science programmes. Rowe outlined two types of wait time as being; (a) the time between a teacher question and a student answer, and (b) the time between when a student answers and the following teacher feedback or teacher question. In the case that the student remained silent, the teacher was found to apply strategies such as repeating the initial question, rephrasing, asking a different question or calling on another student (1974: 81). Rowe found that when mean wait time between a teacher question and a student answer was increased from one second to between three to five seconds, the quality of student participation was enhanced as well as the number and type of questions asked by the teachers. Among other things, Rowe noted that the length of responses increased, unsolicited responses increased, failure to respond decreased and the frequency of student questions increased (1974: 81). These findings are supported by Tobin (1987) who surmised that when average wait time was greater than three seconds, a higher cognitive level of learning was achieved and this influenced the quality of teacher and student discourse. With increased wait time, Tobin suggests that teacher questioning strategies tend to be more varied and flexible and there is greater attention to the quality and variety of teacher questions as opposed to quantity. For example, Tobin notes that teachers asked additional questions that required more complex information processing and higher-level thinking on the part of students.

In agreement with these findings, Maroni's (2011) examination of interaction in primary school classes found that wait time promoted students' involvement and the quality of their answers. Student involvement was found to be further enhanced if wait time was accompanied by teacher interventions encouraging student collaborative participation. Maroni, stressing the need for the teacher to instigate long pauses in order for students to produce a turn, intimates that the chief problem is one of calibration. The point being that determining when and for how long to pause is critical to providing students enough time to take their turn and respond to the question. Researchers have demonstrated that wait times are influenced by sociocultural factors that impact on perceptions as to what constitutes appropriate timing (Du-Babcock & Tanaka, 2010; Hess & Azumi, 1991; Maroni *et al.*, 2008; Nelson & Harper, 2006). An example of cultural divergence is offered by Scollon and Scollon (1990) in relation to the differing norms regarding pausing at transitions observed in Athabaskan and English.

The length of pause that the Athabaskan takes while expecting to continue is just about the length of pause the English speaker takes in exchanging turns. If an Athabaskan has in mind a series of sentences to say, it is most likely that at the end of the first one the English speaker will think that he has finished because of the length of the pause and will begin speaking. The Athabaskan feels he has been interrupted and the English speaker feels the Athabaskan never makes sense, never says a whole coherent idea. Much of this misunderstanding is the result of something like a one half second difference in the timing of conversational pauses, but it can result in strong stereotypical responses to the opposite ethnic group. (Scollon & Scollon, 1990: 273)

The students sense of frustration as expressed in comments such as *'"eh" mitai'* (It's like 'Huh? What?') indicated that the teacher's wait-time was viewed as being distinct from familiar practices. Moreover, explicit reference to confusion as being shared among the students *'minna'* (everybody) draws attention to linguistic and affective bonds of solidarity which align the class through mutual opposition to the teacher's demands. In the subsequent excerpt the students are asked to look around the classroom in order to identify English objects for a word search activity.

[Classroom excerpt 35: The teacher (T) asks the students (Ss) to identify classroom objects for an activity.]

1T: Let's start with classroom objects (2) I want you to find the longest words you can (2) like whiteboard ((gestures around classroom with hand sweep)) OK (.) what's a LONG English word? ((looks around classroom at Ss))

2S: (17) ((Ss glance at each other, look around classroom))

3T: ((T makes sweeping gesture with hands around classroom)) Look around (2) ((holds hands palms upward with fingers curling inward to invite contributions)) what's a LO::NG English word?

4S: (9) ((Ss look around classroom and at classmates))

5T: ((T clicks ball point pen quickly and repeatedly)) Come on (3) QUICK ((gestures with hands in circular motion, clicks pen))

6S: (16) ((Ss look at each other and around classroom))

7T: ((T clicks ball point pen rapidly and repeatedly)) Quick (3) what's a long English word? (1) QUICK

8S: (12) ((Ss look around classroom and at classmates))

9T: ((T clicks ball point pen rapidly and repeatedly)) Just say a word (.) anybody (1) say a word (1) what's a LONG English word? (.) QUICK (2) ANY WORD

Supplementing a textbook activity, in turn 1, the teacher indicates that the focus of the activity is on identifying 'Classroom objects' in English and informs the students that 'I want you to find the longest words you can' proffering 'whiteboard' as a suitable response. The teacher's request is followed by an extended pause during which the students can be seen actively looking at each other and around the classroom in order to ascertain potential responses (turn 2). In turn 3 the teacher, deciding sufficient time has transpired, makes a sweeping gesture around the classroom with his arms while encouraging the students to 'look around'. He then gestures with his fingers curling inward inviting responses while repeating the question, 'What's a long English word?' When the repeated question fails to stimulate the desired response (turn 4) the teacher does not conceal his frustration as he rapidly clicks a ballpoint pen and impatiently instructs the class 'Come on quick' (turn 5). A sense of urgency conveyed in the inference that students are working below expectations is further implied when reacting to silence, the teacher again demands 'Quick! What's a long English word? Quick!' (turn 7). The teacher's verbal interjections interwoven with dynamic gestures assert that the students' failure to contribute responses is viewed as a matter of deficient participation rather than task complexity A final attempt is made to encourage a student response when the teacher, implying that the task is simple and can be carried out by 'Anybody' solicits contributions asking, 'Just say a word. Anybody! Say a word. What's a long English word? Quick! Any word!'

Providing insight into her interpretation of the above exchange student Ami commented: 'sensei ga "isoide" to iu to isoganakucha to omou (...) sonna ni isogasaretaku nai (...) nani ka kangaenaito mitai na (...) jikan kakaru' (When the teacher says 'quickly' I feel that I have to hurry. I don't want to be so rushed. I feel like I've got to think of something. This takes time [to think of something]). Ami, while not verbally partaking in the way envisaged by the teacher, illustrates that she was engaged through actively considering viable responses. Ami, her face threatened by the implication that her performance is inadequate, illustrates that her ability to process the information and respond is obstructed by the sense of urgency communicated through the teacher's verbal and non-verbal interaction. Defiantly reflecting on the exchange, Ami forcefully concluded by stating 'yukkuri kangaetai' (I want to take my time to think about it) revealing that she was prepared to resist teacher pressure to perform within time limits and was prepared to use silence as a means of negotiating her own terms of engagement even if aligned with a negative identity. Similarly, the desire for the teacher to not only allocate more time, but to also take additional time when instructing was noted by student Hikari who commented, 'isogasaretaku nai (...) sensei *motto yukkuri shite hoshii'* (I don't want to be hurried. I want the teacher to take his time). In the final excerpt students are admonished when they fail to respond to the teacher's request for participation.

[Classroom excerpt 36: The teacher (T) instructs students (Ss) to identify the missing day from a sequence.]

1T: ((T reads from T/B)) Monday (.) Tuesday (.) Wednesday (.) Friday (.) Saturday (.) Sunday (.) Monday (2) ((looks at Ss)) what's the <u>missing day</u>⸮

2S: (8) ((S silence))

3T: Anybody⸮ ((T looks around at Ss))

4S: (6) ((S silence))

5T: ((T scratches head)) What's the missing day⸮ ((places hands on hips, looks around at Ss))

6S: (7) ((S silence))

7T: <u>Lis::ten</u> ((cups hand against his ear)) (2) Monday (.) Tuesday (.) Wednesday (.) Friday (.) Saturday (.) Sunday (.) Monday (4) ((looks at Ss)) <u>wake-up</u> ((closes eyes places, hands next to head to gesture sleeping, snores, slowly stretches as if waking from sleep)) (7) come one YOU KNOW (2) what's the <u>missing day</u>⸮

Throughout the exchange the teacher's mounting frustration culminates in a brief mimed performance during which he acts out sleeping, gradually awakens, stretches and looks around disorientated (turn 7). The pantomime of students waking from a metaphorical slumber insinuates that they are underperforming and directly projects a threat to the face as it questions motivation and participation levels. When the class fails to identify the missing day from the sequence (turn 1) the teacher initially encourages the students by indicating that he will not be nominating a student, and they are free to contribute at will, 'anybody⸮' (turn 3). When silence follows the teacher's forceful tone of voice and hands placed on his hips discloses his frustration as he repeats the initial question, 'What's the missing day⸮' (turn 5). In turn 7, the teacher is visibly agitated when in addition to his rather blunt performance, he projects a threat to the students face by admonishing them to 'Listen' and to 'Wake-up'. The rebuke illustrates that the students' silence is not only interpreted as constituting a lack of attentiveness, but is face threatening for the teacher who is unable to persuade the students to engage in the way in which he desires. What is important to note here is that the lack of a verbal response does not necessarily designate limitations in the students' abilities to comprehend or respond to the teacher's question as is indicated in Hikari's retrospective comment, *'nan'youbi na no ka o kangaeteta* (...) *sensei ga mou sukoshi nagaku matsu no ga futsuu'* (I was thinking about what day it should be. It's normal for the teacher to wait a little longer). As stated, from Hikari's perspective the lack of time allotted is not what she views as standard and threatens her face by impugning her ability to identify and respond in a timely fashion.

Classroom recordings demonstrated that, even following teacher intervention and demands for faster participation, the students did not refrain from using verbal and non-verbal *aizuchi* or noticeably speed up their response times. In other words, the teacher's intervention did not achieve the desired shift in classroom behaviour in regard to the frequency and situations in which the students employed silence. In addition to potential teacher/student variance regarding expectations surrounding the use of *aizuchi*, there may have been additional cultural factors which impacted on the Japanese students' tendency to employ silence. For example, Nakane (2005) notes that Japanese students can find themselves silenced during situations in which peers or the lecturer take over the floor from a designated speaker who requires time to organise a response. Nakane makes the point that 'once the floor is taken by others and the direction of talk is shifted, it can be difficult for Japanese students who are not familiar with voluntary participation in class to come back to the interaction without an explicit cue for participation' (2005: 94). Wong (2003) makes a similar observation in suggesting that when a Japanese keeps quiet in a seminar it does not mean that he has no opinion on the topic under discussion, but rather that he may be waiting to be nominated to speak. The sense of vulnerability associated with teacher/student power imbalance is highlighted by student feedback such as *'asecchaimasu'* (I felt rushed) which illustrated that the panic the student experiences at times obstructed ability to rationally process and respond to the lesson material.

The implication that the teacher views the absence of student talk as the absence of meaningful interaction was evident in his visible agitation and the frequency and force of his discursive intervention. The threat to student face and the negative identity alignment associated with the teacher's intervention during periods of student silence, such as directive to work 'quickly', was recognised by student Marin who notes *'"quick" toka sore wa tabun isoide datta you na ki ga suru kara amari sekasa nai de hoshii* (...) *isoide tte iwareru to nan ka "yabai kangaenakya" "yabai" mitai na kanji ni naru'* (I think words such as 'quick' meant to hurry so I didn't want [the teacher] to hurry me too much. When I'm told to hurry, I feel like 'Oh no! I have to think of something. Oh no!'). Indicating her desire to avoid being directed to work quickly Marin noted *'hayaku tte iware nai you ni kotae o ganbatte kangaeta* (...) *dokidoki shichau'* (I was doing my best to think of the answer so that I wouldn't be told to hurry. I get nervous). Moreover, retrospective interviews illustrated that the students resented being negatively positioned when they were on task and performing in a capacity consistent with how they viewed their classroom role. The cross-cultural disparity may have been intensified by the teacher's failure to recognise that the imposing of time restraints impacted on the students' ability to enact identities in line with their intentions. For example, Nakane (2006) found that student silence as a face-saving strategy is a standard practice within Japanese classrooms and therefore Japanese teachers do not appear to find silence as face-threatening as Australian lecturers do. This would suggest that from the Japanese students' perspective, the non-Japanese teacher's intervention during silence imposed a set of beliefs that were not necessarily shared.

Implications: Classroom Silence

The Japanese students' recourse to silence, and the ensuing discursive intervention employed by the teacher, represented an ongoing source of cross-cultural classroom misunderstanding. Points of disparity regarding interpretations of silence threatened students' face given that they indicated feeling compelled to speak, or else to endure a negative teacher evaluation. While non-verbal communicative practices corresponded to the Japanese students' cultural codes of acceptable L2 interaction, the teacher critically aligned the absence of student speech with fear of failure, reticence, and inability to comprehend lesson content. While fear of failure was indeed cited by students as a cause of silence, it is important to note that this was but one of many functions and that silence was not regarded by students as being an inappropriate strategy for negotiating this fear. Given that silence was viewed by the teacher as undesirable and unproductive, he therefore sought to modify silence orientations by means of demanding verbal contributions. The implication that they had violated classroom protocol rejected that for the students silence was viewed as a highly valued and multifunctional communicative tool.

Unaware of and/or impervious to the students' interactive use of silence, the teacher endeavoured to prevent silence and to deter offending students through verbal admonishment, body language, and insistence on oral classroom contributions. Teacher intervention strategies publicised the teacher's dissatisfaction and demanded students embrace communicative practices that retrospection revealed did not always feel appropriate or comfortable. Of note here is that silence research has demonstrated that within the Japanese classroom silence is not regarded as a threat to face or as obstructive behaviour (Nakane, 2006). On the contrary, silence represents a conventionalised politeness strategy by which to uphold an interlocutor's face through a diverse range of politeness orientated communicative functions such as expressing interest, respect and consent. Participating students revealed that periods of silence were at times associated with a lack of appropriate response options being made available. For example, when a student, directed by the teacher to respond either 'Yes' or 'No', felt that a definitive response failed to adequately account for his status, he noted feeling uncertain as to how to accurately respond and elected to remain silent. In addition, data revealed a distinct gap in student/teacher assumptions as to what constituted an appropriate waiting period between the teacher asking a question and the student responding. The teacher assumed a shorter processing time was required and as a result, when students failed to meet these unstated time demands, the assumption was that the silent student was unable or unwilling to respond. By contrast, students noted that there were moments at which they had comprehended content and were in the process of formulating responses when the teacher unexpectedly intervened and demanded verbal participation. Students favoured a longer time to process and formulate responses prior to classroom participation by means of verbal response.

Finally, retrospective feedback underscored a gap in student/teacher perceptions of what constitutes silence. While non-talk was associated by the teacher with the absence of communication, student feedback demonstrated that communication was not always to be regarded as exclusively verbal. The point being that the students recurrently employed *aizuchi* (backchannel) communication strategies often in combination with other gestures such as to *'unazuku'* (to nod in assent) and *'kubi kashigeru'* (to tilt one's head). While viewed by the students as appropriate and obvious indications of active participation, these non-verbal cues were not always recognised or indeed, permitted by the teacher. This requires attention given that not only does the teacher deny the students use of *aizuchi,* but also is unable to employ *aizuchi* in a way that the students may have found to be demonstrative of his desire to uphold communicative exchanges.To recap, the data findings illustrate that a central problem lies in conflicting interpretations of not only the appropriateness of moments of silences, but what should essentially be considered silence. The students were not permitted to employ silence in ways that they felt to be situationally appropriate due in part to the teacher's limited understanding of Japanese silence orientations, Moreover, the teacher expected that students would modify their interactional patterns to reflect the classroom behavioural norms he valued. Attention to silence as a communicative practice needs to be incorporated within curriculum in ways that respect student beliefs, behaviours and values which do not always reflect those norms the teacher may associate with the use of the L2.

Part 4

Reflection and Modification: Teacher Professional Development Model

11 Professional Development Conclusions and Implications

The findings presented in this book draw attention to the challenges that students encounter within the language classroom as they strive to manage face while forging and performing new identities. Student interpretations of classroom interaction offers persuasive evidence that students felt threatened by certain verbal and non-verbal features of the English language classroom that the teacher assumed to be standard practice. This was particularly so in cases when student language use or behaviour was not recognised or rejected by the teacher as violating L2 classroom expectations. Of significance here is that the data underscores that language and issues of identity are closely bound together, as too are language and the management and negotiation of face. As students claim and enact new identities their socio-culturally shaped worldviews are contested as they mediate elements of the L1/L2 cultures and languages. Participant insights highlight that while language was employed so as to confront issues of face and to enact specific identities, meanings attributed to such language were rooted in socio-cultural and individual affiliations that were not always mutually recognised. Participant reflections provide access to pervasive patterns of language use, attitudes, and behaviour from which a picture of the Japanese students' face, as a construct of identity, materialises.

In addressing issues of socio-cultural variance in the negotiation of face and alignment with identities, we argue that it is critical for language teachers to recognise how misconceptions associated with preconceived cultural stereotypes may influence divergence in the interpretation of communicative intentions. There is a pressing need for teachers to be trained to acknowledge and pedagogically respond to pragmatic divergence in the performance of illocutionary acts and behaviour in a culturally sensitive manner. In short, L2 teachers require training to recognise the pragmatic underpinnings of the views and beliefs that they and their students may hold. This is critical to building teacher awareness of their verbal and non-verbal actions in the class-room, and how these are being interpreted by students. Ishihara (2010), citing a gap between what is known about pragmatics in language use and how this information is conveyed to the student, denotes the teacher as 'the main agent in creating this bridge' (2010: 21). Referring to the pivotal role played by the teacher, Ishihara cautions that the teaching of pragmatics is impacted by teachers' backgrounds, knowledge, experiences and beliefs and therefore recommends monitoring, reasoning of teaching practices, and reflection. In order to serve as an effective 'bridge' we argue that the teacher requires knowledge as to the linguistic properties of the L1 and L2 and how these potentially relate to socio-cultural factors that support the negotiation of face and alignment with identities in order to reduce inadvertent, yet highly damaging miscommunication.

With this in mind, the final chapter begins with an examination of the interwoven relationship between structural knowledge and pragmatic knowledge of language. We then outline a model for teacher professional development and classroom practice which focuses on initially building teacher awareness through consciousness-raising tasks, and finally, the implementation of modifications to teaching practices and behaviours that can benefit the students. The model, a data-driven programme, is based on the premise that before teachers can be expected to change their beliefs, they need to first be made aware of them (Crandall, 2000), as beliefs, often held unconsciously, play an important role in the approach to teaching. This model, following a pedagogic and exploratory cycle of teaching and learning phases is employed in the context of professional communication develop-ment tasks built around the five phases of: Awareness, Knowledge Building, Critique, Action and Evaluation (see Candlin et al., 1995; Candlin, 1997; O'Grady, 2011) with a fifth Evaluation phase included. Following this, and in the light of the outcomes of the study, the chapter turns to a discussion of culturally sensitive teaching strategies and draws attention to a number of key implications in regard to the instruction of pragmatic forms within the classroom.

Structural Knowledge and Pragmatic Competence

The Japanese classroom, like any classroom, incorporates specific social and cultural notions of relative social status and membership which students are expected to acknowledge and maintain. While it is important to avoid oversimplifying, or generalising from particular instances of classroom behaviour, we may discern recurring patterns of verbal and non-verbal disparity as impacting on the students and teacher's ability to interpret communicative intentions, or express themselves as intended. These issues pose a challenge for the non-Japanese language teacher who must make decisions about not only what and how to teach, but also consider how instruction impacts on student face and the social and cultural identities performed within the learning environment. Student input is critical to classroom-based instruction in pragmatics given that in many cases pragmatic features of the L1/L2 may not come to light unless varying perspectives are voiced. Moreover, in order to provide meaningful pragmatic instruction, it is imperative that the teacher develop social and cultural knowledge relevant to pragmatic choices associated with both the native tongue and target language. This may be more challenging than it appears given that communicative practices are often so engrained in L1 communicative practices that we may not even consciously recognise them.

Attention to pragmatics and its principles, while rising, fails to garner the awareness in language teacher education programmes that other areas of language do with pragmatically related instructional materials and activities underrepresented in ESL and EFL settings. Moreover, the area of pragmatics and practical strategies for teaching pragmatics in the language classroom are not adequately addressed by many TESOL teacher preparation programmes (Bardovi-Harlig & Mahan-Taylor, 2003; Eslami-Rasekh, 2005; Ishihara, 2007; Ishihara & Cohen; 2010; Vásquez & Sharpless, 2009). A point in case being the results from a survey of approximately 100 MA-TESOL programmes around the United States (Vásquez & Sharpless, 2009) which found that while programmes have specific courses dedicated to phonology and syntax, the majority do not have a course dedicated to pragmatics. The survey found that while many MA-TESOL faculties expressed interest in exposing students to pragmatics, they had yet to determine where pragmatics should 'fit' in their curriculum. In many cases, the programmes surveyed were found to address issues of pragmatics in a piecemeal fashion as opposed to establishing comprehensive courses.

A lack of cross-cultural pragmatic awareness can seriously impede an individual's ability to express oneself or understand interlocutors intended communicative messages in situations when the language employed is by all accounts grammatically accurate and structurally comprehensible. For classroom pragmatic instruction to be successful, it is essential that pragmatics forms a part of the language teacher's content and pedagogical knowledge base. As a first step, language teachers require opportunities to build and/or update pragmatic knowledge relevant to their specific teaching/learning contexts in order to effectively identify and creatively integrate awareness raising activities into L2 curriculum. To achieve this, among other issues, requires that the teacher becomes accustomed to how the L1 is potentially used in classroom contexts by students, and how such use may differ from what he believes to represent target language norms. By means of demonstrating an awareness of structural and pragmatic knowledge of the L1 and L2, and how these relate to the classroom and beyond the classroom context, the teacher can communicate openness and respect towards the students' native tongue and culture. Moreover, through appropriate instruction, teachers can foster appreciation and awareness of one's own culture while at the same time, sensitising students to expect and be open to varying pragmatic interpretations consistent with the sensitivities of people from differing cultural, social and linguistic backgrounds. The importance for students is aptly captured by Ishihara (2010) who maintains that it is essential that teachers 'know how to communicate to their students the importance of having pragmatic ability in the L2, how to direct students' attention to features of socio-cultural context, and how to elicit and assess students' pragmatic use of language' (2010: 25).

A critical issue that needs to be considered is that students may prefer their own social and cultural values to those of the target language, even when explicitly instructed to perform in a specific way. For example, student Kaori, reserves her right to collaborate with peers and indicates that she will continue to resist the teacher's demand for individual work even when directly rebuked, stating, *'kotae ga wakatteru toki wa sono hito ni oshiete ageru'* (When I know the answer then I will tell the person being asked). In other words, students may resist altering their speech strategies even when aware that those strategies are not positively interpreted by the teacher within the L2 context. For this reason, it is essential for language students to be made aware of pragmatic divergence and to be urged to recognise that variation exists both across cultures and within communities of NSs, without however the student being forced to align with the L2 pragmatic expectations held by the teacher. Language students require opportunities within the classroom to develop the pragmatic linguistic tools and resources necessary to communicate and present themselves as they intend to within the target language. These include raising awareness of the potential for miscommunication when students elect not to embrace L2 pragmatic norms, particularly in situations when failure to do so may negatively impact on the speaker's ability to present himself in accord with his intentions. While the teacher has a responsibility to instruct students to use the target language in a situationally and culturally appropriate manner, students should be encouraged to make personally relevant choices reflecting their own values and their own desires concerning self-presentation in the target language.

Attention to pragmatics within L2 instruction does not have to be delayed until students have achieved specific levels of communicative competence.

Bardovi-Harlig and Mahan-Taylor (2003) make the point that while there is no single best approach to pragmatics instruction, there is the need for authentic language samples, and the need for input to precede student interpretation or production. Beyond exposure, explicit instruction in pragmatics is advocated as a way forward as students may not acquire the pragmatic features of the target language simply through identification. Instruction targeting pragmatic competence can be provided through an explanatory approach in order to provide students with perspective on language use in social and cultural contexts (Ishihara & Cohen, 2010) with instruction focusing on awareness activities, contextually authentic output practice, and production in real-world communication tasks (Archer *et al.*, 2012). Ishihara and Cohen (2010) argue that in order to provide effective instruction in pragmatics, teachers require; (a) an awareness of diverse pragmatic norms in a speech community, (b) the ability to provide metapragmatic information about target language pragmatic norms, (c) the ability to develop and assess L2 students' pragmatic competence, (d) sensitivity to students' subjective and cultural being. Awareness raising activities can involve demonstrations in both L1 and L2 in order to present cases of divergence in a context in which students have control over the language (Bardovi-Harlig & Mahan-Taylor, 2003) or personal anecdotes to illustrate pragmatic failure which serve to 'communicate the importance of learning about pragmatics' while also build solidarity between the teacher and the students (Ishihara & Cohen, 2010: 193). Cross-cultural discussion is advocated as an approach by which students can be aided in identifying variance that exists between the cultural and pragmatic norms associated with the native language and the target language (Bardovi-Harlig & Mahan-Taylor, 2003) based on the position that the student has to notice the pragmatic information in the input and understand its function in the surrounding context (Tagashira *et al.*, 2011). Teachers can then involve students in activities that prepare them for interaction outside of the classroom while at the same time giving them the confidence and the skills required to engage in activities within the classroom.

Reconceptualising the Nature of Language Teaching and Learning

> The 'best' teacher is neither the native nor the non-native speaker, but the person who can help learners see relationships between their own and other cultures, can help them acquire interest in and curiosity about 'otherness', and an awareness of themselves and their own cultures seen from other people's perspectives.
>
> (Byram *et al.*, 2002: 10)

Within the cross-cultural classroom context, it cannot be assumed that patterns of language use, verbal and non-verbal, will routinely be interpreted in the same way by students and their teachers. In order to avoid unintentionally imposing cultural values, among other things, teachers require professional development opportunities to reflect on how they are employing communication strategies within the language classroom, and the potential impact these strategies have on their students. In addition, to guard against ethnocentric generalizations, teachers require focused training to extend their awareness of the pragmatic features associated with students' native tongues, particularly when these may differ from assumed L2 standards. McKay (2002) makes the obvious yet essential point that, 'An understanding of the local culture of learning should not be based on stereotypes, or a received view of culture, in which assertions are made about the traditional roles of teachers and students and approaches to learning, often in reference to western culture. Rather, it should depend on an examination of particular classrooms' (2002: 129). The pragmatically informed teacher serves as a bridge between the chiefly controlled world of the classroom and the diverse and dynamic communicative challenges that lay beyond the classroom walls through promoting student openness to different pragmatic interpretations consistent to sensitivities of various cultures and social groups.

Knowledge of socio-cultural divergence in cross-cultural interaction practices enables the teacher to synthesise elements of different cultures, and thereby build an understanding of cultural differences that can be applied to teaching practices. By means of building teacher awareness of socio-cultural pragmatic distinctions through a process that begins with awareness raising reflection and ultimately leads to action, teachers can transfer their knowledge of pragmatic diversity into teaching practices. The goal is for teachers to be effectively equipped with knowledge and practical teaching skills by which to inspire students to examine the socio-cultural worlds of both the L1 and L2 beyond the classroom. The potential benefits for students are highlighted by Kawai (2007) who recommends a contextualised approach to English education in which students are helped to 'view the world critically, reflexively and multi-dimensionally' (2007: 52). Stressing that classroom practices represent an opportunity to establish supportive classroom norms, Dörnyei (2007) advocates implementing a norm of tolerance in order to ensure that the classroom experience is directed towards motivating students through promoting acceptance and cohesiveness. This notion of acceptance is a non-evaluative and positive regard of others acknowledging that humans are both complex and imperfect, while cohesiveness is the result of acceptance, commitment to the task, and group pride (2007: 721). Embracing culturally responsive teaching, Gay (2000: 29) recommends harnessing cultural knowledge, prior experiences, and performance styles of students to make learning more appropriate and effective. Gay makes the point that culturally responsive teaching acknowledges that cultural heritage impacts students' dispositions, attitudes, and approaches to learning, and necessitates pedagogical attention within the classroom.

Within the Japan context, comprehensive teacher training is imperative given that non-Japanese teachers of English employed by MEXT and in private *eikaiwa* (English conversation schools) are often on short term contracts, lack formal teacher training and often have limited opportunities for professional development (Ohtani, 2010). As Hammond (2007) points out, these teachers 'have a unique opportunity to adapt their lessons and activities to be responsive to Japanese culture' and go deeper than superficial cultural comparisons (2007: 41). In this way, the teacher can create meaningful links between the socio-cultural realities of the home and language learning. With the official inclusion of English as a compulsory subject in the elementary school curriculum along with the nomination of Tokyo Japan to serve as the host city for the 2020 Olympic Games, the number of English teacher's employed in Japan is expected to increase considerably. Accordingly, the need for an analytical approach to understanding socio-cultural features of language use in order to build non-Japanese language teachers awareness of what they are doing within the classroom, and how teaching practices and language use are being interpreted by students, has to be addressed in a methodical, meaningful, and economic manner.

Teacher Professional Development

For the L2 teacher, receptiveness to the identities students claim can be supported through facework that is attentive to the social and cultural practices, beliefs, traditions, customs and values which contribute to the expectations of all participants within the classroom. Such a goal demands considerable knowledge and experience of the practices employed and expected by both teacher and students within the context of the classroom. Among other matters, this requires in turn that the language teacher be provided with opportunities to build knowledge of socio-cultural features associated with use of the L1 and L2 within the classroom context. The objective of building knowledge is to promote teacher acceptance of potential disparity and to encourage flexible and tolerant approaches to instruction during English activities. Through teacher action, students can be systematically exposed to cultural diversity, and teachers can be urged to establish initiatives within their pedagogical practices to promote tolerance, understanding, and respect for cultural differences. At the same time, awareness of cultural values and societal characteristics associated with the target language is not tantamount to a call for the student to achieve an idealised native-like competence or conform to specific target language values. Rather, opportunities to compare and contrast L1 and L2 language usage serve as an important teaching/learning tool in the sense that teachers can be encouraged to actively explore linguistic divergence in order to develop and promote acceptance of varying communicative practices and cultural paradigms.

In order to enhance teacher professional judgment and performance within the classroom, the following model for professional development and classroom practice is directed at functional and focused reflection from authentic sites of engagement. The model composition takes into account the dearth in practical and fiscally viable teacher development programmes suitable for English language teachers from an increasingly diverse range of socio-cultural, professional and educational backgrounds. Whereas conventional teacher professional development often involves an independent expert providing information and guidance, this model follows a pedagogic and exploratory cycle of teaching and learning in which the teacher and real communicative exchanges within the classroom are central. This is achieved through judicial use of video/audio recordings employed to focus attention directly on real situations well-known to teachers which are then explored through attention to the five phases of: Awareness, Knowledge Building, Critique, Action and Evaluation (see Candlin et al., 1995; Candlin, 1997; O'Grady, 2011). Critically, the five phases each draw on the previous phase and leads to the next. The final phase produces data which can then be employed to begin a second interactive cycle of professional development. Designed to be simple and intuitive, this professional development programme is intended to supplement teacher training process models, not replace them. With this objective, the model provides teachers with an application-oriented approach to building socio-cultural awareness, content knowledge and understanding of the classroom and students through reflecting on teaching beliefs and practices that may not always be perceptible to the teacher on a conscious level. In addition, the model encourages teachers to observe and identify pertinent pragmatic features of the L1 and the L2 that can be introduced into English learning activities in a timely fashion in order to systematically nurture the growth of students' pragmatic competence.

The development model embraces the position that for a teacher development programme to be effective, it must inculcate in teachers the need to inquire and question existing practice (Karavas-Doukas, 1998). In other words, it should not be limited to the focus of the programme, but motivate teachers to become reflective, to evolve and seek new understandings in order to bring about meaningful, effective, long term educational reform.

The model empowers teachers by instilling in them an awareness of the need to routinely question their existing professional practices through embracing critically reflective teaching processes. Reflection provides the basis from which teachers are emboldened to evolve and to seek new understandings in order to bring about consequential, effective and durable educational transformation. The programme is designed to encourage teachers to reflect on the impact of their own background, assumptions, behaviour and language use on their teaching practices, while attending to the possible impact of these practices on their students. This can have profound effects on classroom practices as it gives the teacher practical tools by which to understand their beliefs and how these are being played out in the classroom. The programme addresses how the outcomes can productively activate classroom innovation through working together with teachers to implement changes within their classrooms. Fook and Askeland (2006) emphasise that the focus of critical reflection should be on connecting individual identity and social context: 'Part of the power of critical reflection in opening up new perspectives and choices about practice may only be realized if the connections between individual thinking and identity, and dominant social beliefs are articulated and realized' (2006: 53). The objective being for teachers to become more flexible through encouraging them to reflect on, and expand their range of strategic options for managing their verbal and non-verbal communication strategies and those of their students. In short, the informed and self-aware teacher has the capacity to discern if, when and how to adopt, modify, or where deemed appropriate, discontinue specific teaching practices in order to better meet students' needs. Reflective practice is understood as the process of learning through and from experience in order to gain new insights of self and/or practice, and frequently involves examining assumptions of everyday practice (see Boyd & Fales, 1983; Mezirow, 1981). Schön's (1983) *The Reflective Practitioner: How Professionals Think in Action*' identified ways in which professionals could become aware of their implicit knowledge and learn from their experience through being self-aware and critically evaluating their responses to situations through reflection-in-action and reflection-on-action. The former refers to the thinking we do while actually practicing, while the latter refers to reflection after the event where we review our experience, make sense of it and learn from it. In both types of reflection, practitioners seek to connect with their feelings and address relevant theory so as to construct new understandings to shape their action in the unfolding situation.

The programme focuses on delivery of professional development to teachers through a school-based strategy where teachers learn with and from their colleagues. Acknowledging that teachers will inevitably have different needs, interests and requirements, voluntary participation is regarded as positively influencing the success of the programme. The need for choice in order to make personal commitment is noted by Robb (2000) who emphasises that 'choice is at the heart of making a commitment ... it allows teachers who are skeptical about change to be observers and listeners and to talk to colleagues who are actively involved in professional learning before making a personal commitment' (2000: 3). As the process is a cyclical professional development programme, it necessitates sufficient time and a supportive environment in order for teachers to comfortably and actively achieve critical awareness without concern that their teaching practices are being critically evaluated. Time demands will be unique to each institution and therefore timelines should be agreed upon by teaching staff and school management prior to the commencement of the programme. The model is organised around teachers playing active roles by including:

- teacher interaction;
- authentic classroom data;
- reflective discussion;
- modification of teaching approaches;
- development of innovative teaching approaches;
- lessons or assessments.

The Awareness phase involves a deliberate examination of self, beliefs, attitudes, and behaviours framed in reference to authentic classroom data in order to better understand one's classroom practices. The awareness stage as employed by Candlin *et al.* (1995) in professional development programmes for practicing lawyers, is initiated by asking the question: 'What do we know?' This approach is based on the premise that it is only when teachers become aware of their own tacitly held beliefs and their routinised practice that they can articulate their beliefs and use them to reflect on their teaching practices. Teachers take part in consciousness-raising tasks through the observation of authentic classroom data sources which have been audio/video recorded and transcribed. During this process, the teachers observe recordings of classroom activities in small focus groups with a neutral moderator controlling technical equipment and stimulating discussion when required. Teachers are encouraged to draw on personal experiential commentary relevant to the specific theme of the programme during critical reflection. Themes which would be relevant to the current study are the four areas of student peer collaboration, characteristics of Japanese identities, use of the L1 (Japanese), occasions of student silence. Because of the potentially large scope of each of these themes, we recommend that each be considered as an independent area of examination and reduced to further subcategories for professional development seminars.

For example, in the case of our data regarding the theme of student collaboration, separate teacher development seminars would target key functions of collaboration exhibited by students during learning activities such as; (a) to compare and/or confirm responses to classroom tasks with peers, (b) to solicit answers from peers in order to complete learning exercises, and (c) to compare/solicit/verify responses with peers in order to avoid failure.

During the Awareness phase, critical reflection is seen as necessary for teachers to understand themselves as individuals and as professionals, and to make sense of their professional experiences. With reflection-in-action, teachers examine their experiences and responses as they occur in order to build new understandings to shape their action within the classroom. In Schön's words:

> The practitioner allows himself to experience surprise, puzzlement, or confusion in a situation which he finds uncertain or unique. He reflects on the phenomenon before him, and on the prior understandings which have been implicit in his behaviour. He carries out an experiment which serves to generate both a new understanding of the phenomenon and a change in the situation. (Schön, 1983: 68)

Schön argues that the novice practitioner lacks knowledge-in-action, and therefore is inclined to be dependent on rules and procedures which are mechanically applied. In contrast, as professionals become more expert in their practice, they develop the skill of being able to monitor and adapt their practice simultaneously, perhaps even intuitively. As noted by Gebhard and Oprandy (1999), '[t]he more we observe and develop our teaching, the freer we become to make our own informed teaching decisions' (1999: 38). In addition, the researchers point out that the more aware teachers become of their teaching practices, the more they can consider their beliefs about learning and teaching. Research demonstrates that constant reflection plays a critical role in empowering teachers to raise their awareness to a level of metaconsciousness and a further level of critical awareness. (Bailey *et al.*, 2001; Ross & Bruce, 2007). The Awareness phase is central to the overall success of the model, and requires both adequate time and a supportive environment in order for teachers to critically examine self, beliefs and practices that surface during learning activities. Teacher reflections are audio/video recorded and key areas of discussion transcribed for further reference.

The Knowledge phase begins with the question: 'What do we need to learn?' (Candlin *et al.*, 1995). During this stage, transcriptions from the *Awareness phase*, or extended texts either in the form of classroom recordings or transcripts, are examined by the teachers. These extended examples of actual classroom interaction form the basis by which to determine what needs to be learnt. Key areas can be explored through group exchange as discussed by the participants to enable a fuller and more focused discussion of what appears to the teachers to be occurring in the original audio/video recorded and transcribed data excerpts examined during the Awareness phase. Where appropriate, group knowledge is to be supplemented by drawing on print resources such as papers in academic publications, teaching resources or other material. Teachers are urged to identify specific questions they have regarding what the students were thinking and doing. In this phase, the 'participants come to determine and adopt a common analytical language in terms of which the data in question can be described, interpreted and explained' (Candlin & Candlin, 2013: 27).

In the Critique phase we turn to the question of: 'Why are matters as they are?' At this phase, we focus on developing an understanding of the students' perspectives regarding classroom interaction and behaviour. This phase of the discussion focuses on developing a better understanding of the reasons behind the particular performances in question, and how these may or may not relate to the situation-specific practices. In the Action phase, teachers now draw on, and engage with their own recorded and transcribed data obtained from their own professional practice, addressing the questions: 'What can be done?' and 'What should be done?' This is the phase in which theory is enacted, practiced, and realised through engaging, applying, exercising, realising or practicing ideas. We are reminded here of the need for the initial change proposals of a teacher development programme to be specific, limited and small in order to maximise the benefits. As Candlin and Candlin (2013: 27) point out, such personally relevant data, made suitably anonymous and with the ethical permissions of all involved, can then be recycled as input to the initial phases of any subsequent programme. In this way, the model is a continuing and practice-generating cycle of description, interpretation and explanation aimed at enhancing teacher professional judgment and performance within the classroom. As a complement to the above four phases, an Evaluation phase is employed in order to assess; (a) participant satisfaction, (b) gains in teacher knowledge, (c) changes in classroom practices, and (d) student achievement/awareness in relation to the specific pragmatic areas under investigation. Participating teachers take part in discussing these evaluative criteria which are assessed by teachers through observations of classroom recordings. Recordings drawn from the Action phase provide in-depth qualitative data which enable teachers to systematically reflect on modifications to classroom practice through repeated viewings. Taken as a whole, the professional development model introduces teachers to the socio-cultural dimensions of teaching and learning through providing opportunities to examine their own assumptions and how they impact classroom practice, as well as assisting them to examine how socio-cultural factors influence learning and student attitudes. Such an approach sheds light on potential variability in student/teacher expectations regarding values and beliefs. Yero (2002) compares changing an old established belief to trying to open a window that has been painted shut. It requires a great deal of prying, poking and prodding before it will loosen and break free from the frame. This is a consequence of the comfort of established habit that provides consistency and stability in people's lives. The open window brings about the winds of change as fresh air is welcomed and the stale atmosphere reinvigorated.

The professional development model advocated here concurs with Lortie (1998) who, when revisiting some issues in his seminal work *School-teacher*, aptly commented 'that considerably more research is needed on teachers and their work' (1998: 161). In order to encourage teachers to reflect on and interpret their teaching practices, a final yet crucial characteristic of our approach to teacher professional development is the promotion of a nonjudgmental stance towards participants. In other words, participating teachers are urged to work collaboratively and are not subject to external supervision or evaluation. Such a nonjudgmental stance empowers participating teachers to feel comfortable in interpreting, and where appropriate potentially reconstructing their approach to English activities through taking risks (Gebhard & Oprandy, 1999). In addition, in order to promote meaningful discussion, teachers are encouraged to take a nonjudgmental stance towards each other so that all teachers can express themselves openly in a collaborative and equal format. For effective collaborative learning to take place, the model outlined recognises that it is important to keep in mind that interpretations of optimal conditions will vary among teachers. Consequently, it is necessary for teachers to be made aware of the collaborative nature of the professional development model, and informed that this provides a platform from which to transmit wide ranging and mutually beneficial knowledge and skills.

Model Professional Development Seminar

Drawing on the analysis of our research data, we identify the following key aims for professional development programmes:

- To encourage teachers to reconceptualise the nature of language teaching and learning and their role.
- To raise teachers' awareness of the verbal and non-verbal communicative strategies they are employing in the classroom.
- To raise teachers' awareness of how their verbal and non-verbal communicative strategies are interpreted by Japanese students.

- To raise teachers' awareness of the verbal and non-verbal communicative strategies students are employing in the classroom.
- To sensitise teachers' to the need for explicit attention to pragmatic features of the L1/L2 and for these to be pedagogically incorporated within learning activities.
- To generate an awareness and knowledge base from which teachers can develop learning activities and/or adjust their teaching practices in order to better meet their students' needs.

The research outlined in this book provides insight into pervasive patterns of language use, attitudes and behaviours from which an image and appreciation of the Japanese students' conceptions of face as a construct of identity emerges. These findings underscore the need for teacher awareness of key characteristics of the L2 classroom:

- Varying socio-cultural backgrounds of students and teachers.
- Potential for variance in cross-cultural negotiations of face.
- Potential for variance in the enactment of identities.
- Potential for variance in cross-cultural pragmatic meaning beyond the literal interpretation of what is said.
- Potential for variance in cross-cultural assumptions concerning standards of classroom appropriateness in regards to language use and behaviour.
- Potential for variance regarding the different roles played by teachers and students at different moments.

The analysis of the data explores cross-cultural pragmatic divergence seen from the perspective of the students' and their teacher as revealed through student identities and the pragmatics of face. These characteristics are realised and defined by the ways the teachers address key issues of communication:

- How face is negotiated during English learning activities.
- How students align with, and enact identities during English learning activities.
- How the pragmatics of the L2 may be expressed and addressed in English learning activities.
- How the pragmatics of the L1 may be addressed and expressed in English learning activities.

Integral to these issues of classroom participation are a number of key areas which reveal specific moments during learning activities where the teacher's interpretations of classroom communication deviate from the students' communicative intentions. Similarly, data reveals points during activities where the students' interpretations of classroom communication deviate from the teacher's communicative intentions. Organised around recurring themes explored in our study, these four areas constitute the key areas of content for the professional development programme as outlined above:

- Peer collaboration – spontaneous collaboration between the Japanese students.
- Japanese identities – students' resistance to classroom practices deemed to be inconsistent with Japanese classroom behaviour or language use.
- Use of the L1 (Japanese) – students' interpretations of the teacher's use of Japanese.
- Recourse to, and maintenance of, silence – students' reflections on periods of extended silence and/or the teacher intervention.

Seminars may choose to focus on one of the above four themes, or alternatively, attend to one of the sub-themes revealed as being sources of misunderstanding related to verbal and/or non-verbal communicative styles. It should be noted that the model is equally applicable to examining critical moments that arise within the cross-cultural classroom that we have not directly raised within this study. Whatever the focus of the professional development seminar, we emphasise the need to follow a number of key pedagogic principles adopted from the professional development programme outlined by Candlin *et al.* (1995: 49):

- Seminars should work with authentic classroom data.
- Participating teachers should be encouraged to draw from real-life experiences within the classroom at all four phases of the model.
- The focus should be on the nature of the best practice.
- It should reflect both the teacher and the student perspectives.
- It should be cyclical in order to build a sustainable model for ongoing teacher development.
- It should be voluntary in terms of participation and collaboratively managed.

Model Seminar: Silence and *Aizuchi* (Backchannels)

Seminar Focus: *Aizuchi* (backchannels) communication strategies. This programme is to be conducted in small groups of four to six teachers with participants made up of either or both Japanese and non-Japanese teachers.

Definition: *Aizuchi* (backchannels) communication strategies, verbal and non-verbal, serve a range of communicative functions, are pervasive in their occurrence within Japanese communication, and take on a number of forms (Maynard, 1989; Horiguchi, 1997; Ishida, 2006; Kita & Ide, 2007). During interaction in Japanese, *aizuchi* perform as supportive behaviours with which a listener can engage in functions such as responding to questions, shifting topics or demonstrating support for the speaker. If the non-Japanese speaker is unaware of the prevalence and communicative function of verbal/non-verbal *aizuchi* in Japanese, points at which *aizuchi* are employed may not be recognised for the communicative function intended by the speaker.

Phase One: Awareness

Input: It is at this phase that we outline that interest in cultural variation in the communicative functions of *aizuchi* in daily life draws attention to potential differences in socio-cultural attitudes towards the functions and frequency of *aizuchi* employed in the Japanese language. In addition, we point out that a similar use of *aizuchi* is observed in the English produced by Japanese English speakers (Maynard, 1986, 1990) with these backchannels potentially representing a source of cross-cultural communicative misunderstanding (Ike, 2010). As a distinctive feature of Japanese English, we note that backchannel behaviour needs to be methodically examined in order to have successful cross-cultural communication.

We would note that attitudes, influenced by an array of socio-cultural and individual factors, are integral to understanding how *aizuchi* are employed and interpreted in order to achieve specific communicative goals. Moreover, understanding socio-cultural attitudes towards the communicative functions of *aizuchi* may provide insights into both what is said, and what is left unsaid during cross-cultural communication. We would explain that *aizuchi* are a form of communication that may not always be recognised or incorrectly identified by the non-Japanese teacher unfamiliar with Japanese language use. We would make the point that while *aizuchi* play a key role in signalling support and empathy towards the speaker, they can only be truly effective if the communicative intentions are evident to the interlocutors (Cutrone, 2005; Katagiri, 2007; Kita & Ide, 2007). In terms of its formal characteristics we would note that non-verbal and verbal forms of *aizuchi* can occur either alone, or simultaneously. We would point out that *aizuchi* when used in Japanese signal the current speaker to continue his turn and do not require him to respond (Iwasaki, 1997). We would suggest that a useful, but not the only, definition of a backchannel is as follows:

(1) A backchannel is a short vocal and/or non-vocal utterance by the listener to the content of another interlocutor's speech. Head movements such as nodding and head shakes are included as long as such movements display one of the backchannel functions. That is, the head movement does not contradict what the speaker is saying, nor answer any particular question.

(2) A backchannel does not require the floor. That is, it does not initiate the direction of conversation.

(3) Acknowledgement of a backchannel is optional.

(4) Main functions of backchannels are categorised as continuer, acknowledgement, agreement, judgment, and emotional reaction.

(Ike, 2010: 206)

This would be followed by the presentation of several short video recorded classroom excerpts. Presented with transcriptions, these recordings and texts are selected to provide examples of the functional use of *aizuchi* as an interactional strategy within the language classroom.

Example text: Taken from Classroom excerpt 32: The teacher (T) asks Kaori (K) to indicate if she can count from 1 to 100.

1T: ((T points at K)) OK (1) next (1) can you count from 1 to 100?

2K: (2) *u::n :*((nods))
'Yes'

3T: (5) ((T moves toward K)) Can you? ((raises shoulders)) (2) ((K glances at classmates, then looks up at T))

4K: (6) ((K looks at classmates, looks up at T, nods)) *u::n*
'Yes'

5T: (6) ((T looks at K, takes step forward)) Is that YES or NO? ((looks around at Ss, shrugs, quizzical expression))

6K: (8) *U::n* ((T frowns, places hands on hips)) (5) yes ((K looks at T then down and shuffles through notes))
'Yes'

7T: ((T folds arms, moves directly in front of K, taps desk with hand)) (3) Do you <u>understand the question</u>? (1) *ima no shitsumon <u>wakarimashita ka</u>?*
'Did you understand this question?'

8K: (6) ((K looks at classmates, then up at T)) (1) Yes ((T shrugs, furrows forehead, turns away))

Action: Here the teachers would be asked to reflect on the nature of *aizuchi* as viewed in the recordings. In addition, teachers would be asked to reflect on *aizuchi* as a strategy employed by Japanese speakers through reflecting on their teaching experience. They would be asked to discuss:

*   What communicative functions do you feel these *aizuchi* are intended to serve in the recordings?
*   How did the teacher react to the use of *aizuchi*?
*   How do you feel about the teacher's response?
*   Are these examples of *aizuchi* in the recordings what you would categorise as being standard occurrences within the classroom?
*   Are these examples of *aizuchi* in the recordings what you would categorise as being standard occurrences outside of the classroom?

Phase Two: Knowledge

Input: At this stage, teachers would be presented with a more extended video recording of a classroom. To obtain these samples, teachers would be asked to record their own classes and identify and transcribe short samples of *aizuchi* use within classroom interaction. Teachers would be asked to identify particular uses of *aizuchi* by Japanese students within the recordings. It is at this stage that the teachers would be encouraged to view the area of examination through attention to the Japanese students' perspectives. To assist teachers in identifying and understanding *aizuchi* we would present classifications and where appropriate, functional frameworks. Alternatively, teachers would be welcomed to draw from colleague knowledge, access journals or other publications to determine a relevant framework. It is in this phase, that the teachers determine and adopt a common analytical language in terms of which the data in question can be described and interpreted.

For example, we would present Horiguchi's (1997) framework which classifies *aizuchi* into three types: (1) a fixed set of short expressions called *aizuchi-shi*, such as *hai, ee, hoo, fuun, hee, soo desu ne, naruhodo,* and *hontou*; (2) a repetition; and (3) a short reformulation of a part or all of the immediately preceding speaker's utterance. Secondly, we would present Iwasaki's (1997) model for understanding *aizuchi* which notes three types of *aizuchi* as: nonlexical, phrasal, and substantive. Non-lexical *aizuchi* refer to a closed set of short sounds with little or no referential meaning such as *ee, soo, aa*. Phrasal *aizuchi* are expressions with meaning, such as *naruhodo* and *uso*, and substantive *aizuchi* are an open class of expressions with full referential content. Non-lexical *aizuchi* tend to be treated as continuers while phrasal and substantive backchannels are interpreted as reactive backchannels.

In addition, teachers would be instructed to be aware of the use of non-verbal forms of *aizuchi* such as *unazuku* (to nod in assent) and *kubi kashigeru* (to tilt one's head to the side to demonstrate uncertainty) or other non-verbal *aizuchi* behaviours, including smiling, and eye movement (Kogure, 2007). Finally, we would present Ike's (2010) framework for identifying and classifying *aizuchi* as practical means of identify three broad types:

- Vocal type – backchannel consists of a vocal utterance alone.
- Non-Vocal – backchannel consists of head movement alone.
- Vocal + Non-Vocal – backchannel consists of a vocal utterance accompanied by head movement.

In order to identify and categorise the functions of *aizuchi* the teachers would be directed towards Horiguchi's (1988) five functional categories: (1) display of listening; (2) display of understanding; (3) display of agreement; (4) display of disagreement; and (5) expression of emotion. In addition, teachers would be introduced to Maynard's (1993a) six categories: (1) continuer; (2) display of understanding of content; (3) support and empathy toward the speaker; (4) agreement; (5) strong emotional response; and (6) minor additions, corrections or requests for information. These categories are intended to instill in the teacher recognition that *aizuchi* serve diverse communicative functions. Teachers would be advised to employ a framework they felt appropriate and practical, or alternatively, to develop their own framework.

Teachers would be instructed to use their framework in order to identify examples of *aizuchi* as used by the students within their classroom recordings. Video recordings of these examples would be presented to the group along with basic transcriptions. Here the teachers would be asked:

- To identify the use of *aizuchi* by students.
- To identify the frequency of particular types of *aizuchi* employed by students within the recording.
- To determine the communicative function of the *aizuchi* employed by students.
- To discuss whether the communicative function of the *aizuchi* employed by students was correctly interpreted by the teacher.

Phase Three: Critique

Here the purpose is to encourage the teachers to raise critical questions surrounding the use of *aizuchi* by students. Teachers would be asked to consider how *aizuchi* could potentially result in misunderstanding regarding communicative intent in cross-cultural situations. In addition, teachers would be asked to consider how students could be made aware of the potential for misunderstanding, and what action should be taken as a result.

Issues to consider are:

- There is a danger that non-Japanese teachers, failing to recognise students' *aizuchi* as a form of communication may incorrectly assume that students have not comprehended lesson content.
- There is a danger that non-Japanese teachers, failing to recognise students' *aizuchi* as a form of communication may assume that students are not participating in activities as expected.
- There is a danger of non-Japanese teachers misinterpreting the extended range of functions served by *aizuchi*.
- There is a danger that non-Japanese teachers' rejection of *aizuchi* and demands for verbal response strategies may be interpreted by students as a rejection of *aizuchi* as a valid, and important form of Japanese communication.
- Failure to acknowledge *aizuchi* may be viewed as the teacher imposing cultural values, either on a conscious or unconscious level, on the students.
- There is a danger of students assuming that the communicative intentions behind *aizuchi* will be evident to non-Japanese.
- There is a danger of students assuming that that their communicative intentions through the use of *aizuchi* have been correctly interpreted by a non-Japanese interlocutor.

Phase Four: Action

Here the purpose is to move the discussion to the practical level of teacher/student interaction within, and outside of the classroom. There are two main foci: Firstly, to implement modifications to teaching practices that have been identified as resulting in misunderstanding, and secondly, to make appropriate pedagogic inclusions or modifications to learning activities which address pragmatic features of the L1 and L2 regarding *aizuchi*. The objective here is to identify and introduce students to pragmatic aspects of the target and native languages regarding *aizuchi* through raising pragmatic awareness, and creating opportunities to engage pragmatic features of the target language. In this way, both teachers and students can be encouraged to view the L1 and L2 through each other's cultural lens. In particular, the focus would be on:

- Exposing teachers to specific *aizuchi* and the communicative intent as viewed by the Japanese students as a way to foster appreciation and awareness of one's own culture and tolerance of others.

- Building students' awareness of the pragmatic features of Japanese *aizuchi* as a way to foster appreciation and awareness of one's own culture and tolerance of others.
- Identifying classroom activities so as to raise students' pragmatic awareness of L1 *aizuchi.*
- Building students' awareness of L2 backchannel options, verbal and non-verbal, to provide students with the means to express themselves as intended within the L2.
- Provide students with opportunities to practice English backchannels in a variety of interactive communication activities.

Phase Five: Evaluation

Here, the purpose is to move the discussion to; (a) the overall effectiveness of the professional development seminar, and (b) the practical measures that have been implemented during the action phase. The *Evaluation phase* is designed with four specific evaluation targets; (a) participant satisfaction, (b) gains in teacher knowledge, (c) changes in classroom practices, and (d) increases in student achievement/awareness in relation to the specific pragmatic areas of investigation.

Participant satisfaction and gains in teacher knowledge will be appraised through the analysis of data drawn from focus group discussion. The participating teachers will be asked to comment on:

- What have you learned in the teacher education programme?
- Do you feel the development seminar was useful?
- What have you learned about *aizuchi*?
- Do you plan to make any changes to your teaching practices as a result of knowledge gained from the programme?
- How do you feel that any changes you make will benefit your students?

Changes in classroom practices, and increase in student achievement/awareness in relation to the use of *aizuchi* and L2 backchannel strategies will be further appraised by the participating teachers by means of video/audio recordings of classroom observations. Recordings are to be made following the *Action* phase during which students' have been presented with L2 backchannel options and participated in backchannel interactive communication activities. Teachers will be asked to discuss:

- How did students respond to pragmatic instruction regarding *aizuchi*?
- Were students able to recognise their use of L1 *aizuchi*?
- How did students perform on L2 backchannel activities?

- Were students open to adopting L2 backchannels?
- How do you feel student awareness of L1/L2 backchannels impacts on the students' ability to employ L2 backchannels during English activities?

The proposed professional development seminar maintains that *aizuchi* behaviour, verbal and non-verbal, is a distinctive feature of the Japanese language which is open to misinterpretation when employed in differing socio-cultural or linguistic contexts. The seminar asserts the need for *aizuchi* to be accurately recognised by both Japanese speakers of English and their English teachers in order to avoid misunderstanding, and increase the effectiveness of cross-cultural communication.

A Final Word: Approaching the Student

A limitation of the study is that we focus on one research location, and trace the work of a single teacher as he instructs two small groups of young students. While the study is directed at an examination of classroom discourse as interpreted through the voices of the often neglected perspectives of younger students, it should be noted that compulsory English activities at public Japanese elementary schools have only been implemented at the fifth and sixth grade levels from April of 2011. Given the infancy of mandatory English curriculum there remains minimal research available and we therefore draw from data examining Japanese secondary school and university classrooms. Furthermore, when the students make comparative statements such as references to Japanese teachers being *'motto yasashii'* (kinder) and more considerate than their non-Japanese English teacher, these comparisons are largely, though not exclusively, based on their experiences within the elementary school classroom. Given the close rapport the teacher and students often share at the elementary school level (see Rohlen & LeTendre, 1996) it is assumed that this bond will influence comparative reflections.

A further feature of the research site worth noting is that the non-Japanese English teacher is unaccompanied within the classroom. While this is commonplace within an *eikaiwa* English conversation schools setting, within elementary school English activities it is standard practice for a native speaker to instruct in a team-teaching arrangement with a Japanese teacher. Consequently, points of divergence such as outlined in this study may not have arisen as the Japanese teacher acts as a go-between to facilitate understanding and to smooth over potential conflict or confusion between the non-Japanese teacher and the students. On the other hand, it is this very presence of the Japanese teacher as mediator that may inhibit students from really learning about and negotiating the kind of pragmatic issues discussed in this book, and may be one of the weaknesses of the team-teaching method. While the data and conclusions outlined in this book are derived from a small-scale study, they may provide an important context for future research on pragmatic disparity, as well as insight into how pragmatics can be addressed in teacher training in order to build a constructive and supportive learning environment for students.

The relationship between face and identities underscores the need for heightened reflection on classroom practices through attention to authentic classroom data and associated responses from participants involved. Negotiation of face within the L2 classroom represents a significant challenge as students work to carve out their own place while at the same time ascertaining when to align with or to reject imposed identities which may not always present as being appropriate to the context or assumed roles. The potential for misunderstanding associated with differences in socio-cultural pragmatic verbal and non-verbal forms of communication revealed through the interplay of face and identities requires careful reflection, and appropriate pedagogical intervention. Of importance here is that it is inevitable that misunderstanding associated with the use and interpretation of language will at times occur between interlocutors of differing socio-cultural backgrounds. Moreover, the communication and interpretation of meaning is shaped by factors that may be so engrained that they are neither known nor evident to the speaker when communicating information, or the listener when assigning meaning.

> Communication between speakers of different languages is fraught with difficulty, even between speakers who appear to know each other's languages well. We find that there are considerable cultural differences operating at all levels of behavior, verbal and non-verbal, and that these affect our ability to communicate. (Archer et al., 2012: 225)

The L2 classroom is a setting for identity construction and consequently tests students as they seek to align with identities they value, while at the same time resisting, or at times rejecting, positions they find untenable. Crucially, the issues raised by this examination highlight that it cannot be assumed that teachers, even by virtue of factors such as exposure to the L1 culture, teaching experience, proficiency in the students' L1, or good intentions, will automatically be able to predict and control how their use of language and behavioural actions will be interpreted by students within the classroom.

Retrospective interviews illustrate that the meanings attributed to the verbal and non-verbal communicative strategies employed by the teacher are rooted in socio-cultural and individual affiliations of the students, ones which did not always align with the teacher's communicative intentions. Similarly, a number of ways in which the students employed culturally, socially and individually informed communicative strategies and behavioural actions were misinterpreted or at times disallowed by the teacher. In short, the communicative strategies employed by both students and teacher, in order to demonstrate individual worth and to maintain socio-cultural appropriateness, were not always mutually recognised as such. Differing interpretations of classroom events exposed pervasive patterns of shared student language, behaviour, and attitudes during the L2 English activities. Further, data illustrates that the students at times responded negatively towards linguistic and non-linguistic features of the teacher's classroom interactions which they interpreted as being at odds with what they viewed as being Japanese classroom norms. Among other matters, this negative reaction was evident in the students' reticence, avoidance of participation and overt criticism of the teacher.

Research data illustrates that while the teacher had the students' best intentions at heart, the verbal and non-verbal communicative strategies he employed undermined his positive intentions by contradicting what the students identified as constituting the behavioural norms governing the language classroom. Interview feedback revealed that the teacher expressed a high degree of satisfaction with the classes and was unaware of any friction which might interfere with the conduct and process of activities. Of importance here is that teacher failure to recognise the potential for variance in the production and interpretation of language within the classroom can lead to stereotyping and the imposition of the teacher's value system. Consequently, it is critical for the teacher to develop an awareness of factors which shape such values and beliefs, together with an understanding of how these various factors may influence the use and interpretation of both the native and the target languages. This knowledge can then be employed within the classroom to encourage students to identify, respect and value their own and others cultures. As Byram (1997) points out:

> In an educational framework which aims to develop critical cultural awareness, relativisation of one's own and valuing of others' meanings, beliefs and behaviours does not happen without a reflective and analytical challenge to the ways in which they have been formed and the complex of social forces within which they are experienced. (Byram, 1997: 35)

This examination has shed light on the Japanese students' interpretation of English activities underscoring how differing linguistic and cultural norms within the classroom can inadvertently alienate and silence such students. Of note here is that teacher imposed identity alignment threatens to undermine students views regarding their positive social value and influences communicative strategies employed when carrying out facework in order to maintain, enhance, protect and possibly restore losses to face. As educators, we have a responsibility to empower our students through creating opportunities for students to express and share opinions in the course of reflecting on L2 learning activities. In addition, we have a responsibility to initiate, establish and maintain positive and supportive classroom practices through working jointly with students in order to develop classroom environments that recognise the inherent value of our students. In order to achieve this goal, reflective teaching practices are necessary to develop a deeper teacher awareness of what we expect of our students, and how this may align with or potentially contradict what students want for themselves. As Boxer (2002) states, 'In an age in which cross-cultural interaction is the norm not only across societies but also within them, different rules of speaking have the potential to cause stereotypes, prejudice, and discrimination against entire groups of people' (2002: 150). In reference to the cross-cultural classroom in which interpretations of normative roles and rank may differ, it is crucial that the teacher avoid alienating students through deliberate or unintentional rejection of what may be unfamiliar classroom behaviour or language practices. Through teacher attention to cultural and linguistic diversity students can be encouraged to embrace global identities that are not derived from a sense of having to protect one's culture.

With this in mind, a classroom built on mutual respect and trust can be aspired to through conscious teacher attention to face and the identities that students both bring to and seek to develop through the acquisition of English. Through recognising and embracing the identities students seek to align to within the classroom, the teacher can communicate a powerful message that the acquisition of a L2 does not in any way compete for space with attitudes and values associated with the mother tongue. As Dörnyei (2007) points out, 'The language classroom is an inherently face-threatening environment because students are required to take continuous risks as they need to communicate using a severely restricted language code' (2007: 723). For language learners the ability to control the target language can be life changing. The challenges faced by the student are significant given that language acquisition involves exposure to unfamiliar social and cultural behaviours which challenge the learner to be receptive to potential changes in the creation and merging of identities.

Second language acquisition should not be viewed by young students as diminishing or threatening their sense of individual or national identities, but on the contrary, can serve to expand identities and possibilities they claim for the future. Through awareness of, and interest in cross-cultural pragmatic features of language acquisition, teachers can be trained to recognise and act in response to the diverse and shifting needs of students. Given that students' L2 communicative competence cannot be judged solely by grammatical precision, it follows that teachers should be encouraged to reconceptualise their professional role within a broader framework. It is here that we advocate teacher attention to communicative manifestations of culture, both differences and similarities, and the impact on the process of teaching and learning. Through attention to the implementation of culturally responsive teaching practices, curriculum and learning activities, teachers and their students can observe, value and celebrate socio-cultural diversity and individuality within the classroom and beyond.

References

Alegria de la Colina, A. and Del Pilar Garcia Mayo, M. (2009) Oral interaction in task-based EFL learning: The use of the L1 as a cognitive tool. *International Review of Applied Linguistics in Language Teaching* 47 (3/4), 325–345.

Al-Issa, A. (2003) Sociocultural transfer in L2 speech behaviors: Evidence and motivating factors. *International Journal of Intercultural Relations* 27 (5), 581–601.

Antrim, N.M. (ed.) (2007) *Seeking Identity: Language in Society.* Cambridge: Cambridge Scholars Publishing.

Archer, D., Aijmer, K. and Wichmann, A. (2012) *Pragmatics: An Advanced Resource Book.* London and New York: Routledge.

Arundale, R.B. (2006) Face as relational and interactional: A communication framework for research on face, facework, and politeness. *Journal of Politeness Research* 2 (2), 193–216.

Arundale, R.B. (2009) Face as emergent in interpersonal communication: An alternative to Goffman. In F. Bargiela-Chiappini and M. Haugh (eds) *Face, Communication and Social Interaction* (pp. 33–54). London: Equinox.

Arundale, R.B. (2010) Constituting face in conversation: Face, facework, and interactional achievement. *Journal of Pragmatics* 42 (8), 2078–2105.

Aspinall, R. (2006) Using the paradigm of 'small cultures' to explain policy failure in the case of foreign language education in Japan. *Japan Forum* 18 (2), 255–274.

Astor, A. (2000) A qualified nonnative English-speaking teacher is second to none in the field. *TESOL Matters* 10 (2), 18–19.

Atkinson, D. (2002) Toward a sociocognitive approach to second language acquisition. *The Modern Language Journal* 86 (4), 525–545.

Auerbach, E. (1993) Reexamining English only in the ESL classroom. *TESOL Quarterly* 27 (1), 9–32.

Auerbach, E. and Wallerstein, N. (1987) *ESL for Action: Problem-Posing at Work.* Reading, MA: Addison-Wesley.

Bachman, L.F. (1990) *Fundamental Considerations in Language Testing.* Oxford: Oxford University Press.

Bachnik, J.M. (1994) Challenging our conceptualizations of self, social order, and language. In J.M. Bachnik and C.J. Quinn (eds) *Situated Meaning: Inside and Outside in Japanese Self, Society, and Language* (pp. 3–37). Princeton, NJ: Princeton University.

Bailey, K.M., Curtis, A. and Nunan, D. (2001) *Pursuing Professional Development: The Self as Source.* Boston: Heinle & Heinle.

Bakhtin, M.M. (1981) Discourse in the novel (M. Holquist and C. Emerson, Trans.). In M. Holquist (ed.) *The Dialogic Imagination: Four Essays* (pp. 259–422). Austin, TX: University of Texas Press.

Bakhtin, M.M. (1986) The problem of speech genres (V. McGee, Trans.). In C. Emerson and M. Holquist (eds) *Speech Genres and Other Late Essays* (pp. 60–102). Austin, TX: University of Texas Press.
Bardovi-Harlig, K. and Mahan-Taylor, R. (eds) (2003) *Teaching Pragmatics*. Washington, DC: United States Department of State.
Bargiela-Chiappini, F. (2003) Face and politeness: New (insights) for (old) concepts. *Journal of Pragmatics* 35 (10–11), 1453–1469.
Bargiela-Chiappini, F. and Haugh. M (eds) (2009) *Face, Communication and Social Interaction* (pp. 1–30). London: Equinox.
Bar-Hillel, Y. (1971) Out of the pragmatic wastebasket. *Linguistic Inquiry* 2 (3), 401–407.
Barnes, M. (2004) The Use of Positioning Theory in Studying Student Participation in Collaborative Learning Activities. Paper presented at the Annual Meeting of the Australian Association for Research in Education, Melbourne.
Barron, A. (2003) *Acquisition in Interlanguage Pragmatics: Learning How to do Things with Words in a Study Abroad Context*. Amsterdam and Philadelphia: John Benjamins.
Befu, H. (1993) Nationalism and nihonjinron. In H. Befu (ed.) *Cultural Nationalism in East Asia: Representation and Identity* (pp. 107–133). Berkeley, CA: Institute of East Asian Studies.
Befu, H. (2001) *Hegemony of Homogeneity: An Anthropological Analysis of Nihonjinron*. Melbourne: Trans Pacific Press.
Beneke, J. (2000) Intercultural competence. In U. Bliesener (ed.) *Training the Trainers. International Business Communication* (vol. 5, pp. 108–109). Köln: Carl Duisberg Verlag.
Bennett, J.M., Bennett, M.J. and Allen, W. (2003) Developing intercultural competence in the language classroom. In D.L. Lange and R.M. Paige (eds) *Culture as the Core: Perspectives on Culture in Second Language Learning* (pp. 237–270). Greenwich, CT: Information Age Publishing.
Biggs, J.B. (1994) Asian learners through Western eyes: An astigmatic paradox. *Australian and New Zealand Journal of Vocational Educational Research* 2 (2), 40–63.
Biggs, J.B. (1998) Learning from the Confucian heritage: So size doesn't matter? *International Journal of Educational Research* 29 (8), 723–738.
Biggs, J.B. (1999) What the student does: Teaching for enhanced learning. *Higher Education Research and Development* 18 (1), 57–75.
Block, D. (2003) *The Social Turn in Second Language Acquisition*. Edinburgh: Edinburgh University Press.
Block, D. (2007) The rise of identity in SLA research, post Firth and Wagner (1997). *The Modern Language Journal* 91 (5), 863–876.
Borg, S. (2006) *Teacher Cognition and Language Education: Research and Practice*. London and New York: Continuum.
Borg, S. (2013) *Teacher Research in Language Teaching: A Critical Analysis*. Cambridge: Cambridge University Press.
Bouchard, J. (2011) Pragmatic failures and language ideologies: Challenges in the Japanese EFL context. *Studies in Culture* 49, 69–141.
Bourdieu, P. (1977) The economics of linguistic exchanges. *Social Science Information* 16 (6), 645–668.
Bourdieu, P. (1984) *Distinction: A Social Critique of the Judgment of Taste* (R. Nice, trans.). London: Routledge & Kegan Paul.
Bourdieu, P. (1991) *Language and Symbolic Power* (J.B. Thompson, ed.; G. Raymond & M. Adamson, trans.). Cambridge: Polity Press. (Original work published in 1982.)

Boxer, D. (2002) Discourse issues in cross-cultural pragmatics. *Annual Review of Applied Linguistics* 22, 150–167.

Boyd, E.M. and Fales, A.W. (1983) Reflective learning: Key to learning from experience. *Journal of Humanistic Psychology* 23 (2), 99–117.

Brown, H.D. (2007) *Principles of Language Learning and Teaching* (5th edn). White Plains, NY: Longman and Pearson Education.

Brown, I.B. (2007) The applicability of Brown and Levinson's theory of politeness to Japanese: A review of the English literature. *Bulletin of Joetsu University of Education* 26, 31–41.

Brown, P. and Levinson, S.C. (1978) *Politeness. Some Universals in Language Usage.* Cambridge: Cambridge University Press.

Brown, P. and Levinson, S.C. (1987) *Politeness: Some Universals in Language Use.* Cambridge: Cambridge University Press.

Butler, Y.G. (2004) What level of English proficiency do elementary school teachers need to attain in order to teach EFL? Case studies from Korea, Taiwan, and Japan. *TESOL Quarterly* 38 (2), 245–278.

Butler, Y.G. (2007a) Foreign language education at elementary schools in Japan: Searching for solutions amidst growing diversification. *Current Issues in Language Planning* 8 (2), 129–147.

Butler, Y.G. (2007b) Factors associated with the notion that native speakers are the ideal language teachers: An examination of elementary school teachers in Japan. *JALT Journal* 29 (1), 7–40.

Butzkamm, W. (2003) We only learn language once. The role of the mother tongue in FL classrooms: Death of a dogma. *The Language Learning Journal* 28 (1), 29–39.

Butzkamm, W. and Caldwell, J.A.W. (2009) The bilingual reform: A paradigm shift in foreign language teaching. Tübingen: Narr.

Byram, M. (1997) *Teaching and Assessing Intercultural Communicative Competence.* Clevedon: Multilingual Matters.

Byram. M. (2006) *Language Teaching for Intercultural Citizenship: The European Situation.* Paper presented at the NZALT Conference, University of Auckland.

Byram, M. (2012) Language awareness and (critical) cultural awareness – relationships, comparisons and contrasts. *Language Awareness* 21 (1–2), 5–13.

Byram. M., Gribkova, B. and Starkey, H. (2002) *Developing the Intercultural Dimension in Language Teaching: A Practical Introduction for Teachers.* The Council of Europe. See http://lrc.cornell.edu/director/intercultural.pdf (accessed 09 November 2015).

Byram. M. and Zarate, G. (1997) Defining and assessing intercultural competence: Some principles and proposals for the European context. *Language Teaching* 29, 14–18.

Canale, M. and Swain, M. (1980) Theoretical bases of communicative approaches to second language teaching and testing. *Applied Linguistics* 1, 1–47.

Canale, M. and Swain, M. (1981) A theoretical framework for communicative competence. In A. Palmer, P. Groot and G. Trosper (eds) *The Construct Validation of Tests of Communicative Competence: Including Proceedings of a Colloquium at TESOL 79* (pp. 31–36). Washington, DC: TESOL.

Candlin, C.N. (1987) Explaining moments of conflict in discourse. In R. Steele and T. Threadgold (eds) *Language Topics: Proceedings of the 1987 AILA Congress* (vol. 2, pp. 412–429). Sydney and Amsterdam: John Benjamins.

Candlin, C.N. (1997) Editorial preface. In B. Gunnarsson, P. Linell and B. Nordberg (eds) *The Construction of Professional Discourse,* (pp. ix–xiv). London: Longman.

Candlin, C.N. and Lucas, J. (1986) Interpretations and explanations in discourse: Modes of 'advising' in family planning. In T. Ensink, A. van Essen and T. van derGeest (eds) *Discourse Analysis and Public Life* (pp. 13–38). Dordrecht: Foris Publications.

Candlin, C.N., Maley, Y., Koster, P. and Crichton, J. (1995) *Lawyer-client Conferencing: Report to the Law Foundation of NSW.* Sydney, Law Foundation of NSW.

Candlin, S. (1997) Towards excellence in nursing: An analysis of the discourses of nurses and patients in the context of health assessments. Unpublished doctoral dissertation. University of Lancaster (UK).

Candlin, S. and Candlin, C.N. (2013) *Presencing* in the context of enhancing patient well-being in nursing care. In H. Hamilton and S. Chou (eds) *The Routledge Handbook of Language and Health Communication.* London: Routledge.

Celce-Murcia, M., Dörnyei, Z. and Thurrell, S. (1995) Communicative competence: A pedagogically motivated model with content specifications. *Issues in Applied Linguistics* 6 (2), 5–35.

Chávez, M. (2006) Classroom-language use in teacher-led instruction and teachers' self-perceived roles. *International Review of Applied Linguistics in Language Teaching* 44 (1), 49–102.

Chávez, M. (2007) The orientation of learner language use in peer work: Teacher role, learner role and individual identity. *Language Teaching Research* 11 (2), 161–188.

Childs, M. (2005) The place of pragmatics in language learning. In D. Tatsuki (ed.) *Pragmatics in Language Learning, Theory and Practice* (pp. 13–24). Tokyo: JALT Pragmatics SIG.

Chomsky, N. (1965) *Aspects of the Theory of Syntax.* Cambridge, MA: MIT Press.

Christensen, C.P. (1992) Training for cross-cultural social work with immigrants, refugees, and minorities: A course model. *Journal of Multicultural Social Work* 2 (1), 79–97.

Clarke, D. (2001) Complementary accounts methodology. In D. Clarke (ed.) *Perspectives on Practice and Meaning in Mathematics and Science Classrooms* (pp. 13–32). Dordrecht, Netherlands: Kluwer Academic Press.

Coates, J. (1993) *Women, Men and Language: A Sociolinguistic Account of Gender Differences in Language* (2nd edn). London: Longman.

Cohen, A.D. (2004) Assessing speech acts in a second language. In D. Boxer and A.D. Cohen (eds) *Studying Speaking to Inform Second Language Learning* (pp. 302–327). Clevedon: Multilingual Matters.

Cohen, A.D. (2008) Teaching and assessing L2 pragmatics: What can we expect from learners? *Language Teaching* 41 (2), 215–237.

Cohen, L., Manion, L. and Morrison, K. (2000) *Research Methods in Education* (5th edn). London and New York: Routledge.

Cook, H.M. (2011) Are honorifics polite? Uses of referent honorifics in a Japanese committee meeting. *Journal of Pragmatics* 43 (15), 3655–3762.

Cook, V. (1999) Going beyond the native speaker in language teaching. *TESOL Quarterly* 33 (2), 185–209.

Cook, V. (2001) *Second Language Learning and Language Teaching.* London: Edward Arnold.

Coupland, N., Wiemann, J.M. and Giles, H. (1991) Talk as 'problem' and communication as 'miscommunication': An integrative analysis. In N. Coupland, H. Giles and J.M. Wiemann (eds) *Miscommunication and Problematic Talk* (pp. 1–17). Thousand Oaks, California: Sage Publications.

Crandall, J. (2000) Language teacher education. *Annual Review of Applied Linguistics* 20, 34–55.

Creswell, J.W. (1998) *Qualitative Inquiry and Research Design: Choosing Among Five Traditions.* Thousand Oaks, CA: Sage Publications.

Crichton, H. (2009) 'Value added' modern languages teaching in the classroom: An investigation into how teachers' use of classroom target language can aid pupils' communication skills. *The Language Learning Journal* 37 (1), 19–34.

Crozet, C. (2007) *Culture Knowledge and Intercultural Learning*. In Intercultural Language Teaching and Learning in Practice: Professional Learning Programme Resource for Participants (ILTLP). Research Centre for Languages and Cultures Education (RCLCE), University of South Australia.

Cutrone, P. (2005) A case study examining backchannels in conversations between Japanese-British dyads. *Multilingua* 24 (3), 237–274.

Cutrone, P. (2009) Overcoming Japanese EFL learners' fear of speaking. *University of Reading Language Studies Working Papers* 1, 55–63.

Cutrone, P. (2011) Politeness and face theory: Implications for the backchannel style of Japanese L1/L2 speakers. *University of Reading Language Studies Working Papers* 3, 51–57.

Davis, K. (1995) Qualitative theory and methods in applied linguistics research. *TESOL Quarterly* 29 (3), 427–453.

Day, E.M. (2002) *Identity and the Young English Language Learner*. Clevedon: Multilingual Matters.

Delamont, S. (1992) *Fieldwork in Educational Settings: Methods, Pitfalls and Perspectives*. London: Falmer Press.

Derry, S.J., Pea, R.D., Barron, B., Engle, R.A., Erickson, F., Goldman, R., Hall, R., Koschmann, T., Lemke, J.L., Sherin, M.G. and Sherin, B.L. (2010) Conducting video research in the learning sciences: Guidance on selection, analysis, technology, and ethics. *Journal of the Learning Sciences* 19 (1), 3–53.

Dewaele, J.M. (2008) 'Appropriateness' in foreign language acquisition and use: Some theoretical, methodological and ethical considerations. *International Review of Applied Linguistics in Language Teaching* 46 (3), 235–255.

Diaz-Rico, L.T. and Weed, K.Z. (2006) *The Crosscultural, Language, and Academic Development Handbook* (3rd edn). Boston: Pearson Allyn and Bacon.

Dörnyei, Z. (2007) *Research Methods in Applied Linguistics: Quantitative, Qualitative and Mixed Methodologies*. Oxford: Oxford University Press.

Dörnyei, Z. and Skehan, P. (2003) Individual differences in second language learning. In C.J. Doughty and M.H. Long (eds) *The Handbook of Second Language Acquisition* (pp. 589–630). Oxford: Blackwell.

Du-Babcock, B. and Tanaka, H. (2010) Turn-taking behavior and topic management strategies of Chinese and Japanese business professionals: A comparison of intercultural group communication. *Proceedings of the 75th Annual Convention of the Association for Business Communication*. Chicago, Illinois.

Duff, P.A. and Polio, C.G. (1990) How much foreign language is there in the foreign language classroom? *The Modern Language Journal* 74 (2), 154–166.

DuFon, M.A. (2002) Video recording in ethnographic SLA research: Some issues of validity in data collection. *Language, Learning and Technology* 6 (1), 40–59.

Dwyer, E. and Heller-Murphy, A. (1996) Japanese learners in speaking classes. *Edinburgh Working Papers in Applied Linguistics* 7, 46–55.

Ellwood, C. (2008) Questions of classroom identity: What can be learned from codeswitching in classroom peer group talk? *The Modern Language Journal* 92 (3), 538–557.

Erickson, F. (1986) Qualitative methods in research on teaching. In M. Wittrock (ed.) *Handbook of Research on Teaching* (3rd edn, pp. 119–161). New York: Macmillan.

Ericsson, K.A. and Simon, H.A. (1993) *Protocol Analysis: Verbal Reports as Data* (2nd edn). Cambridge, MA: MIT Press.

Eslami-Rasekh, Z. (2005) Raising the pragmatic awareness of language learners. *ELT Journal* 59 (3), 199–208.

Félix-Brasdefer, J.C. (2006) Linguistic politeness in Mexico: Refusal strategies among male speakers of Mexican Spanish. *Journal of Pragmatics* 38 (12), 2158–2187.

Fook, J. and Askeland, G.A. (2006) The 'critical' in critical reflection. In S. White, J. Fook and F. Gardner (eds) *Critical Reflection in Health and Social Care* (pp. 40–53). Buckingham: Open University Press.

Foster, P. (1998) A classroom perspective on the negotiation of meaning. *Applied Linguistics* 19 (1), 1–23.

Foster, P. and Snyder Ohta, A. (2005) Negotiation for meaning and peer assistance in second language classrooms. *Applied Linguistics* 26 (3), 402–430.

Fujita-Round, S. and Maher, J. (2008) Language education policy in Japan. In S. May and N. Hornberger (eds) *Encyclopedia of Language and Education: Language Policy and Political Issues in Education* (vol. 1, pp. 393–405). New York: Springer.

Fukada, A. and Asato, N. (2004) Universal politeness theory: Application to the use of Japanese honorifics. *Journal of Pragmatics* 36 (11), 1991–2002.

Fukushima, S. (2000) *Requests and Culture: Politeness in British English and Japanese*. Frankfurt: Peter Lang.

García, O. (2009) *Bilingual Education in the 21st Century: A Global Perspective*. Malden, MA: Wiley/Blackwell.

Gardner-Chloros, P. (1995) Code-switching in community, regional and national repertoires: The myth of the discreteness of linguistic systems. In L. Milroy and P. Muysken (eds) *One Speaker, Two Languages: Cross-Disciplinary Perspectives on Code-Switching* (pp. 68–90). Cambridge: Cambridge University Press.

Gass, S.M. and Mackey, A. (2000) *Stimulated Recall Methodology in Second Language Research*. Mahwah, NJ: Lawrence Erlbaum.

Gay, G. (2000) *Culturally Responsive Teaching: Theory, Research, and Practice*. New York: Teachers College Press.

Gebhard, J.G. and Oprandy, R. (1999) *Language Teaching Awareness: A Guide to Exploring Beliefs and Practices*. New York: Cambridge University Press.

Gee, J.P. (1999) *An Introduction to Discourse Analysis: Theory and Method*. London and New York: Routledge.

Gee, J.P. and Handford, M. (eds) (2011) *The Routledge Handbook of Discourse Analysis*. London and New York: Routledge.

Geertz, C. (1973) *The Interpretation of Cultures: Selected Essays*. New York: Basic Books.

Geyer, N. (2008) *Discourse and Politeness: Ambivalent Face in Japanese*. London: Continuum.

Goffman, E. (1955) On face-work: An analysis of ritual elements in social interaction. *Psychiatry: Journal for the Study of Interpersonal Processes* 18, 213–231.

Goffman, E. (1967) *Interaction Ritual. Essays on Face-to-Face Behaviour*. New York: Pantheon Books.

Gottlieb, N. (1994) Language and polities: The reversal of postwar script reform policy in Japan. *The Journal of Asian Studies* 53 (4), 1175–1198.

Gottlieb, N. (2005) *Language and Society in Japan*. Cambridge: Cambridge University Press.

Grice, H.P. (1975) Logic and conversation. In P. Cole and J.L. Morgan (eds) *Syntax and Semantics: Speech Acts* (vol. 3, pp. 41–58). New York: Academic Press.

Gu, Y. (1990) Politeness phenomena in modern Chinese. *Journal of Pragmatics* 14 (2), 237–257.

De Guerrero, M.C.M. and Villamil, O.S. (2000) Activating the ZPD: Mutual scaffolding in L2 peer revision. *The Modern Language Journal* 84 (1), 51–68.

Gumperz, J.J. (1982) *Discourse Strategies*. Cambridge: Cambridge University Press.

Hacking, I. (1986) Making up people. In T.C. Heller, M. Sosna and D.E. Wellbery (eds) *Reconstructing Individualism: Autonomy, Individuality, and the Self in Western Thought* (pp. 222–36). Stanford, California: Stanford University Press.

Hagerman, C. (2009) English language policy and practice in Japan. *Osaka Jogakuin University College Kiyo Journal* 6, 47–64.

Hall, S. (1990) Cultural identity and diaspora. In J. Rutherford (ed.) *Identity, Community, Culture, Difference* (pp. 222–237). London: Lawrence and Wishart.

Hammond, C. (2007) Culturally responsive teaching in the Japanese classroom: A comparative analysis of cultural teaching and learning styles in Japan and the United States. *Journal of the Faculty of Economics* 17, 41–50.

Harada, S. (1976) Honorifics. In M. Shibatani (ed.) *Syntax and Semantics. Japanese Generative Grammar.* (vol. 5, pp. 499–563). New York and Tokyo: Academic Press.

Harlow, L.L. (1990) Do they mean what they say? Sociopragmatic competence and second language learners. *The Modern Language Journal* 74 (3), 328–351.

Hasegawa, Y. (2010) The sentence-final particles *ne* and *yo* in soliloquial Japanese. *Pragmatics* 20 (1), 71–89.

Hasegawa, Y. (2012) Against the social constructionist account of Japanese politeness. *Journal of Politeness Research* 8 (2), 245–268.

Hashimoto, K. (2009) Cultivating 'Japanese who can use English': Problems and contradictions in government policy. *Asian Studies Review* 33 (1), 21–43.

Hashimoto, K. (2011) Compulsory 'foreign language activities' in Japanese primary schools. *Current Issues in Language Planning* 12 (2), 167–184.

Haugh, M. (2005) The importance of 'place' in Japanese politeness: Implications for cross-cultural and intercultural analyses. *Intercultural Pragmatics* 2 (1), 41–68.

Haugh, M. (2007) Emic conceptualisations of (im)politeness and face in Japanese: Implications for the discursive negotiation of second language learner identities. *Journal of Pragmatics* 39 (4), 657–680.

Haugh, M. and Bargiela-Chiappini, F. (2010) Face in interaction. *Journal of Pragmatics,* 42 (8), 2073–2077.

Haugh, M. and Hinze, C. (2003) A metalinguistic approach to deconstructing the concepts of 'face' and 'politeness' in Chinese, English and Japanese. *Journal of Pragmatics* 35 (10/11), 1581–1611.

Hayashi, M. (2010) An overview of the question-response system in Japanese. *Journal of Pragmatics* 42 (10), 2685–2702.

Hess, R.D. and Azuma, H. (1991) Cultural support for schooling: Contrasts between Japan and the United States. *Educational Researcher* 20 (9), 2–8.

Hill, B., Ide. S., Ikuta, S., Kawasaki, A. and Ogino, T. (1986) Universals of linguistic politeness: Quantitative evidence from Japanese and American English. *Journal of Pragmatics* 10 (3), 347–371.

Hinenoya, K. and Gatbonton, E. (2000) Ethnocentrism, cultural traits, beliefs, and English proficiency: A Japanese sample. *The Modern Language Journal* 84 (2), 225–240.

Hinkel, E. (2001) Building awareness and practical skills to facilitate cross-cultural communication. In M. Celce-Murcia (ed.) *Teaching English as a Second or Foreign Language* (pp. 443–458). Boston: Heinle & Heinle.

Horiguchi, S. (1988) *Komyunikeshon ni okeru kikite no gengo koudou* [Listeners' Behavior in Communication]. *Nihongokyoiku, 64*, 13–26. Tokyo: Nihongokyoikugakkai.

Horiguchi, S. (1997) *Nihongo kyooiku to kaiwa bunseki.* [Japanese Language Teaching and Conversation Analysis]. Tokyo: Kuroshio Shuppan.

Hosoki, Y. (2011) English language education in Japan: Transitions and challenges. *Kokusai Kankeigaku Bulletin* 6 (1), 199–215.

Hu, H. (1944) The Chinese concepts of face. *American Anthropologist* 46 (1), 45–64.

Huang, Y. (2007) *Pragmatics.* Oxford: Oxford University Press.

Hughes, H.J. (1999) Cultivating the walled garden: English in Japan. *English Studies* 80 (6), 556–68.

Hughes, C.E., Shaunessy, E.S. and Brice, A.R. (2006) Code switching among bilingual and limited English proficient students: Possible indicators of giftedness. *Journal for the Education of the Gifted* 30 (1), 7–28.

Hymes, D. (1966) On Communicative Competence. Paper presented at the Research Planning Conference on Language Development among Disadvantaged Children. Yeshiva University.

Ide, R. (1998) 'Sorry for your kindness': Japanese interactional ritual in public discourse. *Journal of Pragmatics* 29 (5), 509–529.

Ide, S. (1989) Formal forms and discernment: Two neglected aspects of universals of linguistic politeness. *Multilingua* 2 (3), 223–248.

Ide, S., Hill, B., Carnes, Y., Ogino, T. and Kawasaki, A. (1992) The concept of politeness: An empirical study of American English and Japanese. In R. Watts, S. Ide and K. Ehlich (eds) *Politeness in Language. Studies in its History, Theory and Practice* (pp. 281–297). Berlin and New York: Mouton de Gruyter.

Ide, S. and Yoshida, M. (1999) Sociolinguistics: Honorifics and gender differences. In N. Tsujimura (ed.) *The Handbook of Japanese Linguistics* (pp. 444–480). Oxford: Blackwell.

Iino, M. (1999) Issues of video recording in language studies. *Obirin Studies in Language and Literature* 39, 65–85.

Ike, M. (1995) A historical review of English in Japan (1600–1880). *World Englishes* 14 (1), 3–11.

Ike, S. (2010) Backchannel: A feature of Japanese English. In A.M. Stoke (ed.) *JALT 2009 Conference Proceedings.* Tokyo: JALT.

Ikuta, S. (1983) Speech level shift and conversational strategy in Japanese discourse. *Language Sciences* 5 (1), 37–53.

Imura, M. (1997) *Palmer to Nihon no Eigo kyouiku* [Harold E. Palmer and teaching English in Japan]. Tokyo: Taishukan Shoten.

Imura, M. (2003) *Nihon no Eigo kyouiku nihyaku nen* [200 Years of English Education in Japan]. Tokyo: Taishukan Shoten.

Ishida, H. (2006) Learners' perception and interpretation of contextualization cues in spontaneous Japanese conversation: Back-channel cue *Uun. Journal of Pragmatics* 38 (11), 1943–1981.

Ishihara, N. (2007) Web-based curriculum for pragmatics instruction in Japanese as a foreign language: An explicit awareness-raising approach. *Language Awareness* 16 (1), 21–40.

Ishihara, N. (2010) Teachers' pragmatics: Knowledge, beliefs, and practice. In N. Ishihara and A.D. Cohen (eds) *Teaching and Learning Pragmatics: Where Language and Culture Meet* (pp. 21–36). Harlow: Pearson Education.

Ishihara, N. and Cohen, A.D. (2010) *Teaching and Learning Pragmatics: Where Language and Culture Meet.* Harlow, England: Longman and Pearson Education.

Ishihara, N. and Tarone, E. (2009) Subjectivity and pragmatic choice in L2 Japanese: Emulating and resisting pragmatic norms. In N. Taguchi (ed.) *Pragmatic Competence in Japanese as a Second Language* (pp. 101–128). Berlin and New York: Mouton de Gruyter.

Ishiyama, O. (2009) A note on Matsumoto regarding Japanese verbs of giving and receiving. *Journal of Pragmatics* 41 (5), 1061–1065.

Iwasaki, S. (1997) The Northridge earthquake conversations: The floor structure and the 'loop' sequence in Japanese conversation. *Journal of Pragmatics* 28 (6), 661–693.

Izuhara, E. (2003) *Shuujoshi 'yo', 'yone', 'ne' saikoo* [The sentence-final particles yo, yone, and ne revisited]. *The Journal of Aichi Gakuin University* 51, 1–15.

Jacobs, J.K., Kawanaka, T. and Stigler, J.W. (1999) Integrating qualitative and quantitative approaches to the analysis of video data on classroom teaching. *International Journal of Educational Research* 31 (8), 717–724.

Janes, A. (2000) The interaction of style-shift and particle use in Japanese dialogue. *Journal of Pragmatics* 32 (12), 1823–1853.

Jaworski, A. (1993) *The Power of Silence: Social and Pragmatic Perspectives*. Thousand Oaks, CA: Sage Publications.

Jaworski, A. (2005) Introduction: Silence in institutional and intercultural contexts. *Multilingua* 24 (1–2), 1–6.

Jaworski, A. and Coupland, N. (eds) (1999) *The Discourse Reader*. London and New York: Routledge.

Jaworski, A. and Sachdev, I. (1998) Beliefs about silence in the classroom. *Language and Education* 12 (4), 273–292.

Jaworski, A. and Sachdev, I. (2004) Teachers' beliefs about students' talk and silence: Constructing academic success and failure through metapragmatic comments. In A. Jaworski, N. Coupland and D. Galasinski (eds) *Metalanguage: Social and Ideological Perspectives* (pp. 227–244). Berlin and New York: Mouton de Gruyter.

Jenkins, R. (2004) *Social Identity* (2nd edn). London and New York: Routledge.

Ji, S. (2000) 'Face' and polite verbal behaviors in Chinese culture. *Journal of Pragmatics* 32 (7), 1059–1062.

Jones, R. (2012) *Discourse Analysis: A Resource Book for Students*. London and New York: Routledge.

Joseph, J.E. (2004) *Language and Identity: National, Ethnic, Religious*. Basingstoke: Palgrave Macmillan.

Joseph, J.E. (2013) Identity work and face work across linguistic and cultural boundaries. *Journal of Politeness Research* 9 (1), 35–54.

Kachru, B.B. (1982) *The Other Tongue: English Across Cultures*. Urbana, IL: University of Illinois Press.

Kachru, B.B. (1985) Standards, codification and sociolinguistic realism: The English language in the outer circle. In R. Quirk and H. Widdowson (eds) *English in the World: Teaching and Learning the Language and Literatures* (pp. 11–30). Cambridge: Cambridge University Press.

Kachru, B.B. (1996) World Englishes: Agony and ecstasy. *Journal of Aesthetic Education* 30 (2), 135–155.

Kalin, R. and Berry, J.W. (1994) Ethnic and multicultural attitudes. In J.W. Berry and J.A. Laponce (eds) *Ethnicity and Culture in Canada: The Research Landscape* (pp. 293–321). Toronto: University of Toronto Press.

Kamio, A. (1994) The theory of territory of information: The case of Japanese. *Journal of Pragmatics* 21 (1), 67–100.

Kang, K.-H. (2001) Korean's politeness strategies. *Korean Journal of Journalism and Communication Studies, Special English Edition* 2001, 7–27.

Kang, K.-H. (2002) Cross-cultural differences in face (*che-myun*) between Korea and the United States. Paper presented at 52nd Annual International Communication Association Conference, Seoul, Korea.

Kanno, Y. (2003) *Negotiating Bilingual and Bicultural Identities: Japanese Returnees Betwixt Two Worlds.* Mahwah, NJ: Lawrence Erlbaum Associates.
Kanno, Y. and Norton, B. (2003) Imagined communities and educational possibilities: Introduction. *Journal of Language, Identity and Education* 2 (4), 241–249.
Karavas-Doukas, K. (1998) Evaluating the implementation of educational innovations: Lessons from the past. In P. Rea-Dickins and K.P. Germaine (eds) *Managing Evaluation and Innovation in Language Teaching: Building Bridges* (pp. 25–50). New York: Longman.
Kasper, G. (1997) The role of pragmatics in language teacher education. In K. Bardovi-Harlig and B. Hartford (eds) *Beyond Methods: Components of Second Language Education* (pp.113–136). New York: MacGraw-Hill.
Kasper, G. (2001) Four perspectives on L2 pragmatic development. *Applied Linguistics* 22 (4), 502–530.
Kasper, G. and Roever, C. (2005) Pragmatics in second language learning. In E. Hinkel (ed.) *Handbook of Research in Second Language Teaching and Learning* (pp. 317–334). Mahwah, New Jersey: Lawrence Erlbaum.
Kasper, G. and Rose, K. (1999) Pragmatics and SLA. *Annual Review of Applied Linguistics* 19, 81–104.
Kasper, G. and Rose, K. (2002) *Pragmatic Development in a Second Language.* Malden, MA: Blackwell.
Katagiri, Y. (2007) Dialogue functions of Japanese sentence-final particles 'Yo' and 'Ne'. *Journal of Pragmatics* 39 (7), 1313–1323.
Kato, F. (2000) Integrating Learning Strategies, Time Management, and Anxiety-Free Learning in a Tertiary Level Course in Basic Japanese: An Intervention Study. Unpublished doctoral dissertation, The University of Sydney. Australia, Sydney.
Kato, Y. (2002) 'Chigai ga wakaru otoko' wa donna otoko ka [What kind of person is someone who is called 'chigai ga wakaru otoko'?]. *Bulletin of the International Student Center Gifu University,* 97–109. See http://ci.nii.ac.jp/vol_issue/nels/AA11584135/ISS0000343073_en.html (accessed 12 November 2015).
Kawai, Y. (2007) Japanese nationalism and the global spread of English: An analysis of Japanese governmental and public discourses on English. *Language and Intercultural Communication* 7 (1), 37–55.
Keyes, C. (2000) The early childhood teacher's voice in the research community. *International Journal of Early Years Education* 8 (1), 3–13.
Kinginger, C. (2013) Identity and language learning in study abroad. *Foreign Language Annals* 46 (3), 339–358.
Kita, S. and Ide, S. (2007) Nodding, *aizuchi,* and final particles in Japanese conversation: How conversation reflects the ideology of communication and social relationships. *Journal of Pragmatics* 39 (7), 1242–1254.
Kobayashi, M. (2003) The role of peer support in ESL students' accomplishment of oral academic tasks. *Canadian Modern Language Review* 59 (3), 337–369.
Kobayashi, Y. (2000) Japanese Social Influences on Academic High School Students' Attitudes Toward Long-Term English Learning. Unpublished doctoral dissertation. University of Toronto.
Kobayashi, Y. (2011) Global Englishes and the discourse on Japaneseness. *Journal of Intercultural Studies* 32 (1), 1–14.
Kogure, M. (2007) Nodding and smiling in silence during the loop sequence of backchannels in Japanese conversation. *Journal of Pragmatics* 39 (7), 1275–1289.

Koike, D. and Pearson, L. (2005) The effect of instruction and feedback in the development of pragmatic competence. *System* 33 (3), 481–501.

Koike, I. and Tanaka, H. (1995) English in foreign language education policy in Japan: Toward the twenty-first century. *World Englishes* 14 (1), 13–25.

Kondo, S. (2008) Effects on pragmatic development through awareness-raising instruction: Refusals by Japanese EFL learners. In E. Alcón and A. Martínez-Flor (eds) *Investigating Pragmatics in Foreign Language Learning, Teaching and Testing* (pp. 153–177). Bristol: Multilingual Matters.

Kramsch, C. (1993) *Context and Culture in Language Teaching*. Oxford: Oxford University Press.

Kramsch, C. (2003) Identity, role, and voice in cross-cultural (mis)-communication. In J. House, G. Kasper and S. Ross (eds) *Misunderstanding in Social Life: Discourse Approaches to Problematic Talk* (pp. 129–153). Harlow: Longman and Pearson Education.

Kramsch, C. (2004) Language, thought and culture. In A. Davies and C. Elder (eds) *The Handbook of Applied Linguistics* (pp. 235–261). Malden, MA: Blackwell Publishing.

Kramsch, C. (2009) Third culture and language education. In V. Cook and L. Wei (eds) *Contemporary Applied Linguistics* (pp. 233–254). London: Continuum.

Krashen, S.D. (1982) *Principles and Practice in Second Language Acquisition*. Oxford: Pergamon Press.

Krashen, S.D. (1985) *The Input Hypothesis: Issues and Implications*. New York: Longman.

Krieger, D. (2005) Teaching ESL versus EFL: Principles and practices. *English Teaching Forum* 43 (2), 8–16.

Kubota, R. (1998) Ideologies of English in Japan. *World Englishes* 17 (3), 295–306.

Kubota, R. (1999) Japanese culture constructed by discourses: Implications for applied linguistic research and English language teaching. *TESOL Quarterly* 33 (1), 9–35.

Kubota, R. (2002) The impact of globalization on language teaching in Japan. In D. Block and D. Cameron (eds) *Globalization and Language Teaching* (pp. 13–28). London and New York: Routledge.

Kubota, R. (2003) Critical teaching of Japanese culture. *Japanese Language and Literature* 37 (1), 67–87.

Kubota, R. and Lin, A. (eds) (2009) *Race, Culture, and Identity in Second Language Education: Exploring Critically Engaged Practice*. London and New York: Routledge.

Kumatoridani, T. (1999) Alternation and co-occurrence in Japanese thanks. *Journal of Pragmatics* 31 (5), 623–642.

Kurzon, D. (1995) The right of silence: A socio-pragmatic model of interpretation. *Journal of Pragmatics* 23 (1), 55–69.

Kurzon, D. (2007) Towards a typology of silence. *Journal of Pragmatics* 39 (10), 1673–1688.

Kushima, C. and Nishihori, Y. (2006) Reconsidering the role of the ALT: Effective preparation for ALTs based on the questionnaire survey. *Annual Review of English Language Education in Japan Journal* 17, 221–230.

Kvale, S. (2007) *Doing Interviews*. Thousand Oaks, CA: Sage Publications.

Labov, W. (1972) *Sociolinguistic Patterns*. Oxford: Blackwell.

Lazaraton, A. (2003) Evaluative criteria for qualitative research in applied linguistics: Whose criteria and whose research? *The Modern Language Journal* 87 (1), 1–12.

Lebra, T.S. (1976) *Japanese Patterns of Behavior*. Honolulu: University of Hawaii Press.

Lederach, J.P. (1995) *Preparing for peace: Conflict Transformation Across Cultures*. Syracuse, NY: Syracuse University Press.

Lee, K. (2006) Territory of information theory and emotive expressions in Japanese: A case observed in *shiranai* and *wakaranai*. In S. Suzuki (ed.) *Emotive Communication in Japanese* (pp. 191–207). Amsterdam and Philadelphia: John Benjamins.

Lee, E. (2008) The 'other(ing)' costs of ESL: A Canadian case study. *Journal of Asian Pacific Communication* 18 (1), 91–108.

Leech, G. (1983) *Principles of Pragmatics*. London: Longman.

Leech, G. (2005) Politeness: Is there an East-West divide? *Journal of Foreign Languages* 6, 3–31.

LePage, R.B. and Tabouret-Keller, A. (1985) *Acts of Identity*. Cambridge: Cambridge University Press.

Levine, G.S. (2003) Student and instructor beliefs and attitudes about target language use, first language use, and anxiety: Report of a questionnaire study. *The Modern Language Journal* 87 (3), 343–364.

Levinson, S.C. (1983) *Pragmatics*. Cambridge: Cambridge University Press.

Levinson, S.C. (1988) Putting linguistics on a proper footing: Explorations in Goffman's concepts of participation. In P. Drew and A. Wootton (eds) *Erving Goffman: Exploring the Interaction Order* (pp. 161–227). Oxford: Polity Press.

Liddicoat, A.J. (2002) Static and dynamic views of culture and intercultural language acquisition. *Babel* 36 (3) 4–11, 37.

Liddicoat, A.J. (2004a) The conceptualisation of the cultural component of language teaching in Australian language-in-education policy. *Journal of Multilingual and Multicultural Development* 25 (4), 297–317.

Liddicoat, A.J. (2004b) Language planning for literacy: Issues and implications. *Current Issues in Language Planning* 5 (1), 1–17.

Liddicoat, A.J. (2005) Teaching languages for intercultural communication. In D. Cunningham and A. Hatoss (eds) *An International Perspective on Language Policies, Practices and Proficiencies* (pp. 201–214). Belgrave: Editura Fundaţiei Academice AXIS & Fédération Internationale des Professeurs de Langues Vivantes.

Liddicoat, A.J. (2007) Internationalising Japan: Nihonjinron and the intercultural in Japanese language-in-education policy. *Journal of Multicultural Discourses* 2 (1), 32–46.

Liddicoat, A.J. (2009) Communication as a culturally contexted practice: A view from intercultural communication. *Australian Journal of Linguistics* 29 (1), 115–133.

Liddicoat, A.J., Papademetre, L., Scarino, A. and Kohler, M. (2003) *Report on Intercultural Language Learning*. Canberra: Department of Education Science and Training, Australian Government.

Lightbown, P.M. (2001) L2 Instruction: Time to teach. *TESOL Quarterly* 35 (4), 598–99.

Lincoln, Y.S. and Guba, E.G. (1985) *Naturalistic Inquiry*. Thousand Oaks, CA: Sage Publications.

Lincoln, Y.S. and Guba, E.G. (2000) Paradigmatic controversies, contradictions, and emerging confluences. In N. Denzin and Y. Lincoln (eds) *Handbook of Qualitative Research* (2nd edn, pp. 163–188). Thousand Oaks, CA: Sage Publications.

Linehan, C. and McCarthy, J. (2000) Positioning in practice: Understanding participation in the social world. *Journal for the Theory of Social Behaviour* 30 (4), 435–453.

Liu, J. (2001) Constructing Chinese faces in American classrooms. *Asian Journal of English Language Teaching* 11, 1–18.

Liu, J. (2002) Negotiating silence in American classrooms: Three Chinese cases. *Language and Intercultural Communication* 2 (1), 37–54.

LoCastro, V. (1987) Aizuchi: A Japanese conversational routine. In L.E. Smith (ed.) *Discourse Across Cultures: Strategies in World Englishes* (pp. 101–112). New York: Prentice Hall.

LoCastro, V. (1998) Learner Subjectivity and Pragmatic Competence Development. Paper presented at the annual meeting of the American Association for Applied Linguistics, Seattle, WA, March 14–17, 1998.

LoCastro, V. (2001) Individual differences in second language acquisition: Attitudes, learner subjectivity, and L2 pragmatic norms. *System* 29 (1), 69–89.

LoCastro, V. (2003) *An Introduction to Pragmatics: Social Action for Language Teachers.* Ann Arbor, MI: The University of Michigan Press.

LoCastro, V. (2012) *Pragmatics for Language Educators.* London and New York: Routledge.

Long, M.H. (1985) Input and second language acquisition theory. In S. Gass and C. Madden (eds) *Input and Second Language Acquisition* (pp. 377–393). Rowley, MA: Newbury House.

Long, M.H. (1996) The role of the linguistic environment in second language acquisition. In W.C. Ritchie and T.K. Bahtia (eds) *Handbook of Second Language Acquisition* (pp. 413–468). San Diego, CA: Academic Press.

Lortie, D. (1998) Unfinished work: Reflections on schoolteacher. In A. Hargreaves, A. Lieberman, M. Fullan and D. Hopkins (eds) *International Handbook of Educational Change* (pp. 145–162). Dordrecht: Kluwer Academic Publishers.

Lutz, F. (1981) Ethnography: The holistic approach to understanding schooling. In J. Green and C. Wallat (eds) *Ethnography and Language in Educational Settings. Advances in Discourse Processes* (pp. 51–63). Norwood, New Jersey: Ablex.

Macaro, E. (2001) Analysing student teachers' codeswitching in foreign language classrooms: Theories and decision making. *The Modern Language Journal* 85 (4), 531–548.

Mackey, A. and Gass, S.M. (2005) *Second Language Research: Methodology and Design.* Mahwah, NJ: Lawrence Erlbaum.

Mackey, A., Gass, S.M. and McDonough, K. (2000) How do learners perceive interactional feedback? *Studies in Second Language Acquisition* 22 (4), 471–497.

MacMartin, C., Wood, L. and Kroger, R. (2001) Facework. In W. Robinson and H. Giles (eds) *The New Handbook of Language and Social Psychology* (pp. 221–237). Chichester: John Wiley and Sons, Ltd.

Makino, S. and Tsutsui, M. (1986) *A Dictionary of Basic Japanese Grammar.* Tokyo: Japan Times.

Manita, E. and Blagdon, J. (2010) *Japanese Grammar in Use: Practical Grammar for English Speakers.* Tokyo: Maria Shobo.

Manning, P. (1992) *Erving Goffman and modern sociology.* Cambridge: Polity Press.

Mao, L. (1994) Beyond politeness theory: 'Face' revisited and renewed. *Journal of Pragmatics* 21 (5), 451–486.

Maroni, B., Gnisci, A. and Pontecorvo, C. (2008) Turn-taking in classroom interactions: Overlapping, interruptions and pauses in primary school. *European Journal of Psychology of Education* 23 (1), 59–76.

Maroni, B. (2011) Pauses, gaps and wait time in classroom interaction in primary schools. *Journal of Pragmatics* 43 (7), 2081–2093.

Martínez-Flor, A. and Usó-Juan, E. (2006) A comprehensive pedagogical framework to develop pragmatics in the foreign language classroom: The 6Rs approach. *Applied Language Learning* 16 (2), 39–64.

Matsuda, A. (2002) 'International understanding' through teaching world Englishes, *World Englishes* 21 (3), 436–440.

Matsuda, A. (2003) Incorporating world Englishes in teaching English as an international language, *TESOL Quarterly* 37 (4), 719–729.

Matsugu, Y. (2005) Japanese epistemic sentence-final particle *kana*: Its function as a 'mitigation marker' in discourse data. *Pragmatics* 15 (4), 423–436.

Matsumoto, Y. (1988) Reexamination of the universality of face: Politeness phenomena in Japanese. *Journal of Pragmatics* 12 (4), 403–426.

Matsumoto, Y. (1989) Politeness and conversational universals. *Multilingua* 8 (2/3), 207–221.

Matsumoto, Y. (1993) Linguistic politeness and cultural style: Observations from Japanese. In P.M. Clancy (ed.) *Japanese and Korean Linguistics* (vol. 2, pp. 55–67). Center for the Study of Language and Information: Stanford University.

Matsumoto, Y. (2003) Reply to Pizziconi. *Journal of Pragmatics* 35 (10–11), 1515–1521.

Mattioli, G. (2004) On native language intrusions and making do with words: Linguistically homogeneous classrooms and native language use. *English Teaching Forum* 42 (4), 20–25.

Maynard, S.K. (1986) On back-channel behavior in Japanese and English casual conversation. *Linguistics* 24 (6), 1079–1108.

Maynard, S.K. (1987) Interactional functions of a nonverbal sign: Head movement in Japanese dyadic casual conversation. *Journal of Pragmatics* 11 (5), 589–606.

Maynard, S.K. (1989) *Japanese Conversation: Self-Contextualization Through Structure and Interactional Management*. Norwood, NJ: Ablex.

Maynard, S.K. (1990) Conversation management in contrast: Listener response in Japanese and American English. *Journal of Pragmatics* 14 (3), 397–412.

Maynard, S.K. (1991) Pragmatics of discourse modality: A case of da and desu/masu forms in Japanese. *Journal of Pragmatics* 15, 551–582.

Maynard, S.K. (1993a) *Discourse Modality: Subjectivity, Emotion, and Voice in the Japanese Language*. Amsterdam and Philadelphia: John Benjamins.

Maynard, S.K. (1993b) *Kaiwa Bunseki* [Conversation Analysis]. Tokyo: Kuroshio Shuppan.

Maynard, S.K. (1997) Analyzing interactional management in native/non-native English conversation: A case of listener response. *International Review of Applied Linguistics in Language Teaching* 35 (1), 37–60.

McConnell, D. (1996) Education for global integration in Japan: A case study of the JET program. *Human Organization* 55 (4), 446–57.

McConnell, D. (2000) *Importing Diversity: Inside Japan's JET Program*. Berkeley, CA: University of California Press.

McKay, S. (2002) *Teaching English as an International Language: Rethinking Goals and Approaches*. Oxford: Oxford University Press.

McKenzie, R.M. (2010) *The Social Psychology of English as a Global Language*. Dordrecht and New York: Springer.

McVeigh, B.J. (2002) *Japanese Higher Education as Myth*. New York and London: M.E. Sharpe.

McVeigh, B.J. (2004b) *Nationalisms of Japan: Managing and Mystifying Identity*. Lanham, MD: Rowman and Littlefield.

Mendoza-Denton, N. (2002) Language and identity. In J.K. Chambers, P. Trudgill and N. Schilling-Estes (eds) *The Handbook of Language Variation and Change* (pp. 475–499). Oxford: Blackwell.

Mercer, N. (1992) Culture, context and the construction of knowledge in the classroom. In P. Light and G. Butterworth (eds) *Context and Cognition: Ways of Learning and Knowing* (pp. 28–46). Mahwah, NJ: Lawrence Erlbaum.

Merry, S.E. (1990) *Getting Justice and Getting Even*. Chicago, IL: University of Chicago Press.

Meyer, H. (2008) The pedagogical implications of L1 use in the L2 classroom. *Maebashi Kyodai Gakuen College Ronsyu* 8, 147–159.

Mezirow, J. (1981) A critical theory of adult learning and education. *Adult Education* 32 (1), 3–24.

Miller, E. and Kubota, R. (2013) Second language learning and identity construction. In J. Herschensohn, and M. Young-Scholten (eds) *The Cambridge Handbook of Second Language Acquisition* (pp. 230–250). New York: Cambridge University Press.

Ministry of Education, Culture, Sports, Science and Technology (2003) Regarding the establishment of an action plan to cultivate 'Japanese with English abilities.' See www.mext.go.jp/english/topics/03072801.htm (accessed 2 June 2009).

Ministry of Education, Culture, Sports, Science and Technology (2011) Five Proposals and Specific Measures for Developing Proficiency in English for International Communication (Provisional translation). See http://www.mext.go.jp/component/english/_icsFiles/afieldfile/2012/07/09/1319707_1.pdf (accessed 12 November 2015).

Mitchell, R and Myles, F. (2004) *Second Language Learning Theories* (2nd edn). London: Arnold.

Miura, A. (1983) *Japanese Words and their Uses*. Rutland, VT: Charles E. Tuttle.

Miyata, S. and Nisisawa, H. (2007) The acquisition of Japanese backchanneling behavior: Observing the emergence of *aizuchi* in a Japanese boy. *Journal of Pragmatics* 39 (11), 1255–1274.

Mizutani, N. (1983) *Aizuchi to ootoo* [Aizuchi and Response]. In O. Mizutani (ed.) *Hanashi Kotoba no Hyoogen* (pp. 37–44). Tokyo: Chikuma Shoboo.

Mizutani, N. (1988) *Aizuchiron* [On aizuchi]. *Nihongogaku* 7 (12), 4–11.

Morita, N. (2004) Negotiating participation and identity in second language academic communities. *TESOL Quarterly* 38 (4), 573–603.

Morris, F.A. and Tarone, E.E. (2003) Impact of classroom dynamics on the effectiveness of recasts in second language acquisition. *Language Learning* 53 (2), 325–68.

Morrow, P.R. (2004) English in Japan: The World Englishes perspective. *JALT Journal* 26 (1), 79–100.

Mouer, R. and Sugimoto, Y. (1986) *Images of Japanese Society: A Study in the Structure of Social Reality*. London and New York: Kegan Paul International.

Mouer, R. and Sugimoto, Y. (1995) Nihonjinron at the end of the twentieth century: A multicultural perspective. In J.P. Arnason and Y. Sugimoto (eds) *Japanese Encounters with Postmodernity* (pp. 237–269). London and New York: Kegan Paul International.

Murata, K. (1994) Intrusive or co-operative? A cross-cultural study of interruption. *Journal of Pragmatics* 21, 385–400.

Murata, K. (2011) Voices from the unvoiced: A comparative study of hidden values and attitudes in opinion-giving. *Language and Intercultural Communication* 11 (1), 6–25.

Muysken, P. (2000) *Bilingual Speech: A Typology of Code-mixing*. Cambridge: Cambridge University Press.

Nakane, I. (2003) Silence in Japanese-Australian Classroom Interaction: Perceptions and Performance. (Unpublished doctoral dissertation). University of Sydney, New South Wales, Australia.

Nakane, I. (2005) Negotiating silence and speech in the classroom. *Multilingua* 24 (1–2), 75–100.

Nakane, I. (2006) Silence and politeness in intercultural communication in university seminars. *Journal of Pragmatics* 38 (11), 1811–1835.

Nation, P. (2003) The role of first language in foreign language learning. *The Asian EFL Journal* 5 (2), 1–8.

Nelson, C. and Harper, V. (2006) A pedagogy of difficulty: Preparing teachers to understand and integrate complexity in teaching and learning. *Teacher Education Quarterly* 33 (2), 7–21.

Neustupny, J. and Tanaka, S. (2004) English in Japan: An overview. In V. Makarova and T. Rodgers (eds) *English Language Teaching: The Case of Japan* (pp. 11–28). Munich: Lincom Europa.

Newton, J., Yates, E., Shearn, S. and Nowitzki, W. (2010) *An Introduction to the Concept of Intercultural Communicative Language Teaching and Learning: A Summary for Teachers.* Wellington: New Zealand Ministry of Education.

Nihalani, P. (2010) Globalization and international intelligibility. In M. Saxena and T. Omoniyi (eds) *Contending with Globalization in World Englishes* (pp. 23–44). Bristol: Multilingual Matters.

Niyekawa, A.M. (1991) *Minimum Essential Politeness: A Guide to the Japanese Honorific Language.* Tokyo: Kodansha International.

Norman, J. (2008) Benefits and drawbacks to L1 use in the L2 classroom. In K. Bradford Watts, T. Muller and M. Swanson (eds) *JALT 2007 Conference Proceedings. Challenging Assumptions: Looking in, Looking out* (pp. 691–701). Tokyo: JALT.

Norton, B. (1997) Language, identity, and the ownership of English. *TESOL Quarterly* 31 (3), 409–429.

Norton, B. (2000) *Identity and Language Learning: Gender, Ethnicity and Educational Change.* Harlow: Longman and Pearson Education.

Norton, B. (2006) Identity: Second language. In K. Brown (ed.) *Encyclopedia of Language and Linguistics* (2nd edn, vol. 5, pp. 502–507). Oxford: Elsevier.

Norton, B. (2010) Identity, literacy, and English-language teaching. *TESL Canada Journal* 28 (1), 1–13.

Norton, B. (2013) *Identity and Language Learning: Extending the Conversation* (2nd edn). Bristol: Multilingual Matters.

Norton, B. and Toohey, K. (2002) Identity and language learning. In R. Kaplan (ed.) *The Oxford Handbook of Applied Linguistics* (pp. 115–123). Oxford: Oxford University Press.

Norton, B. and Toohey, K. (2011) State-of-the-Art article: Identity, language learning and social change. *Language Teaching* 44 (4), 412–446.

Norton Peirce, B. (1993) Language Learning, Social Identity, and Immigrant Women. Unpublished doctoral dissertation. University of Toronto, Canada.

Norton Peirce, B. (1995) Social identity, investment, and language learning. *TESOL Quarterly* 29 (1), 9–31.

Nwoye, O. (1992) Linguistic politeness and socio-cultural variations of the notion of face. *Journal of Pragmatics* 18 (4), 309–328.

O'Driscoll, J. (1996) About face: A defence and elaboration of universal dualism. *Journal of Pragmatics* 25 (1), 1–32.

O'Grady, C. (2011) Teaching the communication of empathy in patient-centred medicine. In B. Hoekje and S. Tipton (eds) *English Language and the Medical Profession: Instructing and Assessing the Communication Skills of International Physicians* (pp. 43–72). Bingley: Emerald.

Ohashi, J. (2003) Japanese culture specific face and politeness orientation: A pragmatic investigation of yoroshiku onegaishimasu. *Multilingua* 22 (3), 257–274.

Ohtani, C. (2010) Problems in the assistant language teacher system and English activity at Japanese public elementary schools. *Educational Perspectives* 43 (1/2), 38–45.

Ohzeki, A., Koguchi, N., Toyama, T., Fukuda, S. and Muramatsu, H. (2012) *Eigo de hasshin Tochigi no rekishi* [Let's Enjoy Tochigi History]. Tochigi: Shimotsuke Newspaper Inc.

Okamoto, S. (1998) The use and non-use of honorifics in sales talk in Kyoto and Osaka: Are they rude or friendly? *Japanese/Korean Linguistics* 7, 141–157. Stanford, CA: Center for the study of language and information.

Okuno, H. (2007) A critical discussion on the action plan to cultivate 'Japanese with English abilities'. *The Journal of Asia TEFL* 4 (4), 133–158.

Ortega, L. (2013) SLA for the 21st century: Disciplinary progress, transdisciplinary relevance, and the bi/multilingual turn. *Language Learning* 63, 1–24.

Ortega, L. (2014) Ways forward for a bi/multilingual turn in SLA. In S. May (ed.) *The Multilingual Turn: Implications for SLA, TESOL and Bilingual Education* (pp. 32–53). London and New York: Routledge.

Park, Y. (2005) Culture as deficit: A critical discourse analysis of the concept of culture in contemporary social work discourse. *Journal of Sociology and Social Welfare* 32 (3), 11–33.

Parmenter, L. (1999) Constructing national identity in a changing world: Perspectives in Japanese education. *British Journal of Sociology of Education* 20 (4), 453–63.

Pavlenko, A. (2003) 'I never knew I was bilingual': Reimagining identities in TESOL classes. *Journal of Language, Identity, and Education* 2 (4), 251–268.

Pavlenko, A. and Blackledge, A. (2004) New theoretical approaches to the study of negotiation of identities in multilingual contexts. In A. Pavlenko and A. Blackledge (eds) *Negotiation of Identities in Multilingual Contexts* (pp. 1–33). Clevedon: Multilingual Matters.

Pavlenko, A. and Norton, B. (2007) Imagined communities, identity, and English language learning. In J. Cummins and C. Davison (eds) *International Handbook of English Language Teaching* (pp. 669–680). New York: Springer.

Pavlidou, T.S. (2001) Politeness in the classroom? Evidence from a Greek high school. In A. Bayraktaroglu and M. Sifianou (eds) *Linguistic Politeness: The Case of Greece and Turkey* (pp. 105–136). Amsterdam and Philadelphia: John Benjamins.

Pennycook, A. (2001) *Critical Applied Linguistics: A Critical Introduction*. Mahwah, NJ: Lawrence Erlbaum.

Pizziconi, B. (2003) Re-examining politeness, face and the Japanese language. *Journal of Pragmatics* 35 (10–11), 1471–1506.

Placencia, M.E. (1996) Politeness in Ecuadorian Spanish. *Multilingua* 15 (1), 13–34.

Plaut, S. (2006) 'I just don't get it': Teachers' and students' conceptions of confusion and implications for teaching and learning in the high school English classroom. *Curriculum Inquiry* 36 (4), 391–421.

Polio, C.G. and Duff, P.A. (1994) Teachers' language use in university foreign language classrooms: A qualitative analysis of English and target language alternation. *The Modern Language Journal* 78 (3), 313–326.

Pomerantz, A. (2005) Using participants' video stimulated comments to complement analyses of interactional practices. In H. te Molder and J. Potter (eds) *Talk and Cognition: Discourse, Mind and Social Interaction* (pp. 93–113). Cambridge: Cambridge University Press.

Poplack, S. (1980) Sometimes I'll start a sentence in Spanish y termino en Espanol: Toward a typology of code-switching. *Linguistics* 18 (7/8), 581–616.

Reesor, M. (2002) The bear and the honeycomb: A history of Japanese English language policy. *NUCBA Journal of Language, Culture and Communication* 4 (1), 41–52.

Reischauer, E.O. and Jansen, M.B. (1988) *The Japanese Today: Change and Continuity*. Cambridge, MA: Belknap Press.

Richards, K. (2003) *Qualitative Inquiry in TESOL*. New York: Palgrave Macmillan.

Riley, P. (2006) Self-expression and the negotiation of identity in a foreign language. *International Journal of Applied Linguistics* 16 (3), 295–318.

Rivers, D.J. (2011a) Intercultural processes in accented English. *World Englishes* 30 (3), 375–391.

Rivers, D.J. (2011b) Politics without pedagogy: Questioning linguistic exclusion. *ELT Journal* 65 (2), 103–113.

Robb, L. (2000) *Redefining Staff Development: A Collaborative Model for Teachers and Administrators*. Portsmouth, NH: Heinemann.

Roberts, C. (1997) Transcribing talk: Issues of representation. *TESOL Quarterly* 31 (1), 167–172.

Roberts, C. and Sarangi, S. (2005) Theme-oriented discourse analysis of medical encounters. *Medical Education* 39 (6), 632–640.

Rohlen, T. and LeTendre, G. (eds) (1996) *Teaching and Learning in Japan*. Cambridge: Cambridge University Press.

Rolin-Ianziti, J. and Brownlie, S. (2002) Teacher use of learners' native language in the foreign language Classroom. *The Canadian Modern Language Review* 58 (3), 402–426.

Rolin-Ianziti, J. and Varshney, R. (2008) Students' views regarding the use of the first language: An exploratory study in a tertiary context maximising target language use. *The Canadian Modern Language Review* 65 (2), 249–273.

Rose, K. and Kasper, G. (eds) (2001) *Pragmatics in Language Teaching*. Cambridge: Cambridge University Press.

Ros i Solé, C. (2003) Culture for beginners: A subjective and realistic approach for adult language learners. *Language and Intercultural Communication* 3 (2), 141–150.

Ross, J.A. and Bruce, C. (2007) Professional development effects on teacher efficacy; Results of randomized field trial. *The Journal of Educational Research* 101 (1), 50–66.

Ross, S. and Kasper, G. (eds) (2013) *Assessing Second Language Pragmatics*. Basingstoke: Palgrave Macmillan.

Rowe, M.B. (1974) Wait-time and rewards as instructional variables; their influence on language, logic, and fate control. *Journal of Research in Science Teaching* 11 (2), 81–94.

Sadler, M. (2010) Subjective and intersubjective uses of Japanese verbs of cognition in conversation. *Pragmatics* 20 (1), 109–128.

Sarangi, S. and Candlin, C.N. (eds) (2003) Categorization and explanation of risk: A discourse analytical perspective. *Health, Risk and Society* 5 (2), 115–128.

Saville-Troike, M. (1996) The ethnography of communication. In S.L. McKay and N.H. Hornberger (eds) *Sociolinguistics and Language Teaching* (pp. 351–382). Cambridge: Cambridge University Press.

Scarino, A. (2009) Assessing intercultural competence in language learning: Some issues and considerations. *Language Teaching* 42 (1), 67–80.

Schlenker, B.R. andPontari, B.A. (2000) The strategic control of information: Impression management and self-presentation in daily life. In A. Tesser, R.B. Felson and J.M. Suls (eds) *Psychological Perspectives on Self and Identity*(pp. 199–232). Washington, DC: American Psychological Association.

Schmidt, R. (1983) Interaction, acculturation, and the acquisition of communicative competence. In N. Wolfson and E. Judd (eds) *Sociolinguistics and Language Acquisition* (pp. 137–174). Rowley, Massachusetts: Newbury House.

Schneer, D. (2007) (Inter)nationalism and English textbooks endorsed by the Ministry of Education in Japan. *TESOL Quarterly* 41 (3), 600–607.

Schneider, K.P. and Barron, A. (2008) Where pragmatics and dialectology meet: Introducing variational pragmatics. In K.P. Schneider and A. Barron (eds) *Variational Pragmatics: A Focus on Regional Varieties in Pluricentric Languages* (pp. 1–32). Amsterdam and Philadelphia: John Benjamins.

Schön, D. (1983) *The Reflective Practitioner: How Professionals Think in Action*. New York: Basic Books.

Scollon, R. (2001) *Mediated Discourse: The Nexus of Practice*. London: Routledge.

Scollon, R. and Scollon, S. (1983) Face in interethnic communication. In J.C. Richards and R.W. Schmidt (eds) *Language and Communication* (pp. 156–190). London: Longman.

Scollon, R. and Scollon, S. (1990) Athabaskan-English interethnic communication. In D. Carbaugh (ed.) *Cultural Communication and Intercultural Contact* (pp. 259–286). Hillsdale, NJ: Lawrence Erlbaum.

Scollon, R. and Scollon, S. (1995[2001]) *Intercultural Communication: A Discourse Approach*. Malden, Massachusetts: Blackwell Publishing.

Scott, V.M. and de la Fuente, M.J. (2008) What's the problem? L2 learners' use of the L1 during consciousness-raising, form focused tasks. *The Modern Language Journal* 92 (1), 100–113.

Shimahara. N.K. (1979) *Adaptation and Education in Japan*. New York: Praeger.

Shohamy, E. (2006) *Language Policy: Hidden Agendas and New Approaches*. London and New York: Routledge.

Shulman, L.S. and Shulman, J.H. (2004) How and what teachers learn: A shifting perspective. *Journal of Curriculum Studies* 36 (2), 257–271.

Siegal, M. (1996) The role of learner subjectivity in second language sociolinguistic competency: Western women learning Japanese. *Applied Linguistics* 17 (3), 356–382.

Sifianou, M. (1992) The use of diminutives in expressing politeness: Modern Greek versus English. *Journal of Pragmatics* 17 (22), 155–173.

Sifianou, M. (1995) Do we need to be silent to be extremely polite? Silence and FTAs. *International Journal of Applied Linguistics* 5 (1), 95–110.

Sifianou, M. (1997) Silence and politeness. In A. Jaworski (ed.) *Silence: Interdisciplinary Perspectives* (pp. 63–84). Berlin and New York: Mouton de Gruyter.

Sime, D. (2006) What do learners make of teachers' gestures in the language classroom? *International Review of Applied Linguistics in Language Teaching* 44 (2), 211–230.

Simon, B. (2004) *Identity in Modern Society: A Social Psychological Perspective*. Oxford: Blackwell.

Stough, L.M. (2001, April) *Using Stimulated Recall in Classroom Observation and Professional Development*. Paper presented at the meeting of the American Educational Research Association, Seattle, Washington.

Smith, R. and Imura, M. (2002) Harold E. Palmer, 1877–1949. In H. Cortazzi (ed.) *Britain and Japan: Biographical Portraits*, (vol. 1V pp. 233–46). London: Japan Library (Taylor & Francis).

Smith, R. and Imura, M. (2004) Lessons from the past: Traditions and reforms. In V. Makarova and T. Rodgers (eds) *English Language Teaching: The Case of Japan* (pp. 29–48). Munich: Lincom Europa.

Spencer-Oatey, H. (2000) Rapport management: A framework for analysis. In H. Spencer-Oatey (ed.) *Culturally Speaking: Managing Rapport Through Talk Across Cultures* (pp. 11–46). London New York: Continuum.

Spencer-Oatey, H. (2005) (Im)Politeness, face and perceptions of rapport: Unpackaging their bases and interrelationships. *Journal of Politeness Research* 1 (1), 95–119.

Spencer-Oatey, H. (2007) Theories of identity and the analysis of face. *Journal of Pragmatics* 39 (4), 639–656.

Spencer-Oatey, H. (2008) *Culturally Speaking: Culture, Communication and Politeness Theory* (2nd edn). London & New York: Continuum.

Spencer-Oatey, H. and Franklin, P. (2009) *Intercultural Interaction: A Multidisciplinary Approach to Intercultural Communication*. Basingstoke: Palgrave Macmillan.

Spencer-Oatey, H. and Xing, J. (2005) Managing talk and non-talk in intercultural interactions: Insights from two Chinese–British business meetings. *Multilingua* 24 (1/2), 55–74.

Stake, R.E. (1995) *The Art of Case Study Research*. Thousand Oaks, CA: Sage Publications.

Storch, N. and Wigglesworth, G. (2003) Is there a role for the use of the L1 in an L2 setting? *TESOL Quarterly* 37 (4), 760–770.

Streeck, J. (2002) Culture, meaning, and interpersonal communication. In M.L. Knapp and J.A. Daly (eds) *Handbook of Interpersonal Communication* (pp. 300–335). Thousand Oaks, CA: Sage Publications.

Swain, M. (1985) Communicative competence: Some roles of comprehensible input and comprehensible output in its development. In S.M. Gass and C.G. Madden (eds) *Input in Second Language Acquisition* (pp. 235–253). Rowley, MA: Newbury House.

Szatrowski, P. (2000) Relation between gaze, head nodding and *aizuti* 'back channel' at a Japanese company meeting. *Berkeley Linguistics Society* 26, 283–294. Berkeley, CA: Berkeley Linguistics Society.

Szatrowski, P. (2003) Gaze, head nodding and *aizuti* 'back channel utterances' in information presenting activities. In P.M. Clancy (ed.) *Japanese/Korean Linguistics* 11, 119–132. Stanford, CA: Center for the Study of Language and Information.

Tagashira, K., Yamato, K. and Isoda, T. (2011) Japanese EFL learners' pragmatic awareness through the looking glass of motivational profiles. *JALT Journal* 33 (1), 5–26.

Taguchi, N. (2012) *Context, Individual Differences, and Pragmatic Competence*. Bristol: Multilingual Matters.

Takano, S. (2005) Re-examining linguistic power: Strategic uses of directives by professional Japanese women in positions of authority and leadership. *Journal of Pragmatics* 37, 633–666.

Takayama, K. (2008) Beyond orientalism in comparative education: Challenging the binary opposition between Japanese and American education. *Asia Pacific Journal of Education* 28 (1), 19–34.

Tang, K.C.C. (1993) Spontaneous collaborative learning: A new dimension in student learning experience? *Higher Education Research and Development* 12 (2), 115–130.

Tani, M. (2008) Raising the in-class participation of Asian students through a writing tool. *Higher Education Research and Development* 27 (4), 345–356.

Tannen, D. (1985) Silence: Anything but. In D. Tannen and M. Saville-Troike (eds) *Perspectives on Silence* (pp. 93–111). Norwood, NJ: Ablex.

Tateyama, Y. and Kasper, G. (2008) Talking with a classroom guest: Opportunities for learning Japanese pragmatics. In E. Alcón and A. Martínez-Flor (eds) *Investigating Pragmatics in Foreign Language Learning, Teaching, and Testing* (pp. 45–71). Bristol: Multilingual Matters.

Terkourafi, M. (2007) Toward a universal notion of face for a universal notion of cooperation. In I. Kecskes and L. Horn (eds) *Explorations in Pragmatics: Linguistic, Cognitive and Intercultural Aspects* (pp. 313–344). Berlin and New York: Mouton de Gruyter.

Theobald, M. (2008) Methodological issues arising from video-stimulated recall with young children. *Australian Association for Research in Education*.

Thomas, J. (1983) Cross-cultural pragmatic failure. *Applied Linguistics* 4 (2), 91–112.

Thomas, J. (1995) *Meaning in Interaction: An Introduction to Pragmatics*. London: Longman.

Tobin, K.G. (1987) The role of wait time in higher cognitive level learning. *Review of Educational Research* 57 (1), 69–95.

Tobin, J. (1999) Method and meaning in comparative classroom ethnography. In R. Alexander, P. Broadfoot and D. Phillips (eds) *Learning from Comparing: New Directions in Comparative Educational Research* (pp. 113–134). Oxford, England: Symposium Books.

Trappes-Lomax, H. (2004) Discourse analysis. In A. Davies and C. Elder (eds) *The Handbook of Applied Linguistics* (pp. 133–164). Malden, MA: Blackwell Publishing.

Tsuda, Y. (1990) *Eigo shihai no kozo* [The Structure of English Domination]. Tokyo: Daisan Shokan.

Tsui, A.B.M. (1996) Reticence and anxiety in second language learning. In K.M. Bailey and D. Nunan (eds) *Voices from the Language Classroom* (pp. 145–167). New York: Cambridge University Press.

Tukahara, N. (2002) The sociolinguistic situation of English in Japan. *Revista de Sociolinguistica*.

Turnbull, M. and Arnett, K. (2002) Teachers' uses of the target and first languages in second and foreign language classrooms. *Annual Review of Applied Linguistics* 22, 204–218.

Turnbull, M. and Dailey-O'Cain, J. (eds) (2009) *First Language Use in Second and Foreign Language Learning*. Bristol: Multilingual Matters.

Ushioda, E. (2011) Motivating learners to speak as themselves. In G. Murray, X. Gao and T. Lamb (eds) *Identity, Motivation and Autonomy in Language Learning* (pp. 11–24). Bristol: Multilingual Matters.

Valdes, J.M. (1986) *Culture Bound: Bridging the Cultural Gap in Language Teaching*. Cambridge: Cambridge University Press.

Vásquez, C. and Sharpless, D. (2009) The role of pragmatics in the master's TESOL curriculum: Findings from a nationwide survey. *TESOL Quarterly* 43 (1), 5–28.

von Dietze, A., von Dietze, H. and Joyce, P. (2009) Researching the role of L1 (Japanese) in the English (EFL) classroom. *Interdisciplinary Educational Research Institute Journal* 5, 35–52.

von Dietze, A., von Dietze, H. and Joyce, P. (2010) Inviting students to use their L1 in the EFL classroom. *Kinki University English Journal* 6, 11–33.

Walsh, S. (2006) *Investigating Classroom Discourse*. London and New York: Routledge.

Watson-Gegeo, K.A. (1988) Ethnography in ESL: Defining the essentials. *TESOL Quarterly* 22 (4), 575–592.

Watts, R. (2003) *Politeness*. Cambridge: Cambridge University Press.

Weaver. G.R. (1986) Understanding and coping with cross-cultural adjustment stress. In R.M. Paige (ed.) *Cross-Cultural Orientation, New Conceptualizations and Applications*. Lanham MD: University Press of America.

Wenger, E. (1998) *Communities of Practice: Learning, Meaning, and Identity*. Cambridge: Cambridge University Press.

Werkhofer, K. (1992) Traditional and modern views: The social constitution and the power of politeness. In R.J. Watts, S. Ide and K. Ehlich (eds) *Politeness in Language* (2nd edn, pp. 155–199). Berlin and New York: Mouton de Gruyter.

Wetzel, P.J. (1994) Contemporary Japanese attitudes toward honorifics (keigo). *Language Variation and Change* 6 (2), 113–147.

Wierzbicka, A. (1991) *Cross-Cultural Pragmatics: The Semantics of Human Interaction*. Berlin and New York: Mouton de Gruyter.

Wilkerson, C. (2008) Instructors' use of English in the modern language classroom. *Foreign Language Annals* 41 (2), 310–320.

Wong, N.L. (2003) The communicative meanings and functions of silence: An analysis of cross cultural views. *Journal of Tagen Bunka* 3, 125–146. Japan: Nagoya University, Graduate School of Languages and Cultures.

Wong, N.L. (2010) *Silent Communication of Japanese Society*. Kuala Lumpur: University of Malaya Press.

Wood, L.A. and Kroger, R.O. (2000) *Doing Discourse Analysis: Methods for Studying Action in Talk and Text*. Thousand Oaks, CA: Sage Publications.

Woolard, K.A. (2004) Codeswitching. In A. Duranti (ed.) *A Companion to Linguistic Anthropology* (pp. 73–94). Malden, MA: Blackwell Publishers.

Yero, J.L. (2002) *Teaching in Mind: How Teacher Thinking Shapes Education*. Hamilton, MT: MindFlight Publishing.

Yoneyama, S. (1999) *The Japanese High School: Silence and Resistance*. London and New York: Routledge.

Yoshida, R. (2008) Learners' perception of corrective feedback in pair work. *Foreign Language Annals* 41 (3), 525–541.

Yoshimi, D. (1999) The language of interdependence in Japanese vertical relationships. In J. Verschueren (ed.) *Pragmatics in 1998. Selected Papers from the 6th* International Pragmatics Conference (vol. 2, pp. 606–619). Antwerp: International Pragmatics Association.

Yoshino, K. (1992) *Cultural Nationalism in Contemporary Japan: A Sociological Enquiry*. London and New York: Routledge.

Yoshino, K. (2002) English and nationalism in Japan: The role of the intercultural-communication industry. In S. Wilson (ed.) *Nation and Nationalism in Japan* (pp. 135–145). London and New York: Routledge.

Zimmerman, D.H. (1998) Discoursal identities and social identities. In C. Antaki and S. Widdicombe (eds) *Identities in Talk* (pp. 87–106). Thousand Oaks, CA: Sage Publications.

Index

321

'western' bias 25, 49–51, 58, 93, 241
Western versus Japanese identities
141, 142–143
'we-they' distinctions 161, 168, 170
Wheaton, Mr 82
white culture as 'standard' 19–20, 21, 22
Wierzbicka, A. 28
Wigglesworth, G. 181
Wong, N.L. 230, 268
Wood, L.A. 88, 89
Woolard, K.A. 182
word-by-word translation techniques 88
World Englishes 20–21

World War II 15, 82
writing systems 14
wrong face, being in the 42

xenophobia 144–145
Xing, J. 226, 228

Yero, J.L. 285
yo particle 205, 207, 208, 209–210, 212
Yoshida, M. 56, 85
Yoshino, K. 143, 144, 174

Zimmerman, D.H. 67–68